D1472553

They Builded Better
Than They Knew

JULIUS HENRY COHEN

Books

The Law: Business or Profession?

Law and Order in Industry

An American Labor Policy

Commercial Arbitration and the Law

Papers

The Contingent Fee

The Obligation of the United States to Return Enemy Alien Property

The Law of Commercial Arbitration and the New York Statute

The Old Port and the New

Arbitration and Public Policy

A New Federal Tax on the States and Their Municipalities

"Government of the People, By the People, For the People" . . . Shall It Perish?

A League to Enforce Industrial Peace

A Letter from a Lawyer on the Subject of Health

Doctors of Medicine *vs.* Doctors of Health

Ice (Discussion of the United States Supreme Court decision in *New State Ice Co.* vs. *Liebmann.*)

They Builded Better Than They Knew

By JULIUS HENRY COHEN

JULIAN MESSNER, Inc.
New York

To my friends—
Portraits within.

PUBLISHED BY JULIAN MESSNER, INC.
8 WEST 40TH STREET, NEW YORK 18

COPYRIGHT, 1946
BY JULIUS HENRY COHEN

PRINTED IN THE UNITED STATES OF AMERICA
AMERICAN BOOK-STRATFORD PRESS, INC., NEW YORK

Contents

PAGE

Foreword   vii

BOOK I

BENDING THE TWIG

CHAPTER

1. Everett V. Abbot   3
2. Robert C. Taylor   15
3. A Tragedy and Two Lessons Gleaned Therefrom   18
4. Horace E. Deming   21
5. Dr. Felix Adler   32
6. Dr. John P. Peters   41
7. Frank Damrosch   50
8. William Travers Jerome   64

BOOK II

ORCHIDS GROW IN SWAMPY GROUNDS

9. Theodore Roosevelt   73
10. William M. Ivins   91
11. Alfred E. Smith   108

BOOK III

THE WOMEN TAKE OVER

12. Rosalie Loew Whitney   131
13. I. S. C.   137

BOOK IV

THE LAW MOVES FORWARD

14. Charles L. Bernheimer   149
15. Rent Cases   162

BOOK V

Trial and Error in Industry

CHAPTER	PAGE
16. Max Meyer	179
17. Louis D. Brandeis	190
18. Morris Hillquit	201
19. Meyer London	215
20. John A. Dyche	223
21. Dr. George M. Price	238
22. Belle Lindner Moskowitz	245

BOOK VI

New Times—New Instrumentalities

23. Alexander J. Shamberg	257
24. Eugenius H. Outerbridge	271
25. The Port of New York Authority	289
26. Samuel L. Fuller	307
27. Conference on State Defense	317
28. St. Lawrence Power Authority	329
Notes	343
Index	365

Foreword

A WISE COUNSELOR and friend who knows much about the writing and publishing of books told me that an introduction should not be prepared by the author until he had completed his book. He was right.

As one writes, his book grows under his hand. If, as in my case, one surveys fifty years of experience and reflects, he puts two and two together to make sense. We were still in World War II when this book was begun. The war ended before the last chapter was completed. During its writing, the book fell into a pattern of its own. It became more than a portrait gallery of interesting people, or a simple chronicle of events and incidents. From the survey there emerged a vindication of ideas and principles.

Through the fifty years could be seen clearly the change from the imperialism of Theodore Roosevelt—attacked as it was during and after the Spanish-American War by Felix Adler—to the withdrawal by Great Britain from its own "White Man's Burden" policy. Tragic events proved that imperialism anywhere is an unsound doctrine. By her examples America herself had contributed in part to bringing about World Wars I and II.

Another thought: My belief in people—all people, was the belief of the leaders who shaped my thinking in the formative days.

Who are God's Chosen People? They are *all* peoples, all races—yellow, black, brown, red and white. We see that clearly now. But Felix Adler taught that doctrine fifty years ago. Other moral leaders delivered the same preachment—*the sanctity of the human soul*. Great statesmen found in the same doctrine the moral basis for democracy in government. But it was lost in the cynicism to which we succumbed all over our land. The tragedy of World War II became a crucible for proving this elementary truth. President Truman—after publication of the report on Pearl Harbor in September, 1945—blamed that tragedy on the American people—blamed the people for ignorance and stupidity. He could have gone farther and said that the American people had followed the wrong leaders from the days of the Spanish-American War. The truth came from my teachers in the nineties. I learned that leaders must have vision—must see at least fifty years ahead and must have the courage to lead—*to sacrifice themselves for principle, if need be.* And to tell the truth as they see it regardless of the effect on their own fortunes. Yet for half a century the American people followed another kind—chieftains who thought in terms of their own political advancement until we reached a state of mind where we distrusted all leadership. The leaders who did set principle above expediency and who did speak out relied on history to vindicate them—and it has now begun to do so. Some of these leaders are portrayed in this book.

Now America is faced, as all intelligent observers agree, with the simple choice of annihilation or cooperation in friendship with the rest of the world. Can such a working together be achieved? The story of cooperation between two sovereign states of these United States—which we know—is based on earlier international cooperation.

Another matter: We shall have politics with us for a long time to come. Are men bred in political schools bad *in toto?* On the basis of actual experience, I give you my answer.

How much is knowledge of human nature—good and bad—a factor in successful leadership?

Does the law stand still? Can it be improved? How? What of lawyers? I knew leaders of the Bar who in their lives made great contributions to the public good. Here are portraits of them.

What of labor and capital? Can they work together? In tragic defeat we shared in the experiment in the Garment Industry. What guideposts do these experiences set up?

Are bankers bad men? Not all of them. I saw some do a great piece of constructive work.

The war is over now and we face a new world. Once more we need pathfinders—men of creative leadership. What trails are already blazed for them? What lines can be extended? These teachers at whose feet I sat, have something to give to this new world. Many of the men and women portrayed here are already well-known—others deserve to be placed in a gallery of portraits of American leaders.

As for the author himself, though he did not intend to write his memoirs, he was bound to tell you something of himself. He hopes not too much to disturb the story.

JULIUS HENRY COHEN

BOOK I

BENDING THE TWIG

CHAPTER ONE

Et quasi cursores vitae lampada tradunt.
Like runners in a race they hand on the lamps of life.
LUCRETIUS. (*"Caesar and Christ,"* WILL DURANT)

Everett V. Abbot

A group of young men make their way to the Bar—
One of them meets a professor of law who gives him
his first job and leads him into the field of Municipal
and Law Reform—Some leading cases—Should the
Courts correct their own mistakes—The Supreme
Court is asked to reverse its prior ruling that the
Eighteenth Amendment is constitutional.

I

IN THE SECOND HALF of the gay nineties, something was going on in Clinton Hall, the building on Astor Place near the present Wanamaker Store, cat-a-corner to Cooper Union. It was running in the evening when "Ta-Ra-Ra-Boom-Der-E" was Lottie Collins' big success. The enterprise of which I speak was the *Metropolis Law School,* a show of all stars, though few of them were comedians. Life was serious business for them.

This Metropolis Law School afterwards merged with the Law School of New York University, which had among its eminent graduates such men as Elihu Root and Samuel J. Tilden and such Deans as Benjamin F. Butler, John Norton Pomeroy and Austin Abbott.

This night law school was started by Clarence D. Ashley. Professor Ashley followed his partner, William A. Keener, in the development of the teaching of law by the *case system.* That is, in Dean Ashley's classes the discussion of actual cases brought about "vigorous, forthright encounter between student and instructor in an intellectual struggle to extract the law from the decisions of the courts. Any loose use of words or faulty reasoning, be it by judge or student, was remorselessly exposed." [1]

Abbot came into the faculty to take over the subjects of *agency* and *torts*. What are *torts*?

A colored woman lay upon the pavement all smashed up after being hit by an automobile. An ambulance-chaser rushed up, put his card in her hand and said, "Mammy, you can recover damages for this." "Go 'way, man," she answered. "I don't want damages, I want repairs."

The subject of *torts* deals with the matter of personal injuries to persons or property and damages recoverable therefor.

The subject of *agency* covers a broad field, but the underlying principle comes out in the following anecdote: The late Judge Alfonso T. Clearwater once visited former Senator William Evarts at his farm in Vermont. Evarts raised pedigreed cattle. While showing Clearwater around the farm, Evarts pointed out the animals and said, "You know, Judge, I get as much satisfaction out of propagating a fine heifer as I do in winning a big case." To which Clearwater said, "Senator, for a man who is as meticulous as you are in the use of English, I am a little astonished that you use the verb 'propagate.'" Quick as a flash, Evarts said, "Qui facit per alium facit per se." Which means that whatever somebody else does on my behalf, is the same as if I did it myself.

That's the law of *agency*.

The members of the faculty were fated to meet keen minds in my class as well as in the classes preceding and succeeding mine.

In the classes ahead of '96 there was Frank H. Sommer, later to become distinguished at the Bar of New Jersey and Dean of the Law School in 1916. Tasker L. Oddie, Senator from Nevada, was in the Class of '95.

In '96 there was Michael Schaap, who left the profession after twenty years for a highly successful business career, first as head of Bamberger's in Newark, and then of Bloomingdale's in New York.

Then there was Theodore Prince, who first joined his brother's banking firm and later made money (I hope) for his client-investors by careful analysis of the value of stocks and bonds. Besides there were Burch and Frank R. Foraker, both related to Governor Foraker of Ohio, and Samuel Koenig, later the Republican leader of New York County for many years. By the way, Koenig worked during the day at Ansorge's wholesale clothing establishment, at Third and Mercer Streets, next door to No. Six where my father had his tailor shop. There was, too, Henry A. Rubino, afterwards a partner in Kenneson, Ashley, Emley and Rubino, and largely responsible for my entering the law school. We attended the Thirtieth Street Evening

High School together. General John F. O'Ryan was in this class, too. There were many others who, during the day, worked in business, in law, in engineering, in accounting, or as private secretaries. Justice Oliver Wendell Holmes believed that facing hardship is good training. One sails "better with the wind on the quarter than when it is directly astern." [2] We think, too, defeat and frustration—if properly accepted for what they are, strengthen character and bring out the best there is in a man.

But the fellows at Metropolis '96 knew at first hand the subjects of *notes, bills,* and *sales* and other legal situations in the business world. Moreover, they met people of all kinds, races and previous conditions of servitude, and, hence, while not realizing it, were getting educated in the school of life—an education quite as essential for their vocation as Greek or Latin.

There was a wit in the class. A fat fellow who with cassock would have made a genial little priest, Shields. He grew up from office boy to useful assistant in one of the first real estate law firms in New York City. One night Professor Thomas was quizzing us in the course on *real estate.* We were supposed to have read our Blackstone and to know the three kinds of death in the law. It was Shields' turn. Professor Thomas asked: "Mr. Shields, what is 'civil death'?" Quickly Shields replied, "I think, Professor, a good example would be when a monk enters a nunnery. That would mean civil death."

For this escapade, Shields deserved instant execution. (So do I now for repeating it.)

After class, some of us went over to Third Avenue and had coffee and cheesecake and trial bouts over the *cases* assigned for class discussion the next evening. I always found when I got home some cheese, a Bermuda onion and a bottle of beer—which a fond mother left for her son. I was on an eight hour shift then: eight hours for work, eight for study and eight for sleep.

Let me give you a picture of Abbot: About the size of Governor Dewey and about his weight. Clear blue eyes, a beard, a definite blond. Why he wore a beard I do not know. Perhaps for the same reason it was said Charles Evans Hughes wore one, or as doctors did in my day—to seem older than they really were.

Naturally, I looked at men's clothes. I was brought up in the shop of a man who made clothes for men. We believed, father and I, that "The apparel oft proclaims the man." I learned in the shop in my early teens the differences between serges and cheviots, flannels and worsteds, meltons, vicunas and kerseys. Plaids and stripes and greys, blues and browns. A well-tailored man appealed to me. I still see some of the rough tweeds, the warm, friendly mixtures of brown and grey—never anything conspicuous—that Abbot wore. He was the first man I ever met who had his shirts made to order and his choice revealed his conservative taste.* Neat red, blue and brown stripes and always immaculately laundered. I do not think that any tie he wore had anything of the gay abandon in it, but he did get the joy that men get who know the real pleasure of buying a new necktie. (When you are down in the dumps, buy a new tie, it will pep you up just as buying a new hat helps a woman's morale.)

He wore a neat little pin in his scarf. Handkerchiefs always of fine linen which just peeped out of his pocket. I doubt if anyone, except someone in the business, would have noticed anything save that here was a gentleman to his very fingertips.

His handwriting was a joy to anyone who had to copy it on a typewriter. Bold, fearless, written with a stub pen, each letter had its own character. (In those days, I, too, wrote longhand legibly. Of course, shorthand is quicker. It was stenography that spoiled my fine Spencerian style. Why write out *ing* when a concave curve in the third position or even a dot at the end of another hieroglyphic will answer?)

Abbot's thinking was as clear as his handwriting. He had the lawyer's greatest asset—a logical, analytical mind. He thought things through. He did not get his law "by ear" but by good hard digging. When he sat at his desk at 55 William Street, or at the law school, and one put a question to him, he did not answer at once. He carefully formulated his thinking and gave his answer lucidly. He was a minister's son, a Unitarian minister and a philosopher.

Abbot never told us about his high honors at Harvard, but his education was superb. He differed much from Professor Abner C. Thomas, afterwards Surrogate of New York, who, under beetling brows, once said to us with Yankee shrewdness, "Young men, when you open your office, always arrange your desk and your client's chair so that your client is in the light and you can see every expression on his face, but he can't see yours."

II

About two years before graduation I began looking for a job in a law office. I had to earn a living, and to serve a year's clerkship in a law office was required for admission to the Bar.

Abbot gave me a letter to Lloyd McKim Garrison, a classmate of

* It will be news to most of us that the American male "* * * spends two dollars on his shirts for every three dollars on his suits, the giddy thing." [3]

his. For a long time I treasured Garrison's reply, which though it told me there was no vacancy at the moment, encouraged me to go on. I showed it with delight to my father. He had long been convinced that no man could earn a living unless he had a trade. Whenever he found his son reading a book he was disappointed. A really worthwhile boy with proper standards of usefulness would have been whisking a brush over the hanging clothes or the rolls of cloth in the shop. He told mother, not once, but many times, "That boy of yours will die in the gutter." And as he saw it then, he was right.

In addition to teaching at the law school, Abbot had been managing clerk for the law firm of Miller, Peckham and Dixon. The name Peckham brings up a picture of one of the mountain peaks of my day, Wheeler H. Peckham, who like William B. Hornblower came near reaching the United States Supreme Court bench.

Does enchanting distance make us all think of the mountain size of the leaders of fifty years ago? There were James C. Carter, Joseph H. Choate, Elihu Root, John E. Parsons, Edward M. Shepard, Joseph Larocque, William M. Evarts—their portraits all hang in the Bar Association rooms—they all moved across the stage in my time.[4] Down on the plains, we youngsters looked up and wondered if we climbed and climbed real hard, whether we might ever reach the heights of Mount Marcy.

To be managing clerk for Peckham's firm—that was a high peak in itself.

At the same time that Abbot was with the Peckham firm, John Morris Perry was managing clerk for Parsons, Shepard and Ogden over at 111 Broadway, the Trinity Building—not the building into which my firm moved some thirty years later, but the old building in which they had open fireplaces and burned cannel coal.

William Manice was first assistant to David B. Ogden, the leading adviser of that day to the large real estate owners in New York, one of the old type of gentleman of the '80s and '90s. John E. Parsons was then regarded as one of the smartest lawyers in town—what laymen used to mean when they spoke of a "Philadelphia lawyer."

These three, Abbot, Perry and Manice, were to leave their jobs and build and sail their own craft, under the name of Manice, Abbot and Perry. They were my first bosses. They were all as straight as Perry was in his walk. I never knew them to break a promise. I have met handsome men in my time, but Manice was one of the two handsomest men I ever have known. The other was Eugenius H. Outerbridge.* Mrs. Manice was one of the reigning beauties of that day. She was Sarah Remsen. Manice carried himself as the real aristocrat he was,

coming from one of the best families in New York. And one may
get a clue to the early prosperity of Manice, Abbot and Perry when
I say that my first typing work was done in the *Remsen Estate* and
later in the *Manice Estate*. But under the surface of a Knickerbocker
aristocrat, I soon discovered a gallant, appreciative and genial friend.
When I learned that Manice kept double entry books I found an
affinity. You see, under father's challenge to do something in the
world, I had gone from grammar school to night school and there
learned bookkeeping. Indeed, I kept a full set of books for father,
perfectly balanced, regularly showing him that he was running deeper
and deeper into the red—a fact he did not need my books to tell him
about. He had it all in his head. Like Frances Place's customers in
London, father too made clothes to order for men who regarded it as
proper and fashionable to let the tailor wait for payment of his bill.
Father's "bad debts," if collected, could easily have paid for my law
school training.

After I had finished the bookkeeping course at the First Street
Night School, I took a course in stenography from Charles Schekeler,
who became my friend. That shorthand was a great help at the Law
School in taking notes. Later, it was still more helpful. As a witness
testified, one could keep notes of what he said and on cross-examination, if he contradicted himself, could confront him with his exact
words and, with safety, turn to the official stenographer for confirma-
tion.

In my second year at law school, Abbot came to me one evening
after class and asked if I could write shorthand. Perhaps he had noticed my doing it in class. I said "yes," but I told him I could not
type. But that training I got quickly a little later with Schekeler's
help by pounding, under his guidance, a hired typewriter at his
house.

That evening Abbot told me in detail of the plans for the new
firm and asked me whether I would like to come in as combination
law clerk and stenographer. Fifteen dollars a week in those days was
great pay.

III

Charles Dickens started as a stenographer, when he was nineteen, reporting the proceedings of Parliament. In my day two other men
climbed up the ladder as stenographers. One, George B. Cortelyou,
secretary to Presidents McKinley and Theodore Roosevelt, later became President of the Consolidated Gas Company. He started as a

* See Chapter 24.

general law stenographer at five dollars per diem when employed. And William Loeb, Jr., successor to Cortelyou as secretary to President Theodore Roosevelt, later became President of the American Smelting and Refining Company.

My stenography was the key that opened the door for me to No. 55 William Street, tenth floor. Manice had the largest office of the three, facing south and east. Perry's office was in the center. Then came Abbot's room, next to the outer office, which was reception room and clerk's office combined. We had an office boy from the beginning, Sidney Curtis—I still remember his name. He was charming. He came near running the whole shebang. Something like the boy at James, Shell and Elkus, who attended the telephone and answered all the calls with, "This is *James*, of James, Shell and Elkus."

Then, there was a law clerk. A little too highhat and collegiate for me. His name began with an H and he came from Harvard. On September 28, 1944, the following "ad" appeared in the East Hampton "Star":

"Young Boar—Name, Herman; sex, male; age, 5 months. Excellent pedigree, charming personality, double inoculated, Virginia stock, Poland China-Durock. Fertility guaranteed (maybe)." (sic)

Our H. came highly recommended too. Like Herman, he was of the male sex, doubly inoculated and his pedigree was just as good —even superior. Like Herman, the boar, *fertility (maybe)*—there were quite a few of them in the market those days. Five dollars a week! They looked down on a male stenographer or typist who had no comparable pedigree. Outside of H., the five of us, Manice, Abbot, Perry, Sidney and I, made a happy family. My bosses were patient with me.

Later I was to learn what it was like to get back typewritten material that had only a nodding acquaintance with what I had dictated, and to find substituted for my carefully phrased sentences some original composition by the young lady who thought my vocabulary was "just awful" and did her damnedest to improve upon it. Abbot was meticulous in his English. He had vouched for me to his partners. I was raw, very raw, but they forgave me my gaucheries. I must have tried Abbot severely many times. He should have fired me, for one thing, for my satires on his poetry.

When I failed to answer the call of the calendar in one of Perry's cases—an action for damages against the City for injuries resulting from failure to remove ice from the streets—Perry was kinder than any person I had met in the business world, but Perry had been a managing clerk in a law office. He knew how easily one could make a slip. He told me how he had awakened in the middle of the night and come in all the way from Brooklyn to 111 Broadway (no subways in those days) to get out and mail a legal paper that had to be served by the following morning or there would be a default.

We had a great time at "55," and it was Abbot who gave me my first introduction to Law Reform and Municipal Politics.

IV

On the subject of the administration of the law—Cardozo called it "the judicial process"—Abbot was ahead of his time. We have in recent days witnessed substantial changes in the law made through judicial reversals. What are we coming to if we cannot rely on what the courts have already decided? The doctrine of *stare decisis* is the doctrine of *standing by decisions*—the following of precedents. In our Anglo-American system of jurisprudence, precedents play a vital part. They enable a lawyer to look up the law, and make some reasonably approximate prophecy of what the courts will decide in a given case. Thus, for example, I could advise the Port of New York Authority that its bonds as well as all bonds issued by states and municipalities were immune from federal taxation. Investors could then rely upon such advice and buy such bonds, paying a higher price for them (or taking a lower rate of interest). But if they could not rely upon the courts following their own decisions, what was there to rely upon? Of what value are such rulings if they are subject to change every time there is a change in the personnel of the court?

However, this dilemma the courts must face: Is the law ever wrong? Are there decisions which are really unsound? Have modern conditions made these precedents obsolete? For example, the long line of decisions holding for three centuries that an arbitration agreement was revocable played havoc with the development of the practice of commercial arbitration both in England and in this country. It went counter to sound commercial usage. I urged in "Commercial Arbitration and the Law" that this error should have been corrected by the courts themselves and I cited Abbot liberally. The older technique, both in England and in our country, of meeting changed social conditions was the practice of "distinguishing" cases on the facts. Very often the distinctions were tenuous. But it was the accepted method for correcting decisions which the courts had come to believe were unsound. Our whole Anglo-Saxon jurisprudence is replete with fictions invented by judges to adjust precedents to new conditions. By this method they give continuity to the law. Abbot found a way out of this dilemma.

Under the title "Judicial Correction of Judicial Error" he wrote an article for the Yale Law Journal from which I take but one paragraph:

> "Of all methods of correcting judicial errors, the judicial method is obviously the wisest, the most effective, and the most just. The mere fact that there has been error signifies that there has been injustice and the courts are better fitted to cope with injustice than any other department of an organized state. Our courts should always be ready, therefore, to apply to their own errors and injustices the judicial method of correction. A frank acknowledgment that they can be, and are, on occasion, mistaken, and an open-minded reception of lawyer-like and respectful arguments tending to point out errors, will not in the slightest degree undermine their authority, or diminish the respect in which they are held. On the contrary, the more tolerant and approachable the court is, the greater will be the popular confidence in its decisions. In fact, the strongest bulwark which the courts can erect against the recall and other insidious attacks upon our judicial system will be found in the recognized practice by the courts themselves of the principle that judicial errors are to be judicially corrected." [5]

This idea was carried to other minds.

In *United States v. Sprague* [6] a group of lawyers believing the United States Supreme Court had made a mistake should reverse itself. It had declared that the Eighteenth Amendment was constitutionally adopted. The Constitution of the United States was ratified in *Conventions of the People*. The Eighteenth Amendment was ratified only by *Legislatures*. Article V, if liberally interpreted, would seem to give a choice of either method. And so the Supreme Court had held. But the founding fathers had insisted in the Philadelphia Convention that the Constitution would not be valid without the action of the people themselves, and the states joined in the view that nothing less than ratification by the people in *conventions assembled* would bring that document into legal existence. Only in that way would the powers granted be derived from the "consent of the people." The group of lawyers who appeared for the defendant in the Sprague case * asked the Court to reverse its prior ruling and to hold that the Eighteenth Amendment had not been authorized by the *people* since it had been ratified only by *Legislatures*.

If in those days the court had been in the mood to follow Abbot's teaching, it would have reversed itself. Two decades later, it overturned a lot of prior decisions. I still think that if the court had reversed itself in the *Sprague* case, it would have "added to its own prestige," as Abbot said it would in such cases.

The court, however, preferred to stand by its prior ruling and leave to the people themselves the task of repealing the Amendment.

* Frederic M. P. Pearse, Daniel F. Cohalan, Selden Bacon, the writer and his two partners, Kenneth Dayton and Burton A. Zorn.

Future writers on constitutional law will read the briefs filed in that case and may agree that in this field there was judicial error which should have been *judicially corrected*. Since that time this doctrine of correction of judicial error has been applied in many cases by the United States Supreme Court. It is difficult to say whether this attitude of the court was directly influenced by Abbot's article, but I have been impressed with the way in which birds carry seeds from one place to another. There is a wild growth of bittersweet on the road near us up in Westchester. My wife, who knows her botany, explains that this growth came from berries carried by the birds from our own front door and dropped by them in new ground, there to take root and prosper. One may not be able always to trace the spread of ideas as we did the spread of this bittersweet. But that they do spread is unquestionable.

V

It was through Abbot that I was led into the field of Municipal Reform. He and his friends were active in the Good Government Clubs of that day. Through Abbot and his friends I was started in a field of independent political activity which colored my whole career from that time on.

The Citizens Union was organized in 1897. As part of the task of securing better government in New York City, it watched zealously all legislation in Albany dealing with the city's affairs and formulated legislation such as the Home Rule Amendment, giving the city freedom to manage its own affairs. From 1902 to 1913 I was chairman of that committee. It included men who already had made places for themselves in the profession, like Joseph M. Proskauer, later Judge of the Appellate Division; William L. Ransom, later Counsel for the Public Service Commission; Goldthwaite H. Dorr; Laurence A. Tanzer; and others. Each Friday night we would meet at dinner at the City Club, go over every piece of legislation then pending affecting the city in any wise, and make our recommendations. Members of the committee became specialists. Abbot was one of the ablest men in that committee.

A third field in which Abbot made a distinct contribution was that of judicial reform. For the group on legal ethics which Felix Adler inspired,* Abbot prepared a plan for statewide organization of our judicial system. It was based upon the conception that the administration of justice required effective business administration and required judges uninfluenced by political considerations. Though this plan was

* See Chapter 5.

presented to the Constitutional Convention of 1915 and failed of acceptance then, the ideas have since found acceptance. Impetus to these reforms has been given by the revelations of the scandals in nominations in New York County in 1943 and the conduct of judges in Albany County in 1944.

A Jesuit priest once said, "You can do a lot of good in the world if you are not too particular who gets the credit for it." Little credit has been given to Abbot for the good work he did.

The contributions made by Abbot should have entitled him to high professional honors. Abbot had qualities which should have made him a success. He had charm, he had an excellent education, he had a fine background. He had fine friends—men like Albert Sprague Bard, Lloyd McKim Garrison, Judge Augustus N. Hand and many others whom I came to meet through him. Abbot could have been an alternate to Southmayd of Evarts, Choate and Beaman, or to Stone of Davies, Stone and Auerbach—both great legal scholars.

Abbot never cared for money. He never cared for honors. He did crave the esteem of his friends. He should have continued at the law school, teaching law, devoting himself to writing in his spare time. He would have had a satisfactory income if he had done this. His venture into the private practice of the law was not a success. As a matter of fact he died of starvation in his own office. Like the man at Montauk who got caught in the undertow and was swallowed up in the great Atlantic, Abbot disappeared. The knack of getting clients is something in the nature of a special quality, but if one does not possess that gift it is necessary to get "lucky breaks." The importance of "happenstance" will be developed in later chapters.

VI

I had read, while in the Thirtieth Street Evening High School, under the inspiration of Dr. Gustave Simonson, teacher of political science, books on economy and philosophy—Charles Darwin and Herbert Spencer, and English and American history, in connection with law school studies and in preparation for Regents examinations. But Abbot introduced me to fine literature and broadened my reading.

In addition to the fifteen dollars a week, I was promised one-third of any fees from the cases that came in to Manice, Abbot and Perry through me. But where would they come from? I had no rich family connections. No connections whatever which would normally produce professional employment. Oh yes, I did draw a will the first year— that I think brought in ten dollars, or maybe fifteen. It was for John Hayes, the horse-shoer around the corner from father's shop—our village blacksmith. In 1945, I met his son, William H. Hayes, who is now a successful lawyer. Young Hayes then reminded me how his father and mine played poker in father's shop every Saturday afternoon. John Hayes thought if a tailor's son could make a living at the law, so could the son of a horse-shoer.

Into my father's shop one day came Mrs. "K". She stopped at the Grand Central Hotel around the corner. She lived in Cincinnati. The hotel brought in quite a bit of revenue to father's shop, mostly for repairing and cleaning and pressing jobs. It made for me, also, when I worked in the shop, what seemed a large revenue—the ten cent pieces and the quarters given to me as tips from kind customers when I made deliveries of the cleaned and pressed suits.

Mrs. "K" had a son. Her son had gotten into "trouble" with a servant girl and was in court to be held accountable for the support of the child, "bastardy proceedings" they are called.

"How can I find a good lawyer?" asked Mrs. "K" of my father. Well, of course, he knew the very best and most talented one in town. I was shocked, however, when I was asked to take the case. Manice, Abbot and Perry would never handle such a line of merchandise! But they did. And Perry said, "Why should not self-respecting lawyers handle any case where the client needs sound advice and presentation of his case by someone who enjoys the courts' confidence?" He was right. I netted about fifty dollars out of the case. It was in connection with the research work in that case that I came across a remark by that old buzzard, Judge Arthur H. Van Brunt, who, in my early days, bullied us all at General Term. He said in a minority opinion in a bastardy case (I paraphrase): "This child seems to be the result of the efforts of a syndicate, not of one single individual."

By 1898, two years after graduation from the law school and after my admission to the Bar, work began coming in to me, sufficient to make it difficult to carry on as a clerk for Manice, Abbot and Perry and still build up my own practice.

If my principals had followed then the fashion of today, they might have taken me in as a partner. But they did not, and that is how I came to find my second friend at the Bar.

CHAPTER TWO

Qui uti scit, ei bona.
Good things to him who knows how to use them.

Robert C. Taylor

We hang out our shingle—Sweet are the uses of pro-
fanity—We learn how to cross-examine a lying witness.

I

IN THE ELEVATOR of "No. 55" I met Robert C. Taylor. Let me draw
his picture, the second in this gallery. Deep, dark eyes, black hair,
mustache and a bit of a goatee. He came from one of the best families
in Virginia. He had married Postmaster James Albert Gary's daughter.
He had nothing to worry about so far as money or position were
concerned.

One day as I was leaving my office, I ran into Taylor in the elevator
and in the course of conversation I said to him: "I am going to leave
the building."

"Why?" he asked. I explained.

"What do they pay you?" I told him.

"Well," said he, "I'll tell you what I'll do. I need some help. I have
a vacant room. Come in and help me. Build up your own practice
and you can have the fifteen dollars a week that you got before. That
will keep you going, and besides you can keep your own fees. I want
none of them."

So my first shingle was hung out under Taylor's name, painted on
the one-door entrance at 55 William Street. My father knew at last
that I was going to practice law and became resigned to it. Father
always thought that he had made a mistake in adopting his middle
name, Cohen, instead of his last name, Garnot. He thought I should
not repeat the error. But I had been admitted to the Bar under the
name of Cohen. I would stick it out. The change would require a
lot of explanation. Since there were quite a few Julius Cohens, I did
impose upon my friends the writing out of all three names. Father

accepted this as a compromise. My middle name and his first name became the same.

Taylor differed from either Abbot, Perry or Manice, although in their strict adherence to high moral standards, they differed not at all. He was the first man I ever knew who attended the opera regularly. He knew the entire score of "Aida" by heart. It was his favorite. He sang some of it at the office. I trace back my love of opera to Taylor's inspiration.

Though I disliked all kinds of manual labor, even today, I did get to putting Taylor's files in order and I kept them that way. He was brought up to have other people do the dishwashing and drying.

Taylor read the decisions in the Law Journal every day—the daily report of local judicial decisions—and made elaborate notes. Before there were any digests of these day-to-day decisions, he had put together a set of valuable precedents. Over and over again I saw an adversary stumped by one of these cases. No one else troubled to digest these day-to-day decisions in the Law Journal. (Many years later a publication was created which now does this job of reporting.)

Another trait of Taylor's—he used big black type for the points in his briefs. He also used italics as frequently as periods, commas or semicolons and every once in a while, for good measure, he would throw in an exclamation point. It was his theory that most of the judges never took time to read the briefs. "If they don't catch them quickly, as the readers in the subways catch the headlines, you never get your point across."

One of Taylor's strong qualities was his profanity. It was beautiful. It was comprehensive. It was devastating. Here was blended bourbon, aged in the wood. I thank my stars I picked up some of it. It stood by me and helped me over many rough places when I needed to explode. When Taylor lost a case his profanity solaced him. Did he let fly at the "goddam fools" at General Term and in the Court of Appeals! When I worked on his briefs I agreed with him.

Taylor always expressed himself on the occasions when someone tried to trick him, "I don't mind his trying to put one over on me. What I do mind is the goddam insult to my intelligence which made him think he could succeed."

II

When reform came in and the District Attorney's office was cleaned up, first by Eugene A. Philbin and later by William Travers Jerome, Taylor was made head of the Appeal Bureau. In that position he had charge of all the arguments in the Appelate Division and in the Court of Appeals. It was not the place for drama or for getting one's name in the headlines as William Rand did in the Thaw case or Arthur Train did in some of his highly dramatized works in the courtroom.

Taylor was counsel to the County Medical Society. He prosecuted both men and women who practiced medicine without licenses. These included druggists, abortionists and the like—all were his game. Here is a sample of his cross-examination: A certain Rothbart was arrested for practicing medicine illegally. He advertised as "Dr. Rothbart" and ran some sort of "abortion shop." The charge was that he held himself out as a doctor of medicine. His alibi was that the "Dr." did not mean "doctor" at all. It meant only "director."

In the Magistrate's Court, Taylor asked:

"Can you read?"

"Yes," said Rothbart.

"Well, let us see. Take this newspaper. Read this column of advertisements."

When he got to his own, Rothbart read, *"Doctor* Rothbart." His goose was cooked. I can still hear Taylor's chuckle when he came back to the office and related how he had shot his bird on the wing. The judges liked him. Many of them were his personal friends.

And this is how in Taylor's office I acquired a University of Virginia training as postgraduate course to Abbot's Harvard training. I always felt that Taylor merited advancement to the Bench. But he would not pull strings or run after anything. If it did not come on recognition of merit—"to hell with it." He enjoyed his work, every moment of it. He kept true to the course he set for himself. A proud man, always holding his head high.

CHAPTER THREE

Res ipsa loquitor.
The thing speaks for itself.

A Tragedy and Two Lessons Gleaned Therefrom

*Counterweights crash through the cage of an elevator
—The writer escapes but his neighbor is killed—The
value of contemporaneous records.*

I

ON THE SIXTH OF DECEMBER, 1898, when I had the room in Taylor's
suite on the sixth floor of "55," the United States Fire Insurance
Company had offices on the seventh and eighth floors of the same
building. After a meeting of the Board of Directors, Mr. Griffen, the
Secretary of the United States Fire Insurance Company, boarded the
elevator. I got in on the sixth floor. Besides Mr. Griffen, there were
three or four fellow directors in the car—one of them Mr. Cauldwell.
The elevator struck the bottom of the shaft with such force as to re-
bound. The counterweights, pieces of iron of from forty to sixty
pounds, fell down the shaft breaking through the cage of the elevator.
One of these struck Mr. Griffen on the head and killed him instantly.
Mr. Cauldwell was thrown to the floor of the car and severely in-
jured. I stood directly next to Mr. Griffen, yet escaped with nothing
but a sprained shoulder and shock.

For whatever it is worth, I now believe that chance plays a greater
role in the shaping of men's lives than most of us will admit. The
notion that by one's will, one can wholly shape one's life, I do not
now accept. Probably up to the time of this accident, I did believe that
if I worked hard I was bound to succeed, but now I know that much
of it depends upon the breaks one gets. How much of a man is really
self-made? How much is merely the result of accident?

II

Griffen v. Manice [1] is one of the turning points in our law. The case
was tried before Judge Emery E. Chase and a jury. Mrs. Griffen, the

widow, secured a verdict of $22,500. John E. Parsons tried the case for the defendant and elected to stand on the testimony offered by the plaintiff. That is, he offered no evidence for the defendant.

I was not called as a witness in the trial. Judge Chase charged the jury:

"* * * the rule that where an accident happens, which in the ordinary course of business would not happen if the required degree of care was observed, the presumption is that such care was wanting; and if you find in this case that this accident was one which, in the ordinary course of business, would not have happened if the required degree of care was observed, you have a right to presume that such care was wanting."

The Appellate Division affirmed Judge Chase, but the Court of Appeals reversed. I thought then and still think that Judge Chase's opinion was the sound opinion.

Judge Bartlett said in the Court of Appeals (dissenting):

"In these days of lofty buildings and the annual transportation of millions of passengers in elevators by interested owners, who could not otherwise rent their property, public policy requires them to exercise the same degree of care as is imposed on common carriers."

An incident occurred in connection with the trial of the case that taught me a valuable lesson. I think its telling may prove of value to layman and lawyer alike. The building was owned by William D. F. Manice, the father of William Manice, and Manice, Abbot and Perry, my former employers, took over the defense of the case. After I returned to my office, only a few days after the accident, Perry sent for me and said, "Cohen, while the thing is fresh in your mind, I wish you would write out, in your own hand, your recollection of what occurred." I did that, on plain yellow office draft paper. Later I was called at the coroner's inquest on Griffen's death and gave my testimony.

When the case came up for trial in the Supreme Court a year or so later and Perry was preparing for trial, he asked me to come over to his office and go over my testimony. When I started to describe the accident, I said that after the elevator stopped for me it went faster and faster until it came down with a bump. Now, note this "faster and faster." Perry looked at me in astonishment. "But Cohen," he said, "that isn't what you testified to at the coroner's inquest." "Well, if I testified otherwise, Mr. Perry, I was mistaken. I am telling you the God's truth now."

Perry asked me to think it over. A few days later he called me again. Overnight he had recalled those yellow sheets of paper. There were not more than two or three men written in my own hand immediately after the accident. There appeared clearly these words: "There was no perceptible increase in speed." Of course, when Perry showed this to me I said at once that as it was a contemporaneous record made while the event was fresh in my memory, it would be controlling with me. Perry told me afterwards that he had assured John E. Parsons who was to try the case that I had not been "bought up" by the other side.

III

Since that experience I have read Muensterberg's "On the Witness Stand," and other works on psychology. I have learned to understand the difference between what may be called the *historical* memory and the *logical* memory. Man after man whom I have examined in my office has told me his recollection of events as he honestly believed them to have occurred, only to be confounded later with letters that he had written, putting the events in just the opposite way. This kind of technique—confronting a witness with his own record—is something done on cross-examination, but the examiner should be very careful if he means to be fair, to distinguish between the honest witness who has relied on a *logical* instead of an *historical* memory and the witness who is a deliberate liar.

Two lessons, then, I learned from this elevator accident. First, the importance of accident in its effect in shaping one's life. Second, the importance of records, so that frail, human memory may not be the sole reliance for true record of facts. "Keep records and look at them" —is sound advice.

55 William Street is just across the way from my present office. From my window I now look over into what fifty years ago was William Manice's room. The building, it is true, is only 17 x 67 —a narrow building——but it was a broad one for me. My first bosses were in that building and by example and inspiration they influenced me.

CHAPTER FOUR

Bis vivit qui bene.
He lives twice who lives well.

Horace E. Deming

My third preceptor—The Home Rule Movement for Cities—"Government responsible and responsive to the people"—How much of a fortune can one leave?—The prosecution of a District Attorney.

I

WHILE I WAS STILL at law school, a case made the headlines in the New York newspapers—*Belasco v. Fairbanks*. It was the trial of a suit brought by David Belasco, the playwright and producer, against N. K. Fairbanks, the soap manufacturer. It was brought to recover compensation from Fairbanks which Belasco claimed Fairbanks agreed to pay for his work in training Mrs. Leslie Carter to become a leading actress.

The lawyer for the plaintiff was Horace E. Deming. Not for this case alone, but for many others, he was recognized as one of the outstanding trial lawyers of his day. Since nearly all of his contemporaries are gone, few remember his achievements, both at the Bar and in public work.

About 1899, after I had been with Taylor about a year, Abbot sent for me and said that Horace E. Deming was looking for somebody to aid him in his practice and Abbot had recommended me for the place.

I went down to see Deming and we made the association. My predecessor was Joseph G. Deane, who afterwards became the partner of Charles S. Whitman.

Let me give you a picture of Deming. He differed entirely from Abbot or Taylor. When I first met him, his hair was already white. It was parted in the center. His face was smooth and despite his white hair it was a young face. His lips were thin, there was no mustache. He never really was an old man. A Connecticut Yankee—a gleam in his eye and a laugh that was like that of Will Rogers—dry and under-standing.

Deming was generous. He asked me to take the room that Deane had occupied. I was free to have my own practice. All he wanted was first call on my time. I was given the use of all the staff services I needed. I was guaranteed $2,400 a year and was to divide, half and half, with Deming, all income from my own law practice. On the strength of this financial set-up, I got married.

Deming did not have to learn the Chinese philosophy of life from Lin Yutang. He knew the importance of living—though he preferred to work until the wee hours of the morning and come down about eleven the next day with a sheaf of manuscript developed during the night.

His handwriting was even worse than mine is today, and that is saying a lot. There were only two people who could read it. "S" who was his secretary, and I. But he had style. He would take the material I prepared and rewrite it. When he was through, there were so many interlineations and additions that it was not recognizable as mine. He had made it his own and added to my vocabulary. Deming was a Phillips-Andover man and a graduate of Harvard Law School. A com-plete Cambridge background, with all the best in the traditions of both Phillips-Andover and Harvard.

Deming loved fast horses and up at Putnam he drove at such a pace that he was known throughout the country for his speed. His horses were of fine breed. Indeed, he had a friend in Kentucky who found horses for him and he showed their pedigrees with great pride. After I had been with him for a year, part of my job in the summer con-sisted in looking for new coachmen and hostlers. Deming fired one regularly every two months.

Deming was a perfectionist. If people did not measure up to his high standards, he just "wiped them off the slate." But if I said this and nothing more, one would get a distorted picture of the man. It was my good fortune to hear him read letters sent him by his sons, Harold and Guy, while they were at school. Harold is now a successful admiralty lawyer, a member of one of the leading law firms. No father ever gave his son or daughter a better training than Deming gave his children. He taught them never to shoot an animal. With great pride he read to me letters from Harold describing in great detail how he had sat in a tree for hours, finally catching his bird on the wing—in the camera.

II

The first country place I ever visited was Nip Net, at South Wood-stock, Connecticut. The name is of Indian origin. Among other things, Deming taught his children to read all about Indian life, especially around South Woodstock. Nip Net was simple, pleasantly furnished in the best of taste; the atmosphere was homey, just as was the Deming apartment in New York City. I recall the words over the fireplace in the dining room: "Some Hae Meat And Canna Eat. Some Can Eat And Hae No Meat. But We Hae Meat And We Can Eat. So Let The Lord Be Thankit." Deming was the first real epicure I ever met. Often we would work at the office until long after mid-night and then go off on a search for some restaurant which featured a special delicacy. Mouquin's on Fulton Street was a favorite. I think the first devilled pigs' feet I ever ate he bought for me. I think also that my introduction to tripe came through Deming.

But Deming introduced me to more than food for the body. He dealt with the most vital principles of government—with the funda-mental basis of democracy and the machinery by which to achieve it— the principle which a few years ago was completely forgotten by the "blueprint" boys and the advocates of a "planned society." Dem-ing stands out today for these principles. I came to accept his phi-losophy of government. Forty years after my association with him, when we were writing the brief in the *Shamberg* case for use in the United States Tax Court,* we argued that the Courts should not de-stroy our federal system of government but should continue to recog-nize the great value of the states and of the cities as part of our dual system. Among Deming's papers I found the whole applied philosophy of local self-government. I remember particularly Dem-ing's phrase, "government responsible and responsive to the people." I recognized in these writings some of the original manuscripts which Deming had shown me forty years before. They are as fresh and timely as if they were written today.

Deming knew his John Stuart Mill and he knew his De Tocque-ville.

"* * * Municipal institutions constitute the strength of free nations. Town meetings are to liberty what primary schools are to science; they bring it within the people's reach, they teach men how to use and how to enjoy it. A nation may establish a free government, but without municipal institutions it cannot have the spirit of liberty." [1]

* See Chapter 21.

While Deming was writing, "The Shame of the Cities" by Lincoln Steffens came into print. All over the country graft, avarice and political corruption were rampant in municipal government. "McClures" became a popular magazine in those days, largely because of Lincoln Steffens' and Ray Stannard Baker's exposures of these conditions. The cities of the country seemed to be destined to the fate of Sodom and Gomorrah.[2] Yet a small handful of men believed then that democracy could live on a pattern of local self-government, free from state interference and free from federal domination. They were the *pathfinders* of Municipal Reform. Through them came the plans for municipal self-government; the constitutional amendments guaranteeing home rule to cities; the fusion movements that brought about in New York City elections of mayors like Seth Low, William L. Strong, John Purroy Mitchel and Fiorello La Guardia. Their company was congenial to me.

In 1903, in a banquet speech, Deming said:

"Following the civil war the people began a determined struggle to do away with the abuse of arbitrary power through the centralizing tendencies in government which the storm and stress of war and reconstruction had done so much to foster."

This is true of the present day.

"What is needed in our cities," said Deming, "is a government truly representative of the people of the cities adapted to their local needs and honestly and efficiently administered." How could you expect people to take an interest in local affairs unless they had the power to carry out their plans? To get rid of misgovernment, you must get *local self-government,* free from federal or state interference. His words were prophetic. True statesmanship requires vision. Deming had it.

English writers now see the difference between this distinctively American approach and their own.[3]

The supervision which is exercised over municipal finances in Great Britain has naturally resulted over there in an almost complete loss of free local government. Thus, in Great Britain municipal corporations are treated as on a parity with private corporations and are actually compelled to pay income taxes on their revenues and upon the rental value of their property.[4]

Deming wrote the outstanding work on this subject, "Government of American Cities." He was the Chairman of the Executive Committee of the National Municipal League. Among his most active associates were Clinton Rogers Woodruff, Frank J. Goodnow, William

Dudley Foulke and J. Hampden Dougherty—all outstanding figures in the field of municipal good government—fellow *pathfinders* with Deming.

III

Deming took lickings, a great many of them, in some of which I participated. The first important one I remember was the *Dows* case. That case went to the United States Supreme Court and was the companion to the *Vanderbilt* case. Both were decided together.[5]

I worked on the case with Deming. The question, stated simply, was whether or not the exercise of a power of appointment granted by will furnished a basis for inheritance tax upon the exercise of the power.

David Dows, the father, left his estate to his son, David, Jr., for life, with remainder over to his grandchildren, granting to David, Jr. the power by will to carve out the amount which each grandchild might receive. Under the law, as it then stood, if the power was not exercised by the son, title vested in the grandchild under the grandfather's will. The same situation was involved in the *Vanderbilt* case.

It was in preparing this case that I learned for the first time the clear rule of law that there is no such thing as an *absolute right of inheritance*. Upon his death, the property which a man owns vests legally in the state, with the only qualification that the state may *permit* him to dispose of it by will or by statute, giving his widow and his children in the absence of a will, a share. But this is a *privilege,* not a *right* granted by the state, which it can take away in whole or in part. I have often thought how little the layman appreciates that the state can take all of the property which is owned by him at his death and leave nothing whatever to be distributed to his children. Let the Communists control Congress and the United States government might well, under an Inheritance Tax Law, take over all the private wealth in the country and no amendment to the United States Constitution would be required. In short, Congress can abolish all inheritance of wealth and take over the property by taxation, and even eliminate the right of a state to take over any of the property.

The *Dows* and *Vanderbilt* cases were the first sign in this country of the trend in the direction of breaking up inherited wealth. With the heavy inheritance taxes of today, we are going fast in that direction. How much will the Russian and English experience in collectivism affect our future legal and political development in this field? The extent to which we have already gone is shown by the figures of the William K. Vanderbilt estate. He left an estate of $35,000,000.

Federal inheritance taxes took out $25,000,000, New York State took another $5,000,000—so the heir gets (1945) $5,000,000.[6]

It is entirely within the realm of practical experience that the inheritance taxes of an estate (both federal and state) may exceed the actual realizable value of an entire estate. For example, the appraisal of the value of the good will of a closely held family corporation might far exceed for tax purposes the realizable value of the interest in the business when sold after the decedent's death. Especially is this so where the decedent was the leading spirit in the business itself. His very death might reduce the realizable value of the interest he owned. Inheritance tax appraisals are governed by artificial rules. On the other hand, sales of stock in closely held corporations are governed by actual realty.

My first introduction to the United States Supreme Court came when I went to Washington to file the papers on appeal in the *Dows* case and to be admitted to the Bar of that Court.

Two weeks after my return, I was taken down with typhoid. I drank the water of the Potomac River and at that time it was not filtered. And so I lost the opportunity of helping with the brief or hearing the argument in the United States Supreme Court.

When the case was lost, Deming only smiled—a Coolidge smile. One of his favorite sayings was "live and learn." But his best—which has stayed with me for forty-five years was, "Time holds the trump card."

Hentz v. Havemeyer involved a claim for a million dollars compensation for services performed by Hentz in the organization of the Sugar Trust. Hentz was the father of the "trust" idea. He was the organizer of the tobacco and several other great trusts. All the others had paid him for his services but the sugar magnates would not. So Deming sued them for Hentz. Austen G. Fox tried the case against Deming. Hentz had brought Havemeyer, John E. Searles and all the big sugar refiners together into one combination. For the trial memorandum, I traced through the whole history of the organization of the sugar trust from its very inception. It was an education in itself.

We lost that case. John E. Parsons had advised Havemeyer and his colleagues against the specific form of trust suggested by Hentz. He formed instead for them the American Sugar Refining Company. When he was over eighty years of age, he was indicted along with the other directors of the American Sugar Refining Company for alleged violation of the Sherman Anti-Trust Law. Joseph H. Choate, in his memorial to Parsons, stigmatized that action as "a travesty of justice" and as "government by indictment." [7] By this time what Hentz had tried to do was treated as against the public interest, i.e., as a combination in restraint of trade. Times change.

The court held in Deming's suit that since Hentz could not prove that he had been the final procuring cause of the combination, he was not entitled to the compensation. We argued that he did bring them together and the legal form which they adopted was only a matter of detail. The court held against us.

IV

Charges were presented in October, 1899, to the Governor of New York State—Theodore Roosevelt—by the City Club asking for the removal of the District Attorney, Asa Bird Gardiner. To those who have seen a really honest administration of a district attorney's office under Thomas E. Dewey and Frank S. Hogan, it must be difficult to grasp the realities of the days of Asa Bird Gardiner's administration of the office.

In spite of the proof of Tammany misrule and "Boss" Croker's barefaced admission upon the witness stand that as dictator of the city's affairs he was working for his own pocket all the time, he won in the November, 1900 elections by a large majority.

Deming was named as Special Attorney-General of the State to prosecute these charges and to secure Gardiner's removal from office. The Governor had on his staff in Cuba, a Rough Rider named Captain "C." Roosevelt recommended "C" as an assistant to Deming. Unfortunately, the Captain had little or no experience in trial work. I remember once lunching with him at the City Club and he told me, "This is as exciting as war."

But preparation of a case is not like the G.I.'s work on the battlefront. It is *organization*. It involves something of General Brehon Somervell's job in World War II. It is *logistics*. The senior has to have just the kind of material he needs and has to have it just as and when he needs it on the battlefront.

Some assistants know how to click with their chiefs. Others are either too stupid or too smart. I have been most fortunate in having men of ability assist me, who since, on their own, have achieved positions of distinction. These include Kenneth Dayton, now in Berlin helping to establish order; Theodore B. Richter; Burton Zorn, now a leader in Industrial Relations Law; William Victor Goldberg; Samuel Conrad Cohen; and when I was with Deming, Ralph W. Gwinn, now in Congress from Westchester County, and J. Ard Haughwout—not omitting those on my staff in the law department of the Port of New York Authority—Leander I. Shelley, my successor as General Counsel; Austin J. Tobin, now Executive Director; Sidney Goldstein; Mortimer S. Edelstein; Daniel B. Goldberg; C. Thomas Schettino; Walter Caughlin; William Worksman; John S. Dudley; William Pallme and Charles S. Horowitz. Without their help my own record would be poor indeed, in accomplishment.

Captain "C" was not of this type. And Deming, with his standards of perfection, got to a point where he just could not have him around. I regret to say that Deming did not use profanity. In this respect he fell far below Taylor. When Deming was called in to try the Gardiner case, we both knew that it would take him away from the office for at least a month. It became my job then to take over and carry on the rest of his practice. By that time I knew Deming's clients and they knew me. However, one afternoon, tired and worn out, my white-haired chief came down to 15 William Street and said: "This case will fail unless you can manage somehow to come in and help me." Of course, this would involve night and day work, but having been on the night shift for a number of years, this was not disturbing.

So once more I got into two shifts. I remember in the preparation of the summing up, which was printed for the press, Deming and I worked until four in the morning. Samuel Untermyer was counsel for Gardiner. Untermyer was a master of strategy and could wield a bludgeon, but with the rapier he was no match at all for Deming. Ansley Wilcox was designated by Theodore Roosevelt as the Commissioner to take testimony and make recommendations on the charges. Untermyer's play was to ridicule the entire proceedings and make a farce of the hearings. He was successful. If you got the picture from the news columns, it was a "bear garden" and not a serious proceeding. Untermyer was adept in this kind of tactic. He soon discovered that Wilcox was not a man of firm will, so he played with the Commissioner as many other trial lawyers have done with trial judges. If he had had a stronger trial judge, Deming would have been more successful. He was quick at repartee and ready always on his feet.

One morning Untermyer made a statement. In the afternoon he contradicted himself. Deming observed quietly, "That is not what you stated this morning." Untermyer snarled, "I said nothing of the sort." Deming retorted: "Then your memory is shorter than your tongue." Silence from the other side.

Ansley Wilcox sent in a report to Governor Roosevelt which, while not vindicating Gardiner, was in the nature of a Scotch verdict. However, Roosevelt definitely wanted to remove Gardiner. Accordingly, within two months after he received the Wilcox report, on his own action, he did remove Gardiner. On November 5th, 1900, he sent a letter to Gardiner calling upon him "to assist in the orderly enforcement of the law * * *." [8]

Roosevelt wrote, "The District Attorney refused to heed my letter, and assumed an attitude of defiance, and I removed him from office." [9]

Accordingly, the removal which the City Club sought on evidence supporting definitive charges was achieved. The Governor carried out his purpose to get rid of Gardiner. He named Eugene A. Philbin, an able, high-minded member of the Bar, to succeed Gardiner. Philbin changed the entire color of the office.

V

Deming did fine professional work and knew its value in dollars and cents. His annual income was substantial. Compared with what Samuel Untermyer or William Nelson Cromwell received in fees, Deming's was not large. He did not die a rich man.

Once I drew a will for a client. It involved disposition of an estate running into seven figures. I was to be named as executor. Obviously, the charge should be one that would satisfy the client. Those who read "Country Lawyer" by Bellamy Partridge know that in the city of Phelps, the author's father (who in many ways reminded me of Deming) used to draw wills for his clients for the customary charge of one dollar and for safety he would keep the will in his own safe. Then, when the testator died, the administration of the estate naturally fell into the Partridge law office. Bellamy Partridge says that thirty estates came into the office as the result of this practice and one of his father's one dollar wills brought in an estate from which he drew fees for over twenty years and when Bellamy came into his father's office, he found in the safe a bundle containing more than one hundred wills of people still living. When "Old Tick," a prospective client, was told by Partridge's father that his price for drawing a will was one dollar, he said, "Jees Cri! No reason for a man to die untestate [sic] when he can get a will for a dollar!" [10]

There were lawyers in New York who were shrewd enough to follow a similar course and drew wills for small fees. Later the trust companies, until the Bar stopped them, drew wills without charge for the same reason—in order to get in the business of executorships and trusteeships. After drawing this particular will for my client, I wanted him to fix the charge so that he would be entirely satisfied. I wrote out a brief summary of the work done, the amount involved and the problems presented and asked a few friends at the Bar, confidentially, for an appraisal of the value of the services. I remember the wide margin between Deming's figures and the figures of other lawyers.

My recollection is that Deming suggested $1,500. The lowest estimate came from the man who afterwards became my partner. He was brought up in another type of office, one like that of Partridge's father.

My work in Deming's office gave me training both in court and in office work. Deming was shrewd. Up in "Pootman" as the natives called it, he was known as a good trader. Many a deal he cleared to a business client's delight. But he believed that a private client who got value out of his lawyer's work should pay for it. He never exploited anyone, and no one ever exploited him. The fees he received from private clients did enable him to give the larger part of his time to public work, as he did in the Gardiner case and in the National Municipal League. Deming had no hankering for public office. He never expressed even the hint of an ambition to become a judge. Of course, it is true that his private practice afforded him not less than three times the income which a justice of our Supreme Court then received. But I think Deming enjoyed his freedom.

According to all standards, usual or otherwise, I think the estimate would be that Horace E. Deming was a successful lawyer. He was, in essence, a teacher. If he had not practiced law, he would have been a leading educator. As a matter of fact, he was what John Jay Chapman called his "crack tutor." Indeed, in his early days, Deming did teach school when he was working his way through college. He trained his daughter, Eleanor, and his two sons how to live. Mrs. Deming (Caroline Springstead), was one of the finest and most beloved women of that day. Her children adored her. No place that I have ever been in has ever surpassed Nip Net as a home, filled as it was with culture and simplicity and good humor. Anyone visiting this household, even for a few days, would understand why such people as the Demings make American history. They are the salt of the earth.

VI

Defeat never fazed Deming. The story told of Daniel Webster and Chief Justice Marshall is apposite here.

Webster had been taking one beating after another from the United States Supreme Court. One day he won. At recess he happened to run into Marshall, his friend.

The Chief Justice said, "Well, Daniel, I see you have won a case." Webster replied, "Well, the Court can't be wrong all the time."

Much of success in the law turns upon the "breaks" you get. So the Deming way is the only way to take either success or failure in a lawsuit. You are entitled always to stick to your own opinion and to continue to disagree with the court, even if you go down. Or your client may be actually wrong and you may have deservedly lost the case. But if you had lived with Horace E. Deming, you would have learned that the lawyer who is called in to handle difficult situations starts with the odds against him. He must do his best, even if he knows that the chances are that he will lose. He is not unlike the doctor who knows that the patient may die under his knife, but still must do his best.

Deming had exceptional talent. Indeed, he had the knowledge and the skill which would have made him a great governor, a great senator, an outstanding member of a president's cabinet or even a great president. He was well grounded in the principles of American government and its history. He had a gift for handling men. However, Deming would never have entered the White House by the route trodden by Theodore Roosevelt or Warren G. Harding. To be the independent he was in politics, to find iniquity in municipal government and to fight against it, closed the doors almost completely to any political preferment.

Dickens colorfully pictures lawyers of his day and Arthur Train pictures some of ours. They make delightful reading for those who want color in their drama. The characters are all of one type. In nearly all the motion pictures where a lawyer plays a part, the directors seem to think that the audience prefers lawyers who are scurvy and tricky. Yet if this book does anything, it should reveal to the lay reader that there are lawyers of different types who live with great satisfaction to themselves and render great service to others. Someday the drama of a great lawyer of character will find its appeal in the movies. It has already found such appeal upon occasion, as in "The Life of Emile Zola," where the defense of Captain Dreyfus is well portrayed. "For the Defense," the life of Marshall Hall, the great English barrister, contains many chapters which would make a splendid movie.

Deming made his choices deliberately. He held his head high. He deliberately chose the career of a gentleman, a scholar, a fine father, a fine husband, an independent citizen and a great lawyer. And he had a fine time doing it.

CHAPTER FIVE

*"Orthodoxy, my Lord," said Bishop Warburton, in a whisper,—
"orthodoxy is my doxy,—heterodoxy is another man's doxy."*
"Memoirs," JOSEPH PRIESTLY, Vol. I, page 572.

Dr. Felix Adler

---

*"Learn by doing"—A great moral leader beats out a
new trail—A man of philosophy and wit—Tenement
house and law reform—Influence of an idea upon the
legal profession.*

I

EVERY LEADER NEEDS A COMPASS. The former Chief Rabbi of Rome,
after the release of Rome by the Allies, told Herbert L. Matthews, of
"The New York Times" that "Mussolini voyaged on the great sea of
history without a compass." [1] Felix Adler was the greatest of the
moral leaders of our day. He found a compass for himself and others.

In religion and philosophy he wanted but one compass—that was
a compass pointing in the direction of truth. It was to be adequate
for all persons of all creeds and all races.

He was called "atheist" and though he never quite satisfied orthodox Jews, in later life he came to be respected by the leaders of all
faiths. Through his study of the Orient, he knew the life and teachings of Buddha, Confucius, Mohammed and Christ.

Before World War I, he called together a Congress of Religions.
The purpose was to find agreements on the principles common to all
religious faiths and to achieve a better mutual respect.

Bound by no ties of formal religion he was influenced by all of
them. No one who listened with his mind to the Doctor could preach
or adopt a defeatist attitude toward life. Albert Jay Nock's friend,
Edward Epstean, reasoned with Nock:

"When God created man, * * * He created man part divine, part bestial, and
the two elements have been at war within the individual ever since. When the
bestial side gets the better of it for the moment, as it will every now and then,
and you go wrong, don't bother over repenting and nagging yourself about it.

Let it go,—forget it,—to hell with it!—and put your energy harder than ever on building up the divine side. Don't try to repress the bestial side. Repression is negative, enervating. Put all your work on the positive job, and you can afford to let the bestial side take its chances." [2]

Felix Adler would be inclined on the whole to agree with this, but he also taught that to "build up on the divine side," you must *apply the rule in action,* putting all your heart and soul into doing the thing that was set before you. You *must fight* against wrong and whether you liked it or not, you fulfilled your own destiny only by constantly doing your best. By acting this way, you got the only satisfaction out of life that is really worth while.

Nock finds that Jesus' teaching was reasonable because it was based upon experience as a way of life. That was the nub of Adler's faith. Speaking of Jesus, Nock says:

"His way of life is not to be followed because He recommended it, or because He was virgin-born, or was a part of the Godhead, or could work miracles, or for any other reason than that experience will prove that it is a good way, none better, if one have but the understanding and tenacity of purpose to cleave to it; neither of which I have, and I believe very few have." [3]

It is in the end of this sentence that Nock falls down. Felix Adler— like a good golf professional—taught you to "follow through." Nock apologizes for not doing it himself. But it was the hard, gritty, common sense of Felix Adler which led him to apply his positive philosophy to every act of life. He always taught that the means you used were as important as the end.

In the eighties, Dr. Adler started, with the assistance of Professor Edwin R. A. Seligman, new model tenement houses erected by the Ethical Culture Society on Cherry Street. This marked the beginning of Tenement House Reform in America. At that time Stanton Coit was a young assistant to Dr. Adler.

Teaching in the school he founded, or in the seminars he led at Columbia, from which many great moral leaders graduated, as well as preaching on Sundays from his own platform, Felix Adler urged his hearers always to believe that there was a Godhead in all of us, that there was something *divine* in us, but that it was to be found only by reaching down into ourselves and bringing it up. By bringing out the best in others, he taught, we bring out the best that is in ourselves. "To put forth power in such a way as to be provocative of power in others is the ethical aim that should guide men in all vocations and in all their relations." [4]

Dr. Adler and Judge Oliver Wendell Holmes were in complete accord on two points. Holmes said: "Life is action and passion, * * * I think it is required of a man that he should share the action and the passion of his time at peril of being judged not to have lived." [5]

Again, "If I were dying," Holmes wrote at eighty-odd to a young man, "my last words would be, 'Have faith and pursue the unknown end.' " [6] And, "To know is not less than to feel," he said. "A valid idea is worth a regiment any day." [7] Adler said the same thing over and over.

II

Dr. Adler was bald. He had a well rounded head, a strong Roman nose—suggestive of Savanarola in profile. He wore a mustache and a scraggly beard—something like an oriental's. In physical size he seemed diminutive when he came near but on the platform he seemed twice his height.

Arthur Eisig went to his residence on Sixtieth Street near Third Avenue to ask him to perform his wedding ceremony. After all the arrangements were made for the wedding, the Doctor asked Arthur to go for a walk with him. As they walked from the house, which was between Lexington and Third Avenues, toward Fifth Avenue, and were engaged in general conversation, the Doctor said, "Arthur, you will have to excuse me now. I have some thinking to do."

He had the gift of making one feel at home in his company. If the other fellow had any diffidence, it soon disappeared. The Doctor made him talk about himself and of his work and of his interests. By the way, it was in that very house on Sixtieth Street that I came into the circle of young men whom the Doctor brought together in the late eighties to discuss political ethics. This group included Joseph M. Price, who afterwards played a great part in the movement for better government in New York City and later became President of the City Club; Arthur K. Kuhn, an international law expert; Robert D. Kohn, the architect, afterwards President of the Society for Ethical Culture; Abraham L. Gutman, later one of my partners; John Lovejoy Elliott, one of the assistant leaders of the Society; Benjamin G. Paskus and Edgar A. Hellman.

After the serious business of the evening was covered, we would adjourn to the basement of the Doctor's house. Here, in his dining room, the Doctor would doff his thinking cap and the robes of a divine, and lead us into what became a students' beer and sandwich party. He loved to tell a good story. And here is one of them:

In class the little girls were each asked to select a maxim and write about it. One little girl of seven took as her text "Virtue is its own reward."

"There was a young man who fell in love with a rich candylady's daughter. But he was very, very poor. So when he asked the candylady if he could marry her daughter, she said 'No' because he was poor. So the young man was very sad and he decided to become a drunkard, when suddenly something made him change his mind. He said: 'No, I will not become a drunkard.' But as he walked away from the saloon his foot kicked something and he looked down and what do you suppose he found? A pocketbook containing a million dollars in gold. He picked it up and went back to the rich candylady and showed her the gold and once more asked to marry her daughter. This time the candylady said 'Yes.' And so they got married and had a big wedding and the next day they had twins and so *virtue is its own reward.*"

III

Up near Elmsford, the Fairview Country Club was obliged to give up its golf course when the City decided to take over the property for a filtration plant. The Club was forced to move across the Saw Mill River Road. One day, my wife and I walked over the old grounds. The pear trees were full of ripe pears and they were falling to the ground. This she thought was a great waste. She packed up a couple of bushel baskets, put them in the car, brought them home and then canned them. Later, when the Doctor and Mrs. Adler came to visit us, some of these canned pears were set before us. At dinner, I said very seriously to the Doctor that I had a difficult ethical problem to present to him. He took on his most sober manner. I put in the point that the property belonged to the City and legally the trees and fruit went along with it, at least with the title. I told him where the pears came from. "Now, Doctor, the question is this: Is it moral for us to eat these pears?"

Dead silence. He had started to eat the pears and he went on slowly, until he had spooned the last morsel, then said, "I think it is highly immoral to eat these pears."

He was fuller of real fun, prankish, impish fun than any man I ever met. That is the way he acted when he visited us. But one day just as we were about to finish our dinner the front doorbell rang and some friends came in. Before the doorbell rang, the dining room had been full of joyous laughter. The Doctor had just finished some joke or story. My wife and I never saw such a change in a man as happened at that moment. As soon as our friends entered, he again became the great moral leader, taking on at once all the dignity becoming the head of the Society for Ethical Culture.

His hand was cold, barely touching yours and people did say of him as they said of the Society, that they both lacked the warmth that should accompany a minister or a church. However, when he got up to St. Huberts in the Adirondacks and he came down from his "Eagle's Nest" (Adler is German for "eagle") and met someone he knew and cared for, he was once more just a full-fledged imp of Satan and warm and hearty.

It so happened that Dr. Sigmund S. Goldwater of Mt. Sinai Hospital and one time Commissioner of Health for New York City publicly advanced the idea that the use of liquor, especially whiskey, was bad for the health. Dr. Adler was fond of his highball. When we called at St. Huberts shortly after the Goldwater preachment, Dr. Adler prepared one for himself and one for me. "You see," he said, as he poured the whiskey, "I still like my *gold water.*"

His fondness for puns was notorious. (Like Charles Lamb in this respect.)

We invited him once to come up to Ausable Lake where we were to sleep on pine boughs in a lean-to. It was about fifteen miles away from his place at St. Huberts. Mrs. Adler asked him how he would let us know of any change of plan in case of rain. He promptly replied, "I'll walk up there and tell them I'm not coming."

IV

The name of his institution is "The Society for Ethical Culture." It is a ponderous title. Its meaning is to be found in the words over the platform of the meetinghouse on Central Park West and Sixty-fourth Street: "The Place Where Men Meet to Seek the Highest Is Holy Ground."

Dr. Adler was invited to speak in a southern city. A synopsis of his work was handed to the chairman to aid him in his introduction. The chairman introduced him as the great leader of the "Agriculture Society of New York." The Doctor enjoyed that story, but he never felt that the man who made the introduction was very much to blame.

When Dr. Adler formed his Society, he intended to keep it free of all creed and formalism. "Ethical Culture" meant the constant development of one's character through experience. But it was deeply religious—deeply spiritual. It made no difference what church a person belonged to, if only he believed in that one rule. Unless one lived in the movement and listened to Dr. Adler or the other leaders, like John Lovejoy Elliott or Horace Bridges or David S. Muzzey or Henry Neumann or Algernon D. Black, the name of the Society would mean little or nothing. I believe there are thousands of residents of the City of New York who have not the slightest conception of the nature of the movement. Of course, a great many people do know about the "Ethical Culture School" and it is difficult to say which was the Doctor's greater interest, the School or the Society. He developed the School because he believed that the larger results he aimed at could be best secured through the training of the younger generation. That he was successful is shown by the tribute paid to him by educators. To cite one instance: When an appeal was made to John D. Rockefeller, Jr. to contribute substantially to the School to enable it to carry on its work, he first of all required a very careful study of the School to be made, of its methods as well as its aims. This was done by competent experts. On the basis of their report, Rockefeller made a very handsome contribution. Yet, outside the educational field, I doubt whether many people ever think of the Ethical Culture School as anything but a "good *prep* school." This is unfortunate for its aim is comprehensive and universal.

In applying his philosophy to life, the Doctor believed that professional men should solve their own ethical problems out of their own experiences and that the duty of applying general principles of ethics to their problems was primarily a job for lawyers themselves. This point of view led to the formation of a group of lawyers that came to include deans of law schools, professors in law schools, judges, prosecuting officers, public officials and active practitioners, all members of the Bar, all men of varying but real experience.

I sent out, as its Secretary in December of 1908, the invitations to join this group. Later, it was my job to get the group together at irregular intervals. To name some of the members: Everett V. Abbot, Albert Sprague Bard, Charles A. Boston, Stewart Chaplin, Judge Joseph E. Corrigan, Abraham L. Gutman, Henry W. Jessup, Laurence Arnold Tanzer, Edmond E. Wise, Paul Fuller, Dean George W. Kirchwey, Professors Nathan Abbot and Ralph W. Gifford. It was in this group that there was prepared, largely by Everett V. Abbot, the "draft of a judiciary article for the new constitution" presented to the New York State Constitutional Convention of 1915. Indeed, out of this group, Abbot drew the material for his book, "Justice and the Modern Law," but out of it came also what is known as "The Legal Ethics Clinic"—a very definite and distinct contribution to the legal profession.

After Charles A. Boston had been active in the group for three years, he made the recommendation to the New York County Lawyers Association that its standing committee on professional ethics "be empowered, when consulted, to advise inquirers respecting questions of proper professional conduct * * *" This had been carried on for several years when Dean Ezra R. Thayer of the Harvard Law School wrote of it:

"The New York County Lawyers' Association has given another striking instance of what thoughtful members of the Bar experienced in affairs can do in the way of practical help to their fellow-lawyers and to the community in its so-called 'Legal Ethics Clinic.' This phrase has been aptly used to describe the work of the committee of that association on professional ethics in answering properly formulated questions concerning the application of the recognized principles of ethics to situations actually arising in practice. This undertaking has displayed in a new and interesting way the quality of the common law which Lord Haldane so aptly described 'not as something that waits to be embodied in abstract codes before it can be said to exist, but as what we ourselves are progressively and cooperatively evolving.' The response which has met this new departure and the widespread interest in the committee's work have attested the value of such an attempt to deal with evils by preventive methods; and the committee's published reports of its answers to questions have for a common lawyer the peculiar interest which accompanies the test of any general proposition by its application to concrete realities."

I was a member of this Committee for twenty-four years. Its work still goes on. In many of the law schools of the country its questions and answers are used as the basis for instruction in legal ethics. In "The Law: Business or Profession?" I have given in detail the work the Committee had done up to the time of its writing, and added in an appendix many of the more important questions and answers that it had completed.

The credit for the movement should go to Felix Adler. It was due to him that the Bar was made in this way to feel its responsibility for developing a system of applied professional ethics.

V

In Adler moral wrath came forth like the thunderbolts of Jehovah. When in the nineties he was the leader in the movement for healthier tenement houses, after he had made his own inspection trips and visited tenements owned by the Trinity Corporation, he put his indignation into words. The rafters trembled, the walls shook. Under his spell, you felt that God Himself would at any instant come down from His heaven and slay the men who had so forgotten their duties to their fellowmen as well as the teachings of their own church.

I know of no other man in my day who could vent such indignation upon social wrongdoing. He let it go against political wrongdoing each Sunday just before Election Day. During the wave of imperialism in the Theodore Roosevelt period and at the very time of the seizing of the Philippines and of the Panama Canal, he stood upon the platform of the meeting house and after calm analysis of the facts, his voice rose to a great crescendo. His sentences tingled in one's ears all through the following week. He was a great dramatist. He knew the art of modulating the voice. Sometimes he would play the pipes very soft and low. Sometimes it rose to fortissimo. Then his eyes flashed. No play-acting. But it was well-controlled eloquence suggestive more than anything else I have ever seen of the Prophets of the Old Testament. Of course, he knew that passion played a large part in influencing conduct, and that by appealing on the higher plane you could hope to supplant the appeal of the lower passions. The appeal was from "Richard Drunk" to "Richard Sober."

Frustration meant for this man postponement but for the moment. For him the fight went on just the same. Felix Adler never believed civilization faced destruction. His belief included the faith that there was enough goodness in the world to save it from going to hell.

Given the intimate confidences of many types of men and women, as a lawyer gets them, I have come to know the defeatist in the flesh. This type believes that "you can't change human nature." That you must be "realistic." I have heard defeatists say "I'm all washed up—I'm through." And when clouds came to darken the horizon they saw only rocks upon which their ship was about to smash up. If you had Adler's faith, you could not be a defeatist. You might be too much of an optimist, but never a defeatist. What Bismarck always called "the imponderables," great religious teachers understand. They have found the compass to guide them on the sea of life.

Dr. Adler had the rare gift too, of understanding men and of forecasting events. He knew that *training* rather than *education* was what men needed. And for such training, they need to put their hands to doing things. Out of experience, they would learn the truth.

VI

We who knew him as a member of the Board of Trustees of the Society, knew him as an excellent business man. In this respect he resembled many rabbis. There is a kind of shrewdness which often accompanies great idealism.

When in the summer of 1917, the then Mayor of New York, John Purroy Mitchel, upon the joint recommendation of Morris Hillquit, the lawyer for the union, and myself, lawyer for the employers, called a group of men together as a Council of Conciliation to make recommendations for the settlement of the strike then pending in the Cloak Industry, Hillquit and I, with the approval of our clients, both agreed that Felix Adler was the one man ideally suited to sit as Chairman of that Council. On my part, I counted upon his business sagacity to understand the employer's side. Hillquit relied on his sense of justice. Both of us were right.

It was a hot summer in July, 1917. The Doctor had gone to his place in St. Huberts in the Adirondacks. We believed it was imperative that we should get him back to New York. I recalled then one of his own stories he had told twenty years earlier in the basement of his house on Sixtieth Street. This is the story:

"A colored man went out in the woods to pray. He prayed, 'Lord, please come down to help this sinner. Please, Lord, come, but come yourself. Don't send Your Son. *Dis am no child's play.*' "

I wired the Doctor at St. Huberts, supplementing Mayor Mitchel's call: "Come thou, thyself—this is no child's play." He afterwards told my wife the telegram did the trick. He came not only because of his fine sense of public duty, but because always near that sense of duty was a fine sense of humor. He loved a joke, even if it were at his own expense. And he loved this turning the story on himself. He did come and he made one of the greatest contributions in the history of industrial relations.

In 1944, Catholic cardinals, Jewish rabbis and Protestant ministers joined in a "Pattern of Peace" of which the first basic principle is the *recognition of the supremacy of the moral law*. Adler would be pleased with such a move if he were here. *This was his compass for life.*

CHAPTER SIX

"And thou shall do that which is right and good in the sight of the Lord; that it may be well with thee, and that thou mayest go and possess the good land which the Lord swore unto thy fathers."

Deut. 6:18.

Dr. John P. Peters

The upper West Side—The author joins the City, the Reform, the Twilight, the Good Government Clubs and the Independent Club of the West Side—Dr. Peters' great fight over the Amsterdam Avenue grab— The Transit Committee of One Hundred—The "free transfer fight"—College professors beat a political machine.

I

THERE WAS A TIME when the residents of the upper West Side, especially of that section west of Central Park and between the Nineties and Morningside Heights, shared their habitat with the goats and the squatters. In 1910 I remember an occasion when, to evict an old squatter, it required several marshals of a municipal court and two policemen to carry her out from a rickety old shack on the rocks in the shadow of the Cathedral of St. John the Divine, and the goats paid not the slightest bit of attention to the performance. The owner of the property expected to erect a modern apartment house upon the site. But the old lady thought she had the legal right to continue there because of her long occupancy. Someone must have told her that "possession is nine points in the law," but she had possession *without claim of legal title,* and that could not help her.

The nice ladies standing about thought it was a sheer act of cruelty to put the old lady out in the street. If the landlord or his lawyer could have been identified in the crowd, it would have gone hard with him.

In the Eighties and Nineties transportation consisted of horsecars, later cablecars and then the West Side "L" which stopped at 110th Street. There was a station at Ninety-third Street. I came to know this station in 1896 and 1897. I used it to return to East Twelfth Street where we then lived. You see, the family of my fiancée owned a house on Central Park West between Ninety-fifth and Ninety-sixth Streets, and she lived there. I shall not make any effort to record the hour of my arrival at home or the hour of my departure from Central Park West, except to mention that one of her sisters every so often did drop down into the entrance hall a pitcher of water to accelerate my departure and shorten my "good-nights."

On the upper West Side there lived a lot of fine people. Alfred Corning Clark built a great mansion at Eighty-ninth Street and Riverside Drive, opposite where the Soldiers and Sailors Monument now stands —designed by Charles and Arthur Stoughton—the architects who in 1909 laid out our place at Elmsford, in Westchester. The Clark residence was one of the sights of New York. I remember when my wife and I pretended we were out-of-town visitors and took a sight-seeing bus for the "rubber neck" trip around the Island. The brash young guide, when we reached the Clark mansion, called out through the megaphone, "This is where Bishop Potter lives *with* Mrs. Alfred Corning Clark." Of course, having kept up to date, we knew that the Bishop and the Widow Clark were properly married and that Alfred Corning Clark had died and that both the latter's funeral and the Bishop's wedding were all carried out in fine church style.

But in addition to Bishop and Mrs. Potter, there were other quiet, refined people living in that neighborhood—good citizens.

II

It seems to me that for a young man with a limited income, I did join a lot of clubs. Deming encouraged it. There was the City Club, the Reform Club, and the Twilight Club. There always was good food and good talk. You do make friends that way.

The City Club two years ago celebrated its fiftieth anniversary. It was founded by Edward Kelly. He was a lawyer with a lucrative practice in Paris and came back to New York to stir up his lazy classmates and friends who submitted to being walked over by Tammany. He tried to get artisans and laborers to join the Club, and when he failed, he resigned in despair and turned to Socialism. Kelly was also responsible for the initiation of the Good Government Clubs, nicknamed by the cynics of the day as the "Goo Goos." To be good, and to think of good government as something achievable in Tammany-ruled New York was in those days so highly fantastic as to merit derision and satire.

The family of my future wife thought that way too. They were respectable, regular "silk-stocking Republicans."

But to go back for a moment to the Twilight Club. This was not a political reform club. It was founded by General George W. Wingate, also founder of the Twilight Club in the Catskills. He brought together authors, doctors, lawyers and businessmen who came right uptown from their offices to dine at the St. Denis Hotel, then at 11th Street and Broadway—as famous as Delmonico's for good food.* I shall tell you how I qualified for membership there. I was Deming's guest. The subject was "Tariffs and Subsidies. Oh Lord, Oh Lord, How Long!" The discussion went around the table. Each man was given not more than five minutes.

Being still fresh from Dr. Simonson's influence up at the Thirtieth Street High School—I wrote a paper there on "Free Trade"—I made my little argument and sat down. Opposite me was a Mr. Sperry, who was in the yarn business. One of the "infant industries," requiring a protective tariff—at least Mr. Sperry thought so. When it came to his turn, he pulled out of his pocket a series of tables of statistics—always a delightful piece of pastry at the end of a dinner. As he reeled off the figures, demonstrating to Mr. Sperry's entire satisfaction that business was superbly good under President McKinley's administration and desperately bad under Cleveland's, he turned on me with a devastating glare, and in acid tones said, "Now, put that in your pipe and smoke it, young man." When he did this for about the fifth time, I asked, "Will it burn, Mr. Sperry?" Then quick as a flash came from the old poet Joel Benton, down at the other end of the table, "Of course it will. It's mostly gas."

I was elected on the basis of Benton's wit.

III

Along about 1902, I found that quite a few of my friends belonged to the "Independent Club of the West Side." Good Government Club "C" dissolved and its members went into the Independent Club. Dr. John P. Peters was its head. In this group, besides Deming, there were many other outstanding figures. Edward B. Whitney, one of the ablest lawyers of my time, afterwards a Justice of the Supreme Court, John DeWitt Warner and Meyer D. Rothschild, two of the group who were in the lead in 1898 in the nomination of Theodore Roose-

* Gregory Weinstein in his book, "The Ardent Eighties" [1] says General Wingate "had a talent for picking witty presiding officers as well as brilliant speakers. Their peculiar views didn't worry him. He rather liked cranks or people with hobbies. 'Tell us what your hobby is,' he would say, 'we will either ride it with you, or rid you of it.'"

velt on an independent ticket; the head of Teachers College, Dr. John Russell; the head of the Economics Department of Columbia University, Dr. Edwin R. A. Seligman, and Cyrus L. Sulzberger, father of Arthur Hays Sulzberger, publisher of "The New York Times." Besides, there were Alfred P. W. Seaman, about whom I shall tell you a little later, and Alfred A. Whitman, of the banking firm of Knauth, Nachod and Kuhne—"naughty naked coon" they called the firm downtown. They all became my friends.

I joined Dr. Peters' club about 1902. The club met for dinner every month or so at a hotel on the upper West Side and there I met and came to know the Doctor. Let me describe him.

It seemed to me he had none of the theological difficulties that beset Dr. Felix Adler. He took his religion as he took his cloth—with ease and comfort and in turn gave ease and comfort to his congregation and inspiration to everyone who came within the range of his voice.

Did you ever meet a little round-faced jolly priest—not much taller than a pint, with a bald head and a little black cap, perked rakishly on the back of his head—for all the world like a white bird with a black crest, with the finest sense of humor and fun bubbling all over? Well, that was my friend, Dr. Peters—only he was not a priest. He was the minister at St. Michael's Protestant Episcopal Church at Broadway and 99th Street. Dr. Peters was the friend of priests and rabbis—of Bishop Potter, indeed of all the religious leaders of his day and the professors in the academic world.

In civil life, he was *a little scrapper*. He resembled a little fighting bantam in a cock fight—and how he loved it! He would fight against any evil that showed its head around Ninety-sixth Street and Amsterdam Avenue or for that matter around any part of the upper West Side.

In the late eighties, His Satanic Majesty raised his head over and swished his tail around Dr. Peters' way. He took on the form and garb of the "street railroads." They were pretty bad in those days. If you don't know it, just go down to the library and read up a bit about the "Boodle Alderman" and "Jake" Sharp and the Broadway Street Railway Franchise.[2]

Now, the Metropolitan Street Railway had a car line running up Amsterdam Avenue. The Third Avenue Railway was a competitor. It succeeded in getting a franchise to extend its line up the same avenue. If it had gone on there would have been four railroad tracks on which cable cars would run directly in front of Dr. Peters' chapel. The children going to and from school would have to cross these tracks at least twice daily and once on Sunday. Old Satan could not get away with anything like that as long as Dr. Peters was around.

So began the historic "Amsterdam Avenue Fight." It filled the front pages of the newspapers of that day. *The Doctor won.* He won a complete and authentic victory. The Devil was licked—the Third Avenue Railway did not run those two extra tracks up Amsterdam Avenue.

IV

In that battle, the Doctor drew around him practically every man and woman of the West Side who believed in good government, and their confidence in the Doctor became a sort of powerhouse and generating plant for very large and important reform movements. The whole town was set afire when the "Black Horse Cavalry" began operations in Albany. They were the group of senators and assemblymen who, for a modest, or immodest, pecuniary reward, would pass or defeat any bills as the railroads wanted it done. The Doctor went after them as the Allies went after the Germans in 1944–1945. And he won again.

About the time I joined the Club the "Four Track Fight" had already been won. The Doctor wore his medals quite proudly but with a clergyman's appropriate modesty. He did smile.

He then took up, generally, the transit conditions on the upper west side. They were almost unbearably bad and there was no place where we could hope to get relief. "The public be damned" attitude prevailed. There was, it was true, a Railroad Commission, but it was packed by politicians and the railway companies knew the politicians and the politicians knew the Commissioners. There were not enough elevated trains to accommodate people going to and from their work. You were neither sure of getting downtown in time to keep your morning engagements nor getting home in time for dinner. The cars were dirty. Something had to be done about it. And the Doctor did something.

There was enough independence and fight in that group of his to make up six or seven groups of "vigilantes" such as those who worked on the Pacific Coast in pioneer days. Moreover, there was a whole troupe of lawyers whom the Doctor could call upon. Out of the West Side Independent Club there came the "Transit Reform Committee of 100" (1900–1905).

The Doctor put me in as Secretary and under his inspiration I drew up the proclamation and call—I think in tempo, at least, it resembled the Declaration of Independence. It was a clarion call to arms—it rang like the bell in Independence Hall in Philadelphia before it cracked. But just as in the war, if you are in the marines, or in the air corps, or are just a plain G.I., the fellows along with you in the scrap become your pals and those of you who survive stick together for the rest of your lives. Thus, many of my best friends, though most of them have since passed away, came with this group—particularly through this Transit Group.

We quickly broke up into several committees and started off with our bazookas and rocket bombs. We hunted up the enemy in the hedgerows. I chanced to discover a dump of ammunition left behind, rather carelessly, I must say now. Let me tell you about it.

V

When the street railways were made up of a lot of small units, some financiers came along and decided to form a system—consolidate all the little units into a big one. Thus came about the "Met" and the "Third Avenue" systems. They had no difficulty in putting through at Albany the legislation they needed. But someone had slipped into the Railroad Law a paragraph really intended for the benefit of the public. The railroads never forgave themselves for letting this get by.

There was a section in the railroad laws under which every passenger was entitled to a free transfer at every intersection in any railroad system. So if you got on a streetcar and gave the conductor a nickel and wanted to change cars to go across town, you asked for the transfer to which you were entitled. Worse than that for the companies, this provision in the law entitled you *to collect a penalty of fifty dollars for every refusal to give you a transfer!* There it was right in the statute! If any law student had taken the trouble to look it up he could easily have found it long before. And transfers were being refused several hundred times a day! The railroads treated the provision as if it had no existence and no one had been given the assignment to look up the law on this point.

It fell within the scope of the subcommittee of which I was chairman to look up the law. Browsing through the statutes, I was so astounded to find these "free transfer" provisions that I immediately asked that Edward B. Whitney, Henry B. B. Stapler and several other veteran lawyers on the committee check up on me.

After examination, they confirmed my conclusions but they turned down flat one of my recommendations. (I still think it would have been *good business* to have carried it through.) I recommended that the "Committee of one hundred" bring test cases, establish the law, organize a bureau for the reception of complaints and get in all these claims. We might recover as much as $50,000—I thought—and we could use that money very nicely, thank you, to finance all the other branches of the fight against the railroad companies. But Whitney, Warner, Stapler and all the other older men, did not like this suggestion at all. I guess they were right. People might have thought that we lawyers had some share in the cash proceeds, no matter how many statements we might make that we would devote the money entirely to the cause. These older heads were wiser. We decided to bring a test case and Paul Blume, who was with Whitman's firm, Knauth, Nachod and Kuhne, became our first plaintiff. Later, in mandamus proceedings, James S. Lehmaier was the petitioner.

We won the test cases and established the soundness of the law. A judge in the Municipal Court, Francis J. Worcester, decided our way. Later, the suit in the Supreme Court also was decided in our favor.

Now it just happened that there were other lawyers in town who did not agree with Whitney, Stapler, et al. One of them had an office in the same building with me. He decided that the way to contribute to the public service was to bring many of these suits. So he brought them in wholesale lots to recover the penalties. As the outraged citizens poured into his office, he did a land-office business. How much he made for himself, nobody knew, but I heard stories about gross receipts of $40,000. I think the stories were exaggerated. It was a joke, wasn't it, for Whitney, Lehmaier and the others to supply the legal talent, sustain the law and then for some other lawyer to get the pecuniary benefits of it all? But the result for the Committee of one hundred was that it secured a great deal of favorable publicity and prestige.

The Committee next prepared a bill which was intended to overhaul the entire legislation regulating public utilities in New York. When, as a result of his exposure of the insurance scandals, Charles E. Hughes became Governor of the State, we made so much noise up on the West Side that we were able, with the aid of the Citizens Union Legislation Committee, to draft and secure the passage of the Public Service Commission Law and to have Hughes put in, as the first Chairman, former Ambassador Oscar S. Straus, and, as its first Secretary, Travis Whitney. Now that was progress. It is the simple fact, however, that all this law work was contributed by busy practitioners of the law—not a single one of them with any motive of self-interest.

VI

The "Gay Nineties" was a cynical period, it is true. Of course, there were in those days men who profited from the combination of corrupt politics and rotten business and the people of New York "took it on the chin." The editorials in the "Sun" of that day were perhaps the best editorials, from the point of view of style, that were written, but they reflected the cynical mood of the day.

Against this the incandescence of Dr. Peters' leadership lit up not only Broadway all over the west side, but lit up all of New York. His good humor, his sincerity, his selflessness, the example of "a man of the cloth" playing his part as a good citizen, were inspiring. I have always suspected that his lead in the four track Amsterdam Avenue fight came through his love of little children—he did love them and they loved him. His Parish House was always filled with laughing and joyous boys and girls.

The Peters family was indeed a fine family. The sisters, Marian, Frances and Sally worked with I. S. C.* Out of this independent group under Dr. Peters' leadership came an interesting fight brought on by the Republican leader of the District, Abe Gruber. Little Abe got the legislature to create a wholly unnecessary Municipal Court District right there on the West Side in Dr. Peters' back yard. The only excuse for such a new Municipal Court District was to augment Abe's political power. He got the bill through and signed. We were unable to defeat it and then he induced Mayor Low to appoint William S. Bennet judge of the Court. Bennet was all right, but he had to be beaten. A mere handful of men nominated Alfred P. W. Seaman by petition on an independent ticket. We got the Democrats to endorse him, too. That was an outflanking move against Little Abe. The Democratic leaders had the good sense to see that by joining with us they could win their first Democratic victory in the district. Up to that time, Abe Gruber had carried this "silk stocking" district all in his vest pocket.

Seaman did not want the nomination at all. James S. Lehmaier intended to put the coat on another lawyer, but that lawyer got one jump ahead of him and nominated Seaman—obviously a much more desirable nominee, as he proved to be after his election to the office.

On election day, Gruber had to take his licking. That was a great campaign. College professors from Columbia joined with their students in house-to-house canvasses. Seaman did become a Municipal Court Judge; more than that, he afterwards became head of that Court. He reorganized it from top to bottom—that was another one of the by-products of Dr. Peters' West Side group.

Then came the big fight against the New York Central Railroad— "Death Avenue and Riverside Drive." That story fits into another chapter and with another portrait, but in this fight our little witty leader of the cloth, with the bald head and the little black cap

* See Chapter 14.

perched on his pate, was not only a great *pilot,* but he was a sure fire *bombardier.* He dropped his bombs just where they should be dropped. Going along with him on his flights was a great joy in what Oswald Garrison Villard appropriately calls "Fighting Years."

So here is his portrait. I have not been up to St. Michael's in years, but for me it is the place where Dr. John P. Peters preached and practiced what he regarded as good Christianity—and we all thought so too.

CHAPTER SEVEN

"The man that hath no music in himself,
Nor is not moved by· concord of sweet sounds,
Is fit for treasons, stratagems and spoils.
The motions of his spirit are dull as night,
And his affections dark as Erebus;
Let no such man be trusted."

The Merchant of Venice, SHAKESPEARE.

Frank Damrosch

A man of music brings it to the people—The People's Singing Classes—The People's Choral Union and the Chorus of the Society for Ethical Culture—An incident in the author's life which indissolubly links him and one other with this phase of musical life.

I

WHAT IS THE DISTINCTION between popular and classical music? As Elie Siegmeister tells us:

"Long before the earliest recorded compositions by professional music-makers, the plain people sang and danced, chanted lullabies and work songs and prayers to their gods. * * * people unable to read or write a note of music have been and are rich in their feeling for melody and rhythm. Their music-making defies the rules of the schools, and in many ways it may sound rough and crude to the sophisticated ear; but if all the evidence of history is worth anything, it goes to show that before there ever was such a thing as a trained musician, music was an art and a practice well known and deeply loved by the humble of the earth." [1]

"They All Sang" is the title of Edward B. Marks' first book. In it one will find an account of all the popular songs of the eighties and nineties as well as of a later period. Marks' firm, "The House of Marks," in 1944, celebrated its fiftieth anniversary upon which occasion deserved tributes were paid to the co-author of the "Little Lost Child." In 1944 he also brought out his second book "They All Had Glamour." In these two books one will find portrayed outstanding personalities in the field of music and drama.

One of the happy accidents of my life was meeting Edward B.

Marks. For nearly fifty years now, through representing the firm in litigation, I have become familiar with the run of what is called "popular music." I enjoy most of the popular songs.

Classical music did not come into my life until about 1892, the year I entered law school. My classmate, George Gehrung, and I did go to the opera once or twice a year, but the door to the great things in music was not really opened for me until that year, when Frank Damrosch opened it wide for thousands, of which, fortunately, I chanced to be one.

The three Damrosch Doctors, Leopold, the father, and his two sons, Frank and Walter, each in his own way were great pioneers of music in this country. All three blazed new trails. Damrosch is a name indissolubly associated with the American musical life of the last half-century. Dr. Leopold organized and led the Oratorio Society, the Philharmonic Symphony Orchestra and was director of the Metropolitan Opera. Dr. Walter succeeded him at the Metropolitan as director.

But Dr. Frank is our own hero—my wife's and mine.

He was named Franz after his godfather and his father's friend, Franz Liszt. Frank Damrosch's fame is associated with the Musical Art Society and the Institute of Musical Art, later merged with the Juilliard School of Music; the People's Singing Classes and the People's Choral Union in which we sang and played small parts. It is of this work I shall write more particularly.

When Frank Damrosch brought together, organized and directed the Musical Art Society, finer music was confined mostly to the relatively few who had access to it. There were no phonograph records. *And no radio.* It is not easy to re-create today a musical world so different from the one in existence fifty years ago. Today, on a Sunday afternoon, one may hear the Philharmonic, the Philadelphia, and several other good symphonic concerts. Of an evening, one may listen to the Boston or the Detroit, both great symphonic orchestras. During the season, one may sit comfortably in an easy chair at home of a Saturday and hear the opera broadcast from the Metropolitan. One may listen to future great opera singers auditioning on the air. Anyone who does not recognize the opening bars of Beethoven's Fifth Symphony, or cannot distinguish it from the Seventh or the Ninth, or who cannot distinguish between Debussy's "Clair de Lune" and "Prelude à L'Après-Midi d'un Faune" or is not immediately entranced when the opening strains of "Tristan and Isolde" come over the air, or put in peace of mind by Bach's "Air for the G String," has no one but himself to blame. Besides, Deems Taylor and

Olga Samaroff Stokowsky give a liberal education in music for the
price of tuning in the radio. And with a slight twist—a split hair's
turn—one can either get "Oklahoma" or the music of Gilbert and
Sullivan or a fine symphony. It is possible to plan a program for a
whole month in advance. One can lie in bed of a Sunday morning
and mark up the radio programs for the entire week, selecting the
choicest and the best.

To us of the Damrosch era, the broad scope of this enlarged field
in music is a constant source of wonderment. Jose Iturbi tells an anecdote which eloquently demonstrates how good music over the air is
finding today a larger and more responsive audience:

> "Driving to New York after a concert in Williamstown, Mass., I stopped for
> coffee at a lunch wagon in the Connecticut countryside just as a Sunday eve-
> ning symphonic program went over the air. What happened amused me greatly.
> There was a good deal of clatter and rattle among the diners. First the counter-
> man stopped washing dishes and listened. A man rattling his cup next to me set
> it down carefully—and listened. The waitress, stacking dishes on a small table,
> stopped her activities, sat down—and also listened. The place was comparatively
> quiet, but the counterman wasn't satisfied. He scowled at four hamburgers siz-
> zling on the griddle and carefully removed them one by one. We all sat there
> for the remainder of the program, when the waitress confirmed our verdict by
> remarking: 'Gee, that was swell!' " [2]

II

Now, what Frank Damrosch did was so great a thing that it should
be pictured in front of this backdrop of music generally and his own
life in particular. For he brought music to the *working people.* In
the beginning his project raised grave doubts in the minds of the
classicists, made them shrug their shoulders and lift their skeptical
eyebrows. He was, think of it, going to teach people—the common
people—*how to read music at sight!* That was his idea and his alone.
He had besides his own love for music, a great confidence in the
love of music *by the masses.* Why shouldn't everyone be able to read
music *at sight?* Why should good music be confined only to the elite
or the well-to-do? That was the creative purpose behind the People's
Singing Classes and the People's Choral Union.

Frank Damrosch was aware of the lack of opportunities for thousands to hear good music. Most working men and women could not
even afford the pleasure of membership for a night in the "standees"
—the real elite of music lovers at the Metropolitan Opera House.
There was, indeed, a painful contrast between the opportunities offered to the pampered daughters of the rich and the young men and
women who worked in sweat shops. But one of the greatest of all
shaping events in Frank Damrosch's life was, as it was in mine also,

meeting and working with Dr. Felix Adler. Frank Damrosch took over the organ at the Sunday services of the Society for Ethical Culture. He found Dr. Adler's philosophy congenial to his own. He had received a fine moral but not a religious training. As the Ethical Society and Dr. Adler appealed to both Jews and Gentiles repelled by dogma yet eager to live ethical lives, it appealed to Frank Damrosch. By his very nature and education, Dr. Adler's original and creative thinking was something to which he was predisposed. From the same platform, these two men radiated their influence, Frank Damrosch with his music and Felix Adler with his eloquence.

They became very close friends. Dr. Adler, too, believed in the people. Those of us who were touched by his flame could not feel otherwise. Frank Damrosch gave freely of his time to the Workingmen's School which Dr. Adler founded. Through Dr. Adler, Frank Damrosch came to know of the work for tenement house reform and the whole East Side settlement movement. That is how he came to know Charles B. Stover who administered the model tenements initiated by Dr. Adler.

III

In 1892, when Dr. Damrosch conceived of the People's Singing Classes and set out to bring in working men and women, he laid the project before certain leaders, and set before them a plan.

Among them was a little earnest bowlegged fellow, Edward King, a leader of organized labor; John K. Paulding of the University Settlement and John McGoodale, a lawyer whom I have known now for nearly fifty years. Edward King was a Scotch printer and a Trade Unionist, deeply imbued with the philosophy of August Comte, and he came to be the guide, philosopher and friend of a whole generation of youthful Russian immigrants growing up on the East Side. These three men helped to achieve the Frank Damrosch dream and make it real.

When he conceived of the singing classes, before putting his ideas into execution, Frank Damrosch went first to Stover for advice. Should the lessons be free and the scheme be financed by some of the Doctor's wealthy friends or should they be paid for by the people themselves? Stover put it before King. The latter, well versed in the arts of popular assemblage, arranged for a mass meeting. There in Cooper Union, on October 16, 1892, by unanimous vote, the prospective pupils decided that they themselves should pay for the lessons. Each person attending the class should pay ten cents and receive his sheet music free.

The first meeting of the People's Singing Class was October 23rd.

At this time a sample lesson was given and the first of the series of elementary lessons was started on October 30, 1892. Later, the People's Choral Union was organized from graduates of the advanced classes of 1893 and 1894 and it adopted its own constitution. In all this, Theodore Schorske played an important part, holding nearly every office in connection with the People's Choral Classes or Choral Union. Four pioneers enabled Dr. Damrosch to extend the work to branches in other sections of the city. These included Sara L. Dunning, Sara J. J. McCaffery, Mary S. Doty and Abbie S. Lee. Later, a fifth pioneer came in 1898—Harriet Adams De Puy—to take over the first People's Singing Class in the Bronx. Later came one of its own graduates, Isaac Rosenblatt, an amateur cellist, as one of his assistants. Alfred Hallam and Edward G. Marquand later took on important posts.

The working men and women of New York responded to his call. They got their sheets of music, they paid their dimes, they sang in the classes. They were taught to read at sight. And they sang well. When about 1900 or 1901, Damrosch gave a concert of the Musical Art Society at Carnegie Hall, he prepared a surprise for the musically elite. He put his People's Choral Union up in the gallery. After leading the Municipal Art Society, made up of trained singers from church choirs, the Oratorio Society and other similar groups, in singing the first two verses of "Lo! How a Rose E'er Blooming," he turned to the gallery and, from the stage below, directed the People's Choral Union to sing the third verse. It was stirring to those of us who sat in that gallery, but it was stirring also to the whole musical world. *The people could sing in chorus!* And sing with musicianship.

IV

On Frank Damrosch's seventieth birthday, the People's Choral Union held a reunion. A hundred or more came together to do him honor. Just the year before, on impulse, I took occasion to express what I knew we all felt in gratitude to the Doctor. Mrs. Damrosch made notes of what I said. Later, she asked if I would write it out for her. One forgets these things once they are uttered, and what I said was wholly extemporaneous. I told her I would try.

On the occasion of Dr. Damrosch's seventieth birthday, the Alumni presented Mrs. Damrosch with their own tribute of love and affection for her. I said, "We might have gone outside to the florist's shop and bought some American beauties * * * but in our own garden we found some warm red cosmos, some purple asters and some white chrysanthemums, and in our woods a few violets which somehow seemed to linger on. We've tied them together with one of our own ribbons, we've added some fall leaves * * * and present this bouquet of flowers from our garden for Mrs. Damrosch, with our love."

I quote now from this Home Made Bouquet. It will give you the picture of the Choral Union. Those who have ever gone down to Cooper Union where we met—the place where Lincoln spoke when he came to New York, will recognize it as we knew it who came there Sunday afternoons during the late nineties. I described the place in these words:

> Red covered seats
> A large platform
> A great hall in a basement
> Gas jets, ofttimes leaking
> Thick, round, bulky pillars
> Obscuring the platform
>
> Platform orators
> Great mass meetings
> A school for heckling
> All week long
> Outside to the south
> A statue
> Of Cooper
> Founder of the Institute
> Peter Cooper's Institute.

And these lines I wrote to describe the people whom Frank Damrosch drew to him:

> If you worked all day
> Here you could learn
> At night
> The technique
> Of draftsmanship
> Of engineering
> Of chemistry
> Of other material things.
>
> But Sunday afternoons the scene was changed.
> You came downtown
> Or you came uptown
> Or you came from the East Side or the West
> A thousand more came to join you.
> All week you worked
> At desk, in shop, in store or factory—
> Perhaps at night you went to school.
>
> But Sunday afternoon you came
> To the Great Hall in the basement.
> You were the Choral Union
> You were the People's Choral Union
> Frank Damrosch was your leader.

And this is how we all felt:

All afternoon you held
Sheets of paper with ruled lines
Little black eggs tied to sticks
And curly figures unlike
The dollar signs merchants wrote in check books.

You played with scales
Not market scales to weigh coins or merchandise
You played with magic scales
That weighed and balanced
Flowers and Poetry
And sunbeams and rainbows.

You played with keys
Not locksmiths' keys to open doors to market-places
But keys that opened up
New empires
Great lands of hope and promise.

You took the blue from out the skies
And the sparkles from the stars
And bound them
In heaven's grandest harmonies.

You sang
Full-throated, deep-chested
Not you alone, yourself
But a thousand more with you.
Sopranos
Altos
Tenors
Basses
All as one, you sang under Frank Damrosch.

You were young
You were old
You were blonde
You were brown or black, grey-haired or bearded
It mattered not.
Your voice was young.
So soft it was, you were a child again
So strong it was, the old basement rang with thunder
So exquisite, it made cold critics wonder.
Frank Damrosch was your leader.
You came to him—
No, he came to you
He led you.

For the afternoon
All your drudgeries
All your sorrows
All your despairs
Were gone.

The cruel world outside might howl
The cold frost freeze you there
But in the great Basement Hall
There was warmth and sunshine
The warmth and sunshine
Of great music
Great music
Sung by you, the thousand
   Led by Frank Damrosch.

In front of the booklet which had been printed, there was a fine portrait of the Doctor. Deep, dark eyes, the hair brushed back in pompadour fashion, dark brown when we first met him, but grey by 1935. A pointed beard and a flowing mustache. One would say on meeting him, "Here is a fine doctor of medicine or a great surgeon." But he was "physician to the soul."

Of those hours we spent with her husband, we said on that occasion to Mrs. Damrosch:

Those hours shaped and shaped again
Your life, your very soul
In ways you did not comprehend.
It thrilled you
It moved you on and up
It stirred the deepest things within you.

'Long years have passed,' you sing.
Long years *have* passed
Thirty, yes, or more
All fresh and green in memory.
And though long years have passed
The debt you owe
This friend, this leader
Grows and grows the deeper
The deeper grows
As your eyes become the keener,
   To Frank Damrosch.

For not sheets of music
Nor scales
Nor keys
Nor notes upon them
Nor even great composers
This friend, this leader
Brought to you.

He brought himself.
Himself he gave
Than which no greater gift
Could one man give another.

His generous, modest, winning, charming self he gave
Unconscious all the while
The mighty power
He wielded over you.

His baton magical
More potent
Than the staffs
Of all the kings in all of Christendom.
His glance
His gentle voice
His smile
His cheer
His mocking mirth
Enthralled you
Made every one of you his
Willing servitor.

He bade us believe
In ourselves.
Bade us believe
'Twas we, not he, who scored the triumphs.
Yet all the while we knew
Or should have known if we were wise enough
Or, if we did not then, should know it now
'Twas he who made our song
Who scored our triumph.

He gave us
Of his own great heart and courage.
So giving, he inspired us
Renewed our faltering, wavering faith
In faltering, wavering mankind.
And this it was
That made our song
The Song Triumphant.

Dear to us always,
Dearer now to us
'As long years have passed'
Is 'John Anderson, my Jo'
    Frank Damrosch."

We can do no better today. He was our friend. He did open the door to fine music for us. "Elijah"—"The Messiah"—all the oratorios, selections from the great chorales. If we sang these songs in our homes, in quartettes of sopranos and altos and tenors and basses, we did it because we carried the music home with us.

When I opened my copy of the biography of Frank Damrosch by Lucy Poate and Richard Poate Stebbins,[3] I was, of course, thrilled to find on the page facing Walter Damrosch's introduction, one of the stanzas of my own composition. Undoubtedly the affection of the authors for the Doctor and Mrs. Damrosch led them to give my words a place.

> Monuments may rise
> To great generals
> Halls of Fame
> May house the sculptured forms
> Of great statesmen.
> None shall rise so high
> Nor be so firmly set
> As the monument
> Invisible
> We have builded
>
> In our hearts
> These many years
> To our
>   Frank Damrosch.

But I was saddened, when I read the book through to learn for the first time the undisclosed circumstances which upon that occassion touched the Doctor and his loving wife so deeply. A great misfortune had overtaken them both in the summer. While the Doctor was playing chess with his wife, he suddenly discovered that he could not see out of his right eye. Consultation with an oculist developed that the loss of the eye was permanent. Life now was a different place. But at that reunion, he was very happy. The love and gratitude of his famous People's Choral Union covered him like a warm, soft cloak.

V

But the Doctor did more than organize the People's Singing Classes and the People's Choral Union. The proceedings at the Society for Ethical Culture meetings on Sundays under Dr. Adler always seemed cold to Frank Damrosch, even though there was his fine playing on the Carnegie Hall great organ. Frank Damrosch induced Dr. Adler to permit him to form a chorus, what in a church one would call a choir, and said he would undertake to train and lead it as part of the Sunday morning services.

Frank Damrosch called for volunteers at Cooper Union. An announcement was made by Dr. Adler from the platform of Carnegie Hall at the close of the Sunday morning services. Rehearsals were to be held Friday evenings at Dr. Adler's School on West Fifty-fourth Street—the "working man's school." This was the beginning of the school at Sixty-fourth Street and Central Park West, and later of the still larger school at Riverdale. I became one of the basses in that choir.

My classmate, George Gehrung, who stood by me through thick and thin for sixty years, was really responsible for getting me into the mischief I am about to relate. George did a lot of things to me and for me. For one thing, I recall that he painstakingly taught me to waltz in our basement. We lived a block apart and went to Public School No. 10 together on Wooster Street. When I decided to go to the Thirtieth Street Evening High School, George went along and we joined Dr. Gustave Simonson's class in Political Science. He and I walked up from West Third to Thirtieth Street, five nights a week. Saturday night, we spent all of twenty-five cents at the Empire Theatre to see John Drew or Maude Adams. Once in a great while we sat in the top gallery of the Metropolitan Opera House and on Robert C. Taylor's recommendation, we heard "Aida." George tried his best to teach me to swim, but that was a complete failure. He also led me to the golf course at Van Cortlandt Park. (Some of those with whom I played in later years at Fairview or Metropolis would say that my golf-playing, too, was a disappointment.)

George sang tenor and his brother, Fred, sang bass next to me in the People's Choral Union. Both brothers were strong physically and went to the gymnasium in the Young Men's Institute, a branch of the YMCA on the Bowery. Then they sang there in a quartette. Sometimes, at the shop, for Mother's entertainment, we sang "The Owl and the Pussycat" and other songs.

Along about 1892, I had advanced far enough to sing alone and with considerable lustiness, the "Armorers Song," from "Robin Hood," and, on slight encouragement, I would sing "Oh, Promise Me."

It was George who, somehow or other, heard of the People's Singing Classes and he and Fred and I promptly signed up. In this way, we met each other every Sunday afternoon. We also met some nice sopranos and altos too. Some of them were quite good-looking. Naturally, we chatted with the ones we thought most interesting and sometimes, on a nice Sunday, after the lesson, we would walk up Fifth Avenue with them. That's how my troubles began.

VI

When Abbot suggested that I ought to be looking around for a wife (on fifteen dollars a week), I must have "gone looking." However, it was not until Frank Damrosch organized the chorus for the Ethical Society and we began our rehearsals at the Workingman's School on 54th Street on Friday evenings that I found her.

She had come down to join the Chorus of the "Ethical." Each member was then paid ten cents a week. It came out of the treasury of the Ethical Society and was intended to cover our carfare—we were supposed to need it. After about six months of singing together, there came a movement in the group to plan a holiday together—some kind of an outing, a picnic, lunch somewhere in the nearby country.

One evening, after rehearsal, we met to discuss plans for such an excursion. Now it is always handy to have a friend about, who, having confidence in you, induces others to share it. When we assembled, George Gehrung proposed me for Chairman of the meeting. I was seconded by another friend, Samuel Harrison. Samuel's father ran the delicatessen shop a few doors down from Number Six where I cut and sold sandwiches when the big parades came up Broadway. As I had no competitors in the campaign for this great office, I was unanimously elected and promptly ushered to the chair. I assure you that this campaign for office was one in which the leader was really drafted.

There then came up a suggestion that to pay the expenses of our picnic, we should ask the Society to raise the ten cents as a sort of subsidy. At that very point, a young lady rose up and quite modestly, but firmly, argued against the proposal. It did not comport with her sense of dignity to ask the Society for anything more than the ten cents each we were receiving. I feel quite confident that a number of those in the Society, who did on other occasions hear really good singing thought even then that ten cents was aplenty for what we gave them. Indeed, some of them were heard to suggest that the audience should be paid for listening to us. Of course, neither Dr. Damrosch nor those of us who gave up our Friday evenings for rehearsals agreed with these cynics. We believed in ourselves, in our singing, and in Dr. Damrosch.

But this young lady saw me in the chair and I saw her and heard her speak her mind. (She still does.) It was quite appropriate that the chairman of the meeting should, after the adjournment, go up to the lady and felicitate her on her well-chosen remarks. She had won the debate. Could I take her home?

At first George went along. But I soon put a stop to that. And so I took her home—and so I took her home. And that is how *I married a chorus girl!* That, I say, is how all the mischief began.

It so happened that this lady's family had been listening to fine music for a great many years. At one time they had two pianos in their home and eight hands played piano concertos. Two of her sisters played, Minna and Hannah—and they all sang. Her aunt, Jennie Danzig, sang in Dr. Leopold Damrosch's Oratorio Society and she went down with her sisters to the rehearsals. We never had a piano in my home and we never had any lessons in music. The reason was quite simple. We could not afford it.

I still remember Rubinstein's "Kamenoi Ostrow" as Sister Hannah played it. When thirty years later, she stayed with us at Fir Cones and the music came over the air, though she was then paralyzed and could not speak a word, she followed the music, tapping out each note with her fingertips on her wheel chair.

So there is good reason why Dr. Frank Damrosch means so much to my wife and me. It all formed part of the romance of that day—the music, the law school, the work at 55 William Street, the philosophy of optimism. How could one be a cynic in such an atmosphere? We lived in the sunshine, too, of the romance of Frank and Hetty Damrosch. The example was infectious.

My wife's niece who was four at the time, greeted me at the door with:

> "Needles and Pins
> Needles and Pins
> When a man marries
> His trouble begins."

She was a prophetess. But these troubles have gone on now for forty-five years. I heard Channing Pollock once say that the man who says he never had a quarrel with his wife is just a plain liar. And he said also that out of just such quarrels, happy marriages resulted. That is, if it meant enough to the two of them, they found a way of getting on. And out of my experience, I can say that Pollock is right. But I think there must be some music in the home to make it come true. And that is why we carry Frank Damrosch's picture close to our hearts.

VII

I do not want to end this chapter on a disappointing note, but for the sake of the record, I must " 'fess up." Metropolitan Opera had a very narrow escape. Theresa Mosenthal, the elder sister of Hetty Damrosch, came to visit us at 69 West 88th Street. Mrs. Mosenthal, their mother, was one of the group in Mrs. Cohen's Riverside Branch of the Women's Municipal League. My wife induced me to sing for Miss Theresa. Miss Theresa then and there decided—in her own mind, you understand—that my bass voice had great possibilities. She said she would begin by giving me lessons herself. Before she could carry out her plan, she became ill and, to our sorrow, was taken off. No one ever took her place for me. Caroline Goldberg, wife of William Victor, both good friends, used to accompany me in my singing and did give me a few lessons. But like Governor Dewey, I turned from music to the law. Did I hear anyone say I might have done better if I had stuck to music?

A wit once said of Martin W. Littleton, in introducing him at the Oakland Country Club, "You know, I can't place that fellow Littleton. Down on Wall Street, they say he's a golfer, but out here at the golf club, they say he's a lawyer." And I once turned that story on James N. Rosenberg, the lawyer, who, as part of his double life, paints pictures. But Jimmy gets real money for his pictures, and when I sing, I don't get a cent. Never got a penny—except the dimes the Ethical Culture Society handed out on Sundays.

CHAPTER EIGHT

A homme hardi, fortune tend la main.
Fortune has a helping hand for the daring.

William Travers Jerome

*A prosecuting lawyer exposes rotten politics and sets
an example of how to run a District Attorney's office—
But he never becomes Governor—why?*

I

THE SUCCESSFUL PROSECUTOR of crime is, indeed, the peacetime hero. That is the road Thomas E. Dewey travelled to the Governorship. It is the way James W. Folk followed as St. Louis prosecutor to the office of Governor of Missouri. So, too, Charles S. Whitman became Governor of New York, after a successful career as District Attorney.

The subject of this chapter is William Travers Jerome. During his term, Harry K. Thaw was prosecuted for the killing of Stanford White; Nan Patterson was prosecuted for killing Caesar Young and Albert T. Patrick for the poisoning of William T. Price. These were celebrated cases and occupied the columns of the press, each in turn, almost to the exclusion of all other news. William Travers Jerome had personal talents of high order. Arthur Train was a member of his staff, and he was also his close and intimate friend. Train says:

"He was a picturesque figure, alert, slender but muscular, brusque and by nature an aristocrat, but beneath his cavalier figure burned the wrath of a Hebrew prophet, and for the time being he became both the idol of the slums and the hero of Fifth Avenue. A 'whirlwind campaigner' his harsh voice would reduce an audience to tears or bring it to its feet with indignation." [1]

Jerome created a role that had never been played before on the municipal stage. As a judge, he visited gambling houses—entered, not politely by first sending his card, but by the more compelling method of breaking down the door and coming in with a police escort. Right in the gambling house, he would call in witnesses—from those who were present, swearing them in on the spot, take their testimony and issue warrants as a city magistrate. Ephraim Tutt reminds us of Wallace Irwin's then popular satire:

> " 'Tut, tut!' said Jerome with a grin,
> 'These games are disguised very thin;
>   When you hear a cop snore
>   By a strange-looking door
> It's a cinch there is gambling within.' " 2

It was truly the "gay eighties." In Devery's place there was a new Chief of Police, William McAdoo. Tutt quotes from Irwin again:

> "A district attorney, who knew,
>   Spoke of gamblers to Chief McAdoo.
>   Then to stir up his slumbers
>   He named streets and numbers
> So what could poor McAdoo do?" 3

In 1897 there was no Fusion, and Tammany won. Robert A. Van Wyck became Mayor of New York, his term expired December 31, 1901. Jerome was nominated in that year for District Attorney, this time on a Fusion ticket. He was elected and held office for eight years. I was active in the Citizens Union at that time, both in the municipal campaign and in Jerome's campaign for the office of District Attorney. In 1905 William M. Ivins was nominated for Mayor by the Republicans. About this time, William Randolph Hearst developed his political ambitions. As he owned a great newspaper and had inherited a great fortune, his ambition seemed feasible of achievement. He procured an independent nomination for Mayor. Tammany nominated George B. McClellan, son of the General of Civil War days, later professor of political science at Princeton. They made a bow to decency by nominating him for Mayor. The Citizens Union supported Jerome for the nomination of District Attorney.

The night the Republican convention was being held to nominate a candidate for District Attorney, I was with Jerome when he was waiting for the result. He had entertained the hope that the Republicans would endorse him. He was greatly disappointed when instead, they nominated a comparatively unknown City Magistrate, J. George Flammer.

Jerome asked me, "Now how can I win without an organization?"

I answered: "Build up your own organization and use the Citizens Union as a nucleus."

II

The Citizens Union formed the "Jerome Nominators." The active manager was Howard S. Gans, one of the members of the Political Ethics group formed under Dr. Felix Adler's leadership. Gans threw himself wholeheartedly into the campaign along with Fred M. Stein, another of the younger men active in political reform. A good-sized campaign fund, I should say a couple of hundred thousand dollars, was raised. The President of the Merchants Association, William F. King, was Treasurer. Jerome's was a whirlwind campaign. Great crowds followed him around. One incident of that campaign gave my wife some elementary education in modern journalism. There was a Jerome mass meeting at Columbus Avenue and 100th Street, at which I presided. When Jerome arrived the hall was packed. This was one of the occasions when Jerome jingled some of the brass checks used on the east side as part of the trade in prostitution.

We were afraid the election might be stolen so, before the meeting closed, I made an appeal for volunteer watchers to stand guard at the polls on election day. Perhaps twenty or thirty men came up to the platform in response to my appeal. I hastily tore up slips of paper. They crowded around me to get these slips on which to write their names.

Lindsay Denison, one of the best newspaper men of the time, then on the "Sun," and a close friend and admirer of Jerome, followed Jerome around on his campaign and wrote the daily report for his paper. The day after this meeting, my wife turned to the "Sun" (it was then a morning paper) to read about the meeting. There she found *a* story. It seemed from the "Sun's" account that when her husband called for volunteers, the rush was so great, the volunteers so enthusiastic, that they stripped the chairman's coat right off his back! Now my wife knew I had come home with a sound coat and as she was a stickler—still is—for truthfulness and accuracy of statement, she was provoked. "How could they write a thing so untrue as that?" she asked.

It was said in those days, "What can you expect of a city in which every morning the 'Sun' makes vice attractive, and every night the 'Post' makes virtue odious?" [4]

Next day was Sunday. In the afternoon we went together to Jerome's headquarters at the Gilsey House. As we came in, there stood Lindsay Denison. I said to my wife "There's the man who wrote the story. Go tell him what you think of it." And she did. And she told him aplenty.

Then Lindsay carefully explained. "You see, Mrs. Cohen, if I had written that story exactly as it happened, it would not have made the same dramatic impression on the readers as it did upon me up there in the hall. So I had to tell the story as I visualized it."

Ephraim Tutt reports one of Jerome's favorite sayings: "Exact knowledge is a great handicap to forcible statement!" [5]

III

Jerome was elected. One of his former assistants, later Judge of the Court of General Sessions, Charles C. Nott, wrote:

"* * * on election night, when a milling, roaring throng swept through the lobby for two or three hours, waving flags, blowing horns, while Jerome appeared from time to time at the head of the stairs saying a few hoarse words through a throat well-nigh ruined by overwork." [6]

He organized a fine staff. Among them was Charles A. Perkins, in charge of Indictments; Robert C. Taylor, in charge of Appeals; Charles C. Nott, Charles W. Appleton, afterwards City Magistrate and later General Counsel for the General Electric Company; Lloyd Paul Stryker, who defended Jimmy Hines a few years ago; George W. Whiteside; Karl R. Miner; William Rand; Isidor J. Kresel; Arthur Train; William D. Bosler, and William Dean Embree.

Train received a good deal of first-hand experience in Jerome's office which made for fine color in his books. A vivid description of the criminal bar, as he saw it, especially of those who practiced in the Criminal Courts Building, is given in the "Mr. Tutt" series. Arthur procured the first real success of the District Attorney's office in the prosecution of commercial frauds.[7] Train's work in this case was afterwards sustained by the Court of Appeals. This was a case of fraudulent shipment of women's lace underwear from New York City to Indianapolis. Arthur dramatized the underwear and its movement— from New York to Indianapolis. That made good color.

While the case was on, I sat in Train's office two floors above, reading the minutes of the trial as they were relayed to me from the courtroom.* I was the lawyer for the lace and embroidery merchants who were induced, by false representations, to sell to the defendant, Levin, the laces which ornamented the underwear. It was necessary to keep the lawyer for these merchants away from the courtroom. Such suggestions as he might make, had to be made off-stage to Train. I had secured the evidence Train used in the case.

Train knew even then how to dramatize human situations. He wrote stories and made literature in the courtroom while he was trying cases. His novels are full of incidents picked up in the Criminal Courts Building.

* I was also Special United States Attorney in New York in *United States v. Richard Cohen* and *United States v. Glass* in New Jersey—prosecution of commercial frauds.

The administration of Jerome's office was one of the shining spots in the history of New York. But Jerome stopped with his eight years in the District Attorney's office. It was his misfortune to lose in prosecutions of the insurance heads whom Charles Evans Hughes so thoroughly exposed at that time.

The Hughes investigation had created a public demand for the prosecution of the life insurance men on the basis of what Hughes had disclosed. Because he did not find it possible successfully to prosecute the insurance men, Jerome was put in a bad light before the public. Hughes having become Governor, a number of citizens brought charges against Jerome, hoping to secure his removal as District Attorney. The charges were referred by Governor Hughes to Richard Hand of Elizabethtown, father of Augustus N. Hand of the United States Circuit Court of Appeals. (I remember well the Elizabethtown library and the old homestead where Richard Hand lived and practiced law near the Cobble Hill Golf Course at the foot of the Adirondacks. I spent many delightful days there.)

Richard Hand was a born judge. He understood perfectly the duties of a judge. His son follows in his footsteps. We could all wish that there were more Hands to preside in the courtroom. We have two now—Augustus N. and Learned—both on the United States Circuit Court of Appeals for the Second Circuit.

Richard Hand had this to say in his report to Governor Hughes:

"This favorable estimate of Mr. Jerome was so general and the desire for his continued services so great as to produce his election, for a second term, to the office of District Attorney of the County of New York, under the peculiar circumstances of a candidacy supported by no political organization and confronted by the regular and powerful organizations then existing. This result was accompanied by great enthusiasm for the successful candidate personally, and an extraordinary hero worship on the part of a very large portion of the inhabitants of the city produced the most extravagant expectations of striking and immediate results, which, as might have been and doubtless was foreseen by the more thoughtful and intelligent of the community, were necessarily and unavoidably doomed to a large measure of disappointment, whatever zeal, ability and effort might be brought to bear by the successful candidate for the purpose of this realization." [8]

IV

Jerome did in fact prosecute insurance men. He filed an information before a city magistrate charging George W. Perkins, the vice-president of the New York Life Insurance Company, with larceny. Such an information begins a criminal prosecution. This was based upon the charge that Perkins had taken five thousand dollars of the

Insurance Company's funds and applied it as a campaign contribution to the Republican Party. Perkins was discharged on a write of habeas corpus.[9] The Appellate Division held that it was no crime to take insurance funds and contribute them to a Republican Campaign Fund. Since the question of the propriety of a contribution to a Democratic Campaign Fund was not before the Court, we can only say that if the Court's decision was sound in principle, it should decide the same way in a case where it is a contribution to the Democratic Party. But in these days, it is very hard to say how far a court will feel bound by its own decisions.

The case was argued by four lawyers, all now dead, but prominent in their day. Jerome had the aid of Samuel Untermyer in arguing for the prosecution. William N. Cohen and Lewis L. Delafield argued for Perkins. That was, indeed, a fine array of professional talent. (By the way, I should set at rest once and for all the fiction that has run around now for these many years that I am Judge William N. Cohen's son. Doubtless it was always said as a compliment, but it becomes a near-insult when you know as I do that Judge William Cohen was a confirmed bachelor.)

There were five opinions in that Perkins case—out of a possible seven. Judges Ingraham, McLaughlin, Patterson, Laughlin and Clarke all wrote opinions. There was not a dissent. Either because of the eminence of the distinguished counsel who appeared before them, or because of the public importance of the case, there is no less than fifteen pages of reasoning devoted to establishing the soundness of the decision. Judge John Proctor Clarke was clear that a contribution to a party campaign fund was neither *malum prohibitum,* that is, something wrong simply because the legislature says it is wrong, nor *malum in se,* immoral in itself. But he even went further and said that it was not even wrong ethically to the extent of implying criminality. As if ethically *wrong* could be so qualified at any time!

V

Jerome lived to be seventy-five. As a civic hero, his span of life was about ten years. Within a year after the Hand report, he retired to private practice. If Jerome had been successful in the prosecution of these insurance cases, it is probable that he would have travelled the Empire State route to the Executive Chamber at Albany. There is a good picture of Jerome hanging at the Bar Association, put there by his *boys.* That is, the lawyers who were his assistants in the District Attorney's office. He is still their hero. They are eternally grateful to him. He gave them their start—as Abbot, Taylor and Deming gave me mine.

BOOK II
ORCHIDS GROW IN SWAMPY GROUND

CHAPTER NINE

A ginooine statesman should be on his guard,
Ef he *must* hev beliefs, not to b'lieve 'em tu hard.
LOWELL, *Biglow Papers*

Theodore Roosevelt

*The political background of 1898—The consequences of
a false American ideology—Imperialism—The Spanish-
American War and a great hero—The method T. R.
used to become Governor of New York—The Reformers
enter the political arena and lose their first great battle—The author gets his first bitter disillusionment—
Did the Reformers really lose?*

I

IT WAS IN 1894 that I went down to Manice, Abbot and Perry at 55
William Street. I graduated from the Metropolis Law School in 1896
and was admitted to the Bar in 1897. In 1895, I began my first important suit. It took me until September 17, 1897, to win that case.
My fiancée's family, with striking unanimity, disapproved. It was a
definite step down to marry a man with no prospects, no connections,
and worse still, with no political ambitions. If he was really worthwhile, he would join the Republican Party as a matter of course. That
was the only respectable party with which a young lawyer should be
aligned. Instead, as they got it, he was fooling around with Good Government Clubs, which they joined with the New York Evening "Sun" in
ridiculing as "Goo-Goos." The young man should be more practical, if
he wanted to get on as a lawyer. And if he was not going to get on as
a lawyer, why should he marry into their family? It was a really good
and convincing argument. The only way to meet it was to pay no
attention to it and go right on.

My classmate, Samuel Koenig, did follow the course they thought I
should. And he became first of all, head of the Federal Club on the
East Side and later advanced to the important post of Chairman of
the Republican County Committee, where he wielded great power.*

* Secretary of State of New York, 1908–1910.

When in 1896, McKinley was nominated by the Republicans under Boss Hanna's rule, and Bryan was nominated to run against him on a "free silver" platform, I cast my first presidential vote for Palmer and Buckner. Whether it was listening to Democrats who came into father's shop, or reading Bennett's "Herald" instead of Hearst's "Journal," or listening to Dr. Gustave Simonson at the Thirtieth Street Evening High School, I do not know. Perhaps all three things combined. But I was definitely against the McKinley Tariff, against Bryan's "16 to 1" program and I would have joyously voted for John Stuart Mill for President of the United States if he could have been nominated in this country. During McKinley's and Roosevelt's regimes, I was definitely anti-imperialist.

I read and re-read Mill's "Political Economy." I had also read Herbert Spencer's "First Principles." There is no doubt in my mind now that I was one of a much larger group who in the late '90s accepted completely the philosophy of evolution and held tenaciously to the optimistic view that the world was going steadily to grow better and better if only each one of us just got out and pushed. Those who believed this way had a sublime confidence in the processes of reason and an equally sublime confidence in the processes of education. The world would move to a higher civilization, we were convinced, if people only read, and if they read, we were sure they would think. The emphasis on reason has since been modified, at least for me. The human animal is not often moved by reason. Tragedy seems to be the only school in which the deepest political lessons are learned. From the imperialism of Roosevelt's day and the isolationism of Wilson's, we have travelled far but at a great cost. Moreover, in the company I kept, it was regarded as elementary that a gentleman should keep his word and that while it was permissible, in war or in the courts, to hide one's intention behind a smoke screen, such tactics were not permissible in one's relations with friends and allies. It was not good form to lead a friend along, get him out on a limb, and then saw off the limb.

II

It is now clear that the Spanish-American War need not have occurred. Spain was ready to yield through our Ambassador, Stewart L. Woodward, but the President of the United States, William McKinley, concealed the facts. If he had told the American people the truth, we should never have gone into the Spanish-American War.[1] General John Sherman was Secretary of State during the Spanish-American War under McKinley. On September 3, 1898, Sherman declared that the war was altogether unnecessary and that as Secretary of State he had had several conversations with the Spanish Minister on the subject, and our difficulties could have been adjusted without the loss of blood.

While Sherman was Secretary of State, Theodore Roosevelt was Assistant Secretary of the Navy. He owed his appointment chiefly to Senator Henry Cabot Lodge's close friendship with him. His ambition to go to the front was reported by Secretary of War Alger. The Colonel recruited, through the aid of President McKinley, "a regiment of mounted riflemen to be commanded by Leonard Wood, Colonel; Theodore Roosevelt, Lieutenant-Colonel." He said he wanted "men who were young, sound, good shots and good riders." [2] So came into being the "Rough Riders." The Colonel's exploits in Cuba made him a national hero. When he came back to Montauk Point, Long Island, after the war, along with his Rough Riders, C. T. Yerkes of Chicago, a public utility magnate and a good Republican, too, said: "That man will be a political idol, sure." [3]

The Colonel's imperialistic policies met with very great opposition, not only from men like Dr. Felix Adler and Carl Schurz, but even from Thomas C. Platt himself. From the Colonel's autobiography, we learn that Platt's coolness to him when he returned to Montauk was "largely because he disapproved of the Spanish War and of my (Roosevelt's) part in bringing it about." [4] Thomas C. Platt was "the Easy Boss" for the New York Republicans. He was also senior United States Senator from New York. William Barnes was then Chairman of the Republican State Committee; Lemuel Eli Quigg was the leader of the New York State County organization. Both were right hand assistants to Platt.

The Colonel refers to Quigg in his autobiography as "on good terms with me while he was in Congress and I was Civil Service Commissioner * * * and he had urged my appointment as Police Commissioner on Mayor Strong." [5] Besides, the Colonel had known Quigg for years while he was a reporter on the "Tribune" and when the latter edited a paper in Montana.

Frank Black was then Governor of New York State and expected a renomination. His friends all joined forces with him to keep him and themselves in power. Timothy Woodruff was Lieutenant-Governor and expected also to be renominated. The "yellow dogs" were the lesser politicians, the ones who, under the Platt-Black-Barnes-Woodruff leadership, made up the "Republican Machine" in New York. [6]

On October 7, 1914, Roosevelt made a speech at Saratoga Springs in which he referred to the combination of Barnes and Charles F. Mur-

phy, the leader of Tammany Hall, the successors to the political union
of Platt and Croker. This is what he then said:

> "The principles and practices of politics in which one of them believes are just
> exactly the principles and practices which the other believes. One has been for
> a long time responsible for the government of the City of New York and the
> other for a long time responsible for the government of the City of Albany. It
> is the same type of government that they have been responsible for. One at
> times controls the party and is master over the Legislature at Albany, and at
> times the other is. But you get substantially the same results from both." [7]

Roosevelt was elected to the New York State Legislature of 1881.
He had acted as chairman of the committee which investigated various
phases of New York official life. He had seen what was going on while
in the Assembly:

> "* * * lobbyists come down on the floor itself and draw venal men out into the
> lobbies with almost no pretense of concealing what they were doing." [8]

In his investigation of New York City official life, while he was in
the Legislature, he had observed:

> "* * * A number of able and unscrupulous men were fighting, some for their
> financial lives, and others to keep out of unpleasantly close neighborhood to
> State's prison." [9]

III

About this time a small band of pioneers was beginning to make their
influence felt for good government. There are several whose portraits
I hang here. One of them was a brilliant writer, John Jay Chapman.
His satires on existing political conditions in a magazine entitled the
"Political Nursery" were fine pieces of prose. He had in him great fire
and poetry. He knew Roosevelt from college days and had faith in
him. He communicated that faith to others.

Most of Roosevelt's friends at Harvard remained his friends and
continued to have faith in him. They always saw in Roosevelt the
finer side of his character—the brave, courageous pioneer, the
fine public servant, the daring soldier, the *reformer* in politics. [10]
The chapter I write here is not *the story of the whole of Theodore Roosevelt*. It is the account of a period in his life—an important
period for me, but still more important for the pioneers of good government. The ground was swampy but orchids did grow there. Those
pioneers builded better than they foresaw—and despite all incon-
sistencies and weaknesses. Theodore Roosevelt builded better than he
knew.

The Citizens Union was organized on February 22, 1898, with R.

Fulton Cutting as its chairman. Cutting was a descendant of Robert Fulton—of fine character, a gentleman and a scholar. Paul Fuller [11] was a member of the international law firm of Coudert Brothers, highly honorable and able; Meyer D. Rothschild was a leading lay member of the Ethical Culture Society—a business man dealing in diamonds; Isaac H. Klein was another. Thomas Mott Osborne, of D. M. Osborne and Company was a manufacturer of agricultural implements and Mayor of Auburn, New York, and Edmund H. Titchenor of Binghamton, New York, was a successful business man. They were fired with zeal for the public good.

There are too many to speak about here [12]—there were lawyers, business men, writers and some doctors. Their contributions should be made known to students of government, especially the history of the struggle to attain good government.

These were the political currents at work in the summer of 1898:

1. A strong imperialistic wave led by Theodore Roosevelt.

2. An anti-imperialistic wave led by Dr. Felix Adler and Carl Schurz.

3. A Republican State machine seeking to continue under Governor Black and expecting to secure his renomination for Governor.

4. A Democratic machine led by Richard Croker which had a complete and working alliance with Platt.

5. An election to be held for United States Senator in place of Edward Murphy, Jr., a Democrat.

6. An aroused and indignant public opinion resulting from one of the worst political scandals in the history of New York—the operation of the New York Canal System under George W. Aldridge, part and parcel of the Republican State machine. This scandal had stirred up the wrath of the decent people in New York State to a high pitch.

Now upon this scene comes a picturesque figure, New York's great hero, Colonel Theodore Roosevelt. He arrives with his Rough Riders at Montauk, in August of 1898.

This relatively small band of pioneers—Chapman, Cutting, Fuller, Rothschild, et al.—believed that if Roosevelt could be nominated on an independent ticket and if he agreed to run on that basis, a successful fight could be waged to break up the Platt-Croker combination. When Roosevelt faced the situation in August and early September on his return to Montauk, he was confronted with this problem: If he were going to break up "boss rule" in New York he would have to fight Platt. Quigg, Barnes, Odell, Gruber, Lauterbach, et al. This is precisely what the Chapman-Cutting-Fuller group wanted him to do and just what Platt-Quigg-Barnes-Odell and company would do everything they could to prevent.

But the interesting thing was that Frank Black and his friends were agreed with the Chapman group on this one point. The Chapman group hoped that the Colonel would break up the Republican *machine*. The Black group *feared* that he would. Abe Gruber, one of the Black group, distributed extracts from some of the Colonel's essays at the Saratoga Convention, in which the latter denounced the bosses with his usual vigor. Gruber said then:

> "I give these little free readings because I think they may help Colonel Roosevelt by saving him from being nominated by Platt." [13]

Roosevelt finally declined the nomination of the Independents on September 25, 1898, saying:

> "It seems to me that I would not be acting in good faith toward my fellow candidates if I permitted my name to head a ticket designed for their overthrow * * *
> "I appreciate the importance of the independent vote, but I cannot accept a nomination on terms that would make me feel disloyal to the principles for which I stand or at the cost of acting with what seems to me bad faith toward my associates." [14]

IV

The story divides itself into two essential parts: The conversations which took place between the Colonel and "Jack" Chapman and the latter's colleagues in the month of September, 1898; the conversations which took place between the Colonel and his friend Quigg, and later between him and Platt—about the same time or earlier.

Though what occurred between the Colonel and "Jack" Chapman was freely disclosed in 1898, what took place between the Colonel and Quigg and Platt did not come out until seventeen years later in the trial of the famous libel suit, which Roosevelt's former friend, William Barnes, brought against him. The events of the trial in Syracuse were reported in the newspapers of that day, but it is to be found in more complete detail in the printed record of the trial. (I may say, in passing, that I have never gotten so much entertainment out of reading a record on appeal, and never so much joy in reading history in the making as in re-reading the current newspapers of that day, the "Times," "Sun," "Herald," "World" and "Post" of August and September, 1898.) [15] In this trial in Syracuse there was brought to light the actual correspondence that passed between Lemuel Eli Quigg and Theodore Roosevelt in September, 1898.

These are contemporaneous records. Obviously, they record the operations of the minds of the correspondents at the time they were written. The letters were written after Quigg had had preliminary conversations with the Colonel. Prior to writing the letters Quigg had conversations with his chief, Platt, and he reduced to writing, for the record, exactly what he had said to Platt and what he had said to the Colonel at Montauk.

To begin with, there is the wire from Quigg to Roosevelt on September 14, 1898:

"* * * There is no difference whatever between us as to that report. It is perfectly understood and understood just as you indicate." [16]

Accordingly, Quigg and the Colonel and Platt came to a *complete understanding* by September 18th.

What was that understanding? (It should be remembered that Quigg was arranging a conference between the Colonel and Platt for the ensuing Saturday.) What took place we can get clearly now from this correspondence.

Quigg wrote Roosevelt:

"He (Platt) has said that he would prevent your nomination if he could see any fair reason to believe that your administration would be injurious to the organization; * * *" [17]

* * * * *

"I told him that you would like to be nominated; that you understood perfectly that if you were nominated it would be as the result of his support; that you were not the sort of man who would accept a nomination directly out of the hands of the organization without realizing the obligation thereby assumed, to sustain the organization and to promote and uphold it; and that you were perfectly prepared to meet that obligation and to discharge it justly; * * *" [18]

Quigg said then that they did not expect him to be a figurehead but that, too, was qualified by his clear statement that Platt understood

"* * * that you would take the office, if at all, intending in good faith to act the part of his (Platt's) friend, personally and politically; to accept and respect his position as the head of the Republican organization and as the Republican Senator from the State of New York; * * *" [19]

And as indicative of his great and genuine friendship for Roosevelt, Quigg said further:

"I want you, my dear Roosevelt, to go on and on. You are a rare good fellow and you have got the American spirit, which, with the multitude, I greatly admire." [20]

Of course, Quigg showed the correspondence to Platt, and it may be assumed, showed it also to Odell and Barnes, who were helping Platt to "steer things right." That is, kill the efforts of Black and his friends and get Roosevelt into commitments that would save the machine. But the public would have no opportunity to see this correspondence.

Now, let us "look at the record"—as Al Smith used to say. It is Ivins cross-examining Roosevelt.

First of all, the Colonel admitted that he knew Quigg was the "local boss of New York City." [21]

Ivins then asked the Colonel:
"Q. And working in co-operation with Senator Platt who was the 'easy boss' of the State?
A. Working, as you say, in co-operation with Senator Platt who was the 'easy boss' of New York State.[22]

* * * * * *

Q. At that time you knew of Mr. Platt's reputation as the leader or boss of the party in this state.
A. As the boss of the party in this state, yes.
Q. And you deliberately, by agreement, met him for the purpose of discussing your nomination at the coming convention by the Republican Party?
A. I did.[23]

* * * * * *

Q. Now, at the time that you wrote that letter to Mr. John Jay Chapman, your associates had not yet been nominated, had they?
A. No; but the Independents had told me that they were going to nominate an entirely separate ticket.
Q. I do not mean that. Your associates on the Republican ticket had not been nominated?
A. I think not; you can tell from the date of the letters.[24]

* * * * * *

Q. So you declined an independent nomination in order to stand by associates who had not yet been nominated, knowing that nominations would be fixed by Mr. Platt and Mr. Odell?
A. By the Republican machine under the control of Mr. Platt as boss." [25]

That makes it clear that Roosevelt owed his nomination to the "machine" and that the "machine" was Platt's.

By September, 1898, the Republican leaders were asking the public, "How could Roosevelt accept the Republican nomination and also accept a nomination from a faction whose object is the overthrow of that organization?" Of course, the answer was clear. Platt and Quigg and Barnes knew the answer all along. The Independents were just banking on Roosevelt's playing the role of Saint Patrick slaying all the snakes in Ireland. But Platt and Quigg had different plans. The object of the Republican machine politicians was clear—to get a ticket named by Platt, preserve the machine and secure a complete endorsement of the Black administration. And that is just what they did get. *(The Independents expected Roosevelt to run on the regular ticket at the same time he ran on theirs. They said so. And they believed it could happen.)*

It was perfectly obvious in August and September that Roosevelt would have to be loyal to something and to somebody. If he were

going to be loyal to his party, how could he attack the party's ticket?
Of course, it was possible for him to insist upon a ticket of which he
could approve, but he did not do this. On the contrary, after he got
his nomination, he not only supported the "yellow dogs" but defended
them. Now let us turn to the Barnes record:

Ivins:
"Q. Did you during that campaign in any way in any of your speeches attack
machine politics or boss rule?"
Roosevelt:
A. Not at all.
Q. Not at all?
A. It was not in issue.
Q. Why was not it at issue if there was a machine and there was boss rule?
A. Because there was no feeling against it at that time—nothing in the shape
of an important Independent movement.
Q. Then you do not attack anything unless there is a feeling against it, is
that what you mean to say?
A. I attack—I attack iniquities. I attack wrong-doing. *I try to choose the time
for an attack when I can get the bulk of the people to accept the principles for
which I stand. I believe that you can only accomplish reforms of a permanent
character when you can educate the people up to the point of standing by
them.**
Q. I think you have answered the question. You stand by righteousness, do
you not?
A. I do.
Q. With due regard to opportunism?
A. I stand by righteousness, always.
Q. With due regard to opportunism?
A. No sir; I stand by righteousness always.
Q. With due regard to opportunism?
A. No, sir; not when it comes to righteousness.
Q. Does not your last answer state that?
A. It does not, sir. I say I believe emphatically that you must have a due re-
gard for opportunism in the choice of the time and methods of making the
attack. But you must stand for righteousness, whether you are going to be sup-
ported or not. * * *" 26

V

"The New York Times" of August 28, 1898, in its leading editorial,
"Platt and Black," pointed out that victory was necessary to Platt and
that Roosevelt was probably the only Republican who could be
elected running against a Democrat of high character. A day later it
said that the people were indignant over the war scandals and this
would have a decided effect upon the state gubernatorial campaign.
The people "want to punish Alger."

On September 11, 1898, the "Times" editorial expressed the view
that an independent nomination was neither necessary nor desirable
and hoped that the Independents would not "mistake the mind and

* Italics supplied.

character of Col. Roosevelt as to believe that he would care to expend his energies in battling against both the political parties this Fall." That their moves might make Roosevelt's nomination distasteful to organization Republicans and diminish Roosevelt's chances of getting the Republican nomination.

On September 24th, the "Times" editorially said:

> "Why do the Independents pester Col. Roosevelt with their nomination? He is not an Independent. He is a Republican, and never has been anything but a Republican, * * *. His relations to the Republican Party and its principles will be those of devoted loyalty."

On August 20, 1898, the "Evening Post" in an editorial headed "Platt and Roosevelt," said:

> "* * * the boss is contemplating the necessity of taking Roosevelt. And well he may be. * * * Yesterday, he (Platt) sent his errand-boy Quigg to see the Colonel of the Rough Riders at Montauk Point, report of the interview being made at Manhattan Beach—to Platt."

By August 23, the "Times" was assuring its readers that the Republican Party leaders expected Roosevelt to decline the Independent nomination then in contemplation.

VI

Now, let us see what happened with the Independents. Paul Fuller gave out a statement on September 25th.[27] He summarized their position.

> "In August last it was known that many voters of all parties in this State were ready to support for State officers candidates who should take office free from partisan obligation.
> "Certain of Mr. Roosevelt's friends believed that he would be an ideal head for such a ticket. They were confident, also, in the exigency in which the Republican Party found itself, that an independent uprising would force it to nominate him without pledges; they believed that with an independent ticket in the field, his election would be assured, and at the same time that Republican boss rule, which they believed he detested, would be deprived of the use of his war record to elect its other candidates. They presented this view to a conference of independents * * * Their suggestions were favorably received, but with special insistence on the part of those present that it must be made clear that, though no objection would be made to Mr. Roosevelt's acceptance of the Republican nomination, the remainder of the ticket to be supported by the independents should be selected by them."

On September 21, Chapman wrote, "Dear Teddy," reminding him that at their very first interview, he, Chapman, had made it clear "that the Independents could not be placed in the position of voting for you if that involved strengthening the Republican machine * * * that the Independents would by this prospect of your nomination by the machine, themselves be placed in an embarrassing position. * * * I spared no pains to explain to you our own aim in the matter and the way we felt at seeing the hero worship elicited by your war record made use to build up what we called the powers of evil."

The letter Roosevelt sent to Preble Tucker in September is referred to by Chapman as "gratifying" because it assured him, Chapman, "that [he] had not misrepresented your position to the men throughout the State and whose knowledge of the state of your candidacy rested right on the hands of Klein and myself."

Now, returning to the Fuller statement:

"An adjournment was then taken that the situation might be fully laid before Mr. Roosevelt.

On the reassembling of the conference Mr. Chapman and Mr. Klein reported that they had fully conferred with Mr. Roosevelt, and that the plan above noted was approved by him, but with the express limitation *that in case * * * he should not receive the Republican nomination, he must then be free to accept or decline the independent nomination,* * * *.

The conference acceded to this, * * *." *

The New York "Herald" of September 11, 1898, had published a statement by Lovell Jerome, a personal friend of Roosevelt's, in which it was said that Colonel Roosevelt

"will not nibble at the Gubernatorial apple which some republican and democratic independents dangled before his eyes yesterday."

And when the Colonel refers to his nomination for Governor, said Jerome,

"He means the regular nomination of the republican party by the delegates at the Saratoga Convention. Should he receive the nomination and be elected, *he would be a republican Governor.*" *

This gives point to the following in the Fuller statement:

"On Sunday, the 11th inst., there appeared in the press an interview with Col. Jerome. * * *

Appreciating that if authentic the closing words lessened the eligibility of Mr. Roosevelt as an independent candidate, a representative of our conference, Mr. Rothschild * * * called upon him at Montauk on Monday, the 12th inst. * * * and asked for such an explanation as he might give of the Jerome interview, * * *.

* Italics supplied.

Mr. Rothschild reported Mr. Roosevelt's explanation that he had not used the specially partisan language referred to; that Mr. Roosevelt's position remained precisely as when Klein and Chapman saw him, and that he had made suggestions to Mr. Roosevelt as to circulating nominating petitions.

* * * on the following or second day thereafter those in charge of the canvass were further reassured by Mr. Roosevelt's approval over his signature of the address in question (issued by the Citizens Union).

* * * * *

On the 20th inst. word was received from Mr. Roosevelt that he found himself in an 'impossible position' with reference to our nomination and suggested an interview, * * * at the City Club on the 23rd inst.

* * * * *

After taking what we believed to be every reasonable precaution to be sure that we were acting in full accord with Mr. Roosevelt's views, we have to thank our friends throughout the State for the prompt support in funds and in work, with which the independent canvass has been supported, and to regret that any confidence which they may have acquired, through us, in the entire willingness of their proposed candidate for Governor to accept their nomination should have proved mistaken."

Clearly, Roosevelt could have had the nomination from the Republicans anyway. He could have dictated the party platform. He could have conditioned his acceptance upon the naming of associates on the ticket who were men of high character. *He did none of these things.*

Edmund H. Titchenor of Binghamton, New York, the nominee of the Independents for State Treasurer, has sent me his files. Among these papers is a duplicate copy of a letter from Paul Fuller as Chairman of the Citizens Union General Committee. (I knew his signature well.) It is addressed to Jacob H. Schiff, Seth Low, J. Kennedy Tod and others—all supporters of Theodore Roosevelt's candidacy on the Republican ticket. They had quoted from a letter from Colonel Waring to Theodore Roosevelt. This letter of Fuller's is the reply distributed widely at the time.

"When the New York Evening 'Sun,' * in its issue of Sunday, October 23rd, resurrected a dead man's letter to bolster up the character of its candidate for Governor, knowing that the estimate contained in that letter had been absolutely repudiated, no one paid attention to the vile expedient, for none other was expected from that quarter; but when, over your honorable names, the same expedient under date of 29th of August, is circulated with your assistance, it is time that you should be informed and the public with you, that the conduct of Colonel Roosevelt in rejecting an independent nomination, which he had welcomed and encouraged, and in placing himself under the orders of a Boss, moved Colonel Waring to apologize for the recommendation given in his letter of August 29th. This he did in a letter to Colonel Roosevelt, of which that gentleman will doubtless furnish you a copy, and in which Colonel Waring expressed his painful disappointment that the friend whom he had always considered a man of honor and of courage, should have forfeited his claim to both of those qualities."

* The Morning "Sun" of 1898 was not the Evening "Sun" of today. The management and editorial board were wholly different.

On July 22, 1914, sixteen years after these incidents of 1898, the Colonel himself wrote:

"It is impossible to secure the economic, social and industrial reforms to which we are pledged until this invisible government of the party bosses working through the alliance between crooked business and crooked politics is rooted out of our governmental system. In New York State the two political machines are completely dominated, the one by Mr. Barnes, the other by Mr. Murphy. The State Government is rotten throughout in almost all its departments; and this is directly due to the dominance in politics of Mr. Murphy and his sub-bosses, acting through such entirely subservient agents as Governors Dix and Glynn, aided and abetted when necessary by Mr. Barnes, and the sub-bosses of Mr. Barnes. Mr. Murphy and Mr. Barnes are of exactly the same moral and political type. * * * The interests of Mr. Barnes and Mr. Murphy are funda-' mentally identical, and when the issue between popular rights and corrupt and machine ruled government is clearly drawn, the two bosses will always be found fighting on the same side openly or covertly, giving one another such support as can with safety be rendered. * * * Yet they really form the all-powerful invisible government which is responsible for the maladministration and corruption in the public offices of the State." [28]

This is precisely what the Independents said in 1898.
Again, in 1914, Roosevelt said:

"It is idle for a man to pretend that he is against machine politics unless he will with straightforward good faith, openly and by name attack Mr. Barnes and Mr. Murphy and pledge himself to do all he can to eliminate them from the control of political affairs, and in destroying them to destroy the system which renders possible such pernicious activities as theirs." [29]

This, too, is what the Independents said in 1898 to the Colonel of the Rough Riders, but in 1914, it became the libel upon which Barnes sued the Colonel. In the trial, Roosevelt put it in evidence to prove that it was true not only in 1914, but in 1898.

VII

In 1898, the Citizens Union offered the voters of New York State as candidate for Governor, Theodore Roosevelt of Oyster Bay; for Lieutenant-Governor, Thomas M. Osborne of Auburn; for Secretary of State, Oren E. Wilson of Albany; for Comptroller, Thomas E. Kinney of Utica; for Treasurer, Edmund H. Titchenor of Binghamton; for Attorney-General, Frederick W. Hinrichs of Brooklyn; and for State Engineer and Surveyor, George E. Waring, Jr., of New York.
This is their Declaration of Faith:

"Whereas, in the State of New York the control of the great political parties has fallen into the hands of unscrupulous men who have so entrenched themselves in power that party government has ceased to be representative government, and the parties themselves are no longer reliable agencies of good government, the promotion of the public welfare being subordinated to the attainment of personal ends; and

Whereas, this intolerable condition is evidenced by frequent coalitions between the machines of both parties in order to maintain the ascendancy of one or the other political ring; by the enactment of laws wholly at variance with the spirit and genius of the Constitution of the State; and by the appointment of notoriously unfit persons to positions of public honor and trust; whereby the good name of the State has been disgraced; and

Whereas, the only remedy for this intolerable condition lies in an appeal from the bosses who have created it to the people who have power to correct it.

Therefore, the voters of the State are invited to cooperate in the nomination and election at the coming election of the following ticket which shall stand pre-eminently for the principle of honesty in office, and which is composed of men free from the corrupting influence of the boss and whose character and abilities guarantee the honest and intelligent administration of their trust."

This is the basis upon which the group procured the signatures to the petition putting the Independent ticket in the field. There is not the slightest difference, save in language, between the statement of the Citizens Union in 1898 and Roosevelt's "libel" of William Barnes in 1914. In 1898 it was Thomas C. Platt and Richard Croker. In 1914 it was William Barnes and Charles F. Murphy. The bosses changed in sixteen years but the system remained the same.

Roosevelt wrote in 1897, in his "Essays":

"An ideal machine has for its officers men of marked force, cunning and unscrupulous, and for its common soldiers men who may be either corrupt or moderately honest, but who must be of low intelligence. This is the reason why such a large proportion of the members of every political machine are recruited from the lower grades of the foreign population." [30]

(This is the extract that was distributed at the Saratoga Convention by Abraham Gruber in an effort to beat Roosevelt.)

And in the "libel" on Barnes, Roosevelt said:

"If the political conditions in New York were such as they are in California, then our public need could best be met by rallying behind such a man as Hiram Johnson and supporting him and his associates; but in New York the two strongest parties numerically are both in such shape that the rank and file are tied hand and foot by the bosses." [31]

The Colonel of the Rough Riders in August and September, 1898, was a greater figure in New York State than Hiram Johnson ever was in California. Moreover, the Colonel was a great national hero. He could have had anything in the way of political preferment. In August of 1898 Platt was obliged to nominate Roosevelt on whatever terms Roosevelt imposed. Yet it is the simple historical fact that the Colonel declined the call of his reformer friends to become their leader in the anti-boss-ship fight. The Colonel turned down one set of friends, the

Independents, and went along with another set, the Republican politicians.

Call my friends—Cutting, Fuller, Chapman, Rothschild—naive; describe them, if you please, as Roosevelt did—"the lunatic fringe" [32] or "mollycoddles." At this juncture in the political history of New York, Theodore Roosevelt not only failed to respond to this high call to leadership but by his conduct furthered the machine and supported the Bosses.[33] From his admissions in the Barnes' libel suit, it is clear that he regarded it as expedient to turn down the Reformers and go along with Platt, Quigg, Barnes and company. But the hopes of those who believed in him in 1898 rested upon confidence in him as a reformer. Fifteen years later, after he had become President, after he had turned on his friends Taft, Root and Hughes and was running on an anti-Republican, anti-Democratic ticket, he then undertook to break up not only the machines of the party, but to break up the party itself. But the truth is that with his support from 1898 to 1914, the machine had grown more firmly entrenched.

Carl Schurz said on November 3, 1898:

"Roosevelt tells us we must 'dare to be great.' I tell him that in order to be truly great we must first dare to be honest." [34]

Roosevelt got 661,707 votes on Election Day. Van Wyck, the Democratic candidate, got 643,921 and the Independent ticket got only 2,103. It was surprising—in those days—that there were so many willing to stand up and be counted, knowing that their votes would be regarded as "thrown away."

Dr. Felix Adler opposed the Colonel at the big mass meeting of the Citizens Union on October 25, 1898, saying:

"* * * because he seems to have done more to hurt the prosperity of the independent movement than any other man in the State. * * * It is very easy to go with the swim, pleasant to vote with a party. But if we have a real spark of American manhood in us let us not believe that this government * * * will come down through a long line of statesmen into the hands of the Platts and Crokers." [35]

VIII

Now I came into the picture in this way:

In late August or September of 1898, Abbot called me into his office and presented the program of the Independents in substantially these words: "Some of my friends have gotten Colonel Roosevelt to agree to run on an Independent Ticket for Governor and we all think it furnishes a great opportunity to break up the Platt-Croker combination. We propose to get him nominated and that requires fifty signa-

tures to a petition from each county in the State. How would you like
to take two or three counties?"

This was like offering me a place in the chorus at the Metropolitan
with Caruso in the star part. It came as part of the romance and adventure of my young life.

So in September I went off "on tour." I covered three counties,
Rockland, Orange and Delaware. I would corral fifty or a hundred
people at a corner or in a store and make a speech. I remember especially Lasher's grocery store at Griffin's Corners in Delaware County.
I was spellbound myself, so I could spellbind my audience. Of course, I
made the most of Colonel Roosevelt as a hero, as a great Police Commissioner, as the enemy of all evil in politics and I pictured the glori-
ous opportunity offered to break up the wicked combination of Platt
and Croker and so get some decent politics into New York State.

Some of those who went through other parts of the State were suggested by the Colonel himself. Under the Roosevelt spell, every one of
my audience signed on the dotted line. I found it easier than selling
a suit of clothes to a reluctant customer. True it is, there were some
skeptics. "The New York Times" reported what I had done.[36] I got
what I was sent out for—the signatures.

That is, I got sixty signatures in each of the three counties and that
with hardly any trouble at all. By telephone, I learned that others in
other parts of the State were getting on quite as well. At the end of
my trip, I landed at the Eagle Hotel at Kingston, tired out and glad
of a good night's rest.

Next morning I read in the New York "Herald" that Theodore
Roosevelt had declined our nomination and would run only on the
Republican Party ticket!

I was sick. I had pinned my faith on a hero and he had let me
down. I might have become a skeptic and joined those who believed
that success wipes out everything else. Because of the influence of the
men with whom I associated I kept marching along with them.

IX

Roosevelt's friend and public relations adviser when he was Governor, Joseph Bucklin Bishop, wrote what was offered as the authentic
biography of Theodore Roosevelt, entitled "Theodore Roosevelt and
His Time." You will not find in it any part of the Ivins cross-
examination. Nor will you find the text of the Quigg-Roosevelt correspondence.

Bishop left the impression that in the game of foxes in 1898, his
friend very decisively out-foxed Platt, Barnes and Quigg and that the

Independents were just beneath contempt. He admits, however, that Roosevelt did say to Quigg that he would like to be nominated for Governor and that, if nominated, he would not make war on Platt. Bishop added, "if war could be avoided." [37] Bishop is of the opinion that the Independents were unkind to his friend, the Colonel, in nominating a complete State ticket with Roosevelt at its head; that their action would, if Roosevelt had accepted it, put out "an anti-Republican ticket throughout" and would have compelled Roosevelt "if he should accept the nomination, to run as an out-and-out Independent candidate without hope of support from the Republican party and consequently without hope of election. The inevitable result of his candidacy under these conditions would have been the election of the Democratic ticket." [38] Bishop gives the Independents a good scolding for persisting "in accusing him [Roosevelt] of deserting his principles even after he became President." [39]

But when Roosevelt failed to get the renomination for President and Taft was nominated, he then turned on the machine and created and led the Progressive Party—a real reform party.

Ultimately, good government was secured in New York State and in New York City. Cutting, Fuller and the other trail blazers ultimately won. Not one of these friends of mine was a cynic or a defeatist. They had faith. Roosevelt, too, dared to be great—to use his own phrase. True, he was an opportunist—but he never was a cynic.

That explains why, in spite of his record in 1898 he succeeded in securing his leadership in 1914 and why, in spite of his weaknesses, he continues to appeal to Americans. He is, indeed, part of the great American tradition. In simple truth, he was at his best when he led a great cause to victory. If he failed in 1898 in New York State to measure up to his highest standards—well, that was his defeat, as well as ours.

Why did he turn his back on his Harvard friends in 1898? The answer is simple: He believed in himself. He believed that he could make the politicians dance to his fiddle and he compromised with them in the confident belief that he could do great good for his state—and if he were ambitious to become President—for his country.

But to understand the times, and even Theodore Roosevelt, the story of how he became Governor of New York should be told in its entirety. He was a great mixture of characters. In 1912 on his way to deliver an oration, he was shot, dangerously shot. But he delivered the speech for over and hour and a half and then went to the doctor for treatment. In 1917, upon the country entering World War I, he wanted to raise a division and fight. As the Bull Moose candidate, he drew to his side men like Frederick M. Davenport, my classmate, Michael Schaap and Dr. Henry Moskowitz. At the convention an enthusiastic group marched around the hall to the hymn "Onward, Christian Soldiers." He was their inspiring leader. Then he was the *Reformer* once more.

But in 1898 he was the *Politician*.

He was a challenge to the ideals of my friends and though Cutting, Fuller, Chapman, et al., went down to political defeat in 1898, what they planted in the swampy ground of those days later blossomed into fine flower. Besides, it is no exaggeration to say that Roosevelt himself profited by the experience and the light of the faith of my friends in good government shone for him as it did for others.

CHAPTER TEN

And the lawyer set out homeward with a very heavy heart. "Poor Harry Jekyll," he thought. "My mind misgives me he is in deep water! He was wild when he was young; a long while ago to be sure; but in the law of God, there is no statute of limitations."
"Dr. Jekyll and Mr. Hyde," ROBERT LOUIS STEVENSON.

William M. Ivins

A trial lawyer par excellence—A great municipal official and leader in Municipal Reform—A believer in the Republican Party—A cause célèbre—Barnes versus Roosevelt—A titan in the law confronts a titan in politics—Who won?

I

TWENTY-SEVEN WILLIAM STREET is at the corner of Exchange Place and William Street. The building is called "Lords' Court." The little girl whose father had his office in the building, told her friends that his office "is in heaven." Fifteen William Street was on the same block, at the corner of Beaver Street. In that building, Deming had his office and I had mine, the Corn Exchange Bank building. Across the way at Beaver and William Street was Delmonico's Restaurant.

On the way from Lords' Court to Delmonico's you might meet any noon an English Squire or K.C.* of the type of Sir Marshall Hall—wearing, if it were spring or fall, a covert topcoat, spats, a brown square top English derby and a gorgeous ascot scarf that must have just come over from Bond Street, London—and an emerald pin. Oh, But that emerald! Both the scarf and the pin—if you were a man—would surely excite your envy. It always did that to me. Only this gentleman was not English at all. He was, in fact, one of the leaders of the New York Bar, and, in my opinion, the cleverest. William M. Ivins knew everybody in New York who was worth knowing, as you would have soon discovered had you followed him down that short block.

* K.C. means King's Counsel. One of the barristers of England who tries cases in English courts.

I met the senior member of the firm of Ivins, Wolff and Hoguet in the Hearst-McClellan election contest in 1905. Then it was I first saw him as a lawyer in action. There were three candidates for Mayor in 1905. Ivins ran as the Republican candidate, George B. McClellan ran as the Democratic candidate, and Hearst ran as an Independent.

In that mayoralty election Hearst *won*—really won. That was my belief then and still is today. The election was stolen from Hearst by false counting of votes. McClellan won over Hearst by a majority of less than 3,000. The then Attorney-General of New York was Julius M. Mayer. Hearst's lawyer was Clarence J. Shearn.

Although the Citizens Union vigorously opposed Hearst's election to the mayoralty, it did stand for clean elections. It so happened that I was assigned to the job of investigating the election frauds for the Citizens Union. Later, James S. Lehmaier was designated by the Attorney-General as Special Deputy Attorney-General. Lehmaier and I knew each other as fellow members of Dr. Peter's West Side Independent Club. We worked together and secured enough material to obtain a half-dozen indictments of election district inspectors. But six months later, on the recommendation of the Attorney-General himself, all these indictments were dismissed. Lehmaier then resigned his position in disgust.

I must say in passing, that his brand of profanity was much inferior to Taylor's. Why some people should think that profanity should be taboo, I cannot understand. G.I.'s don't think so. But why should a good Republican or a good Democrat be sent to jail for keeping Hearst out of the Mayor's office? Stopping Hearst short in his political career was a desirable—if not indeed, a moral end, wasn't it? Now be reasonable, young man, "be practical." That is what they told me.

Mayer was later appointed to the United States District Court and did make a fine record as a judge. He was always a good Republican and loyal to the organization. I think Charles Michaelson would understand why those indictments were dismissed.[1]

Shearn took over for Hearst as his lawyer and brought court proceedings to set aside the certificate of election issued to McClellan. He retained a score of lawyers headed by Ivins, who, as I have said, was the Republican candidate for Mayor. I was given the junior's job of collecting and organizing the evidence. Ivins assigned me a room in his suite at Lords' Court. The evidence we collected was, in my opinion, enough to win the case for Hearst. But the courts thought otherwise.

Now Ivins differed from my chief, Deming, in one important respect. The former remained always a regular Republican and stood by the organization—the latter was not. Deming was very definitely a Reformer.

I came into further professional association with Ivins when the Board of Aldermen of New York City appointed a committee headed by Alderman B. W. B. Brown to investigate the Tammany-controlled Street Cleaning Department. Ivins asked me to come in as junior to organize the evidence and assist him in the hearings. We dug up a lot of dirt.

Ivins was born in Freehold, New Jersey, but moved to Brooklyn, after being admitted to the Bar in 1873—the very year in which I was born. I do not think Ivins had anything against Freehold or New Jersey when he moved to Brooklyn to practice law. But truly great men came from Brooklyn to New York to practice—William M. Ivins, Horace E. Deming, Edward M. Shepard, Benjamin F. Tracy—all giant trees that grew in Brooklyn—fir trees of majestic height. John Morris Perry lived at 1228 Dean Street and my preceptor and guide, Frank Rudd, had a nice little home near Plymouth Church at 45 Orange Street.

"Uncle Frank" was a good and close friend of Deming. He came to our house to dinner one Sunday and the subject turned on old age.

"Uncle Frank, when does a man grow old?" I asked. His answer came swift and true—"When he is no longer receptive to new ideas."

And I might just as well put it down for the record that I, too, was born in Brooklyn,—Bartlett Street (Williamsburg). I allege this, as we lawyers say, "on information and belief." There is no birth record to support my boast! But I am fairly sure that it was not my fault if my parents carried me over on the ferry—I was only a little cone then. Any protestations on my part would have been ineffective. Transplanting me to Bleecker Street, Manhattan, may be the real explanation for the stunting of my growth. If father and mother had only stayed in Brooklyn! Well there's Meier Steinbrink, who became a Supreme Court Judge over there; and Frederick E. Crane, who became a County Judge in Brooklyn and later Chief Judge of the Court of Appeals. Robert H. McCarter always believed that he never would have been the "big shot" that he was in Newark, New Jersey, if he had responded to temptation and moved to New York. He told me so himself. But Ivins moved from Brooklyn to New York and became a leader of the New York Bar.

II

It will help to understand some things of which I shall write if it be kept in mind that Ivins was at one time a partner of Benjamin

F. Tracy and Frank Platt, the son of Thomas C. Platt. These three men constituted a substantial part of the brains of the Republican Party of New York.

In 1890, the Legislature appointed the so-called Fassett Committee to make a general inquiry into the government of cities and Ivins was named as its counsel. "He caused chagrin in such high places by his efforts, that by joint agreement of the State bosses the Committee was presently 'called off.' " [2]

In 1907, he was appointed Chairman of the commission to revise the charter of the City of New York.[3]

Ivins became a partner of William R. Grace, for several years served as president of the United States and Brazil Steamship Company and as counsel for the Cunard Lines. In 1905, at the time he ran for Mayor, the "Times" said of him:

> "* * * No man in the city approached him in intimate knowledge of the machinery of the City Government and its daily working. The Ivins Charter which he prepared was a marvel of logical and systematic exposition of organic municipal law in principle and in detail." [4]

On the day following his death the editor of the "Times" outdid himself. He said:

> "William M. Ivins doubtless surpassed most of those in this or any other age who have had the right to call themselves learned." [5]

I remember a portrait of Nietzsche and a bust of Napoleon in his office in Lords Court. He had a complete collection of medals of the Napoleonic era. He was a collector of rare editions of books, prints and furniture. His published works included: "Money and Politics," "Municipal Finance," "Codification" and "Comparative Jurisdiction." In spare moments he was writing his memories of New York—the City's growth and changes—social, political, geographical and financial.

In 1893, Ivins represented the Brazilian Government in its dispute with the Argentine Republic, concerning the boundaries of the two countries. The case turned largely upon the construction of a decree of Pope Alexander VI, the Borgia Pope.

He acted at one time as special counsel for the Public Service Commission in its investigation of the Interborough-Metropolitan relationships in 1908.

When the Cuban rebel, Garcia, was arrested in New York in 1893 for violation of the Neutrality Act, he volunteered to defend him and in five minutes secured a verdict of the jury of "not guilty." No wonder the editor of the "Times" said:

"The common man finds it hard to believe that such an uncommon man can be practical." [6]

As I saw him daily for over six month, I agree with the "Times" that, "His conversation was extraordinarily stimulating in any circle, whether the discourse was of things political or social, temporal or spiritual, * * *." [7] He was the leader in any group and everybody was quite willing to let him monopolize the conversation.

III

Ivins was a great trial lawyer. The libel suit brought in 1915 by William Barnes against Theodore Roosevelt gave him opportunity to display his talents as a virtuoso in the courtroom. In that trial in Syracuse great drama took place.

Joseph Bucklin Bishop, in his biography of Roosevelt, said:

"Ivins himself made open profession of his absolute confidence in the outcome of the trial. He went about telling his acquaintances that he had Roosevelt's doom in his hands. Among others he said to Elihu Root, on the eve of the trial: 'I am going to Syracuse to-morrow to nail Roosevelt's hide to the fence.' To this Mr. Root replied: 'Ivins, let me give you a piece of advice. I know Roosevelt and you want to be very sure that it is Roosevelt's hide that you get on the fence.' " [8]

Elihu Root was Ivins' friend. He pulled Roosevelt out of a tight pinch in the 1898 campaign for nomination. The Black-Gruber-Lauterbach group had secured from their Tammany friends a copy of an affidavit in which Colonel Roosevelt had sought to escape payment of New York City taxes on the ground that he was then a resident of Washington, D. C. If he was a resident of Washington, D. C., then under the constitution of the State of New York, he could not be nominated for Governor of that state. The Black group thought they held the winning trump, but Elihu Root rendered the opinion that Roosevelt was still a resident of New York. At the convention he made a speech supporting this view. Nevertheless in 1905 when Taft was nominated for the presidency, Roosevelt denounced Root as chairman of the convention and charged him with being the tool of the politicians —including Barnes.

It should be remembered that when Theodore Roosevelt left the Republican Party and ran for the presidency as a Progressive, he denounced all the men with whom up to that time he had worked as a

Republican. The alleged libel against Barnes was planned to destroy the Republican organization in New York State. Every politician, including Barnes, the plaintiff, would be through, if Roosevelt was successful. Even those Republicans who were not interested in the Barnes political machine, but who were loyal to their party, felt that if Roosevelt were to keep getting more power he would do such damage to the G.O.P. that the whole demnition organization might just as well shut up shop and go home.

Now, keep in mind, please, that Ivins was always a regular Republican. Keep in mind, too, that he had been the partner of Benjamin F. Tracy and Frank Platt—son of Tom.

IV

Now what was the trial all about? On its face, a libel suit brought by one William Barnes against one Theodore Roosevelt for $60,000. But as a libel suit alone it was almost certain to be lost.

John M. Bowers, of Bowers and Sands, represented the Colonel. They were counsel for the New York World and were regarded as outstanding specialists in the law of libel. It seems to me in reviewing the facts, that the case properly entitled, should have been called "The Republican Party of the State of New York and the Republican Party of the Nation, plaintiffs, v. Theodore Roosevelt, defendant."

There were men in the Republican Party who felt a deep injury had been done to them by Roosevelt. They knew that it could be established that Roosevelt had been successful as a Republican, just because he had worked with the bosses to get the nomination for Governor. Later as Governor and as President he had worked with them too, and had turned on them only when he failed to get the Republican renomination for President and ran as the Bull Moose candidate against his own party—electing Wilson.

Obviously Ivins did not undertake this case for a fee. Neither did he undertake it for honor or power. Why did he go into the case with such zeal?

Ivins was a sick man all through the trial, yet the record shows that he did not miss a day, even when his junior, Harry Wolff, carried on. The "Times" said that:

> "The past strenuous two weeks has affected Ivins's health. Today he was suffering from a slight attack of la grippe, * * *." 9

He had been advised by his doctors to stop his work in the case. His friends later agreed that the physical strain put upon him brought on his death shortly after the close of the trial. Ivins left a net estate of $14,361 when he died. The gross was $44,439.[10] As he died within several weeks after the trial, it seems a fair inference to say that he received no fee for his services in that case. One hundred thousand dollars would have been a small charge, but it would have been just like Ivins to take the case without a fee.

Ivins believed, besides saving the Republican Party from Roosevelt's devastating blows, that two principles were involved in the case— loyalty and sincerity. Whether "Bill" Barnes was what Roosevelt said he was, or was not, Ivins believed that Roosevelt had clearly violated these two principles. He set out to establish these points out of Roosevelt's own mouth. Did he succeed?

Let us look at the record. Ivins brought out in that trial the famous Barnes "Mugwump letter." Here is what Quigg wrote Roosevelt September 19, 1898:

> "The thing I fear is that these plausible and poisonous Mugwumps will at some time or other involve you in some of their 'good government' entanglements intended, as they always are, to help the Democratic Party and to create dishonest prejudice against decent Republicans, and that the first thing we know there will be a hitch." [11]

In 1912 Theodore Roosevelt turned "Mugwump" and organized the Bull Moose movement, rallying to his support thousands who believed he was then bent on purifying American politics.

But Charles Evans Hughes as Governor fought the machine earlier. Then Theodore Roosevelt stood shoulder to shoulder with Barnes. Ivins brought this out in the trial. Barnes wrote Roosevelt on August 21, 1908:

> "I have burned my bridges on this matter, as you know, last Spring and there is no retreat for me and I shall continue to oppose his [Hughes'] renomination until the result of the convention is known * * *.
> Do not for Heaven's sake put the Republican party in this state in the hands of the Mugwumps.
> You said at luncheon the other day, that you asked your friends once to cut their throats, but you did not feel like asking them to do it again. I think there is a large number of them who will not do it again.
> It is honorable to go into a fight, but it is cowardly to commit suicide." [12]

In the trial Ivins brought out Roosevelt's hostility to Hughes in the Republican Party.[13]

When it was Hughes v. Barnes, Roosevelt was for Barnes.

V

Loyalty as a virtue takes on various tints. Its quality is not a matter of logic. It is a matter of traditional mores. In its higher aspects, it falls into what Lord Haldane, in his great Montreal Address called "Sittlichkeit." Here are some of these elementary kinds of loyalty:

Ivins said to me once that the evening before, he had met So and So, a prominent Republican politician, who urged him to enter actively in a campaign against another So and So and had said: "You know Ivins, you are the very man who could go up and down the State and tear his hide off—go out and expose him."

And Ivins, with a gleam in his eye, had replied: "Yes, I will go up and down the State and say that a man who marries his mistress should not be put in high office."

Ivins knew that the friend who had made the suggestion had in fact married his own mistress and had in fact held high office. Ivins knew, too, that the religious groups of the state would not support such a man for elective office if they knew the fact. But he also knew that men of the world have their own code covering such matters. For example, if the woman is wife in all but name, it is regarded as merely an act of decency for the man to make the relationship legal and thus give the woman the protection of his name. This is one kind of loyalty. Even if the woman's early career had been colorable, it would still be an act of grace—"as long as the light holds out to burn, the vilest sinner may return"—to clear her name by marrying her. Despite its condemnation by the clergy, having three wives in succession is not completely discountenanced, even in high circles. Besides, the man of the world regards the whole matter of sex relationship as a private affair. Hence to him, legalization by wedlock of an *affaire d'amour* is treated as a simple act of loyalty.

Of the same general nature, there is a principle of loyalty among politicians, too. It is not regarded as good form to make promises and break them. That is, when you make promises *to your friends*. Even as in the days of Quintus Cicero, and Marcus, his brother, it is still regarded as permissible to fool the public in a campaign for office by making promises which you know definitely you will not keep.

Theodore Roosevelt himself wrote something like this when he spoke of Platt and campaign contributions.

> "No pledge was needed. It was all a 'gentlemen's understanding.' As the Senator [Platt] once said to me, if a man's character was such that it was necessary to get a promise from him, it was clear proof that his character was such that the promise would not be worth anything after it was made." [14]

It was regarded as bad form, too, to put a friend "out on a limb and then cut off the limb." But the worst charge that any politician can possibly make against another is that "he bit the hand that fed him" or, "he fouled his own nest."

VI

Now we may not like the profession or trade that Bill Barnes followed, but he himself made no bones about it. He was a political boss. He did what he thought a political boss was supposed to do. He was no more ashamed of his profession than Sadie Thompson was of hers. Barnes' hide had been hung on the fence for such a long time it was thoroughly suntanned. His hide so tanned is attached to Roosevelt's answer in the libel suit. Here is what "Collier's" had to say about him:

> "Barnes is the most successful combination of university graduate and strong-arm politician in public life. He is one of the few men of his birth, rearing and education who have conformed successfully to the lowest level of politics. He is head and shoulders in ability over the men he rules. He is dominant and tyrannical—fertile in ideas and brutal in his execution of them. He has quarrelled with practically every Republican Governor of New York of his time, notably with Hughes, Odell and Black. At a festive gathering in Albany, during his fight with Governor Odell, Barnes in a speech parodied Tennyson's lines: 'Governors may come, and Governors may go, But Barnes goes on forever.' " [15]

But suppose the Reverend Davidson had stayed overnight at Sadie's house during that awful period of "Rain" and then had had breakfast with Sadie next morning—it wouldn't have been nice of him, would it now, to have set her house on fire and gone around denouncing her for what she was? Under these circumstances, Sadie would not think much of him *as a gentleman.*

Ivins showed that not only had Tom Platt breakfasted with Roosevelt at the Platt apartment in New York City all the while Roosevelt was Governor of the State, but that Roosevelt had consulted Platt on every point during his administration as Governor, and even after he became President, had invited Barnes to the White House. Under these circumstances, Barnes and Ivins did not think it was cricket nor in good taste for Roosevelt later to denounce Barnes—in effect—as a political prostitute.

But he not only went after Barnes in that fashion, he went after Charles S. Mellen, then president of the New York, New Haven and Hartford Railroad, Clarence H. Mackay, E. T. Stotesbury, John Henry Hammond, Whitelaw Reid, Cornelius N. Bliss, C. D. Borden, T. Coleman du Pont, H. H. Rogers, John D. Archbold of the Standard Oil Company—all financial pillars of the Republican Party. He even said of Charles S. Whitman, then Governor, that he was the tool of the Democratic boss! And though he himself had been the beneficiary, as Ivins showed conclusively, of large campaign contributions from big business, he denounced the alliance between big business and the Republican Party.

VII

Roosevelt testified that Barnes had said to him that it was necessary that the head of a political organization should have complete control of the organization.

"* * * without organization, without leaders, without bosses—he used specifically the word 'bosses'—party government was impossible. And he used this phrase: 'The people are not fit to govern themselves. They have got to be governed by the party organization * * *.' " [16]

That was the theory of that day held by those who ran the political party. Roosevelt believed in it. Read the record:

"Mr. Ivins:
Q. That is, you had to be in alliance with the 'invisible government,' so-called, to get the nominations confirmed?
A. To get the nominations confirmed, I had to have the support of the Senate and the Senate was responsive to Mr. Platt's wishes." [17]

Let me give a fine illustration of expert cross-examination.

Ivins had carefully prepared two horns of a dilemma for the defendant to choose from—either he was a friend of Barnes or he was not. Either he approved of Barnes or he did not. If he was a friend of Barnes, why did he go back on him? If he disapproved of Barnes, why did he treat him as a social equal?

The experienced trial lawyer must, in effect, be able to read the record in print the very instant the witness is answering the question. But a talkative witness—an orator on the witness stand as Roosevelt was—is just meat for a hunter like Ivins. When Roosevelt was put to choose between the horns of the dilemma Ivins put before him, the lawyer then quoted from the President's autobiography. He read this to the witness: "Some of his [Platt's] strongest and most efficient lieutenants were disinterested men of high character." [18]

Then Ivins went on:

"Q. Did you include Mr. Barnes in that list?
A. When I wrote this book?
Q. Did you include him in that list when you formed your opinion, when you were in Albany as Governor?
A. This sentence was not written while I was in Albany as Governor. It was

written in 1912 or 1913, when I wrote the book, and then I did not include Mr. Barnes.

* * * * * *

Q. I want to know whether or not, when you were in Albany in 1899 and 1900, you in your list included Mr. Barnes as one of the efficient lieutenants of Mr. Platt who was a disinterested man of high character?

A. Mr. Ivins, that is not a question that I could answer by yes or no. Do you wish me to answer it exactly as I feel about it?

Q. If you cannot answer it by yes or no, I do not care for your feelings. * * *"

He said after some hesitation:

"A. Then I must answer you no.

* * * * * *

Q. Then I will ask you this: If you did not so regard him as a disinterested man of high character, why did you invite him to the Executive Mansion, why did you consult him in the capitol, why did you associate with him, why did you advise with him?

A. Because I thought he was above the average of the ordinary political leaders, I thought that his morality was at least level with the common political and business morality as I found it expressed at that time. I believed that he had it in him, if he would abandon those standards, to become a most useful public servant of the State, and I believed that there was a good chance for his so becoming."

(He said then that he had discussed Barnes' moral standards with him.)

"A. * * * I said that I thought he could become a very good citizen.

* * * * * *

Q. So that while you were there as Governor you were acting as monitor of Mr. Barnes in the effort to develop his political character, make a good and useful citizen of him; is that what I understand?

A. Only to this extent, Mr. Ivins: That with those men whom I met, I found that they had two characters, a good character and a bad character, a Dr. Jekyll and Mr. Hyde. There were a few of them that were absolutely straight and upright and disinterested. There were a few of them that were hopelessly vile. Most of them were of mixed character. My constant effort was to appeal to the side that was decent and get the man to act rightly and, if he would act rightly, I would not bring up his past against him at all, I would be only too glad to hail him as a decent man and do the best I could in company with him; and I never broke with him, with any man, until I became convinced that it was hopeless to get the good side out of him."

Watch what Ivins did with this Jekyll and Hyde quality of character a little later.

Ivins forced Roosevelt to admit that he twice reappointed Barnes to office. He showed him a letter he had written from the White House, Washington, January 28, 1907:

"My dear Barnes:

* * * * * *

It was a pleasure to send your re-appointment to the Senate today.

Sincerely yours,

Theodore Roosevelt.

Q. In this last sentence you expressed what you meant when you said gladly?
A. Yes sir.
Q. Then which Mr. Barnes, Dr. Jekyll Barnes or Mr. Hyde Barnes, did you appoint to office and express your pleasure in appointing?
A. I appointed Mr. Barnes to the office and until 1910 I hoped that we were going to get the Dr. Jekyll Barnes side uppermost, and I did not abandon hope of it until after 1911.

* * * * * *

Q. This question of severing the ligaments between these Siamese twins, Jekyll and Hyde, did not arise, did it, until you and he had ceased to agree?
A. Oh, no. There was no question of severing the ligaments—it is absorbing one by the other.
Q. You mean absorbing of Mr. Barnes by you, or Mr. Barnes absorbing you?
A. I am not speaking of the absorbing of either of us. I am speaking of the absorption in the man of the good character or the bad. Mr. Barnes was only one of the thousands of public men with whom I was dealing on that basis, trying to get the best I could out of them.

* * * * * *

Q. According to your testimony you were endeavoring to reconstruct Mr. Barnes and in the meantime keeping him in office?
A. I was endeavoring to appeal to what was best in him, and in that sense to reconstruct him." [19]

Ivins continued to hold him on the hook and pull him in. On August 14, 1910, Roosevelt wrote from "The Outlook Office of Theodore Roosevelt":

"Dear Barnes: Can't you come in to see me at the Outlook office Tuesday or Friday of next week, or the week after? I very much wish to see you before I go on my trip west." [20]

Having read this to Roosevelt, Ivins resumed:

"Q. At this time you had not discovered that Mr. Barnes was Mr. Hyde, had you?
A. That there was an element of Mr. Hyde in him?
Q. That is not my question. You have described him as I recollect it, as a double personality, Mr. Hyde and Dr. Jekyll. I want to find out whether at this time in 1910, you had yet discovered a Mr. Hyde element in Mr. Barnes?
A. That I had yet discovered it?
Q. Yes?
A. Wasn't my testimony that I thought that element was in him from the beginning?" [21]

Examining him further with references to his cooperation with Platt, Roosevelt answered:

"* * * at any rate I remember writing to Mr. Platt expressing my appreciation."

Then Ivins put this question to him:

"Q. You did not at that time have an attack of righteousness and chide him for his influence with the Legislature?

A. On the contrary, I praised him for his righteousness in passing the bill, Mr. Ivins, I did my best to get on with Mr. Platt and with all the other members of the organization. I, in good faith, endeavored to keep the organization intact and to make it the responsive servant of the rank and file of the Republican Party and the people as a whole, and I never broke with Mr. Platt or Mr. Barnes or any other leader of the organization until I could not help doing so in order to serve decency as I regarded it. I regarded myself as an organization man." [22]

Ivins closed his cross-examination of Theodore Roosevelt by quoting from an article which Roosevelt himself had written in "Putnam's" magazine during the fall of 1905. "The Man with the Muck-Rake." This is what he read to Roosevelt:

"The liar is no whit better than the thief, and if his mendacity takes the form of slander, he may be worse than most thieves. It puts a premium on knavery untruthfully to attack an honest man, or even with hysterical exaggeration to assail a bad man with untruth. * * *

* * * * * *

The effort to make financial or political profit out of the destruction of character, can only result in public calamity. Gross and reckless assaults on character, whether on the stump or in newspaper, magazine, or book, create a morbid and vicious public sentiment, and at the same time act as a profound deterrent to able men of normal sensitiveness and tend to prevent them from entering the public service at any price.

Q. Do you remember saying that?

A. I do.

Cross-examination closed." [23]

Of course, the unskilled cross-examiner would have asked, "Did you mean it?" And then the witness would have had an opportunity to make another speech.

VIII

Roosevelt won the suit. The jury decided in his favor. John M. Bowers won a great triumph as a libel lawyer. Roosevelt made a nice speech to the jury, thanking them for the verdict. So far as the libel case itself was concerned, it is all summed up in what Judge Andrews, who sat in the case, charged the jury:

"I have held that the article is libelous *per se* in two regards. I have held that it charges a corrupt political alliance between Mr. Barnes and Mr. Murphy in regard to the Government of this State. * * * I have held, in the second place, that it is libelous *per se* because it also charges that Mr. Barnes has worked through a corrupt alliance between crooked business and crooked politics.

* * * * * *

Three witnesses, Mr. William Loeb, Franklin D. Roosevelt and Mr. J. Mayhew Wainwright * * * testified to conversations * * * had with Mr. Barnes. You will remember that Mr. Loeb testified that some time in the winter of 1911 while this Senatorial controversy was on, he had an interview with Mr. Barnes at luncheon at the office of Bache & Co. in New York, and that Mr. Barnes there told him that he had an arrangement with Mr. Murphy that Mr. Barnes was not to interfere with Murphy's plans about the Senate." [24]

Franklin D. Roosevelt testified that he had a conversation with Barnes on February 15th or 20th, 1911. He told Barnes that he understood there was an agreement between the former and Murphy that the Republicans should remain steadfast for Depew so that the Democrats could have full chance to elect Sheehan; and he said that when he made that statement to Mr. Barnes, Mr. Barnes did not answer.

The defendant claimed that:

"Barnes' failure to answer it was equivalent to an admission of the truth of the statement. Mr. Wainright says he was a Republican Senator during the Senatorial contest in 1911; * * * he had an interview with Mr. Barnes; that he proposed a combination between the Republicans and the Independent Democrats, and that after some talk Mr. Barnes finally said to him no, that would be impossible; 'word had been given to the Democrats that we would keep our hands off.' " [25]

Judge Andrews charged the jury:

"Gentlemen, that is a pure question of fact for your determination. The charge is that there was a corrupt alliance between Mr. Barnes and Mr. Murphy. The justification is that the charge is true, that there was such a corrupt alliance, and that this Senatorial situation in 1911 proves it. * * * It is for you to determine what the truth is." [26]

Now, of course, on an issue of veracity between Franklin D. Roosevelt, William Loeb and J. Mayhew Wainright as witnesses and the former President of the United States on one side and William Barnes on the other—the defendant was almost certain to win the case as a libel suit. Crediting Ivins with the skill he clearly possessed, did he have any doubts on this score from the very beginning?

Ivins had a good press until May 7th. The front pages were filled and special articles appeared in the Sunday editions.

And then came one of the worst bad breaks that ever happened to a lawyer! Let a writer for "The New York Times" tell you just what happened:

"*Roosevelt Luck Restored*—There have been some doubts of late—for several years, in fact—about the fidelity of Dame Fortune to her sometime favorite,

Colonel Roosevelt, but evidently her desertion of him was a temporary with-drawal of attention, not a permanent desertion. When this great war was brought on only a column or two could be given * * * to the Colonel's viva-cious rehearsals of political history * * * (when plaintiff Barnes comes) to give his version of the same events * * * the Germans sink the Lusitania, and in-stantly not only the first page, but half a dozen more as well, have no space for anything else, and the Roosevelt-Barnes case is moved so far along in the wilderness of paper that only members of the leisure class have the time for reading on till they reach it. And they haven't the energy for it.

The result is that a considerable part of the public has either forgotten that there ever was a Roosevelt-Barnes libel case, or else it remembers the trial as something that ended when the Colonel's testimony closed. Of course, the Judge and the jurors are presumably listening * * * but what the two former friends and present enemies really wanted to reach in this litigation was the dear public, and only one of them has been permitted to do it. Roosevelt luck again! * * *" [27]

An appeal was taken but Ivins died on July 23, a few weeks after the close of the case. And when he died, the very life went out of the case. And then came the war.

IX

Ivins got a lot out of that case. How do you handle a man whom you must cross-examine and "skin alive" on the witness stand when the man happens to be a former President of the United States, a great orator to boot who takes the stump in the courtroom and orates to the court and jury? Read this exquisite turn by Ivins in the case.

There came a time when the lawyers in the case were examining some account books. Ivins leaned over the shoulder of Colonel Roose-velt, whom he had just been cross-examining, and presented the Colonel with a little green covered book and said with a pervasive smile, "I came across this yesterday, Colonel, and it struck me it was a first-class translation, and that if you cared to amuse yourself with anything of this sort while this uninteresting technical testimony is going on, you might enjoy it." [28]

It was one of Ivins' rare treasures, a translation of "The Acharnians" and other plays by Aristophanes. Roosevelt's face lit up and for the rest of the afternoon his chuckles proclaimed that he had enjoyed Ivins' gift.

Shortly thereafter Ivins had him on the witness stand again, gruel-ling him as wickedly as he could.

And this item:

"Mr. Ivins' fund of good nature seems inexhaustible. Whenever he makes a caustic remark to some opponent he turns and beams upon the audience. At the close of proceedings today several women surrounded him and told him how much they had enjoyed his smile. 'What's the use of getting sour,' the lawyer replied with a grin." [29]

X

What are the lessons to be gleaned from Ivins' life? First of all, note
the variety of his interests—literature, art, botany, politics, philosophy,
government. If you permit one interest to dominate your whole life—
if, for example, you just concentrate on being a lawyer—and you get
a series of "bad breaks," you are apt to find your whole life disappointing and be driven to despair. Active participation in other things
keeps your faith alive. I find that if you get bad breaks in one field,
you are almost always sure to get some good breaks in another. That
is why, if you practice law privately and give—as Ivins and Deming
did, as much as one-third of your time to public service, you really
gain something in the way of a broader base of security—*security of
mind.*

Next, Ivins, like Deming, got a great deal of fun out of just living.
To follow too closely the more austere practice of some religious
faiths—at least as I see it—deprives one of the most valuable elements
requisite to a completely rounded life. Not to be a hedonist, of course,
but to enjoy life *while* you are living is, it seems to me, a sane and a
safe basis for living. You can still believe in life after death.

Then there was this quality which Ivins and Deming, and other
great men whom I knew and worked with, possessed. A certain *sureness* of themselves. That quality which, when the possessor justifies
it by his ability and talents, is neither vanity nor egoism. Dr. Felix
Adler was neither vain nor an egoist. He also had that *sureness*. All
leaders must have it. They inspire confidence in themselves by its
very presence.

XI

Finally, Ivins was expendable. What difference whether a person dies
at 65 or 80—or even at 21? If his life has been spent—even for a single
moment—defending his country on the battlefield—or doing in civic
work some things which take him off too soon to satisfy friends—what
difference? That is what we are here for, isn't it? Leave to the future
to determine whether what we are fighting for is *valid* or not. If it
turns out to be valid while we still live, let us be grateful that we have
have such good fortune. But if what we fought for is invalid and loses
out—well, that's all part of the game, isn't it?

Ivins not only had great gifts, which came from Dame Fortune,
and great opportunities, which also came from the same lady, but he
cultivated those gifts. He was steeped in history and philosophy. He
had a breadth of view which enabled him to see the present in light

of the past and to get some augury of things to come. He was a seer
—he could dream visions, but being practical too, he could make
his dreams come true. I have noticed that with a broad and deep
philosophy, great men develop a fine sense of humor—an almost impish
kind of fun.

As Lord Tweedsmuir said of Lord Milner, "He had what the
French know as *'courage de tête,'* the boldness to trust his reason * * *
it would have been as easy to bully the solar system, since he did not
know the meaning of fear." [30] President or no President, national
hero or no national hero, Roosevelt was just an ordinary human being
after all—and so was Ivins. Roosevelt might win the libel suit—as he
did—but Ivins got the laughs. Ivins was *unbeatable.*

One thing unmistakably Ivins did. He left a record of a great trial
which can be profitably studied by every law student who aims to
become a trial lawyer. Finally, he left an interesting chapter in American political history.

But I wonder who ever got that emerald pin?

CHAPTER ELEVEN

*The history of any public character involves not only the facts
about him but what the public has taken to be facts.*

J. FRANK DOBIE.

Alfred E. Smith *

*A product of New York City—The West Side of New
York is akin to its East Side—The rise and development
of a man from Tammany Hall—Housing Reform and
Port Authority—The Citizens' Union—The statesman's
way to make progress.*

I

"THE SIDEWALKS OF NEW YORK." This was Al Smith's song. So closely
was it identified with him that a great many people thought he wrote
it. He did sing it. I heard him. But the song also runs:

> "East Side, *West* Side,
> All around the town."

This was a concession on the part of the East Side boys that there
were sidewalks over on the West Side of New York too. Broadway was
the dividing line—for us—between the 15th Ward and the 8th Ward.
Anyone belonging to the "15th Warders," was in a higher grade of
schoolboy society, but to the boys of the 8th Ward, he was just plain
snooty. The life on the West Side of Broadway where I lived was not
much different from the life over "Al's" way. My early experiences
enabled me to appreciate him. A picture of the New York of my
neighborhood will help to understand the New York of that day.

My street was originally known as "Amity Street." My friend,
Albert Ulmann, who knows everything about New York history, could
explain how it came by that name. It later was changed to "West
Third Street." But on the other side of Broadway, that same street
was called "Great Jones Street." Ever hear of "Shin Bone Alley," the
lane that ran from Great Jones Street in back of the buildings in

* This chapter was completed before the Governor's death in October 1944. Only
a few supporting details have since been added.

a shin-bone formation and came right out into Bleecker Street? South of Great Jones Street, was Bond Street, where the public library was —a walk of only two blocks. That's where I got my Horatio Alger, my Oliver Optic, as well as Jules Verne in the early schooldays. Later, in the eighties, "Les Miserables" and all of Herbert Spencer's volumes and Charles Darwin's ponderous works.

Ours was a business block. To the east of us, next door, was Saquis' cigar store. The Saquis lived upstairs in a building exactly like ours. At the Broadway end of our block was Coe's photograph gallery.

About fifty years ago, the Iconophiles got out a set of colored pictures of old New York, done by Mielatz. There is a perfect picture of our corner, West Third Street and Broadway. That policeman with the white helmet guiding people across Broadway—I knew him well. There was a pump near by on which I used to sit at night and watch the crowds. Anyone passing that corner could walk three blocks south and reach Niblo's Garden, where Ed Marks made his acquaintance with the glamour of the stage and saw the girls in "Black Crook," from the gallery. I never saw the show. I saw instead, as they moved in a heavy stream past our shop every morning and evening, girls who worked in factories.

II

On the west side of Number Six was a barber shop in the basement. Next to that, another cigar store, Slazenger's. Then a delicatessen store. At the corner of Mercer Street, the "Golden Eagle"—a perfect model of an old English tavern. There we had our pitchers filled with ale and porter—and one Christmas I had my first taste of roast suckling pig, when old John Worden served it for free lunch. Down the street two blocks was "Billy the Oysterman," in a cellar, the floor covered with sawdust. That's where father used to get the box of fried oysters, with a pickle. He would bring them home late at night for mother. And the children got one fried oyster each.

The ground floor of our building was the merchant-tailoring emporium. Up one flight, was the shop itself where the tailors worked, sewing cross-legged or pushing the "goose"—the heavy pressing iron. Another flight up, mother, father, two boys and two girls slept. Up there I remember the open fireplace on which mother, born in London, would turn a roast beef on a spit. Our real dining room, however, was in the basement, where there was little sunlight. Toilet facilities were well hidden under the sidewalk.

When the boys of the 8th Ward decided upon a raid on the "fellers from the 15th," they would advance with bricks and rocks—good-sized ones, and baseball bats. It became then the urgent business of all the boys on our street to rally to the defense of the homeland. Father thought it was funny when he saw his first-born wrap a handkerchief around his hand and heard him say, "Now let them come!" I never could understand why it should be regarded as funny.

Sweet Mamie O'Rourke did not "step the light fantastic" on the sidewalks in front of our house. Nor were there any sweet Rosie O'Gradys around there either. The only girls who lived on our block besides the Hershey girl at the corner and the little Saqui girl at Number Four, were my two sisters, Miriam and Amelia. My sisters were beautiful girls and even as babies, were admired by all passersby. They would stop to look in the baby carriages and give us pennies for their banks.

But if we had no sweet Rosie O'Gradys on our block, we had other girls—not so sweet. On Broadway, at night, they trod the sidewalks and, in the daytime those who went to Public School Number 10 on Wooster Street and passed through that street from Third to Bleecker on the way to school, saw shuttered windows and red lights in the doorways and beckoning fingers behind the shutters. And if we some-times changed and walked through Greene Street, we then saw big, fat, dusky wenches who, we were told, pulled in men and thoroughly despoiled them of their cash and jewelry.

William Travers Jerome, in his campaign for District Attorney, displayed the brass checks that were sold on the sidewalks over on the East Side. These passed the holders into one of these houses, only over there the "houses" were in tenements.

Later, all this "redlight" business, together with its connection with Tammany Hall politics, was exposed by Goff and Jerome for the Lexow Committee and furnished the material for sermons by Dr. Parkhurst who described from the pulpit in full detail some of the performances in these places.

At almost the same time that Tom Foley was leader down Al's way and gave him his start as a subpoena-server, Bernard F. Martin was leader over our way. He was Sheriff long before Al held that office. Al has told how lucrative a job it was. "Barney" Martin was one of father's customers and a good dresser too. How father got there, I never heard, but he became treasurer of the Iroquois Club—the Tam-many Club of our District. Indeed, he helped purchase the property and fit up the club house. It was on Thirteenth Street west of Fifth Avenue. Father was a good treasurer. The men who came into the shop used to tell me, "Be as square as your father, son, and you will be all right." This business of being "square" with one's pals and never "double-crossing" anyone was part of the code of honor of these Tammany men. In "Up to Now," Al relates that Tom Foley said to him: "Don't speak until you have something to say. Men who talk just for the pleasure of it, don't get too far." And Tom added this piece of advice: "Never promise anything that you are not perfectly sure you can deliver. Most people who come to public men are not looking for the truth. They like to be jollied. The safest practice is to tell them the truth, and after they have tried out a dozen other people, they will come to the conclusion that you were right in the beginning." [1] That was good Tammany "dope."

It was through the Iroquois Club that I came to know Thomas C. T. Crain, first Judge and later District Attorney of New York. His confidence in my father was helpful forty years later. In 1933, I represented a man who was in a tight place. My faith in his honesty and Tom Crain's faith in me saved that man from an indictment. I believed in his innocence, and an indictment—as it always does—would have sullied him for the rest of his days.

Father was the captain of our election district. Just the same job in which Al began his political career under Tom Foley. Like Al's job, it was father's job to get out all the Democratic votes, including those that were registered in the Grand Central Hotel around the corner. Before election day, father would bring home from the club house the neatly folded ballots which we children helped him bunch together and fasten with rubber bands. In addition, father had a bag full of something or other, which was to facilitate "getting out the vote." It was father's assignment to put the ballots in the hands of the voters. It was the duty of the captain of the district to see that everybody voted "right." That was at least thirty years before the installation of the voting machines and ballot stuffing was stopped. It was after John Y. McKane down at Gravesend, Coney Island, turned New York State and put its electoral vote into the Democratic column. In this way Grover Cleveland was elected President of the United States.

By the way, I still have the badge that father wore when he marched proudly down Pennsylvania Avenue in Washington in the Cleveland Inaugural Parade with his friends of the Iroquois Club. I still remember, "Maw, Maw, Where's My Paw?" the Republican marching song as it was sung in the parades that passed our corner on Broadway. I understood its full meaning only when I read Allan Nevins' "Grover Cleveland, A Study in Courage," [2] along with "Burn, Burn, Burn, Those Letters"—the song the Democrats used in their campaign as they paraded up Broadway. The Republicans' "Plumed Knight" whose letters should have been burned was, of course, James G. Blaine.

At the same time that Al Smith was getting his education, other boys were getting a different kind of training over at C.C.N.Y.—the College of the City of New York.* There, my Montauk neighbor, Professor William B. Otis, continues to create Edward G. Robinsons and Borrah Minnevitches and there the professor's predecessors helped to give Felix Frankfurter his first start on his way to high judicial position.

III

Accident once more played its part. I chanced to meet Al Smith in the work of the Citizens Union. The "Cits" had been charged with being "just a tail to the Republican kite." That was because in those days if you did not get a Fusion ticket together—and that meant a frank concord with the Republicans—there was not the slightest chance of winning against Tammany. The Legislative Committee of the Citizens Union concentrated wholly on a lawyer's job. The lawyers on this committee gave careful study to every piece of proposed legislation at Albany which in any wise affected the affairs of the city. The committee acted to protect the city's interests. During my term as chairman, we met every Friday at the City Club, had dinner, then canvassed each bill previously referred to a member during the week, received his report, discussed the bill fully and then marked it "A1," "A2" or "A3" if we favored it, or "O1," "O2" or "O3" if we opposed it. "A1" or "O1" meant just a memorandum or letter to the Chairman of the committee in charge; "A2" or "O2" meant attending the hearing at Albany and "A3" or "O3" meant "all out." That is, we were to do everything either to secure the passage of the bill or to defeat it.

We soon found that it was necessary to have somebody in Albany during the legislative session—*a resident lobbyist for good government.* That's how Travis Whitney came into public life and made his

---

* One day a young student whose first name was Borrah and whose last name was Minnevitch came to "Doc" Otis and said: "Doc, I've got to quit college." "Why?" asked the professor. "Well, you see, father died and we have a large family and I must do something to help support them." "Can't you go out and come back again?" asked the professor. "Maybe," said Borrah, "but I don't know what I can work at. I can't do anything." So the professor said, "Well, what do you like to do best in the whole world?" With a little diffidence Borrah answered, "I like best to play the harmonica." So the professor said, "There was a fellow up in New England who once said that if you made the best mousetrap in the world, the whole world would beat a path to your door and buy them. Why don't you go out and make yourself the best harmonica player in the world? You may even play on the Metropolitan Opera stage someday." Two years later the professor was told that somebody wanted to see him and that his name was Minnevitch. It was Borrah all right —and he did play the harmonica on the Metropolitan Opera stage.

contacts with Governor Charles E. Hughes. Hughes came to like and trust him so well, that he made him secretary of the first Public Service Commission under former Ambassador Oscar Straus. Later Travis became a Public Service Commissioner and a mighty good one, too.* He came to know Al equally well.

We engaged first as our Albany representative Lawrence W. Trowbridge, Deming's nephew, and then Robert S. Binkerd, who afterwards became secretary of the City Club and thereafter Joseph Hammitt and Walter Arndt. Through the efforts of these men at Albany, we were able to gather material for a "close-up" picture of every senator and assemblyman who came from New York City. Our representatives were especially able men. Some of them learned how to play their poker at Albany. (They said you had to play poker to learn all about politics.) We watched the votes of all senators and assemblymen from New York City and followed their general record and conduct. We tried to be fair to all, regardless of party and we made a special point to accent the work of Democrats, so as to live down the charge that we were biased in favor of Republicans.

Al Smith began his legislative career in the Assembly in 1903. He was majority leader in 1911, during the administration of Governor Dix and speaker of the Assembly in 1913. He served as minority leader in the three sessions of 1912, 1914 and 1915. About the same time came Robert Wagner, now United States Senator and James A. Foley, late Surrogate of New York. The records of these three men, among others, showed fairness and independence and justified confidence in them as public servants.

IV

Several things came out of the work of the Citizens Union Legislative Committee.[3] First, we passed critical judgment upon the records of Senators and Assemblymen. In some cases we marked them *excellent*. This occurred when they showed ability and a sense of responsibility to the public. They got "certificates of merit," such as we got from teacher at Public School Number 10 when we were good in class. We soon discovered that fine orchids can come from swampy ground.

When Al first came to the Legislature as an Assemblyman, and even later when he was minority leader, the Citizens Union did not regard his record as very commendable. In 1908, in fact, we spoke disparagingly of him as an "experienced and effective legislator" but that he *"voted and worked against the public interest on important issues."* But Al worked hard and by 1915, the Citizens Union report said this:

* See Chapter 12.

"Minority leader. Intelligent and forceful legislator. Strong supporter of desirable industrial and social legislation. Record of votes good." In 1911 in the Assembly Al fostered the creation of the committee of which he became Vice-Chairman, which, following the Triangle fire, framed the factory laws for protection of workers in factories.* In the Constitutional Convention of 1915, Al showed still further improvement. Senator Elihu Root said later that he was the best informed man in New York State upon the subject of government and administration and Delancey Nicoll said of him in the Constitutional Convention: "Smith was the only man who knew what he was talking about."

As the result of our experience the men then in the Legislature learned something—especially in Al Smith's term as Assemblyman. If they knew their records were being watched and they would be "tabbed" on the basis of what they did, they would watch their records closely. They would raise hell with "Travis" or "Joe" or "Bob" if they thought they were not getting a square deal from us. If the records were good, their campaign manager would advertise what the "Cits" said about them in all the newspapers. "C.U. said thus and so of Al Smith or this of Bob Wagner or of Jim Foley."

In short, we put together in our own little shop down in Franklin Square, a piece of political machinery—a sort of Model T Ford—which carried forward and brought to the front, men in *both* of the regular political parties upon the basis of *meritorious* records. I know that Al always valued our opinions and our support. He gave recognition to this work in his book "Up to Now." "* * * it was certainly gratifying * * * to have a non-partisan organization, The Citizens' Union, support me for the new office." ⁴ The new office was Sheriff of New York County in 1915. Our endorsement certainly took from him some of the "curse of Tammany." Hosts of Republicans voted for Al for Governor—and later for President—because they had come to know his worth and believed in him. The Citizens Union's published reports helped to bring this about. Of course, that could not have happened if Al had not been Al. The publicity of the kind the Citizens Union gave him, helped to bring out his natural character and talents and gave him a head start in public life as an independent Democrat.

V

When Charles Michaelson relates, as he does in "The Ghost Talks,"

---

* Abram I. Elkus, later Ambassador to Turkey and Judge of the Court of Appeals, was counsel, and Bernard L. Shientag, now Justice of the Supreme Court of the State of New York, was assistant.

that, in substance, politics is all a game and one must not be squeamish about the means used in fighting the other fellow, he is telling the truth, that is, the truth as *he* saw it. Of course, if anyone were on William Randolph Hearst's staff as Michaelson was, in the days when Hearst was promoting the Spanish-American War, or was engaged in trying to blacken Al Smith in the Milk Campaign, he would see things as Michaelson sees them and would naturally apply that kind of "ethics" to politics—"the game of smear and double-cross."

There could be no greater contrasts in public life than these two men, William Randolph Hearst and Alfred E. Smith. In the past fifty years, no influence in public life, I believe, has been so devastatingly bad as Hearst's and no influence so encouragingly good as Smith's. They were bound to clash. Al knew Hearst through and through and while Al really never hated anyone, he had nothing but contempt for Hearst. When Al's mother was seriously ill of pneumonia, there appeared a cartoon picturing babies deprived of milk by Al as a result of his handling of the milk situation. Al's mother said, "My boy would not do a thing like that." Al always remembered that. As Governor, one of Al's first acts was to settle an upstate milk strike. Hearst in his papers accused Smith of killing the babies of the tenements by his subservience to the Milk Trust. To charge him with the death of the children he loved was more than Al could bear. The Hearst attacks literally struck home, for in her delirium, his mother was heard to say, "My son did not kill the babies."

At a meeting shortly after, in a two hour speech, he said of Hearst: "* * * a man who hasn't a drop of clean, good red blood in his body. I know the color of his liver, * * * and it is whiter * * * than driven snow." [5]

When in 1922 Hearst tried to get the gubernatorial nomination, the party leaders wanted Al for Governor, but were inclined to give Hearst the nomination for United States Senator. Al said to the leaders, "If you put that man on this ticket, * * * I'll * * * leave here and run as an independent. I'll stop that man or wreck the party." [6] Hearst did not get the nomination.

Al Smith is confirming evidence of the truth that you can be a politician and yet accomplish great public good. In spite of the most vigorous campaigns of opposition to him, never a breath of scandal was ever breathed against Al. "But he has gold teeth," said one of the fine ladies who attended the American Bar Association meeting in Philadelphia in 1928 while the Democratic convention was on—even after we told her what Al was really like, as we knew him. The gold teeth were enough for her.

Al had two outstanding characteristics: First, he had a deep religious faith. Second, he loved people. Rupert Brooke once wrote that he could "watch a dirty, middle-aged tradesman in a railway carriage for hours, and love every dirty, greasy, sulky wrinkle in his weak chin, and every button on his spotted, unclean waistcoat." [7]

On the other hand, Ramsay MacDonald, according to Lord Tweedsmuir "lacked this catholic, enjoying zest for human nature, * * *. He was too ready to despise. He loved plain folk, but they must be his own kind of plain folk with his own background. Of the ordinary stupid stuff of democracy he could be as intolerant as Coriolanus." [8]

Al came up from Tammany. But he had qualities of character that brought him the esteem in which he was held. At his death, on October 5, 1944, the 160,000 people who surged around St. Patrick's Cathedral to see him in his coffin included Catholics, Jews and Protestants. He loved his city and his deep ambition was to pay back some of the debt he owed that city. He was always simple "Al" to his friends and his friends were everyone—whether he was Jew, Catholic or Protestant, Irish or German, Roumanian or Italian.

I remember the time when Al visited us the year before he was nominated for President, along with Tom Smith, then Secretary of Tammany Hall and we talked in the locker room of the Fairview Country Club, after a morning of golf. Al and I discussed the possibility of his being nominated for President. I suggested the advisability of his first going to the Senate from the Governor's chair and thus securing a national reputation, before running for the Presidency. He was then thinking about it. But his friend and admirer, W. Bourke Cockran, advised him otherwise and convinced him that he should not wait, but run for President then. Al never thought much of the job of United States Senator anyway. The consequences are now known. Al was beaten, not because he came from the Sidewalks of New York, not because of the South's prejudice against New York, but simply because he was a Catholic.

Al summarized his creed as an American Catholic in the correspondence with Charles C. Marshall which appeared in the "Atlantic Monthly." He wrote:

"I believe in the worship of God according to the faith of the Roman Catholic Church. I recognize no power in the institution of my church to interfere with the operation of the Constitution of the United States, or the enforcement of the law of the land. I believe in absolute freedom of conscience for all men and in equality for all churches." [9]

VI

I sat in Al Smith's rooms at the Biltmore on one occasion when we were discussing the securing of legislation for the creation of the Port of New York Authority. Three other men were present: Eugenius H. Outerbridge, William R. Willcox, Chairman of the New York-New Jersey Port and Harbor Development Commission, the predecessor of the Port Authority, and another member of the Commission, now a judge.

We had agreed upon a line of legislative grand strategy and recommended it to the Governor. He concurred in our recommendation. This strategy might have put the third man in an embarrassing position with the Municipal administration of which he was a part. Said Al to the Commissioner, addressing him by his first name: "Where do you stand?" The Commissioner replied, "I believe in this and I will stand by it, no matter what the consequences may be to me. The Port Commission job does not pay me a cent and my job with the City does, but this is the thing to do." "Good," said Al, clasping the Commissioner's hand, "put it there. You know when I give my word, it sticks."

A gentleman's agreement it was—nothing more. But Al always kept his agreements. If, for any reason, he could not make good because of some change of situation which might embarrass him, he would come and frankly explain the situation and ask to be released from his promise. There are times when a man in public life is obliged to change his policy and may be obliged to change commitments which he had made and upon which others have relied. But Al was a stickler on this point of "keeping a gentleman's agreement" and he had an excellent memory. He never made excuses for himself. His favorite expression in debate was "Let's look at the record." That phrase will stick as part of our vocabulary.

It was the night the New York Legislature convened for final vote on the passage of the Eighteenth Amendment. We were in the Executive Mansion at Albany. I had persuaded Walter Edge, then Governor of New Jersey and later again Governor of that State (1945), to ask Al to arrange a meeting in Albany so that we could get the Port Authority started. Edge was most keen then to get through the tunnel from New York to New Jersey (now the Holland Tunnel) and at the same time, the bridge from Camden to Philadelphia, all as part of his larger program for highway improvement for New Jersey. That job is lastingly to Edge's credit.

At the conference in the Executive Mansion, up in Al's room, besides Edge and Al and Eugenius Outerbridge and myself, there were then present leading Republican and Democratic legislators from both New York and New Jersey.

The first item on the agenda was the *tunnel project*. This took us into late in the night. We then turned to the plan of the treaty between the two states, committing both of them to continuous cooperation in the development of the Port and creating the Port of New York Authority as the agency to do this. This was to provide the definite kind of cooperation which Edge, while Governor had advocated. "I am for marriage and not for divorce," he had said at the Chamber of Commerce meeting in which the plan between the states was under discussion.

The Port Authority we were talking of was to be a *public corporation, self-liquidating and controlled in its membership by the two states*. It was not entirely new in principle, but in form it was new, especially in the use of the compact-making powers reserved to the states. It had some of the virtues and some of the weaknesses of novelty. It was my job to get the idea across and having put two years of intensive study and research into the work, as counsel for the Bi-State Commission, I was full of the subject.

Al was in favor of it. I had gone to him when he lived at 45 Oliver Street, before I made the first draft of the treaty, and had discussed the strategy for overcoming New York City opposition. But that evening, Edge's emphasis was on the *tunnel project*. To him that was something real. The other item was merely an *idea*.

All the men in the room were practical men, especially the legislative leaders. These men, experienced in legislation, wanted not only to know how you got into this enterprise, but how you might get out of it. The first step was the one to be watched. Later on, when the Port Authority plan came up for discussion and Mayor Hylan opposed it, his principal slogan was "Don't buy a pig in a poke." However, that evening in the Executive Mansion, I wanted only to get concurrence in the simple plan of cooperation between the two states and the creation of an agency to bring it about. I knew the first step was the important one, and that if we got into too much detail, we should invite opposition from many quarters.

While we were deep in debate on the subject, Bobby Fitzmaurice, Al's standby, telephoned over from the capitol: "The Eighteenth Amendment has just passed." Al stopped the discussion, told us what had happened and said: "Let's have a drink. Mine's beer, what's yours?" And so was toasted New York State's adherence to the Eighteenth Amendment to which, I believe, everyone in the room was opposed.

Thus refreshed, we went at the debate again. I was making little progress. I argued: "This is like a constitution, the rest will come in the 'by-laws.' You have nothing to risk now." All along the line, both states must agree in the legislation to follow. But we must begin some-where—very simply. Finally, Al said, "It gets down to this, boys. *This is just the wedding ring, what happens afterwards we don't have to talk about tonight.*"

He won. They all came around and got behind us then and there. I am sure that if you have read the "Education of Henry Adams," you will be convinced by now that if Al did not have Henry Adams' education, on the other hand, Henry had little of the education of Al Smith. I ask you now, could Henry Adams have done what Al did with such ease and facility in the making of appropriate illustrations? Could Henry Adams have handled men as Al did? I cannot conceive of Al, as President of the United States, making the tactical errors Wood-row Wilson made in his conferences abroad and in his dealings with the United States Senators. Despite all the blame properly to be at-tached to Senator Lodge and Theodore Roosevelt, Al would have dealt with Lodge as he did with Republican leaders in the Senate of New York State. Al obtained his knowledge of human nature, not from books on psychology or principles of government, but from con-tact with people.

VII

Another incident: One of Dr. Adler's boys, and mine later, is Clarence S. Stein, the architect, who besides all his other achievements, married Aline MacMahon, the actress. Clarence was in the Sunday evening boys' club which John Elliott induced me to take over and where I tried to teach the boys some of the facts of life—and, I fear, taught them very badly. Because of his interest in housing problems, Al ap-pointed Clarence as Chairman of the State Housing Board. There Clarence mixed his architectural skill with his will for the public good. He was convinced that the problems of "slum removal" and "lower cost housing" were face and back of the same coin. Clarence knew of my connection with the Port Authority and knew, as almost every-one else in public life did then, of the self-liquidating nature of the Port Authority. Clarence had the idea that something like the Port Au-thority plan could be made available in the field of housing. He had been doing a great deal of investigation and study with the assistance of George Gove.

Clarence Stein and George Gove came to my apartment one evening and submitted the data they had gathered. The basic fact was simple. It was that, almost exactly to a penny, the figures showed that for every percent in interest rate saved on money borrowed or invested—that is, interest that had to be paid on a first or second mortgage—the rent could be reduced by *one dollar per room per month*. I checked up on these figures with my friend Joseph E. Gilbert who had a wealth of experience in building and real estate.

On this basis we planned a two-sectional enterprise, the "Smith Housing Bank"—I used the word "Bank" advisedly instead of "Authority," because I was averse then to spreading too rapidly the use of the "Authority" idea. Later it became the ruling fashion, especially in the days of the depression, to adopt the name and the form of the institution for all sorts of enterprises.

The next section in the structure that Clarence and I planned was the "Limited Dividend Corporation." This corporation was intended to give investors an opportunity to receive a 6% return on their investment, but no more. It was expected that the money borrowed on first mortgage would not cost more than $3\frac{1}{2}\%$ or 4%. It would be raised through the sale of Housing Bank Bonds—securities of the same general character as Port Authority bonds and, hence, exempt from Federal and State taxation.

A graduate of my office, Harold Riegelman, represented the *other side*. The *other side* was the organized real estate interests in New York City. The realty interests in New York were against the "Smith Housing Bank." We thought they were short-sighted but then they were definitely set against any such scheme. They called it *socialism*. But it was clear even then that private capital alone could not possibly do this kind of a job—the rentals poor people could afford to pay would not stand the burdens of interest charges such as are customarily expected by investors in the real estate field.

The need for extending the technique of the public authority method accompanied by tax exemption, both of the real estate and of the bonds issued for a housing project is now being emphasized.[10]

It is clear that while, ideally, in housing, as in food and clothing, government should not be obligated to intervene, there are two inescapable reasons why such ideal conditions are not now realizable. First, because a large portion of the families of the United States do not have income large enough to own or rent decent places to live in, and second, because the cost of supplying the owner or the tenant a dwelling place that meets minimum standards is too high. Accordingly, the realistic situation is that interest costs must be kept down, taxes must be cut out entirely—even government subsidies must be provided.

In 1917, Clarence Stein, as Chairman of the Commission of Housing and Regional Planning, presented the report to Governor Smith who sent it to the Legislature with a special message. Attached to that report is the proposed State Housing Law drawn by Kenneth Dayton and myself, and my opinion upon the constitutionality of the provisions of the law and of the tax immunity of the securities of the State Housing Bank.[11]

Hearings were held upon the bills, but we were obliged to abandon the Bank. The Legislature was overwhelmingly Republican and Harold Riegelman's clients were more influential with them, even though we were supported by the Governor.

Women played important roles in that fight. Agnes Naumberg, wife of ex-Judge Joseph M. Proskauer, was one, and Dorothy Rosenman,* wife of ex-Judge Samuel Rosenman, was another.

When, after an all-night session, Kenneth Dayton and I revised the bill to make it satisfactory to Harold Riegelman and the interests he represented—by cutting out the Bank—I told the Governor I hoped he would stand for the Bank and veto the bill.

"No, let's get this through," he said. "It's the first stage. The other *will* come. It is bound to come *later*." And it did. Later did come the City Housing Authority in connection with which Aaron Rabinowitz took over as leader and trail blazer and did a fine job. There came also the houses built in cooperation with the Amalgamated Clothing Workers in the Bronx under Sidney Hillman's leadership, the Negro housing project, named after Paul Lawrence Dunbar, at 138th Street in Harlem and "Stuyvesant Town," carried out by the Metropolitan Life Insurance Company in cooperation with the City of New York, in the area bounded by East 14th Street, First Avenue and East 20th Street, East River Drive and Avenue C, in Manhattan.

Business now takes a broader point of view. In 1942, life insurance companies were given power to invest moneys in such projects.[12] Our Court of Appeals said, December 2, 1943, seventeen years after the Smith Housing Bank was proposed:

> "For a long period of years both State and municipal governments have recognized an ever increasing social and economic loss due to conditions in those blighted urban areas where slums exist. It is a fact within common knowledge that conditions prevailing in slum areas affect the health, safety and welfare of the public, causing indirectly a heavy capital loss and a diminishing return of tax revenues."[13]

* She has gone on with this work and become Chairman of the National Committee on Housing and is emphasizing the unhappy, unhealthy living conditions of farm families throughout the nation and urging prompt action to relieve their plight.

In a prior case the Court had said:

"The public evils, social and economic, of such conditions, are unquestioned and unquestionable." [14]

On December 27, 1944, the City Housing Authority presented plans for new public housing to cost $260,000,000, designed to clear away a considerable part of New York City's slum district and to provide modern living quarters for 36,753 additional low income families in the first three years after the war. Edmond B. Butler, Chairman of the New York City Housing Authority, expects that these rooms will be rented below a limit of $7.00 a room and even hopes for an average of $6.00 a room. The projects include five in Manhattan, three in the Bronx, two in Queens and one in Staten Island. Thus, in the City of New York alone, what was projected in his first term as Governor as the "Smith Housing Bank" now lives as the "City Housing Authority," and it has grown to this size.

George Gove, director of the staff of Clarence Stein's Housing and Regional Planning Commission, became third vice-president of the Metropolitan Life Insurance Company, and took charge of its housing program. This company, under the inspiration of Frederick H. Ecker, Chairman of its Board and formerly its president, became the leading life insurance company attacking this problem from the combined point of view of social welfare and private industry. In a public statement, Mr. Ecker said:

"Having due regard to the factor of safety, the Company has always sought to identify the investment policy with sound public need." [15]

Of course, a life insurance company, having so many policy-holders among working people and white-collared folks of moderate income, should take the lead in such a movement.

It was a happy circumstance that George Gove with his initial training in working for the State Housing Board should now be in charge of this work for the company. Six savings banks and the New York Life Insurance Company in 1945 decided to go in for housing projects and follow the lead of the Metropolitan. These projects alone will aggregate $120,000,000.[16] Thus public and private capital is co-operating in low cost housing and slum removal for New York City.

There is a district on the East Side where the "gas house" gang used to flourish and where now gas tanks or old industrial buildings remind New Yorkers of the terrorizing days of the gangsters. A Metropolitan Insurance Company project will wipe out the whole district and create the "Peter Cooper Village" right next to "Stuyvesant Town." [17] Frederick H. Ecker emphasizes the point that this development will not require the tax exemption benefits of the Urban Redevelopment Corporation Law. It is a private housing enterprise under the amended State Insurance Law.

But when Al yielded in 1926 and agreed to accept the bill without the Bank, he added this: "I find that the fellow who insists on getting his bill through without a change is a fellow who does not really care enough to get the main thing." This is a lesson which every zealot must learn. It is indeed the lesson the founding fathers learned when they first framed the Articles of Confederation. Benjamin Franklin and Thomas Jefferson certainly knew that the Articles of Confederation would be inadequate and that we should ultimately have to come to a constitutional form of government. They did what they could to get the country started, believing that the other things would come in due course.

VIII

F. P. Adams in his "Conning Tower" once printed a piece by Milt Gross in the series "Nize Baby" in which Gross said, reporting on the progress of a young girl and her beau, "Gredually they got married."

Borrow a volume entitled "Port of New York Statutes," turn the pages over once and see how from 1917 to 1944, "gredually" the states got married in the field of Port Development. Or perhaps you like better Elihu Root's favorite saying, "Leg over leg, the dog gets to Dover."

I learned the difference between the technique of engineers and the technique of Al Smith when I began to study blueprints and specifications in the work of the Port Authority. I saw, for example, the detailed work which went into the design by Othman H. Ammann before there could be the George Washington Bridge.

> "Here strings are cables, harps a bridge
>   From concrete cliffs to those of granite;
> Here where the Hudson feels the sea
>   Iron is music built upon it.
> Go sail beneath this mile-long arch
>   Of steel and traffic, hear it drone
> Tremendous music, you will find
>   Its iron hymn the city's own." [18]

The engineer prepares every detail. He does not begin construction work until all his plans are tested. For simple illustration: in order to scale a wall, one figures on needing a ladder so high, with so many rungs, so many inches apart. It is designed, built and tested before it is put against the wall. Then and only then does one start up the ladder.

But if there is a statesman's job to do, another method must be evolved. There may be a "blueprint," but only in the mind's eye. One is lucky, indeed, if he can start with but two good strong sides for a ladder and the first rung. The technique is to stand on the first rung and, while standing there, put in the second, then standing on the second, put in the third. So, rung by rung, one builds as he climbs.

When one is young and full of ideals, he has as yet no knowledge of the difficulties to be faced in winning concurrence from others—especially legislators. He thinks that if he can work out a plan—a perfectly logical plan—he can push it across. For short cuts, a "functional" form of government is selected—a strong central regime with a "Big Boss" at the top, that is to say, some big leader who knows what he wants and goes out to get it and who does not let constitutional limitations or any other difficulties stand in the way. He soon becomes contemptuous of the slower processes of our democratic way and impatient of critical minorities. He uses ruses and chicanery to put through his plan. He sometimes induces his chief to take short cuts.

Presently, without knowing it, he has really gone all out for *totalitarianism.* He wants to pack the United States Supreme Court. It will save time if the Court and Congress can be harnessed and one "Big Boss" do the driving. What difference does it make that this is contrary to the principles embraced in the Declaration of Independence and in the United States Constitution? That's all old fogey stuff anyway! But this process is unthinkable to those of us who believe in the checks on powers, and the constitutional restraints put upon the Executive, as well as upon Congress itself. In his short-cut philosophy, if anyone asked the mover what was the difference between his ideology and the European totalitarianism, he might get the answer, "Ours is American and is governed by American ideals." But American ideals are based on solid realities. The founding fathers knew that power anywhere is subject to abuse. Al agreed with them.

Now, the difference between Al's way and the way of the "blueprint" boys, is just this: Al learned early in life that if we are to preserve our democratic ideals, we must hold fast to our American processes—slow as they are. We must preserve the rights of minorities; we must keep government close to the people and must be constantly on the alert, watching both the executive and the legislative branches of government. We must watch our Supreme Court, too. But not to the extent of depriving the Court of its independence. And most of all, we must have Lincoln's faith *in the people.*

Now there is a strong resurgence in this country to the simpler beliefs of the founding fathers. Young men, too, have become older. They are surprised to find out how "father has grown up—he knows something now."

IX

Like every other good executive, Al Smith had an unofficial Cabinet. Among its members was Abram I. Elkus, whom Al later appointed to the Court of Appeals. Also in that Cabinet was Joseph M. Proskauer. Al named him later as Supreme Court Justice and then designated him for the Appellate Division of the First Department.

As one who has known Judge Proskauer for more than forty years, I can say that no lawyer could have been a better adviser to Al. He accompanied Al in the campaign of 1928. They were close friends.

One Friday they sat down for breakfast and the Judge ordered ham and eggs. Al looked at his friend in disgust—"Joe, you aren't anything, are you?" *

In his cabinet, also, was Robert Moses. When Bob scolded "The New York Times" in the election of 1944 for supporting Roosevelt, they reminded him in an editorial that everybody east of the Hudson of any consequence had always been the subject of abuse by Bob.

Here is a good close-up picture of Al and Bob: You know, Bob never was quite convinced that Al was really the Governor. He always talked to Al as though he, Bob, had been the one elected to the office and Al was just a managing clerk. He talked to Al then just as Mayor La Guardia will tell you Bob talked to him.

Now Al was a great actor as a young man. He played in the Dramatic Society of the St. James Parish on the East Side. Among other parts, he played Dion Boucicault's "The Shaughraun." On very little provocation Al would play a role. Indeed, that brown derby of his was a piece of showmanship. So was the tilted cigar and the persistent use of the word "raddio" instead of "raydio," in spite of repeated effort on the part of his purist friends to correct him. His frequent use of the words "baloney" and "crackpot" were all part and parcel of his stage technique.

---

* Of course Proskauer is something. He is Chairman of the American Jewish Committee, in which post he had to take his share of brickbats. Not only is he an outstanding spokesman for American liberal Jews, but by securing the adherence of 1,326 distinguished Americans of all faiths to the proposal for an International Declaration of a Bill of Rights, modeled upon the American Bill of Rights, he did something of far-reaching helpfulness toward the reduction of racial and religious prejudices throughout the world.[19] To him largely goes the credit for persuading the Conferees at San Francisco to adopt the International Bill of Rights—an historic event.

When one day Al was in the little office behind the large executive chamber and Bob was telling him what was what—that is, giving Al his lesson for the day—Bob's tone grew more and more *crescendo* and more and more *fortissimo* and he swung his arms around as though he were addressing a mass meeting at Madison Square Garden—and Al listened and listened. When he thought he had had enough, he crouched down in his chair as though he were thoroughly licked, then slowly slid off the chair and collapsed on the floor!

Everybody, including Bob, had a good laugh, but nothing ever disturbed their close and enduring friendship. Al always rated Bob high for his courage, efficiency and disinterestedness.

Another story about Al: When he and Tom Smith were up at our place in Westchester, he told us of an incident that occurred when he was Sheriff of New York County. Al was very fond of fried eels. He knew a place on Long Island where they were caught and were fried just right. He invited a couple of friends to go one day for fried eels and timed the trip so that he would get there when the eels were ready to serve. The chauffeur had to break traffic regulations to get there in time. He was stopped by a Long Island traffic cop. Al pulled out his gold Sheriff's badge, showed it to the officer and said, "It's all right, officer, these fellows are a couple of crooks that I am taking down to the Suffolk County jail."

X

Here is an incident which is vouched for by his friend, George Sokolsky: After Al was beaten in the 1928 Presidential campaign, his automobile stopped in a town upstate and some children from a Catholic school near by crowded around his car. A Sister came out and said to Al, "You must come inside and make us a speech. These children have never met a Catholic who became a Governor of New York and ran for President."

Al went inside. He picked up a Catholic catechism and said, "Children, this is a catechism. It is the same catechism which I studied when I was a boy. Do you know what it teaches? *Never be a sorehead.* I've been defeated for the Presidency. If I had been elected, it would have been because God, in His wisdom, thought that I should serve. But I've been defeated, which means that God, in His wisdom, had found someone more suitable for the place."

This was his simple faith, genuine and sustaining. He was humble. He was a *good sport*—he learned that in the political field. But more than that he had a *sustaining faith.* He could bow in humility. He had no doubts about his *faith.* Al *knew* that there was a force in the world greater than himself; that he was merely the electrical wire through which that force operated.

Yet, in 1932, when Al was defeated for the nomination of the Presidency, he did take it very much to heart. His enemy, Hearst, sought and secured his revenge. He ganged up on Al with the Ku Kluxers and all the other "antis." But the thing that hurt Al most was the act of a friend. It was the result of Al's recommendation in 1928 that Franklin D. Roosevelt was nominated for Governor of New York. Al and his friends expected Roosevelt to join in giving Al another chance in 1932 to run for the Presidency. Thomas L. Stokes, in his column "Comment" in the "New York World-Telegram," October 5, 1944, entitled "Al Smith, Trail Blazer," says:

> "* * * on the way to the 1932 Chicago convention. I asked what had caused the rift between them." [Alfred E. Smith and Franklin D. Roosevelt] And Al snapped: 'Frank Roosevelt just threw me out of the window.' "

Al never ran out on anyone. He understood what political ambition could do to any man.

However, when he ran for President in 1928, he was attacked by the Ku Klux Klan throughout the country. With fearlessness, in a speech at Oklahoma, he attacked the Ku Klux Klan and openly challenged those who attacked him because of his religious faith. This, of course, brought him support from all who believed in religious tolerance.

Al Smith was elected and served as Governor of New York State for four full terms. It cannot be said truthfully that there is no religious prejudice in New York. But the example of Smith, a Catholic, and Lehman, a Jew, as Governors, substituted respect for what had been misunderstanding based upon ignorance.

Bigotry rests on ignorance. If Al, a Catholic, had become President of the United States and had set the example which he set as Governor of New York and the Catholic Church had given to Al as President the respect it paid him as Governor, what a powerful lesson such an experience would have been for the American people, indeed, for the whole world. Surely it would have dissipated much of the rabid ignorance and stupidity which, through the last two decades, have done so much harm. The process of overcoming racial and religious prejudices is slow and painful. But would it not have been helped if the American people had gone through the experience? The answer leaps at once to one's lips. The time was not yet ripe. Ofttimes things must grow worse before they can grow better.

Now that Al is dead and the lessons of his life are open to all who will read, perhaps the example of his life will contribute to bringing the day of better understanding nearer. In New York State Al Smith did succeed in securing a real confidence in his sincerity. In upstate regions, normally Republican, there were many Freemasons and voters ordinarily strongly prejudiced against Catholics who came to like Al. They liked him for his bluntness. They liked him for his quick wit, his broad diction—"baloney" and "crackpot"—all of it—and for his ability in simplifying complicated questions. All of this brought these "upstaters" to his side. This is the way in which Alfred Emanuel Smith overcame prejudice in his own state. The tribute to him at his death demonstrated the simple fact. Given time and adequate opportunity, if he had occupied the White House, he would have brought the country to his side.

XI

It was fortunate for Al that there were bicycles in his day. For he could follow up his courtship of Catherine Dunn, a pretty fellow-member of the St. James Dramatic Club. When she moved uptown to Third Avenue and 70th Street, a most discouraging distance, Al completed his courtship by bicycle. They were married March 6, 1900. Al dedicated his book: "To my companion on the journey, my wife." [20]

Catherine Smith passed away May 4, 1944. No longer could Al find the solace and comfort she had given him for forty-four years. We knew Catherine Smith. Al and she visited us and we visited them at the Executive Mansion. She consistently followed the rule my mother followed—*she let father do the talking,* while she did her knitting or embroidery work. She was the wife Al found it nice to come home to—in the fullness of his political triumphs or in the depths of his defeat and disappointment. She was a homebody. She was the kind of wife whom thousands of women admired because she was just like them, woman who lives her life in that of her husband and finds her greatest satisfactions in his triumphs. She gave him all those loving kindnesses which soothe and comfort a tired man after a hard day's fighting.

After May, 1944, Al's friends noticed how he began to fail and fade. He was comforted in his last hours by the words of Cardinal (then Archbishop) Spellman:

"I offer you my tribute of gratitude for all that you have done for the welfare of humanity. You have been a blessing to the suffering and the needy. You are a great American, an honor to your church and an inspiration to all who have known you or known of you."

He died smiling. There came to St. Patrick's Cathedral on the morning of his funeral men and women of all races, of all religions, from all walks of life. Al Smith died in the warmth of the deep love of his fellow men whom he loved so well.

BOOK III

THE WOMEN TAKE OVER

CHAPTER TWELVE

What hearts have men! they never mount
As high as woman in her selfless mood.
  "Merlin and Vivien," TENNYSON.

Rosalie Loew Whitney

---

*Woman Suffrage—A debate in which the author was
on the wrong side—The Judges of the debate change
his occupation—The important role a woman lawyer
plays in the trial of a case*

I

IN 1892, I was *particeps criminis* in a joint high school debate. The subject was Woman Suffrage. Henry A. Rubino, who later entered law school with me, and Thomas J. O'Neill, later highly successful as a negligence lawyer, and I, made up the team for the negative side. Because I was captain, I spoke last. And as often happens on the football field, though the team does yeoman's work getting the ball down to the five yard line, the fellow who crosses the line with the ball for the touchdown gets the college cheers. The chairman of the judges, Hon. John W. Goff—after deciding in our favor on the debate—handed over to me a set of books, Macaulay's "Life of Oliver Cromwell." They were provided by the Professor of the Political Science class of the Sixtieth Street High School, which took the affirmative. I could not divide the set with Rubino and O'Neill, though they actually did more to win the debate for our side than I did, so I took the books home.

I took with me also the recommendation of all three of the judges of the debate who, learning that I was then working in a tailor shop, suggested that I take up law. That was not so easy. How could I study law when I had to work during the day? And what interest did the law have in me? Father thought it was a rather poor suggestion for Judges Goff and McCarthy, to make to an impressionable young man.

Rubino, O'Neill and I worked hard in preparation for that debate. We went down to the Astor Library, then on Lafayette Place, and went through Poole's "Index to Periodicals." We got enough material to take either side of the debate. For the negative, we found such outstanding and conclusive arguments as "Woman's Place is in the Home"; "Women are Emotional—Their Judgment is Unreliable"; "Why Drag Women Down into the Mud and Mire of Dirty Politics?" and much more along the same lines.

Just fifty years ago, the New York State Constitutional Convention declined to submit a referendum on woman suffrage to the people for a vote and then it was said that "Women were not educated, knew nothing of politics and were unprepared for the ballot." [1] It resulted in the formation by women of the League for Political Education. There were a few women who wanted the vote, and, in the Fifth Avenue home of Mrs. Eleanor Butler Sanders, they started this movement for *votes for women*.[2]

It is high time I did something by way of atonement for the sins of that debate—apologies, if you please, for contributing to the negative on the subject of Woman Suffrage.

I shall write especially about two women whose work I knew intimately. I shall also put in something about the public work of a third.

Before I get to these two, Rosalie Loew Whitney—the subject of this chapter—and Belle Moskowitz—the subject of a later one, I must make a bow to some others on the distaff side, who in one way or another have contributed to my education. They are striking examples of what women have done and are doing in this modern world of ours.

II

First of all, a word about Anna B. Deringer, the best secretary any man ever had, who endured me and my vagaries for nearly two decades, covering such varied interests as the Protocol Experiences in the Garment Industry, the genesis and early growth of the Port Authority and of Housing—incidentally, severely criticizing the "Smith Housing Bank Plan" because it did not reach down far enough to benefit those who needed it most.

Then there's Mary—Mary Rubin, who succeeded Anna, and lived a life of enforced slavery for another decade or so, escaping from her cage like a bird when I retired in 1942 as General Counsel to the Port Authority to return to general practice. She had, I hope, an easier time in Africa or Italy or somewhere abroad as a member of Ex-Governor Lehman's staff, UNNRA, in a piece of war-peace work she very much wanted to do. Then I surely should write something nice about Olive Ricker, who runs the American Bar Association, mixes with lawyers from all parts of the country, and, as a result, has a whole retinue of friends all over the land. And, nearer home, a piece about Katherine Terry who, Robert Erskine Ely will admit, ran both him and the Economic Club, until she married Theodore M. Riehle. And, about Lillian L. Poses, without whose fine Italian hand, the Trade and Commerce Bar Association would be a dull and inane thing, devoid of both life and humor. And, I must not forget Isabelle Trowbridge, "concertmaster" of the New York State Bar Association. Nor Winifred Notman, who made a special drive to get into our office because she knew of the general outstanding prejudice against women lawyers and picked us as likely liberals who would take her on. Winifred swore, on her oath, in my presence, that she would never give up her professional career. She did make the best managing clerk we ever had. But, later, when called overseas to YWCA work in World War I, she promptly fell in love with a handsome engineer in the Army, David Chandler Prince, now vice-president of General Electric Company in Schenectady, and so her professional career went up in smoke—or, in romance.

A word about Rosaleen Skehan, the first woman lawyer on the staff of the Port Authority who, during World War II, took the place of two or three lawyers called into service. Wouldn't Rosaleen poke fun at me if she could read the notes of that Woman Suffrage debate?

Marion J. Harren narrowly escaped hard labor on our staff when we were at 74 Trinity Place. She became a highly regarded member of the United States Tax Court. She has as fine a brain as can be found anywhere—as some of the males who have practiced before her will confirm.

I must not forget Edna Goeltz, the first woman secretary of the Port Authority, the woman with the John Kieran memory, who never yet has been known to misfile a letter.

It is hard to believe that male prejudice against women lawyers was so thick that up until 1937 the Association of the Bar of the City of New York * would not open its doors to women lawyers, women who were actually admitted to practice on an absolute plane of equality with men! I proposed one of the women members, my friend and my wife's, Emelyn MacKenzie. She can hold her own in any diplomatic situation with a man, I can vouch for that. Her good hard common sense gives the lie to the slander that women cannot reason.

All this I write to offset the superficial prejudice that did much to keep women from even getting a chance to show what they could do—notwithstanding such great achievements as those of Madame Curie and others in the field of science.

* But under the administration of Harrison Tweed, there has come a great change over the Association of the Bar of the City of New York.[3]

III

Rosalie Loew came to the Bar at about the time women began to wear mannish clothes. Some of the women lawyers thought they had to act and dress like men, especially when they appeared in Court. But Rosalie Loew acted and dressed like a woman. She let her brain do the work, expressing in Court precisely what she had to say and always with an intimate knowledge of the law and the facts of her case. So she gained the respect of the judges. I will tell you about one particular case. Her greatest work as a lawyer, however, was as a pioneer in the field of Legal Aid.

In the year 1876, Arthur von Briesen brought together a group of public-spirited citizens to found the Legal Aid Society. It was not then what it is now, having grown to man's estate under the skillful guidance of Harrison Tweed—a national institution aided by the American Bar Association. The Society, in the year 1901, turned to a woman to build up its organization and manage it. This woman was Rosalie Loew. The principle underlying the organization was, of course, that the law should serve those who could not afford to pay lawyers, as well as those who could, and that lawyers primarily, as part of their professional duty, should supply the funds for the support of the institution. Rosalie Loew, during her term of office, organized and ran the Law Department herself. With a woman's intuition and knowledge of the poor—she herself came from poor people—she developed a fine service and it won public acclaim and support. Gradually, she built up a fine staff of young lawyers.

One day, there joined this staff, among others, a Harvard Law School man. He was Travis H. Whitney, who became later not only Rosalie's husband, but the representative of the Citizens Union Legislative Committee and later a Public Service Commissioner.

IV

I shall tell you about one law case in which Rosalie Loew Whitney proved clearly the special value and advantage of the woman lawyer. When I was up at Thirtieth Street High School, I met Tom O'Callaghan and John Fedden. Both started in at the bottom as salesmen and became successful merchants in the hosiery line. O'Callaghan and Fedden were two of the first clients of our firm, and my partner, Theodore B. Richter, remained counsel for both of them until they died. One day, Tom called me up and said he was sending down a lady and wanted us to take her case. She came, and we turned her and the case down. Theo and I did not believe her story. Then, Tom O'Callaghan called me down. "What kind of lawyers are you anyway? Too squeamish to handle a respectable girl's case because it involves charges of rape and seduction?" Well, what happened was that, with the usual prejudice of men, we were dubious of the truth of her story. As, later, her story was told in open court and is part of the printed record on appeal, I may now freely talk about it.

She worked for a Bronx builder and politician. She was his stenographer. One day, he asked her, she said, to come to a hotel north of 125th Street for purposes of dictation. It was a notorious place, but she said she was unaware of that. There, in an alcove bedroom, he assaulted her, and, later, promised to marry her. She went a second time, at his request.

After Tom O'Callaghan had criticized us for refusing to take the case, I thought that perhaps we were wrong. Was she telling the truth? How could we find out?

It was then I thought of Mrs. Whitney. I sent for her and laid the problem before her. She was a wife and mother. The truth turned upon whether the client consented to the act or was physically violated. Only the closest cross-examination could determine. Mrs. Whitney could examine her as no man could do in his private office.

Rosalie Loew Whitney took the assignment; made a thorough investigation, just as she would have done as Counsel for the Legal Aid Society. She reported that it was the truest story she had ever heard. She had gone to the client's house, had seen her mother, and had seen the place where her employer had jumped out of the window to escape a shot from a pistol in the hands of her mother. Rosalie brought a postal card, sent from him, to our client, which showed more than passing interest. She brought the client's diary, written in her own hand. But, more important, she became convinced of the truth of the story. We thereupon changed our minds and took the case, and brought two suits, one for seduction (loss of services) by her mother, and one for breach of promise, by the girl.

V

Two juries believed her. Two judges refused to set aside the verdict. Both cases were appealed to the Appellate Court and the verdicts affirmed. I think the combined judgments were for about $15,000.

When we tried to examine the defendant before trial to ascertain his means or ability to pay, for the purpose of fixing an allowance for counsel fees such as the law allows, the Appellate Division denied our application, indicating clearly that they did not favor this kind of litigation. So, of record, we were criticized, and had our vindication only when our client got hers.

VI

Rosalie Loew Whitney's adversary and mine was none other than Max D. Steuer, a successful trial advocate, whom aspiring lawyers were inclined to follow. Steuer shared with John B. Stanchfield the honors for handling desperate cases. He was adroit.

In this case, Steuer went after me and, in his summing up, charged that to pull a woman into the case to help defeat his poor client was clearly unfair practice and taking a mean advantage of him. The charge that we were taking advantage of him was true, if you accepted his point that our client was a consummate actress, rehearsed for her part by Rosalie or myself.

As a matter of fact, her picture would not quite make the grade as a pin-up girl. There was nothing seductive about her. Just a simple American girl, who dressed quietly and tried to earn an honest living as a secretary.

Rosalie was right in her estimate of the girl. The Appellate Court affirmed the verdict of two juries. The defendant was a huge, burly, heavy-set, powerful man, while our client was slight. That helped our side of the case.

VII

I am convinced that in this field the woman lawyer is invaluable. Rosalie Loew Whitney proved it in this case. We never had occasion to take another case of the kind, but, if we had, we would have followed the same course, if I had anything to say about it.

Definitely, women have a place at our Bar. The Bar Association should hang its head in shame for so long failing to recognize it. All the pet arguments of "smoking" or "men want to be alone together," have now, of course, been dissipated in the light of actual experience. We need women in every walk and activity of life.

Rosalie Loew Whitney was an outstanding example of what a woman can do at the Bar—and be a good wife and mother besides.

CHAPTER THIRTEEN

There is a luxury in self-dispraise;
And inward self-disparagement affords
To meditative spleen a grateful feast.
"The Excursion," WORDSWORTH.

I. S. C.

*The account of a lady who is to be concealed behind
her initials and her friends, as she would want it—The
Women's Municipal League—The Women's City Club
and the "Riverside Branch."*

I

WHILE RIDING IN A TAXI the other day, perhaps you saw, if observant,
boldly challenging your attention, these words:—

OUR CITY
YOURS AND MINE
KEEP IT *CLEAN*

The words appeared painted on the rear end of a large vehicle—*a
garbage collection truck*. As you passed it (and it was winter), you noticed that the men were clad in khaki—they used to be in white, as
they still are clad in summer time. Did you notice how they and the
collection van operated? Did you see them pay a friendly visit to every
apartment house and store on the block, pick up a garbage can, push
it in behind the covered, sliding doors of the collection wagon and
then put it back again politely next to the householder's door? With
no dust to wander all over and decorate the clothes of any passerby?
And no offensive odor permeating the atmosphere?

Perhaps, like most visitors to New York, you took it all as a matter
of course and thought it never had any beginning and, that like
Topsy—it just grew. Well, it did grow—but how?

As we lived in New York, we recall the time, even in the twentieth
century, when there were just little uncovered "toy carts" drawn by
horses running all about New York, into which the ash and garbage

collectors lifted up the cans, dumped the contents, and produced their hernias in the process. If you happened to be on your way to luncheon when this operation took place in those days, you might get such a whiff of garbage smell as would completely spoil your taste for the oysters you expected to order shortly—unless you had a good cocktail beforehand to brace you up. In addition, you could count on a good lather of ashes on your freshly cleaned suit or dress, and would need to stop off at a shoe-shine parlor for a complete brush-off, shoes and all, before you were ready for respectable society. The gray on your clothes made you drab for the rest of the day.

Now here is the story: William L. Strong became Mayor of New York in 1897. He appointed an engineer as head of the Street Cleaning Department—Colonel George E. Waring, Jr. At the same time, he appointed Theodore Roosevelt as Police Commissioner. In their own persons, the one Colonel resembled the other about as closely as a French boulevardier looks like a western broncho-buster. Colonel Waring wore a waxed mustache turned to the sharpest possible point, and had a bald head. One kept sufficiently at a distance in his presence, lest he be pinked with one of those ends. But, above the mustache and under the bald pate, was a brain, and this brain contained in it ideas—*valid* ideas. One of these ideas was to put the street cleaners of New York City into white suits and top them off with white helmets. Immediately, the cynics of that day dubbed them "Waring's White Wings." Think of an engineer—who ought to have some practical sense—putting *white* suits on men who must sweep the city's streets, pick up the droppings from the horses on the highways and gather in the garbage which each day came from the city's kitchens! Of course, the man must be crazy. Like Bernheimer, with his "naive ideas" about arbitration, or Deming, with his "visionary ideas" of local self-government, or Cutting, with his "ridiculous and impractical" belief that you could get rid of Tammany rule, or Shamberg, with his "impossible" vehicular tunnel.*

Immediately, this idea of Waring's, once put into action, stirred the pride of every member of the street cleaning force. Were they going to have a parade each year, too, like New York's "finest" (the police) or New York's "bravest" (the firemen)? Of course—why not? The idea turned out to be a very practical one.

There were women in New York who saw in what Waring was doing the expansion of some very simple principles of good housekeeping. The city is your home, isn't it? Why not encourage the men who do the housework by creating a pride in their jobs?

* See Chapter 23.

For over forty years now these women have worked in cooperation with the Department.

Of course, there are two ways of appealing to the citizens of a city to *clean up*. One is the "shame on you" technique. This was Lincoln Steffen's line. The dedication of his book "The Shame of the Cities" gives you his method: "So this little volume, a record of shame and yet of self-respect, a disgraceful confession, yet a declaration of honor, is dedicated, in all good faith, to the accused—to all the citizens of all the cities in the United States."

The other method is the appeal to the *pride* of the citizen. New Yorkers do have a pride in their city. If you have any doubt on that score, read Simeon Strunsky's "No Mean City." A real New Yorker comes back from a trip and as he drives down Riverside Drive sees the great white lights of the George Washington Bridge or goes to Times Square to see not merely the white lights but the new multi-colored ones, throws back his shoulders and throws out his chest and declares to his visiting friends—"Isn't New York wonderful!" "I love my New York" was one of the favorite phrases of the pioneer whose initials top this chapter.

In the love for their New York, this group of women developed this technique of appeal to the city's pride. They did not go around like Carrie Nation with a hatchet, chopping up city saloons. Instead, they carried deadlier weapons in their pocketbooks. These dug deep but left no wounds. For example, if you dropped your newspaper carelessly on the sidewalk and one of these women happened along, like as not, you would hear: "Excuse me, sir, but would you mind reading this?" And then you were handed a neat little folder and you read:—

"READ AND REFLECT

A Clean City for All of Us"

Don't throw papers or cards or rubbish in the cars or streets.
Of course, it violates the law and you might be punished.
But this is *OUR CITY*, isn't it?
Would you like some one to throw rubbish around your home?
The Women's Municipal League needs your help.

BE A GOOD CITIZEN

Then the women went a little further. They initiated and organized a system of inspection of the city's streets and of the stables of the Street Cleaning Department as well—it is now called the Department of Sanitation. (We used to say in our family in the early days that—I.S.C. meant D.S.C.)

On the basis of reports from paid investigators, the women gave "Waring certificates" and "Waring medals" as awards to the men for the most outstanding performances of the year. They were valued, relatively, as highly as the Pulitzer prize for the best book or the best play, or as the "Oscars" awarded to the best screen stars of the year are today. Of course, it developed competition between district foremen and superintendents. "Medal-giving time" was an event. Just as the servants will clean the house nicely when company is coming—or the ship is made ready for the visit of the Admiral, every thing was conditioned for the day of such inspection in the D.S.C. All this work was done under the auspices of the *Committee on Streets of the Women's Municipal League,* of which the lady we portray here was chairwoman for more than fifteen years.

In the days when the cleanly Dutch ruled Manhattan, there was a lane off Broad Street—which Albert Ulmann reminded the editor of the "Times" [1]—was called the Brewers' Street. It became disgustingly dirty and dusty. On a certain day in 1655 the residents petitioned Peter Stuyvesant, et al., to be allowed to pave the lane with cobblestones—even at their own expense. But nothing was done by those in control. So the housewives met and they decided to act. They got results. The cobblestones were found and placed. *Stone* Street became the first stone-paved street and a feature of New York. The Women's Municipal League did contain some of the Knickerbocker descendants. Perhaps this record inspired them. But perhaps, after all, it was just love of their city, too, which led them to follow the example.

II

Although Colonel Waring got the men and their uniforms, he did not get the machines he wanted. When he died in 1915, they were still twenty years away. But the women were busy and very persistent. They studied what other cities, American and European, were doing; they went to the manufacturers, the sanitary engineers—and asked for designs for *covered* wagons. Moreover, in the lifting of the heavy cans, the men should be saved from ruptures—the "occupational disease" of the department. By sheer persistence, plus acquisition of expert knowledge on the subject, the women were able to support Waring's successors.

Finally, the day of triumph arrived. Such modern wagons as you saw from your taxi came upon New York's streets. However, they did not come in any considerable number until Fiorello La Guardia's first term as Mayor.

In addition to this idea of better men and machines, Waring had some other ideas, equally valid. "Thar's gold in that thar mine" of garbage. Why not salvage it—separate garbage from ashes and paper and waste from both? During the war was heard "Save your fats. We need them for glycerine. Save your garbage. It is good for fertilizer. Save your paper."

The women helped in this campaign. They visited the places where new things were done, and learned at first hand how they were done.

III

When the Lady got into this field of rubbish, ashes and garbage, she went into it deeper, and the deeper she got, the deeper she went.

In 1924, the American and Canadian Bar Associations were invited by the English Bar to visit London, the Inns of Court, and, generally, have a good time. The Berengaria was chartered and the Lady and I went along. I hoped to get some recreation. The party was a great success. My Lady did enjoy seeing Queen Mary and visiting Buckingham Palace, and, with some other ladies, found the conveniences there primitive, as compared with the modern bathroom or "powder-room."

But, all of these things faded into insignificance compared with the accomplishment of the objective she had on this trip. The Lady had heard that in Birmingham, England, there was in operation a very new system of collecting and separating garbage—the latest style in refuse disposal. From the moment of that discovery, the objective which superseded in importance the visits to the Shakespearean country, to Cambridge and to Oxford, to Scotland and to Wales, was *that* Garbage Disposal Dump at Birmingham, England. If we missed seeing it the whole trip would be just one colossal failure.

She induced our old friend, Charles T. Gwynne, then executive secretary of the New York Chamber of Commerce—later its executive vice-president, to write to the secretary of the Chamber of Commerce of Birmingham, England, to tell him we were "coming over, coming over" and that we weren't "coming back" until we saw that plant.

Well, as soon as we got to the railroad station in Birmingham, we went straight to the Disposal Plant—stopping off at the office of the Birmingham Chamber of Commerce just long enough to have the Chamber's secretary transfer us, properly accredited, to the Birmingham Sanitation Department. Oh, yes, I was interested—or made believe I was. But, I cannot truthfully say that, on my own initiative, I would have gone to that particular spot for entertainment or refreshment.

On the other hand, the Lady was highly elated. She made careful notes, and brought them back. Two years earlier, she had dragged me to a place outside Los Angeles to see how garbage was disposed of there. It did seem all very interesting to the pigs. No, I cannot honestly say that this particular spot appealed to me either. I confess I liked very much more seeing Jack Holt making a picture "on the lot" at Hollywood. Or, next door to Jack's picture, those beauties in a bathing pool. Now, there was a place where I could linger. But she didn't let me stay near the pool very long. The Lady, however, got what *she* wanted. She usually does.

A little later, encouraged by Commissioner Featherstone of the Department, she got up a booklet entitled:

> *"What We Should All Know About Our Streets—*
>
> Prepared for the use of our Young Citizens in the City Schools by the Chairman of the Committee on Streets of the Women's Municipal League—and member of Advisory Council, Department of Street Cleaning."

This booklet was later widely distributed under the auspices of the Women's Municipal League to the boys and girls in the City's schools. It became part of the training given for citizenship. (The teachers said it helped. I really think it did. I read some of the letters from the teachers.) On the first page of that booklet is a picture of a giant street-sweeper, all clad in white, dubbed "A Modern Colossus of Roads"—he tells you that he and his friends in arms, sweep every day an area of twenty-eight and a half million yards—as much as would cover a trip from New York to Kansas City. You will find in this booklet several interesting pieces of history of the City's streets, which everyone should know. And then there is this:

> "First of all, we should not throw things into the streets. * * * We should put our papers or skins of fruit in the cans provided * * * by the Department. We should not build fires in the streets—that destroys the pavement. * * * *The sweeper is as much our friend as the doctor who saves us from sickness, for by cleaning the streets, he is keeping away the germs of disease."*

And, at the end, appears the oath of the young man of Athens:

> "We will fight for the ideas and sacred things of the city. * * * We will revere and obey the city's laws and do our best to incite a like respect and reverence in those above us who are prone to annul or set them at nought."

The title "Know Your City" was given to a new movement, sponsored by the City History Club and the Board of Education over WNYC—the City's radio station. 110,000 children took part in an education program designed to teach them the social and historic background of various sections of New York. In ten weeks, 3,000 buttons were awarded. "New York children," said Mrs. Dinkel, have been "trotting right along"—from Coney Island in Brooklyn to Westchester Village in the Bronx.[2]

Besides this, Philip Hunter, over WOR as part of a Port Authority educational program, for more than five years, led children and adults, too, in the same direction—teaching them to know the City. The appeal to the *pride of the people* is strong now. From little acorns, great oaks grow—time does hold the trump card.

IV

This pioneer work was done by women even before they had suffrage. Of course, today, women are all over the place. And they are no longer shy. They know what they can do. In 1945, there were nine women in Congress. There will be more. A friend of the Lady's, Mrs. Genevieve Earle, is an active and respected leader in the Municipal Assembly of New York.

By way of illustration of what women are doing, take two incidents in 1945. There was that stirring achievement by F/O Constance Babbington-Smith of the W.A.A.F. in World War II. In studying reconnaissance photographs, she spotted the flying model for the German robot bomb and located the German experimental station at Pennemuende.[3] This woman's work gave the British Army Intelligence just what they needed to enable them to go after those robots—straight to their very place of origin.

Then, again, there was the world-startling news in August, 1945, that Dr. Lise Meitner, who had been exiled from Germany because of her Jewish ancestry and had fled to Copenhagen, had discovered the important effect of the bombardment of uranium and thus hastened the development of the atomic bomb.

That's the woman of it! There's a job to be done. And she does it. She goes right down to where the dirt is and sweeps it up. In the Presidential campaign of 1944, when there were no chambermaids in a hotel out West, Mrs. Dewey swept up their own bedroom and made the bed.

Now, who but women would make garbage disposal a hobby! Why not collect sea shells or rare pewter! It is a cleaner diversion. Today, there is a whole regiment who follow in the footsteps of this pioneer band of the early nineteen hunderds. How many of these active women of today really know that it was the pathfinders of the Women's Municipal League of New York City who blazed the trail for them?

V

" 'Why don't they keep the streets a little cleaner?'
You ask with keen annoyance not undue;
'Why don't they keep the parks a little greener?'
Did you ever stop to think that 'They' means YOU?" [4]

In 1898, Charles B. Stover [5] began the movement to develop parks
and playgrounds for the children of the lower East Side. The public
authorities had not yet been converted to the playground idea. But,
with the aid of the women, Stover successfully secured and developed
William H. Seward Park, Hamilton Fish Park and Kip's Bay Park.
After Mayor Gaynor appointed Stover Park Commissioner, it became
one of Stover's chief aims to increase the number of these playgrounds.
Acres and acres of park lay buried beneath the Hudson River, in front
of Riverside Park. The City was then paying millions for the boring
of the Catskill Aqueduct through the rocky depths of Manhattan
Island. This excavated rock the contractors were either selling or
wasting. Stover got enough rock from this source to make more than
ten acres of solid land on Riverside Drive waterfront. He was responsible, also, for the creation of the Shakespeare Garden in Central
Park. Overlooking this Garden, on a memorial bench of Vermont
granite, you will find inscribed:—

"Charles B. Stover, 1861–1929, Founder of Outdoor Playgrounds Who Devoted
His Life to Public Service.
IN GRATEFUL RECOGNITION"

But Stover, like Waring, had the help of this fine group of women
and acknowledged it freely. It so happened that under the leadership
of the Lady whose initials top this chaper, there was organized on the
upper West Side an exceptionally active committee of women who,
for over a decade, continued a movement to cover up the then exposed
New York Central tracks along Riverside Drive, and, at the same
time, increase the park and playground area. (When you now drive
over this beautiful highway, you may do so completely unaware of the
public spirit and labor it took to make the highway possible.)

There was a running dog-eat-dog fight with the New York Central
Railroad Company for over a decade. The elimination of "Death
Avenue" is part of that story, and Dr. John P. Peters was in that fight
from the start. So was the Citizens Union. So was the West End Association.

In those days, "the public be damned attitude" had not completely
disappeared from railway executive offices. Patrick Crowley and Fred-

erick Williamson had not yet come into executive leadership in the New York Central. Things changed when they came into power. But in the cynical days of 1900–1910, there was a continuous nuisance operating on Eleventh Avenue—deaths resulting from the grade crossings and the noise of the freight cars coming into the windows along with the smoke—all down Riverside Drive to Seventy-second Street. Ira Place was then the lawyer for the New York Central. He thought the ladies, and the men, too, for that matter, were most unreasonable people. The changes proposed meant a huge capital investment for the New York Central, and the officers of the company had grave misgivings about the financial benefits to accrue to the company. For years, the improvement was blocked.

A few days before the Lusitania sailed, the Lady and I were walking down Riverside Drive with Max Schwarcz, then about to sail for Europe. He was a most comforting and encouraging friend. She talked to him about the great opportunities for beautifying the Hudson River waterfront and how hard she had found it was to make headway. Said he, "Have you ever been to Budapest?" "No," she said. "Well, I am going abroad next week and I shall bring you back some photographs of the waterfront there. They have done a beautiful job. Perhaps the photographs will help you in your campaign." He never came back. (He went down with the Lusitania.)

Then came World War I. That delayed things some more. All this while, the tracks remained uncovered. "Death Avenue" continued. The boys still rode on ponies ahead of the steam locomotives waving warning flags and the noise and smoke still came into the Riverside Drive apartment windows.

But, after thirty years, two events occurred—Commissioner of Parks, Robert Moses, arrived on the scene, and with him the Depression. That Depression was right down Bob's alley. It was a lucky thing for him and for Riverside Drive. It made it possible for Moses to wangle money both out of the United States Treasury and out of the City for park improvements. It was not all used in raking leaves either.

Cutting the story as short as we can, there came into being the greatest river highway in the world. Charles B. Stover has his monument, but Bob Moses has several. Riverside Drive—the Hendrick Hudson Bridge—the Saw Mill River Parkway—Jones Beach—the development of the Island end Park at Montauk. Come down to Hither Hills at Montauk and see something that, for the time being at least, will make you forget all about Bob's blitzkriegs and think only of his creations. However, nothing finer anywhere can be seen than Riverside Drive. Bob should be very grateful for the support of the women.

VI

I could write a good deal more about this particular Lady's work. For years she and a small group have been visiting the old men and women on Welfare Island—the "Poor House." This little band of visitors still bring tokens—symbols of personal interest in the lives of the old—giving them renewed courage.

I could tell you of the many instances of appreciation that came from the cancer and tuberculosis wards. Some of the letters from these friends would tear your heartstrings apart. I mention just one incident: A woman about to undergo an operation received a small bunch of flowers. She said: "I have had no breakfast and I am not going to have any lunch, but I have these flowers."

This work was begun by Mrs. Emma Jacobs. She started the Lady off when the latter was only a young girl. For forty years, her friends, the Morganstern Twins (Birdie * and Louise) have been her dependable assistants. She is the treasurer of this non-sectarian group, "The Fruit and Flower Mission" and the "Women's Conference of the Society for Ethical Culture." People send her checks, without solicitation and ask for no receipt.

As treasurer, the Lady learned that some friend of the Fruit and Flower Mission had left $5,000 for the work. She could find no trace of the money in the Treasury, so she asked her predecessor about it. "Oh, yes, I have it in my safe deposit box." The check was promptly rescued, deposited in the bank and invested in Port Authority bonds. The new treasurer, for some unaccountable reason, believed "Ports" were good.

In line with this incident—Dr. Otis reminded me of the inexperienced young man, who presented a check to the bank unendorsed. When the teller asked him to endorse it, he wrote on the back:—"I cordially endorse this check"—and then failed to affix his signature! But the Lady of this chapter knows all about receiving and depositing money and balancing budgets and gets money easier than I can— either in fees or contributions to public causes or philanthropies.

Then, there is the story of the girls from the Hudson Guild—the Louisa Alcott Club, and what it did for its members. But some of her girls, I am sure, will write about it some day.

* Birdie Morganstern died in 1942. But Louise still carries on.

BOOK IV

THE LAW MOVES FORWARD

CHAPTER FOURTEEN

By this mode of settling disputes, law-suits are nipped in the
bud, the restraints of forms of process are thrown aside, and the
mind of the merchant is not distracted from his own business
by the conduct of the suit.

BALDASSERONI

"I can wait."
(Legend under painting of an old merchant.)

Charles L. Bernheimer

*A public servant who never held public office—The
father of commercial arbitration in the United States—
An error in the law is corrected—Reconversion and
termination of war contracts—An example of persistence in reform.*

I

AL SMITH ONCE SAID TO HIM, "You're a persistent cuss, aren't you?"
And Charles L. Bernheimer was proud of the description. He showed
his delight in the same spirit as the old lady in Barrie's play exhibited
her medals.

His portrait hangs in the Great Hall of the Chamber of Commerce
of the State of New York, along with those of the great merchants and
leaders who lived during the past hundred and fifty years of New
York's business life.

As you enter the Great Hall, your eyes will meet a plaque near the
door. This is what it says:

"Importers Guide Award for the Advancement of Arbitration in Foreign Trade
Presented under the Auspices of the American Arbitration Association to
Chamber of Commerce of the State of New York 1942."

Colonel Charles T. Gwynne,* executive vice-president, always said
that this plaque was really a tribute to Charles L. Bernheimer.

For nearly the whole of its history, it was a cardinal rule of the
Chamber that no president and no chairman of a committee could

* Died January 31, 1945.

serve more than two terms—not because there was any patronage—but because the Chamber believed change in leadership was good. The one exception was Charles L. Bernheimer. The by-laws were amended so as to provide that the Chairman of the Committee on Arbitration should be excepted from this ban; and Bernheimer was re-elected to the office every year.

For some thirty years, in advance of the monthly meetings, he brought the draft of his annual report, written in a clear hand, for me to criticize. During the last five years he regularly said, "Julius, you know, this may be my last." In June, 1944, he desired to report upon the last work in which he participated, and I advised him to delay until September, because the proposed "Contract Settlement Act" had not yet even passed the House.

Charles L. Bernheimer died July 1, 1944. He did not live to read the report which recorded his triumph in the work in which to the end he continued to be the leader.

While he was at the hospital, his daughter, Helen Halle, told me he found great comfort in learning that the bill had passed and would be signed by the President. When he received my letter telling him that the provisions were there, he asked to have it read again.

He was to have been guest of honor at a banquet at which the American Arbitration Association planned to award him its medal of honor for distinguished service in the field of arbitration.

If one met him about 1910, and saw his frail body, one might have said that a man with such physical handicaps could, with good fortune, live to be sixty, but not much beyond that. To live to eighty, was a sheer triumph of spirit over body.

He smoked the worst kind of five cent cigar you ever heard of. He nearly killed me in Washington, D. C. during the winter of 1943 and the spring of 1944, staying up until the early hours of the morning while Paul Fitzpatrick [1] (the night owl) and I worked over drafts and memoranda for Senate committee members. He always found my writings too legalistic. Fitzpatrick would agree with him—said he had to put what I wrote into English—but not until Bernheimer had carefully read every word and clearly understood the meaning of every sentence, would he take the material we produced. But, through it all, Bernheimer smoked these "stinkadoras," as I called them. For Christmas I sent him a box of good cigars and suggested that he might smoke them, at least when he was with me in our dissipations. But, these he gave away to friends.

Bernheimer's method was to turn the other cheek. I never heard him swear. He told me often of his sufferings—but with no rancor, no hatred. Quietly plugging along, his sincerity and intelligence conquered in situations where most other men would have used more belligerent tactics.

His technique was like that of General Wingate's Raiders, whom the natives of Burma call "Chindits," derived from the "chinthe," a mythological griffin in Burmese. To retreat like a chindit means to retreat with courage, showing a brave front to the enemy and so later winning the victory.

II

Bernheimer went on trips to the American Southwest regularly and lived the life of a pack mule. Here in the sharp canyons of Arizona and Colorado, he searched for natural bridges and cliff dwellings known only to the Indians of the region. In 1929, he uncovered the old American basket-weaving industry. A little later, he discovered somewhere in Utah a boomerang. He was a recognized authority an anthropology and botany. One would hardly be aware of all this activity when watching him preside over the Converters Association or at the Board of Trade or saw him at the Chamber of Commerce.

When Charles B. Stover was Park Commissioner of New York City, Bernheimer was appointed to the Park Commissioner's Advisory Board. With Stover's approval and cooperation, Bernheimer called in a company of park-bench idlers and equipped them, at his own expense, with rubber gloves. Under his supervision, they succeeded in extirpating poison ivy from the entire area of the park.

He knew the civic leaders of his day, but he did not join the Reformers. He became and remained a Republican. He had the anti-Franklin Roosevelt fury of a good organization Republican. However, in the Fusion Campaign of 1913, he became the Treasurer of the "Committee of 107," which elected John Purroy Mitchel as Mayor of New York City.

It was Bernheimer who brought me out to make the speeches in favor of Commercial Arbitration. His own strength showed best in a small room, where he spoke in low tones. He enjoyed a grim story—a story that had a point to it. Ofttimes he made up one of his own which he would bring down to the Chamber table. He knew the history of Europe and of America.

Frequently, he would say, "I can wait," reminding himself of a portrait of an old merchant he had seen in his early days, under which those words were written. Resignation and fortitude were characteristics in this portrait. When I urged him to go out and "fight like hell" against some opponent, he would say: "You know I have a different technique than yours—I must stick to my own way of doing things, if you will please forgive me."

He never lost his self-respect. He belonged to the old school and adhered to the Felix Adler philosophy that the end never justifies the means. Deception of an enemy might be justified in the field of war, but was never justified in business or in politics.

He liked those last lines of Sidney Grundy's play, "The Pair of Spectacles"—"It is better to trust and be deceived than suspect and be mistaken." He knew, too, that people who trust are susceptible to *betrayal*. Hence, he accepted "double-crossing" on the part of others as part of the day's work and when it happened to him he would say, almost what Alfred E. Smith said—"The world is made up of such people."

III

The waste of litigation! Charles L. Bernheimer knew how much bad feeling is left behind after any litigation between business men. Besides, he knew that lawsuits did not always achieve justice—real justice. When the lawyer telegraphed his client, "Justice and right have triumphed," the client promptly replied, "Appeal at once." There is much truth in this jibe.

In 1911, Bernheimer was stirred by the cancellation of contracts flooding the country. As head of the cotton converting firm of Bernheimer and Walter, he saw disaster ahead. He looked about to see what substitute could relieve the tension. He did not find it in litigation. In New York City alone, the trial litigation calendar was two or three years behind. Wasn't there some better method? He learned that there had been some system of arbitration in the Chamber of Commerce. Sereno S. Pratt was then secretary and Charles T. Gwynne was his assistant. It was at this point that Bernheimer asked me to look into the history of Commercial Arbitration.

I went back to the musty old records of the Chamber over a period of one hundred and fifty years and found that during the Revolutionary War, when there were no courts functioning in New York City, the Chamber's system of arbitration by business men was actually the only method of administering justice in the City. The story is a long one and need not be repeated here. I shall give you only the highlights.[2]

In 1874, the Chamber secured the passage of a law creating the "Court of Arbitration." Enoch L. Fancher presided over the Court for several years. The principal opposition to the Court, I am sorry to report, came from lawyers. They felt the loss of mercantile cases which could be settled by the methods of arbitration less expensively than by litigation. In 1878, the influence against the Court was so strong that further appropriations by the legislature were blocked and provisions in the prior act providing for salaries to be paid were actually repealed in 1878.

Nevertheless, Judge Fancher continued to serve without pay. Because he had a lawyer's training, he presided over the Court of Arbitration as though it were a court of law. This the business men did not like. They wanted to get away from what they called "the technicalities of the law." When Judge Fancher died in 1900, the Court of Arbitration passed out.

In 1911, Bernheimer and I worked out a scheme, based primarily upon the Chamber's furnishing facilities for carrying on arbitration by bringing together—from pretty nearly all lines of commercial activities—leading business men, who, simply as a matter of public service, act as arbitrators, whenever called upon to function. The business men responded nobly. In this panel ultimately appeared the names of nearly all of the best known business men of New York. Under the system you could pick out from the panel your own arbitrator and have the arbitration conducted and supervised by the Chamber of Commerce. The fees were nominal. Once it was authorized and established, Bernheimer supervised the whole job. His annual reports show the immense volume of cases that was handled by his committee and their importance.

The rules were very simple. The form of submission was one which laymen could easily understand. By 1928, Charles L. Bernheimer's leadership in this field was widely recognized. The New York Times referred to him as "the father of modern commercial arbitration." [8]

IV

But there was one handicap. For three hundred years, there had been operative in our law the deadly rule that an arbitration agreement was *revocable at the pleasure of either party*. This meant, that even if it was agreed to arbitrate a controversy, there was no assurance that the arbitration would go through.

"Commercial Arbitration and the Law" was written with the hope that it would be used by the Bench and Bar to reverse the hoary error. Bernheimer purchased a considerable number of copies from the publishers and distributed them widely among those who we both thought would study the subject sympathetically. I shall not attempt even to summarize what I found and put together in this review of a three-century-old error in the law. It was clearly an error. But based upon the principle of *judicial correction of judicial error,** I hoped we could, on the basis of the complete story, succeed in getting a reversal of this doctrine by the courts themselves. Such a reversal did come twenty-three years later when the Supreme Court of Minnesota by a clear majority held the doctrine of revocability no longer tenable.[4] "For this departure from a doctrine of long standing," the Court declared, "we make no apology." If there is to be apology, it "should be rather for the regrettable fact that our decision law did not promptly reflect the legislative declaration."

One of the ablest Federal Judges of my day was the Hon. Charles M. Hough, of the United States District Court. In 1915, he wrote that he could find no basis in reason for the existing law in this field.

> "There has long been a great variety of available reasons for refusing to give effect to the agreements of men of mature age, and presumably sound judgment, when the intended effect of the agreements was to prevent proceedings in any and all courts and substitute therefor the decision of arbitrators. The remarkably simple nature of this libelant's contract breaking has led me to consider at some length the nature and history of the reasons adduced to justify the sort of conduct, by no means new, but remarkably well illustrated by these libels."[5]

Judge Hough found that the hostility of English speaking courts to arbitration contracts arose out of the "contests of the courts of ancient times for extension of jurisdiction—all of them being opposed to anything that would altogether deprive every one of them of jurisdiction." [6]

In his opinion, Judge Hough went further into the doctrine of revocability, its origin, and said of "the public policy" doctrine:

> "Having built up the doctrine that any contract which involves an 'ouster of jurisdiction' is invalid, the Supreme Court of the United States has been able of late years to give decision without ever going behind that statement."

Maule, a great English judge, called the doctrine of revocability an "inveterate error." [7] Lord Cranworth, Chancellor, in *Drew* v. *Drew,* called it *"an inconvenient,* and, I think I may be allowed to say, *an irrational state of the law* * * * I say that was an absurd state of the law * * *." [8]

Judge Hough never hesitated to express his own opinions, even if he found that they were opposed to settled law, though obviously as a District Court Judge, he was obliged to follow the decisions of the United States Supreme Court. He did this in the *Trinidad* case, but paid his respects to this devastating and unsound policy of the law.

* See Chapter 1.

It was, indeed, this opinion of Judge Hough that first encouraged me to make the studies which later were put into "Commercial Arbitration and the Law" and to gather for that volume the substantial evidence available to establish that there was no basis whatever for the claim that commercial arbitration was against *public policy* or that the law as such was opposed to it. It was easy to find support from many historical references for the definite viewpoint that public policy really *favored* arbitration. It was only some lawyers and judges who thought otherwise.

V

In the year 1916, a committee of the New York State Bar Association was formed to deal with the subject of "Prevention of Unnecessary Litigation." It was headed by Daniel S. Remsen. Among other recommendations it made was that business men should be encouraged to *arbitrate* instead of resorting to litigation. As I was a member of the New York State Bar Association and also a member of the Committee on Commerce of the American Bar Association, I was able to arrange for conferences in which Bernheimer played the lead. The result was, first, passage of the New York State Arbitration Law,[9] then of the New Jersey Arbitration Act,[10] and, later, the United States Arbitration Act.[11]

These acts, very simply told, completely changed the existing law. They reversed the ancient erroneous doctrine. But they also created machinery by which an arbitration award could thereafter be made as effective as a judgment of the Court. They granted power to the arbitrators to subpoena witnesses. Moreover, where a party failed to name his arbitrator, these statutes provided that the Court could name one. If one party failed to proceed with the arbitration, then under these laws a summary order could be secured from a Court directing him to proceed.

The enactment of these statutes gave impetus to the whole movement for arbitration.[12] Through their operation, the relationship of business men with each other, not only in this but in other countries, was very much improved. Through this movement, Bernheimer made friends throughout England, Europe and Latin America, especially with Robert S. Fraser of London who also died in 1944, shortly before Bernheimer. I met Fraser when I visited London in 1924.

Bernheimer was the leader in the movement for the passage of the United States Arbitration Act. I drew the bill for him and he had the support of the American Bar Association under the presidency of Charles E. Hughes. As a good Republican he knew the Congressman from his district, Ogden Mills. Mills became the sponsor for the Act in Congress. Hughes' standing and influence and through him, the support of the American Bar Association, did help to pass the bill.

But the work of breaking down the prejudice and opposition in Congress was done, day in and day out, by Bernheimer. He was in a position to speak for the business men of the entire country. He was so highly appreciated for his work in this field, that along about 1924, his life was insured to the amount of $300,000, the premiums all to be paid by members of the Chamber of Commerce who were friends of his and the fund to be used for the cause. When money for the premiums failed to come in as rapidly as was expected, the Chamber itself made up the difference. The plan ultimately took the form of a paid-up policy of approximately $55,000 to become available to the Chamber on Bernheimer's death. The Chamber will determine how this money is to be used. There is scarcely any doubt that the Chamber will use it to promote the cause of Commercial Arbitration—possibly as a memorial to Bernheimer.

It so happened that a lawyer, Moses H. Grossman, had seen arbitration in action at the Chamber. He was convinced that the principal advantages of arbitration should be more widely spread and that the mechanics of the Chamber for doing this kind of propaganda work were too slow and too old-fashioned. The Chamber has always been and still is a very dignified body. It did not succumb to the arts of publicity which came into play along about the twenties. Grossman proposed that large sums of money should be raised for this promotional work and he himself contributed a substantial sum. Capable publicity experts were secured by him.

The American Arbitration Association was formed in 1926. It was a merger of the Arbitration Foundation of which Bernheimer was the president and of the Arbitration Society of America, which Moses H. Grossman had organized. By the merger, the assets and membership of the two earlier groups passed to the new association, but in its official pamphlet, issued in 1944, the American Arbitration Association gives credit to the Chamber and by implication to Charles L. Bernheimer, in the following sentences:

"While it assumed a new name, it inherited the wisdom, experience and interest of men long associated with arbitration. The Chamber of Commerce of the State of New York, from which the Association has derived constant encouragement, has a history of arbitration experience dating from before the American Revolution." [13]

As I look back upon the picture now, I can see that what happened was bound to happen. There was real merit in the contention that the

Chamber of Commerce was not equipped to cover the broader and more extensive area that should be ploughed up in this field. The movement had to become more national in scope. For this, to be more widely effective, there had to be a trained staff and a substantial annual income. For the educational work, for establishment of panels of arbitrators throughout the country, credit goes to the American Arbitration Association, especially to Frances Keller, its first vice-president; J. Noble Braden, tribunal vice-president, and Paul Fitzpatrick, its administrative vice-president. They have successfully pushed the movement forward.

But, when his Chamber of Commerce was made to "play second fiddle," it is the simple truth that Bernheimer did feel hurt. Besides, the methods of publicity that were used were not entirely to his liking. It went against his nature.

VI

When World War I was nearing the peace stage, Bernheimer saw clearly that great complications would be sure to arise from the sudden termination of the war and the change-over of industry from war to peace time activities. The government had reserved the right of termination in every war contract. There had been, as there came later in World War II, a patriotic appeal from Washington to business men of the country to "avoid all red tape" and supply the needs for the war service promptly. Many informal contracts had been signed. How could they be made valid? Bernheimer envisioned what would happen when peace came. He brought all this to the attention of Eugenius H. Outerbridge, then one of the leaders of the New York State Chamber of Commerce.

I was then General Counsel for the Chamber and because of my position, I was brought into the picture. Legislation was clearly necessary. It was imperative that Congress pass an act validating all informal contracts. Moreover, instead of putting final settlements completely in the hands of war officials, with no right of appeal anywhere for the contractors, save a long drawn-out suit in the Court of Claims, we thought there should be set up a more informal tribunal. We all three believed that there should be created a whole panel of arbitrators operating throughout the country, who could settle promptly and expeditiously such controversies as we foresaw would inevitably arise over the amounts due to the contractors on terminated war contracts.

Bernheimer, Outerbridge and I went to Washington many times on this job. We took a licking—a bad one. We neither got the arbitration system we wanted nor any impartial review nor any act which would save contractors from the results of technical failure to conform with exactitude to the rigorous statutes applicable. Of course, these statutes were enacted to protect the Government, but they could be made to operate with great injustice against those who in good faith had gone ahead, "without red tape" to carry on in the war effort. The failure to get the legislation after World War I actually resulted in great financial damage to business men throughout the country—in many instances resulted in disaster. It happened to business men who had responded in fine public spirit to the patriotic appeal made to them not to wait on formality, but to produce.

When in 1943, once again it appeared that the Government would be totally unprepared to meet the contract termination situations which would surely arise after the close of the war and that repeated injustices would follow precisely along the lines of 1919–1925, Bernheimer again took the lead. He reprinted our memoranda of 1919 and long before Bernard Baruch or his capable deputy, John Hancock, gave their warnings in 1944, Bernheimer was saying, "Hurry, hurry, hurry."

Too bad he did not live until November, 1944. If he had, he would have read in the papers that as a result of the legislation which was passed by Congress by October 31, 1944, the Government had already cancelled and adjusted $21,000,000,000 of war contracts, involving 28,000 contracts, and that it was carrying out the Settlement Act of 1944, fairly and quickly. The settlements with such celerity, resulted in large measure from the spirit in which the negotiations were carried on. But this spirit, in turn, came from the policies declared and the machinery set up under the Act. Undoubtedly, the opportunity for review given to contractors and the knowledge on the part of all departmental officials that contractors were entitled to their day in court and could, if they wanted to, demand arbitration, or in the alternative, sue in the court of claims, resulted in fair settlements.*

The whole movement for arbitration was originally opposed by lawyers, because it was said it took business controversies away from the Courts. Of course, it does not injure lawyers. They can achieve results for their clients more expeditiously. Undoubtedly, there are many lawyers throughout the country who, if they knew that Bernheimer was in large measure responsible for the War Contract Termination Act, would damn him—and his lawyer too—for getting these modern provisions into the War Contract Termination Act. But wiser heads

* According to the report of H. Chapman Rose, director of contract settlements, all but 23,900 of the 312,000 prime contracts terminated since the beginning of war production remained on March 31, 1946 to be settled.

in the practice know that this very machinery helped lawyers to perform professional duties for their clients by producing workable machinery in place of expensive litigation.

By the spring of 1944 a quarter of a century had elapsed from the beginning of the arbitrational movement by Bernheimer—the ground had by then been thoroughly fertilized and many organizations besides the Chamber of Commerce were in the field and pushing hard.

By 1944 it became obvious that the field of arbitration to be covered was still broader. As a member of the Board of Directors of the American Arbitration Association and as General Counsel for the Chamber, I was able to bring together the American Arbitration Association and the Chamber of Commerce in one combined effort. It is too long a story to tell here, but Bernheimer, Paul Fitzpatrick and I became the "Three Musketeers." We had no difficulty at all in enlisting the aid of Senator Warren R. Austin of the Committee on Finance. Through him we saw Senator Walter F. George, the Chairman of the Committee; later we saw Senator James H. Murray of the Sub-Committee of the Senate Military Affairs Committee; Scott Russell, the able lawyer for the Committee on Finance and M. B. Gross, the very competent assistant to Senator Murray.

I should stop to pay a tribute to some of these men in Washington. Senator Warren R. Austin of Vermont is recognized by his colleagues as one of the ablest lawyers in the Senate and one of the great statesmen of our day. He was one of the successful leaders in the fight against isolationism. In the fight of the states and municipalities against the Administration's attempt to tax state and municipal securities he was a tower of strength. His tact, his courage and his intelligence, prepared the way in the Senate for support of the work that Wendell L. Willkie was able to do. If it were not for the fact that Senator Austin comes from the small state of Vermont, he would be the party's candidate for President of the United States. The Senator does not truckle, nor does he pander to popular favor.

Senator George of Georgia is another statesman of giant stature, modest and always open to reason. Scott Russell is a lawyer who left private practice for service to Senator George's Committee. M. B. Gross is a young, constructive economist. The latter two drew up the bills which bore the names of their chiefs, George and Murray. We left our proposed amendments in their hands and had the satisfaction of reading in the Act, as it finally became the law, the very words we had suggested to these draftsmen. The designation of Bernard Baruch and, in turn, his designation of John M. Hancock, brought about the highly praised Baruch-Hancock report.

Bernheimer and Fitzpatrick kept in constant touch with Hancock. Hancock asked for copies of our memoranda and submitted them to the various officers of the Army, Navy and other departments. The Administration, through Baruch, Hancock and James F. Byrnes, was brought into complete coordination with Senators George and Murray and the result was as fine a piece of legislative statesmanship as has been recorded in our day and generation.

In this work of 1943-1944, Charles L. Bernheimer found his complete vindication. The things that he fought for in 1919 and failed then to secure, are now to be found just as he wanted them in the "Contract Settlement Act of 1944." [14]

VII

Yes, we agree with Holmes that "a valid idea is worth a regiment," [15] and with John Stuart Mill that only through conflict do valid ideas prevail. Charles L. Bernheimer's life proves the truth of both points. For three centuries an invalid idea ruled our courts—the so-called doctrine of revocability of arbitration agreements. Men of reason, eminent jurists, sincerely believed in this doctrine, but others saw it only as inveterate error. Why did it persist in the law? Mill, in his essay "On Liberty" says:—

> "The real advantage which truth has, consists in this, that when an opinion is true, it may be extinguished once, twice, or many times, but in the course of ages there will generally be found persons to rediscover it, until some one of its reappearances falls on a time when from favourable circumstances it escapes persecution until it has made such head as to withstand all subsequent attempts to suppress it."

The cynics and defeatists will say, "Oh hell. What's the use? The same damn thing will happen again." If they stop short with examination of the surface of things, they can find much to confirm their cynicism. But the world is moved forward not by the cynics or the defeatists. It is moved by men of faith—deep faith. In Bernheimer's case, the historic fact is that truth did emerge triumphant, after three centuries of error. Those who have Bernheimer's faith must be prepared, however, to take their lickings and go on fighting just the same. If what we are fighting for is not the valid idea, and we do fail, the triumph will not be over us, but over the invalid idea. If, however, the truth we are fighting for is valid, and we triumph, we should be both grateful and humble. For is it not true that hundreds of martyrs have died for the truth—and that those who come after them lived to see the truth ultimately arise triumphant?

VIII

At one time Charles L. Bernheimer was a rich man. He owned a fine home on East 67th Street. During the depression he was obliged to let the property go. When he died, he left only a very modest estate.

A diplomat once said to De Gaulle, "I am sure I am right. I know France well. I lived there thirteen years." "Ah," said the general, "you forget I have lived in France two thousand years." [16]

It is the men who can look back into history, profiting thereby *and act in the present on what will happen in the future,* who are the great leaders of the world. They disregard the appearance of things, the immediate preoccupation, the practical difficulties of the moment and on the basis of this faith and confidence in their convictions, keep on fighting for what they believe in.

Bernheimer had this quality. That is what he meant when he said, "I can wait." Only he was not a warrior like De Gaulle. He did not like a fight, especially a personal one. But his type of mind was not that of most business men who make their decision as speculators do— on "how does the market stand today?" These men do not understand the Bernheimers—"so unrealistic—so impractical." They prefer to follow what has been called the "Gallup Poll" method of planning.

In the industrial field, as well as in the work of the Port Authority, I met this type of mind often—the "ticker-tape" type of mind I called it—thinking only in the present, with no historical background to draw upon and no vision of what the future has in store.

Bernheimer did not fall into this latter group. He worked with such business men, however, and they did like him—just because he was a leader. And they let him lead.

Of all the men and women whose portraits are hung in this gallery, I believe that Bernheimer was the most completely successful in achieving what he set out to do. The result came not only from his breadth and vision, but from that quality of persistence—that dogged determination which was distinctly his outstanding trait, without which quality no cause, good or bad, can make headway at all.

This *stick-to-itiveness,* your deponent avers, is the quality that makes for success, whatever other qualities you may possess.

CHAPTER FIFTEEN

Salus populi suprema est lex
The welfare of the people is the highest law.

Rent Cases

Emergency rent laws of 1920—Rent controls and ceiling prices—The equity of redemption—The equity of renewal—Irish and Jewish sources of the law—Some days in the United States Supreme Court.

I

WE ARE LIVING IN AN ERA where, in the last analysis, public opinion determines the course of government. For democracy to function there must be sound leadership. And such leadership can come only from a two-way stream of knowledge—one from leaders down to the people and the other from the people upwards to the leaders. Hence, while the public need not know all there is to be known about the atomic and the rocket bombs and radar, they should know what it all sums up to. Such articles as the lucid and instructive one by Brigadier-General David Sarnoff [1] should be widely read. Since scientific discoveries, unless properly controlled, mean the power to destroy the whole of civilization, there must be thorough and complete control of the use of these terrifying agencies and that can come only by *law*.

What is law? How does it function?

In the spring of 1945, at a meeting of the Chamber of Commerce, a lay member wanted to know what, indeed, was the constitutional basis for the rent laws. He could see none. The brief answer I then gave seemed helpful and encouraged me to write this chapter.

Law and Equity? What is the interplay between them?

Following both World Wars I and II there came a suspension of building and, in consequence, a severe housing shortage. In 1942–1945, we went through "rationing" and "ceiling prices" and saw the multiplication of alphabetical agencies of government making rules for nearly every act of our daily life. We take it for granted that a war effort requires severe curtailment by law of private action. In a thousand ways the Government regulated our entire life in war time.

II

The problem is not a new one. Conditions arose in Ireland in peace time like those arising here in war time and again in 1942–45. Since, in Ireland, there was but a limited number of farms available for tenants and all of them were owned by English landlords, there was real trouble. Morley, in his "Life of Gladstone," tells the story of rent riots, bloodshed and hardship. It is a long story of recurring troubles between English landlords and Irish tenants. One fact is outstanding. As fast as an Irishman gave evidence of making a move in the direction of material improvement, crack would go the whip of his landlord over his head in the way of a raise in rent. Worst of all, if the tenant occupying the farm did not want to pay the increase, there was always some other Irishman standing by, ready and willing to pay it and thus take away from the occupant his farm, his livelihood and his home. Hence, the Irish lived in hovels.

The rise of temper in Ireland in those days was not unlike that of a tenant in New York City in 1919 and 1945 when his landlord raised rents. His wife tells him that she has looked around all over New York and there are no apartments available within the family budget.

About the time the landlord and tenant situation reached its most acute stage in Ireland, a *Captain Boycott* carried on as the agent for a group of British landlords—so-called absentee landlords. Following his principals' instructions, Captain Boycott raised the rents of the Irish tenants up and up. Mind you now, he was an Irishman himself. And what kind of an Irishman would he be who would go around doing a thing like that to other Irishmen, asked the Irish tenants. The Irish not only have a sense of humor, but they are a fighting race. They did not go about cracking Boycott's skull, but they invented a new weapon. They decided to "cut" this particular gentleman and so make him an outcast from decent Irish society. Thereafter, whenever he appeared, whether in church or at parties, they turned their backs on him. They made him a pariah. He was *boycotted*. So came the word into our language.

The aroused moral indignation of the Irish tenants brought about a new *equitable right*—the *equity of renewal*, first introduced in Ulster, Ireland, and later spread over all of Ireland. Gladstone, as Prime Minister, found it a practicable basis for the control of rents and thus provided for alleviation of distress and avoidance of bloodshed in Ireland.

He developed the judicial machinery for the fixing of rents, taking this very principle of *equity of renewal* as a basis.

It was like this: If a tenant was paying a fair rent, he was not to be ousted by someone else willing to pay more, especially if there was no other place to which the occupant could go and his living depended upon the farm. This new right meant simply that a tenant in possession had an *equitable right* to a renewal of his lease. This equity of renewal, like the *equity of redemption,* became a part of English law.[2]

I might as well stop here and explain what *equity of redemption* means. It will bring out something that is important for laymen to understand. It presents, too, the process of adjustment of the law to constantly broadening moral standards.

III

In the early days of what we call "English common law," from which our "American common law" is derived, when it became necessary to borrow money, if the borrower owned a house and lot, or a farm, he could pledge the property as security for the loan sought. Under the practice, as it prevailed under the older English law, the borrower gave a *deed* of the property as security for his loan. In that way, he turned over the title of his property to the lender, very much as he turned in his overcoat at the shop where hung the "three gold balls," secured ten dollars, and received a ticket evidencing the pledge. If ultimately he could get enough cash to pay "uncle" what he had borrowed, he could get back his overcoat. But if he could not raise the money, he went without his overcoat. "Uncle" had complete title to the coat. It was his for keeps, to sell or to wear, as he chose. In the same way if an owner of a piece of real estate mortgaged it for a loan and did not have the money to pay the lender when the loan was due or did not have enough to pay the interest when due, the lender held the real estate. There was nothing more to it. That was the law. It was "so written" in the bond.

If, by sheer inadvertence, the borrower did not pay the interest— he had forgotten the due date or was short in the bank—he was out of luck. If later he did get sufficient money and found himself in a position to pay the interest on the loan and the loan itself, what happened? It was just too bad. He could not get the property back— that is, as the law then stood.

IV

Now, in the early days, English lawyers believed strongly in the doctrine that *a contract is a contract* and that, with certain rare exceptions, such as fraud or duress, it should be fulfilled to the very letter. Furthermore, they believed that in the fulfillment of contracts in large measure lay the economic safety of the country. And, of course, the English lawyers were right. For how can there be borrowing and lending at all if the lenders cannot be sure that the obligation to repay will be strictly observed—and still more important, unless the courts enforce the rights of the lenders?

In international relations, the great commandment is *Pacta Sunt Servandum*—which translated means, *keep your word.* It is quite obvious that if we ever succeed in establishing peace in this world, it will be because the nations of the world do keep their word with each other. This matter of keeping one's word is even more important than the writing and signing of treaties and the making of decisions by courts, because only when the world is civilized enough to keep promises will we get any kind of international law. If it is just a matter of which nation has the greatest physical power to enforce its will, there is no civilization. We know that now. Hence, you can well understand why English lawyers in the seventeenth and eighteenth centuries held tenaciously to the belief that upon *the sanctity of the contract* lay the basis of civilized society. If that went down, all civilization would go down with it.

All this was good logic, but it was a long distance from home for the fellow about to lose his property because he was in default on his loan. The reality of the situation was this: If the lender who held the title by deed was actually paid what he had loaned, with interest, and in addition enough to cover any real expense he had incurred by reason of the default, that is, was "made whole," what more in good morals should he expect? Why should he profit beyond that point and the borrower suffer?

That is how it happened that when Courts of Equity came into existence and Ecclesiastical law came in to modify the strict laws of the Romans and the Franks, the Chancellors of England put this devil under restraint. Good conscience became the basis of equity jurisprudence. These great Chancellors—and they were great men—devised what we now know as the *equity of redemption*. It means just this: That even if the borrower did not pay the interest on time, he had an *equitable* right to redeem his real estate *upon payment of what he owed to the lender with costs.*

In the course of time, the *equitable right to redeem* the mortgaged real estate became a fixed part of English law. After the Chancellors got this far, they were confronted with another practical difficulty. Developing the law is not like developing medicine. Once sulfanilamide or penicillin is discovered it can be put under control to serve mankind. But, in the law, once one phase of human selfishness is controlled, it turns up in another form. This is so because law deals with human conduct and human conduct—well, is human conduct. And you can take the word of a practicing lawyer that there is still a lot of plain cussedness rampant in this world. Changes in the law come more or less like changes in automobiles, radios or bombers—we learn by experience—by trial and error. Justice Holmes was responsible for the classic phrase, "the life of the law is experience, not logic." (That is something laymen do not quite understand. They get hold of some one point in the law and try to apply it logically. "A little knowledge is a dangerous thing." That is why we lawyers still have justification for our vocation. We may know little, but we do know more than the layman about the law. But we too have to live and learn.)

Having gotten rid of the trend of conduct in one direction of human selfishness, the Chancellors of England were confronted with another. If the borrower had the right to redeem, he could *hold out on the lender.* He could wait and come in at any time he pleased and tender principal and interest, and the lender would then have to give him back his real estate. Meantime, the lender did not have his money and he could not do anything with the real estate. Not a very healthy state of affairs, was it? Well, those old fellows who sat on wool sacks —pillows made of wool for greater comfort for old men to sit in judgment—the same fellows who wore wigs to make them look more elderly, sage and wise—these judges said, "Well, we'll fix that all right. We will give the lender the right to bring a suit in our own courts of Chancery which will end in a decree putting a stop to the right of the borrower to redeem whenever he feels like it. That is why this is a Court of Equity." So came into the law what is now known by lawyers as the *action to foreclose the equity of redemption.*

V

A foreclosure suit is then merely the machinery by which a borrower is estopped from redeeming the liened property at any time. But he still gets the opportunity to redeem, if he simply pays up with costs.

With this brief explanation of the doctrine of equity of redemption, the reader will be helped to understand how by analogous process of reasoning there was produced the doctrine of *equity of renewal.* The two are sisters under the skin. The reader will begin to understand, too, the influence of ecclesiastical thinking upon the law, when he learns that equity is grounded upon principles of morality—which religious leaders do know more about than most lawyers—and do they know it! For centuries, "conscience" through equity *jurisprudence* has been operating upon our common law.

It so happens that just as the *equity of renewal* came into English common law through the experience of the Irish, it came into rabbinical law in the medieval ages through similar experiences of the Jews. In the ghettos in the middle ages, there was limited space available for housing of Jews. Since no Jew could own a piece of real estate, and yet was confined to living in the ghetto, he could get space only as a *tenant*. Just as later in Ireland, farmers were obliged to be tenants since they could not buy any real estate from English owners.

As in the case of the Irish, as fast as the Jew became prosperous, up would go his rent, or his landlord would find someone else ready to take over his place at a higher rent. The ghetto tenant would find himself without a roof over his head. And he liked his landlord then just as much as later the Irish tenant liked his landlord and he liked his competitor quite as much as the Irish tenant liked his.

In those days, for the Jews, the controlling law was made by the rabbis—and it was controlling. The great Rabbi Gershom deduced from the Talmud the law of "Jus Casaca," or the law of Hazakah.[3] Pope Clement VIII legalized the rabbinical law by making evictions practically impossible in the ghettos so long as a reasonable rent was paid. "Jus Casaca" translated means the very same thing as the Irish *equity of renewal*. Rabbi Gershom held that it was against good conscience for one Jew to compete with another for space. Thus, both in Irish and Jewish history, the religious and moral standards of *equity* were worked into the governing law. However, for centuries, the English lawyers fought against it, and some even now are not reconciled.

VI

With this background, the reader will be better able to understand what happened after World War I, especially in crowded cities like New York and Washington. Something had to be done about it. The New York Legislature appointed an investigation committee to look into existing conditions, headed by Charles C. Lockwood, now a Justice of the Supreme Court. Belle Moskowitz, too, helped in this work. The Commission went carefully into all the realities of the situation. Alfred E. Smith was then Governor. He was keen for finding relief. As the legislation was being studied by the Governor, I was consulted about the constitutional points involved. The framers followed substantially the lines of my general advice. The laws were known as the

"Emergency Rent Laws." [4] I shall avoid the use of lawyers' language and explain them simply.

In substance, the State of New York said to the landlords: "You are entitled to rental, but not to *extortionate* rental; you will not be permitted to take advantage of this extraordinary situation at the cost of the public welfare. You shall not have what the market would enable you to get if it had free scope. We will authorize our courts to fix 'fair and reasonable rentals' for such housing and you will take that and no more. We will not permit our courts to be used as instruments of oppression. There will be no dispossessing of tenants for non-payment of rents when our courts determine that the rents are unreasonable."

By 1944, this principle of the law had gone much further—*ceiling* prices, priorities and all the other controls. In essence, all this means that *law is made to serve the public interest* and does not exist for the purpose of giving special advantages to a few who possess power.

The Emergency Rent Laws provoked outcries from real estate owners and especially from mortgagors—just as such protests came in England a century or so before when the *equity of redemption* came in. As a matter of fact, these laws did result in considerable hardship in some instances, especially in the cases of widows dependent upon fixed incomes coming from rentals. Many members of our Bar were opposed to these measures. Among them was a gerat constitutional lawyer of my day, Louis Marshall. He was retained by the real estate interests of New York to contest their validity on constitutional grounds. Though he was not alone in this fight, he was very distinctly their leading lawyer.[5]

Let me tell a story which confirms what I have said about how accident plays a determining part in one's life. In 1919, Abraham L. Gutman was one of my partners. His principal practice in the law lay in the field of real estate and in the handling of estates. He was also at that time an active lay leader in the Ethical Culture Society. He was the legal adviser to the Society as well as Dr. Felix Adler's personal lawyer. I had told Gutman that I had been consulted in the preparation of the "rent laws" and that it had been intimated that I might be called in to defend their constitutionality.

One day Gutman called me and said, "Are you retained by the state in the 'rent cases'?" I said, "No." "Well," said he, "then I am free to represent the landlords and contest the law." "Yes," I answered, "Go ahead." The very day he accepted the retainer, I was called by the representative of the Lockwood Committee and asked to appear for the State to support the constitutionality of the laws. I told him it was now too late as our firm was on the other side. Then I told Gutman about it.

"Call them back right away," he said, "and take that retainer." Those who knew Abraham L. Gutman knew that he was very set in his opinions. "How can I?" I said. "We cannot be on both sides." "We. won't be. I will withdraw from the other side." I said, "You can't do that. Your business is in the real estate field. Your clients will turn on you." "Never mind," said Gutman, "this is a call to public service and you must go on with the case." "But the State will not pay any fee," I said. "The other side will." "What has that got to do with it? You have a public duty to perform," said he.

Of course, had I not yielded, he would have gone right uptown and "told teacher," (Felix Adler) and I would have gotten a good dressing down. So I called the Lockwood representative and accepted the retainer, and from then on had a lot of fun.

Another lawyer of public spirit came into the picture—Bernard Hershkopf. Hershkopf worked on the briefs for William D. Guthrie in great constitutional cases. Guthrie was known throughout the country as a great authority on constitutional law. Hershkopf's fine social instinct put him in complete sympathy with the law. Then, best of all, he persuaded his chief, Guthrie, to come in on our side. This helped a lot, because if Guthrie came with us, we could not be called a *bunch of radicals*.

Guthrie had been for years ace pilot for men of great wealth. He was a partner of Paul D. Cravath and Victor Morawetz. Hershkopf is one of those extraordinary people who can give you the number of the volume, the page reference and even the year any case was decided. Louis Marshall was another one like him. Cardozo could do it, too. I never could. Elbert Hubbard spoiled all that for me. I heard him once in a lecture at Carnegie Hall say that he did not try to remember the combination of his safe, he had a secretary for that.

There were many precedents for the simple proposition that wherever the interest of health or safety of the State is involved, private rights have to give way to the power of the State. This is what is called the "police power."

No one likes to be chaffed by his friends, especially at his luncheon club. It was not easy for Hershkopf to persuade his chief to come into the case, but when Guthrie and I met later at the Downtown Club on Pine Street to confer—after the public announcement that he had come in—friend after friend of his came up to him at the luncheon table and intimated politely that he must be rapidly approaching senility. That was embarrassing to Guthrie. They all predicted a good sound thrashing for us in the United States Supreme Court. (Most lawyers downtown predicted a thrashing for the Port Authority in the Bond Tax case.) I suppose if a Gallup poll had been taken of lawyers on Pine, Wall, Broad Streets and lower Broadway, something like ninety-five per cent would have been for "unconstitutionality" and five for "constitutionality" of the Emergency Rent Laws.

My job was to study the factual, legal phases of the case. I began studying earlier historical precedents in this field. Hershkopf went into the research work and developed more precedents. (In passing, let me stress the point that a lawyer who has a varied practice is constantly improving his education. Justice Holmes once said, "I long have said that there is no such thing as a hard case. I am frightened weekly but always when you walk up to the lion and lay hold the hide comes off and the same old donkey of a question of law is underneath.") [6]

Thus in preparing for the arguments in these rent cases,[7] I reached a broader outlook on Irish and English history and acquired a better understanding of rabbinical law. There is a lot of fun in this business of practicing law—if one knows how and where to look for it.

VII

Three of the judges on the Court of Appeals bench were Judges Hogan, Cardozo and Crane. The last afterwards became Chief Justice. In that Court, after Guthrie had made his argument on the broad constitutional principles involved, I went into the Jewish and Irish precedents. Judge Crane told Judge Luke Stapleton, a day or so after the argument—"They are a clever bunch, Guthrie and Cohen—they cite Irish precedents and get Hogan; they cite Jewish precedents and get Cardozo—and so they bag two of the judges before they even begin their argument." But, it was Hershkopf's view and mine, that if we could get the judges away from the prevailing lawyers' bias against the laws and bring into play the forces of history, we could win the case. We felt sure of liberal judges like Holmes of the U. S. Supreme Court, Cardozo and Pound of the New York Court of Appeals. (Holmes and Pound did write the prevailing opinions.) We also knew with reasonable certainty that we could expect some judges to be against us. In the United States Supreme Court, Mr. Justice McKenna wrote the dissent.

There were two phases of the argument. First, the point that the "police power" of the State is broad enough to meet any emergency. It is not the function of the courts to substitute their opinions for the opinions of the legislature. They may strike down the legislation only if they can say the action of the legislature was *capricious or arbitrary*.

The next point in our argument was that no court could say that the legislative action was capricious or arbitrary, *if on the basis of legislative experience and wisdom,* there was any ground at all for the legislative opinion. Both in the New York courts and in the United States Supreme Court, Guthrie made an unanswerable argument on the first point.[8] After he had finished this part of the argument, I quoted freely from Morley and Gladstone and referred to the Irish *equity of renewal* and the Hebrew "Jus Casaca." At this point, when we were before the Supreme Court, Justice McKenna, who was seated on the right of Chief Justice Taft, and on my left, was quite impatient with my historical presentation. He turned to me and said testily, "I don't think this is a matter of *legislative wisdom or experience* at all. It is just a matter of power." I assured him, as Guthrie had demonstrated, that the power was there. The real question was whether it was exercised *capriciously or arbitrarily* and the Court could not say that it was a capricious or arbitrary action of the legislature, unless on the basis of past experience and wisdom, *it could find no basis whatever to support it.* Accordingly, if we were able to show that at critical points in history, parliaments had resorted to this very method for avoiding riot and disorder, then our point was made. The Supreme Court could not, if it would, strike down the act.

At this point, Holmes, on the Chief Justice's left (whom we naturally expected to be going our way) said, "Mr. Cohen, I am inclined to agree with my brother McKenna. I don't think it is our function to review the wisdom and experience of the legislature." And I replied, "Review not in the sense of substituting *your* judgment for that of the legislature, but in the sense of reviewing the record to see if there is *any* basis for the exercise of the legislative power. You review in the same way as you examine the record in a negligence case, to see if there is any evidence at all upon which the verdict of the jury can be supported, and if you find that there is such evidence, you do not set the verdict aside, you let it stand. This is not substituting the courts' judgment for the jury's, it is reviewing solely for the purpose of determining whether there is *any* evidence at all in the case to support the verdict of the jury."

I thought the old skeptic leaned back satisfied. Then forward advanced the Chief Justice himself. Now what was he going to do to "put me on the spot?" And these are the sententious words which came from the lips of this fun-loving Chief Justice: "My brothers seem to be agreed about that, Mr. Cohen, but you may proceed with your argument upon the assumption that a little *wisdom and experience* will not hurt this court." I went on with the argument. We were gratified when Holmes held that the statute "goes little if at all farther than the restriction put upon the rights of the owner of money by the more debatable usury laws." [9] He had been impressed also with the development in the English law. He said: "The preference given to the tenant in possession is an almost necessary incident of the policy and is traditional in English law." [10]

Of course, McKenna dissented. But Louis Marshall would turn in his grave today if he could see romping around, the children and grandchildren of this ancestor case. But Marshall took his defeat very well. He was a great character—totally different from his partner, Samuel Untermyer. He came here from leadership at the Syracuse bar which he won by clear merit. He and Guthrie had one technique in common—they addressed the court as if the advocate were the court's mentor—the judges were definitely there to learn—to gather "wisdom and experience" and the lawyer was to hand it to them liberally. If one watched from the side lines, one would say their manners were "most pontifical." But all judges, except a curmudgeon like Van Brunt or a bully like Gaynor respect seniority and ability. Hence, older men have an advantage over younger ones in that they may argue with more daring.

VIII

The advocate in an appellate court today must make his argument within a time limit. He must make it terse. He has little time for quotations from the record. If he falls into this error, he will surely hear from the court something like this: "Mr. M., you may assume we shall read the record and study the briefs."

Things were different in Webster's day. A case like the one Guthrie and I argued would take two or three days. Today the lawyer must know every line of his record and, like my friend George Wharton Pepper, must have a ready wit for the sharp questioning of a Jerome Frank from the bench.* He must have a vocabulary as rich as Judge Proskauer's and be as ready as he is on his feet. He must know his economics as well as Henry Epstein does, who—as Solicitor-General of New York State—won many victories in the field involving the exercise of the "police power."

When Taft presided, the judges of the United States Supreme

* Senator Pepper jousted with Judge Jerome Frank on the argument before the United States Circuit Court of Appeals in the *Shamberg* case and successfully won two of the Judges, leaving Judge Frank in the minority.

Court did not take themselves too seriously. They had a little fun on the side. Here are two incidents:

Roscoe H. Hupper was arguing an admiralty case. The libellant had one of those Swedish sixteen-syllable names. Holmes always started writing in his notebook as soon as counsel arose to address the court. When he got to writing his notes for this case, he leaned over and said to Hupper very gravely, "Mr. Hupper, before you begin your argument, would you mind telling the court whether we must be able to pronounce the name of your client in order to decide this case?" Later in his argument, Hupper referred to the case of *Hamlyn & Co.* v. *Talisker Distillery*.[11] "That," said Hupper, "if your Honors please, was a great Scotch case." At once Holmes leaned over and said (the Eighteenth Amendment had just been passed), "One of the kind we may not peer into any longer." But the judges were not always so jolly and often took the lawyers appearing before them "for a ride."

Taft was full of fun, but he ran his court as "The Boss." A few years after my adventure in the rent cases, I appeared before the court in another case. Former Attorney-General George W. Wickersham and John D. Lindabury were pitted against each other—both able advocates. Wickersham was retained by the State of New Jersey and the City of Newark to bring a suit to restrain the Central Railroad of New Jersey from building the present bridge across Newark Bay. Lindabury represented the Central Railroad Company. Wickersham had lost the case below. He had made the Port Authority a party defendant, claiming that its certificate was a prerequisite before the bridge could be built. The Port Treaty had only been signed a short time before. The then Assistant Secretary of War, Jonathan Mayhew Wainright, had asked the Port Authority for its opinion on this bridge. It might or might not be an obstruction to navigation in Newark Bay. For tactical reasons—I thought inadvisedly—the Port Authority referred the matter to the New Jersey Board of Commerce and Navigation of which J. Spencer Smith was then Chairman and at the same time Vice-Chairman of the Port of New York Authority.

I appeared for the Port Authority in the case. I was instructed by my client to prevent, if I could, any narrow interpretation of the Port Authority statutes, but not to take sides in the case itself. I asked for time on the argument. The Chief Justice said, "What side are you on?" "On neither side, sir. We are here to aid the court and to take whatever decision it makes." The Chief Justice persisted, "Do you want us to affirm or reverse the court below?" "We have no opinion on that score. We are merely a public agency and wish to aid the

court in its interpretation of the statutes under which we are operating." The Chief Justice said: "Don't you think it is the business of
a public agency to have an opinion and present it to aid this court?"
Of course, he was right.

At a meeting of the Commissioners of the Port Authority some
years later, when George S. Silzer, former Governor of New Jersey
was presiding, I chanced to be urging the Commissioners to take an
affirmative stand upon something. I referred to this incident in the
Supreme Court, said I was embarrassed then at the Commissioners'
failure to take sides, and I added: *"I was silent."* "And when you
were *silent,"* said one of the Commissioners promptly, *"what did you
say?"* He was Frank C. Ferguson, then a Commissioner but afterward
its Chairman.

IX

I am ready to admit that silence on the part of a lawyer is regarded
as a popular virtue with laymen. Jack Cade said, "First, let's kill all
the lawyers."

It was only two years ago that the New York State Chamber of
Commerce revised its rules and for the first time opened its doors to
lawyers. Present-day members of the Chamber are, as a matter of fact,
not as fearful of lawyers as were their predecessors in olden times.
But the reason assigned by the merchants of olden days was that
"the lawyers will always out-talk us." Such terror has not yet emerged
as a result of the change in the Chamber's tradition. The admission
of quite a few has not given the lawyers much of an advantage. As a
matter of fact, the prejudice against them is so strong that when the
lawyer speaks he starts with two strikes on him before he goes to bat.

This attitude toward lawyers in the Chamber was the rule, however,
when the Port Treaty was signed on April 20, 1921, in the Great Hall
of the Chamber. Governor Nathan L. Miller presided. Each principal
authorized to sign the Treaty stepped forward and made a nice little
speech. Each one of the witnesses made a speech. As I had drawn the
document, it was my place to see that the paper was signed by each
party in the right place, very much as a lawyer supervises the execution
of a last will and testament in his private office. The signing of the
Treaty was a gala occasion. There was a nice luncheon afterwards at
which Darwin P. Kingsley, President of the Chamber and of the
New York Life Insurance Company presided. He opened the luncheon
with this: "We had two historic events here today—the signing of the
Port Treaty and Julius Henry had an opportunity to make a speech
and didn't."

Now, I ask you, in all fairness, is your lawyer to be mute, when it is his duty to speak for you? Judges would answer, "No—but let it be short and snappy."

As for the observation from Chief Justice Taft that a "little wisdom and experience will not hurt this court," I am inclined to think that the bar would say "amen" and so would some of the judges themselves. For do they not now hurl great chunks of wisdom and experience at each other?

BOOK V

TRIAL AND ERROR IN INDUSTRY

CHAPTER SIXTEEN

Ce n'est pas assez de faire entendre ce qu'on dit, il faut encore le faire voir; il faut que la mémoire, l'intelligence et l'imagination s'en accommodent également.

JOUBERT.

It is not enough to make people hear what you say—you must make them understand it; memory, intelligence, and imagination must be equally called into play.

Max Meyer

An industry meets a radical labor union movement— Business men, too, have dreams and visions—One of them makes a great contribution—A new design for industrial education.

I

IF ONE SHOULD see a pint-sized, very serious looking, round-shouldered man, with white hair long on the back of his neck, pushing hard for the 8:36 from White Plains and hurrying to his whist game, with no more greeting to an old friend than "Excuse me, I must make my game today," that would be Max Meyer. But he would rush just as rapidly to attend a meeting in behalf of the Negroes in White Plains —or for that matter in behalf of all the Negroes in the United States— or to meet his good friend, Dr. Stephen P. Duggan, for the planning of a new program of international politics.

If every French private carries a marshal's baton in his knapsack, Max Meyer must have carried a generalship in one of the bundles he carried in the garment industry as a boy.

At a dinner in 1944, employers and labor leaders all joined in paying him tribute for his work as chairman of the Millinery Stabilization Commission—the body that took over the job of bringing about some economic order and stability in that industry.

In 1945, he held also the job of one of Governor Lehman's commissioners on the State Mediation Board. He is rated one of the best arbitrators in the field of labor disputes—was one of Mayor La Guardia's leading advisers in this field.

In 1944, he was named by Governor Dewey on a commission to deal with "after the war" labor problems. He is Chairman of the Educational Foundation for the Apparel Industry. He is always as busy as a flea on three or four hot bricks—jumping from one thing to another.

At his home near White Plains, Max paints pictures. In the depths of his soul he is an artist—a *creative* artist. His banker's role—he is vice-president of a bank—is just a cloak to cover his real self.

If he donned a smock and a French beret and stood before an easel and held a brush in his hand—as he does—he would be recognized for what he is—a runaway from the Latin Quarter in Paris. His love for French literature and his love for his mother country, Alsace-Lorraine, if he can be induced to talk about it, will furnish another clue to his nature.

Max once wrote a sketch of his father and mother, portraying their early life in Alsace-Lorraine. They came to this country—as my father did—to escape the restraints of life in Europe. Both knew the Germans. Even in the eighties my father had strong prejudices against them. But Max's family knew the French too and he loved them. I knew Max's father and mother. They were charming people. Max is witty but not nearly as quick on the trigger as was his mother. One day, when we were visiting her, she asked about our farm in Westchester. In German, she said, "What do you raise on the farm?" I told her. "Do you have any animals?" "Yes. We have a couple of cows, some chickens, some dogs, a horse *and my wife keeps a pig.*" Out of the corner of her eye she looked at me and said, "Ah, yes. The pig that your wife keeps will take the blue ribbon at the next fair." Max would agree about the pig, but not about the blue ribbon—I am sure.

Since propinquity and the accident of relationship have played such a large part in my life, I should report for the record that it was largely through Max that I became active as the lawyer for employers in the women's wear industry. That's how I came to my debut in the field of industrial relations.

II

Along about 1898, Max Meyer's firm, Beller & Company, makers of women's fine coats and suits, met their first strike, brought on by the radical IWW *—"The Wobblies." I was introduced to anarchy in industry. Seidman discusses the technique of their kind of strike in the early nineties. He quotes one of the Union leaders as saying:

* Industrial Workers of the World.

"Our organizing work, * * * we generally carried on in a stereotyped way. We would issue a circular reading somewhat as follows: 'Murder! The exploiters, the bloodsuckers, the manufacturers * * * Pay your dues * * * Down with the capitalists! Hurrah!' " [1]

In the Beller strike, the circulars were headed "War! War! War!" It was, indeed, physical warfare. The papers we submitted to the judge of the court for an injunction set forth plenty of evidence of it. Blood spilt, heads split. The judge who granted the injunction said:

"It is evident that instead of a manly self-respecting demand to right a grievance, whether real or believed to be such, fortified by reason and argument, methods have been employed by the defendants that are un-American, intolerable, abhorrent to all ideas of personal liberty and in defiance of the right of the individual to determine for himself under what conditions he prefers to labor. Every individual is free to exercise any lawful calling without being subjected to acts of terrorism by those who are not in accord with his conception of the manner in which he is pursuing his vocation." [2]

I had no reputation as a specialist in this field. On the basis of merit, if Beller had looked around he could have found other lawyers with much more experience. But it is not a difficult technical job—when one got the hang of it.

The injunction that my partner, Theodore B. Richter, and I secured did stop the strike. But that technique was detested by the union leaders. When in July, 1910, the Great Strike covering the entire women's cloak and suit industry broke out, Max recommended me for the job of counsel to the industry. I helped to form the first employers' organization in the industry—The Cloak, Suit and Skirt Manufacturers Association. A. E. Lefcourt was its first president. It was not long before I met Max Schwarcz, Moses Silberman and Louis Rosenfeld, who with Max Meyer, made up the "Big Four" in the industry. For five years they guided the Association through its troubles.

With the call of the strike, there had been sent out to every manufacturer, a proposed contract containing this clause:

"1. The said Firm hereby engages the Union to perform all the tailoring, operating, pressing, finishing, cutting and buttonhole making work required to be done by the Firm in its cloak and suit business, during the period commencing with the date of this agreement and terminating one year from date, and the Union agrees to perform said work in a good and workmanlike manner."

"The New York Times" of July 16th, 1910, said of this:

"The proposed agreement of the Cloakmakers' Union is a reminder of the padrone system."

From 1910 to 1915, I came into close personal contact with the union leaders—Abraham Rosenberg; John A. Dyche; Meyer London (their first lawyer); and Morris Hillquit, who later succeeded him. I also met Louis D. Brandeis.

There were special circumstances in this industry that in 1910 made it seem possible to succeed in doing what had never been done before. As Seidman says:

> "As parts of the growing Jewish community in New York, they (the employers) were conscious of prejudice and dislike on the part of some of the older groups, and for that reason they were sensitive to criticism. They did not want to be ashamed of their industry, the most distinctively Jewish one of the country." [3]

I can testify to the truth of this. Moreover, these immigrants came from parts of Europe where arbitration was an accepted method of settling disputes. The early successful development of arbitration boards in the needle trades can be traced directly to this experience. Moreover, every orthodox Jew had a thorough training in Jewish law—the Torah. His rabbi was for him always the final arbitrator.

The reader may find in a simple racial sympathy the basis for the optimism which moved Max Meyer, Max Schwarcz, Moses Silberman and Louis Rosenfeld—the "Big Four"—as well as the Jewish philanthropists William Fischman, Reuben Sadowsky and Joseph H. Cohen. I, too, was confident that we could achieve something novel in this industry.

In the first group of immigrants who entered the industry in the eighties were artisans or tradesmen from towns and villages of eastern Europe. These were individualistic, conservative in economics and politics and orthodox in religion. They did not flee from capitalistic oppression. Joel Seidman, in his book "The Needle Trades," says:

> "* * * but rather from feudalism to a land where greater business opportunities were available. Radicals were sensitive to the various limitations upon democracy and civil rights that existed here, but to the average Jewish worker, fresh from the tyranny of Czarist Russia, America seemed freedom and democracy personified. Here, merely by working hard and living frugally, one could save money, enter business, and enable one's sons to be business and professional men instead of factory workers." [4]

The founders of the *men's* clothing industry were seldom more than one generation away from the peddlers who first travelled on foot and then in wagons throughout the country. My wife remembers how her grandfather so won the affection of his New England customers that they invited him to stay as a guest and to bring his grandchildren along—she went to such homes with him.

The names of Adler (Rochester), Benjamin, Goldman, Cohen, Kohn, Rosenberg, Naumburg (all of New York) are familiar to New Yorkers of the nineties. But they were all sons of immigrants. For that matter, too, so were the Strausses—Oscar, Nathan and Isidore, the Gimbels and Saks, and many other of the department store business leaders of the country. They had all the vigor and the enterprise of pioneers. They were creative.

Seidman says of the needle industry as a whole:

"The fact that most employers and workers alike long belonged to the relatively compact Jewish community, where the sufferings of one group could not long escape the attention of the other, *aided understanding*. The more enlightened employers did not wish the needle trades, the most distinctively Jewish industries in America, to remain at a sweatshop level. Prominent Jews had used their influence to bring peace to the industries on a basis fair to all. As a result the needle industries, while contributing some stirring chapters to the history of American industrial strife, have been especially noted for experiments in peaceful industrial relations." [5]

This explains why Max Meyer and Reuben Sadowsky could work with Morris Hillquit and Meyer London and why Louis Brandeis and Louis Marshall should give so freely of their time. They understood and knew the people in the industry. They had different views on economics and on politics but they had a common background.

III

On West Twenty-fourth Street, in New York City, stands the Central High School of the Needle Trades. Let the principal, Mortimer C. Ritter, act as a guide around the classrooms and explain the work that is going on there. The reader will be convinced that this is a work that is to have great consequences in the life of the City of New York; indeed, in the industrial life of the country. Look at the murals by Ernest Fiene which represent the artist's attempt to tell the story of the rise of the "Garment," or, as it is sometimes called, "The Needle Industry," well named because it is built on the work of the needle.

In the garment college now under way * students are being trained to become shop superintendents, designers and technicians. Among the courses are apparel construction, design, industrial scientific management, applied industrial psychology, labor relations, industrial cost accounting, marketing, quality control, applied textiles, identification of fabrics, written and oral English, human relationship and world civilization.[6]

Max Meyer will come on the stage in a few moments—but at a surprise dinner in 1944, Samuel Klein was given a set of resolutions and

* Fashion Institute of Technology.

an appropriately inscribed gold watch. He is the Director of the Industrial Council of the Industry, made up of manufacturers of cloaks and suits. His board of directors wished to pay him a tribute for his work "in fostering constructive management, labor and producer-retailer relationship."

Sam Klein was a "boss," too, in the period 1910–1915, but he was an unusually observant and studious member of the Cloak, Suit and Skirt Manufacturers Association to which I was elected an honorary member. This picture of 1945 is to be put beside the picture of 1910.

Moreover, anyone fortunate enough to have seen "Pins and Needles" in 1942, the show put on by the members of the labor unions in that industry, with a cast made up wholly of young men and young women —members of the union, would have had some knowledge of the latent talent in that industry—talent which Principal Ritter is now developing in that school on Twenty-fourth Street and which we hope now will develop into the garment college.

The note I want to accent at this moment is *that this school came about through frank and open cooperation between labor, management and the public.* But it took thirty-five years before this civilized method was effective.

IV

Such a great industry could not have been built up without business ability. If any of my readers desire a more detailed survey of the industry, I recommend "The Needle Trades" by Joel Seidman (part of the series of "Labor in Twentieth Century America") and especially the very valuable biographical compendium appendix. It is a book studded with facts and figures, a few of which I hope to use to make a background for the personalities whose portraits I shall paint.

At the outset, it should be emphasized that it is true of this industry as it is of the automotive or aviation or chemical industries, that *great industrialists* were needed to give it birth and nurture during its early days. The present state of the garment industry could not have come into being without the great artistic and creative ability of the "bosses." In the mural of Fiene's at the Textile School, the painter has tried to tell the "Saga of the Bundle." The bundle means the package of cut cloth and materials that was carried on the tailor's back from the factory to his home. From my point of view, I must say, Fiene did not, in the mural, give adequate recognition to the contributions made by the *employer-group.* In most of the books written about the industry, the union and its rise have been brought into the highlights, but the part business leaders played is shadowed. There were, indeed, great union leaders and they did make great contributions, but there were also *great leaders among the employers and they made great contributions,* too, without which nothing was possible—even the work done by the union leaders.

Fiene put into his mural Al Smith and Louis Marshall and Louis Brandeis and, besides, stuck in a meek, scrawny, skimpy young fellow. I was not meek. I was not scrawny. But I must admit that in 1910–1915, I was slim. But for Fiene to put the lawyer for the employers in the group and omit the men who actually made it possible for the lawyer to be there at all has always seemed to me to leave the whole picture out of perspective. To correct Fiene, I did secure a picture of Max Schwarcz, which he added to the group.

In dedicating "Law and Order in Industry" in 1916 to Max M. Schwarcz, I said:

> "Of the small band who blazed a trail through the thick forest, he is the first to enter the land of mystery. Proud, brave, loyal, a dear and a good friend to all who labored truly."

That was my testimony then. It is my testimony today, as I look back over these thirty-five years.

Max Schwarcz was but one member of the "Big Four"—the pathfinders. Only one of this group still is living, Max Meyer. The other two, "Mo" Silberman and "Lou" Rosenfeld, were also realistic men and constructive leaders.

There were other men who had the same ideals as the "Big Four," but they followed the "Big Four" as the "Steering Committee." For nearly five years these four were dominant on the employers' side. Max Meyer, like myself, had come under the influence of Dr. Felix Adler. I am sure that Max would agree that the Doctor had much to do with influencing our work.

V

Seidman says: "It is the factor of style around which all else in the needle trades revolves." [7]

These styles originate in the higher priced field in which Max Meyer's firm and Max Schwarcz's firm were outstanding leaders. (If you had known Julius Forstmann as I did—a great artist and business man, too—you would have heard from his own lips how much he counted on these two men for help in the creation of his styles in woolens. A true artist himself, he admired both of the Maxes.)

In addition to the style creators in the higher priced fields, there were competitors who copied their styles almost as soon as they were introduced into the market. This led to bitter competition and a constant turnover of firms. It also brought about the creation of the sweatshop conditions that long disgraced the industries. In men's clothing, style change has always been more moderate and subdued, and not so erratic nor subject to the same caprice or extravagance that has always characterized fashions for women. There came early in the men's garment industry a realistic stabilization in fashions that permitted more minute division of labor and this, in turn, brought about the creation of the larger enterprise—the trade names now so familiar through the country—Hart, Schaffner & Marx, Kuppenheimer, Adler's (of Rochester), Stein-Bloch & Co. and the long line of others.

In the women's industry, slight changes in fashion prevented manufacturing in quantity in advance. This made it necessary for a leader like one of the "Big Four" to be constantly on the jump—to be not less than two or three jumps ahead of his competitor. On the other hand, this same factor of style and quick change created the great problem of seasonal employment for the workers. The needle worker is essentially an *individualist*. However, his talent is not all in his fingers. He must have a head. That accounts for the graduation from the machine to the posts of stylist, executive and administrator and the making of real leaders. These were the creative artists who developed an industry of such magnitude. The men at the top became both style leaders and efficient executives. Naturally, they became leaders in the cloak and suit industry, and later in the dress, waist and millinery industries.

The reader must understand that besides craftsmen who came from abroad, there were business men—immigrants—who found other callings barred to them in the ghetto conditions of Europe. While the garment industry offered no alluring prospects of riches, it seemed to give these hard-driven refugees of the eighties and nineties a start in a new country.

Students, too, came to this country penniless and worked at the bench until they could continue their studies here. Morris Hillquit was such a beginner. And as Hillquit rose from the worker's bench to practicing lawyer, others became great industrial leaders and rose to commanding positions. Here was American opportunity and American resourcefulness at its very best—the "melting pot" in operation.

In the eighties and nineties, not only the style factor but the *personnel* phase of the industry controlled. In that period the greatest development in output took place. During that time large numbers of people migrated to this country. The manufacturers in the popular-priced field, and some even in the higher-priced group began then to cut the cloth in the "inside shop"—so-called—and call in *contractors* to do the sewing, finishing and pressing of the garments. As the contractors wanted work badly, great competition ensued between these bidders for the "bundles." And since there were more contractors than could be kept busy, prices were slashed and in turn forced wages down.

It is this "Saga of the Bundles" which Fiene portrays in his mural. Each painter, like each writer, depicts what is in his eye. And since Fiene finds the drama in the *worker,* we should perhaps not find too much fault with him if he visualizes the employer as the grim, wicked exploiter of labor. There were such employers—I met them as clients—but I happen to have known the other kind—the kind *with ideals.* They had a deep sense of social responsibility.

To those who knew only the workers' side, these business men, like the "Big Four," were all "Bosses." Perhaps not until Samuel Klein took over as manager of the Industrial Council (the employers) did such union leaders as Dubinsky and Zaretsky find real value in working openly in cooperation with these business men. Sidney Hillman saw it early in his collaboration with Hart, Schaffner & Marx in Chicago. Samuel Gompers recognized the value of cooperation with constructive employers. The Gompers philosophy is now coming into its own. But it was the very conditions of the workers which made the needle industries a fertile field for all sorts of *isms* to flourish. Surrounded by and immersed in these conditions, leaders of the East Side turned to Marxian theories. Hillquit did and so did Abraham Cahan, the editor of the "Forward." As we look back upon it now, in 1910 it resembled nothing so much as a jungle where lions and tigers clutched at each other's throats.

VI

There developed quite naturally in the industry, a strong Socialistic movement. It brought a great union upsurge. It made grand theatre in which labor leaders played their roles as stars. And they were stars, make no mistake about it. Only if one gives adequate consideration to the play of human emotions can the events of those days be set in proper perspective. The workers *hated* their employers and had much justification for this feeling. The Socialist labor union leaders and lawyers of that day had *two* objectives. One, the alleviation of immediate distressing working conditions and, second, the finding of a cure for the economic causes producing these conditions. Their enthusiasm for the Marxian philosophy was the result. Naturally it turned into organized opposition to the "capitalists"—the employers. But their philosophy went too far. If there is any one lesson in the experiences of the garment industry, it is that "blueprints" do not solve such human problems. *Isms* are bad when they clash head on with realities. It was essentially a human problem which was met from 1910 to 1945 in the needle industry. To treat strikes as merely the result of the activity of union leaders encouraging a mob, is sheer superficial thinking. As Dr. Oliver Wendell Holmes remarked, "The difference between green and seasoned knowledge, * * * is great. Our American atmosphere is vocal with the flippant loquacity of half knowledge." [8] We confess it—we belonged there, too, in 1910. We had only "half knowledge." We learned as Felix Adler taught us to do—*by doing.*

The simple truth as we see it now is that the conditions of any industry create the kind of union leadership that comes to the top. A labor union leader, like a political leader, gets power because he "delivers the goods." He meets the needs of his constituents. His strength and power lie in making promises of what he intends to do, and to the extent to which he makes good on these promises, he increases his power.

That is the story of John L. Lewis and Sidney Hillman. Making good, the leader must then make more promises to hold his position. And he must keep on making promises and continue making good. And when he believed—as the union leaders did in the nineteenth and early twentieth centuries—that to make good he has to call frequent strikes, he will select such weapons as a matter of course. But, when an intelligent labor leader learns that there are other weapons available he turns to them—or, to change the figure, he plays a diplomat's role and becomes a Dubinsky, a Hillman or a Zaretsky.

The change to political action then is easy. Once control of large numbers of men and a large treasury is secured, and it is found desirable to use it as political power—whatever the aim may be—one cannot avoid the temptation to pit his knowledge and experience against the "Kellys," the "Hagues," the "Flynns" and the "Prendergasts." One feels he can do better than they because of having managed and successfully led large groups of people. The difference between Hillman and Dubinsky is just this: Dubinsky is *astute,* while Hillman is *shrewd.* There is a distinction.

VII

Completing this "back-drop" picture of the garment industry, the reader must understand that the industry was easy of entry for business men. It required but a small amount of capital for an employer to start.

The problems of the industry were complicated still further by immigration. A congressional committee in 1907 made a thorough investigation of this problem.

"The Commission reported that the Irish predominated in the tailoring shops of New York City from 1850 to 1888. After 1865, a few Swedes entered the industry in that city, followed by the Germans in the 1880's. In the early 1890's Russian and Polish Jews entered in large numbers, and were soon followed by Italians, who by 1910 were beginning to supplant the Jews. In Chicago, the first clothing workers were Germans, German Jews, Bohemians, a few Americans, and Poles. About 1895, Scandinavians entered the industry, followed by Russian Jews, Italians, and Lithuanians. In Baltimore the employees in clothing shops were almost exclusively Germans until about 1890. Large numbers of Russian Jews then entered the industry, followed by Lithuanians about 1895 and Bohemians, Poles, Italians, and others about 1900." [9]

During the eighties, the number of Jewish immigrants was 193,000. In the nineties, it rose to 393,000 and, in the following decade, it grew to a migration of a whole people, with 976,000 coming here. In this decade, of the 393,000 of the Jewish arrivals, 145,000 or 37 per cent were tailors and 39,000 were dressmakers. Substantially, half of the skilled workers, therefore, were needle workers before their arrival. Employers of a certain type took advantage of the "greenhorns" as they were called then. A Chicago forelady told a sympathetic college teacher during the 1910 strike:

" 'I want no experienced girls. * * * They know the pay to get. I got to pay them good wages and they make me less work, but these greenhorns, Italian people, Jewish people, all nationalities, they cannot speak English and they don't know where to go and they just come from the old country and I let them work hard, like the devil, and those I get for less wages.' " [10]

Max Meyer and I talked this factor over many times. What was the industry to do for workers when immigration stopped? We finally drew up a plan which we presented to both the employers and the union leaders. We failed to get a start. Max never forgot that plan. He saw what was coming. Most of his colleagues in the industry did not. Many of them still do not. Sam Klein and his present supporters do see it clearly now. So do Dubinsky and Zaretsky.

It is precisely the need for a new type of worker which developed after the flood of immigration was stopped by the Immigration Laws that led Max Meyer, after he withdrew from the industry itself, toward achieving his dream—the Textile School and now also the Fashion Institute of Technology. The school is the realization of Max's dream. It is the product of his 1910–1915 experiences as an employer and leader of employers in the cloak and suit industry. Max's persistence finally won the union and then later the employers to cooperation in the establishment of this school. It is the industry's crowning contribution to all industry. It is a new form of education for our country.

CHAPTER SEVENTEEN

Nemo vir magnus sine aliquo afflatu divino unquam fuit.
No man was ever great without some degree of inspiration.
CICERO.

Louis D. Brandeis

An experiment in industrial arbitration with a great judge at its head—The conflict between the objectives of a radical labor union and the economic needs of an industry—The effort to find a way—The merits of decision as compared with compromise—A discussion of Zionism.

I

MY FIRST CONTACT with Louis D. Brandeis came one hot afternoon at Fir Cones, our house at Elmsford. Max Meyer brought him over to see me. The cloak and suit strike of 1910 was then in full blast. Abraham Rosenberg, John Dyche and Benjamin Schlesinger were the union leaders and Meyer London was their lawyer. Things were going pretty badly—the strikers were losing—the employers were losing—the Hebrew charities were drawn upon for relief—the department stores were not getting deliveries of women's coats and suits.

Among these department stores was Filene's of Boston, of which A. Lincoln Filene was a principal. Filene was then both friend and client of Brandeis. How it came about I do not know precisely, but the leaders of the International Ladies Garment Workers Union were induced in July, 1910, to accept Brandeis as their adviser in this crisis.

Brandeis was a great lawyer in 1910. He had shown the way in Massachusetts for many social improvements. Later when he became a Justice of the United States Supreme Court, he displayed his great natural gifts especially in dissenting opinions. Brandeis not only had constructive ability, but his powers of analysis were unusual. One of the high points in his dissenting opinions was the one in *New State Ice Co.* versus *Liebmann*.[1] I wrote an article "Ice" (published in the Boston University Law Review, January, 1933) in which I said:

"The explanation for Mr. Justice Brandeis' opinion in the Ice case will be found in the footnotes—the unrivalled and encyclopaedic references to economic writings on cognate subjects, as well as the vital grasp of the trend of the times."

In his belief in small business, his warm adherence to the principles of local self-government—Deming's view—his thinking was clear and forceful and here he was an outstanding leader. Judge Learned Hand paid him this tribute (at the memorial ceremonies after Brandeis' death):

"Indeed, his determination to preserve the autonomy of the states—though it went along with an unflinching assertion of federal power in matters which he reckoned truly national—amounted almost to an obsession. Haphazard as they might be in origin, and even devoid of much present significance, the states were the only breakwater against the ever pounding surf which threatened to submerge the individual and destroy the only kind of society in which personality could survive." [2]

His fine Lincoln-like head and his clear speech remains with me. The sculptured head in the lobby of the United States Supreme Court is his best likeness.

II

In July, 1910, the issues in the garment industry were fairly clear. In 1945 they were still the most disturbing issues in industry. Let me summarize the situation in July, 1910:

There were grievances, real grievances, on the part of the working people. Not at all manufacturers were Max Meyers, Max Schwarczes, Moses Silbermans or Louis Rosenfelds. There were men in the industry who exploited labor much as they themselves had been exploited when they worked on the bench. The reaction to these abuses on the part of the workers was a natural one.

As we said, on the East Side of New York the effort to build up a labor organization followed the pattern of the *Socialist* labor union movement. The Jewish Daily "Forward" was published in Yiddish. It was inspired by Abraham Cahan. Benjamin Schlesinger, one of the officers of the union, was on the "Forward's" editorial staff. It was quite normal that the labor union ideology of that day should be built upon the Marxian Socialistic philosophy. Some of its manifestations would be called *Communistic* today. The Socialistic ideology was indeed the only strategy these labor union leaders then knew. It was not in accord with the philosophy of Samuel Gompers or of the American Federation of Labor. A few of them were clearly anarchists, but only a few. By 1945, much of it became the program of the Labor Party in England and of the liberals in the United States.

However noble their purpose, the technique of the labor leaders in the garment industry in 1910 was simply to *beat the bosses and get control of the workers,*—not necessarily for the purpose of immediate conversion of all industry to the Communist state, but because the leaders believed if they could control the jobs, they could get and hold a labor organization together. On the other hand, unless they could get such a control, however noble their aims, they could not achieve them.

There was nothing extraordinary in either the methods or the program of the Political Action Committee of 1944. Sidney Hillman secured his training as a political leader in the years he spent organizing the men's garment industry, first in Chicago and later throughout the country, and he merely applied his education to the political field. "Clear it with Sidney" showed his great power.*

To secure power, the strike was the only weapon known to these leaders in 1910. By July of that year, however, they had agreed upon the grand strategy of abandoning the *shop strike* shop by shop and went in for a *general strike* of the whole industry. Moreover, by adopting the accepted tactics of warfare, they would attack by surprise and in strength. From the start, the public relations aspect of the warfare was better handled by the union than by the employers. The union had a good public relations expert in Benjamin Schlesinger, trained on the "Forward." He told the newspapers the story of the poor working girl and the sweat shop—he told it well and often. It was good propaganda technique. The lessons in publicity he taught the unions have never been lost to his successors.

III

The employers wanted peace and freedom to manage their shops. On this point they could not yield. They hoped they could find some way of securing such freedom of management as industry required. Wisely or unwisely, the leaders of the Association adopted this strategy.

They took the position that they would discuss freely and endeavor to adjust every grievance. They would do what their members collectively could do as an organization to raise the working standards of the industry. They would accept entire responsibility for the employers' end of the industry, but there was one condition. The "closed shop" demanded by the union *must be waived*. Of course, the "Forward" was obdurate. So was the union. The strike went on. Each side stood out for "unconditional surrender."

This was the status of the situation when Louis D. Brandeis was

* This was the phrase attributed to President Roosevelt at the Democratic Convention in 1944 and indicates the high peak of Hillman's political power.

brought in that hot day in July, 1910. We sat out on the grounds up there in Westchester, Max Meyer, Louis D. Brandeis and I.

We did not discuss the general situation. But it was clearly in our minds. Brandeis began by handing me a letter addressed to the Manufacturers Association, signed by the principal officers of the union. It contained a list of grievances which it was proposed would furnish the basis for a conference between both sides and Brandeis hoped we could arrange to bring about such a conference. When I examined the list, I found the *closed shop omitted*. Moreover, it contained no express waiver of the demand—a point of insistence on the part of the Association up to that time. I explained to Brandeis that in the existing state of affairs, I could not advise the Manufacturers to go into a conference such as he suggested, *without an express waiver* on the part of the union of this demand. He told me that he had sat up all the previous night with the union leaders; that he had convinced them that they should yield on this point and that he had their assurance that it would no longer be pressed.

I do not doubt that he thought me then a very obstinate person, but I knew the union leaders better than he did. He said that it was hopeless; that he could do no more.

After a good deal of discussion, I finally said that if *he* would write me a letter, over his own signature, stating definitely that it was his understanding that the issue of the closed shop was waived, I would advise my clients to proceed.

He gave me such a letter. It said:

"* * * All of these officers understand fully that under this proposal the closed shop is not a subject which can be discussed at the conference."

The Association approved. It approved also of my joining with Meyer London, then the lawyer for the union, in asking Brandeis to preside over the conference.

In that very hot July, we sat on two sides of a table in the Metropolitan Life Building day after day in earnest effort to arrive at an agreement, Brandeis presiding.

By his conciliatory tactics, Brandeis aided greatly. We reached a point where everything on the agenda seemed to be cleared satisfactorily. Then, Meyer London, counsel for the union, and John B. Lennon, secretary of the American Federation of Labor, said, in substance:

"Having happily agreed on adjustment of all grievances, there is left only the matter of the methods to be employed for enforcing the agreement." And then both of them asked for the closed shop! They argued that it was the only satisfactory machinery by which the union could be assured of the carrying out of the pledges already agreed upon. I immediately protested. Brandeis then and there sustained my protest. The conference broke up. All of our work seemed to have been in vain. The war was on again. I believed when Brandeis gave me his letter that he was authorized to do so by the leaders of the Union and their counsel. To go back on their word seemed to me then and still does today, as a reversion to the law of the jungle and not what we had the right to expect. I did not realize then that I should have regarded this as evidence of one of the weaknesses in the whole situation—*the lack of adequate respect for the pledged word.*

IV

Since all real grievances were settled in that conference, leaving only the issue of the demand for a monopolistic control of employment in the industry by the union, my partner, Theodore B. Richter and I promptly prepared papers in an injunction suit against the union.

We attached the printed record of the Brandeis conference and secured without delay from Supreme Court Justice John W. Goff, a decision holding that the demand of the union was unlawful. He granted us the injunction. I know of no other injunction of the kind issued before or since. But, of course, it is rare to find a case where the basic issue is so completely disclosed as it was here—*all grievances adjusted, leaving only the demand for the closed shop.*

Let me pause here to observe that this occurred in 1910. In 1945 the same issues came up in various industries. Then, instead of the demand being treated as illegal, under the strategy of the Wagner Act, monopoly of control of workers by a union was actually encouraged and the rights of minorities limited. But union strategy was still the same as in 1910–1915—*to get the workers into a big union and control them.*

After we secured the Goff injunction, Brandeis tried again. It was then that he came forward with the suggestion of the *preferential union shop.*

The preferential union shop was defined by Brandeis. I made a draft and he added a revision. The whole of it is to be found in my letter to Meyer London of August 1st, 1910, from which I quote:

"The manufacturers cannot, of course, surrender the control and management of their factories to the Union. In agreeing to this declaration, the Union indicates that it assents. The manufacturers cannot coerce anyone into joining the Union; to this the Union assents. The manufacturers cannot supervise the Union's business. The Union does not ask that they should. But the manufacturers can let it be known that they are in sympathy with the Union, and that as between a union man and a non-union man of equal ability to do the job, they will employ the Union man. They cannot ask each man seeking a job to show his Union card, nor agree to collect the Union dues. On the other hand, they can and will (if this declaration be accepted) announce to all of their employees that they believe in the Union and that all who desire its benefits should share in its burdens.

In signing this declaration, the union does not seek the 'closed shop' as it is understood by the manufacturers. They seek the 'union shop' by which they mean, a shop where the majority of the men employed are union men, and where the employer is known to be in sympathy with the union. It is not intended that the employer shall not be free to pick and choose his workers. But it is intended that if in bad faith, he discriminates against union men or fails honestly to give preference to union men, then he is not conducting a 'union shop.' It is done *experimentally*, for it has never been tried in this or any other industry."

"* * * but the manufacturers can and will declare in appropriate terms their sympathy with the union, their desire to aid and strengthen the union, and their agreement that as between union men and non-union men of equal ability to do the job, they will employ the union men."

Brandeis' argument for the "preferential union" shop was that it was in the interest of the employers as well as the workers that there be created and maintained with their help, a strong union. That by its adoption it would become possible for the union to preserve the general peace in the industry; that it would help to maintain the standards of the good shops and, at the same time, bring the poorer ones into line. To me it seemed, in substance, nothing more nor less than the "closed shop" and that it would be so construed and practiced by the labor union leaders. The union always understood later that the preferential union shop meant actually the closed shop.[3]

I suggested to Brandeis and to the Executive Committee of the Association that Brandeis present his idea to the Executive Committee and that I would oppose it. This was done. It was a lawyer's argument before a lay tribunal.

I can testify that Brandeis presented the case, as he could, most persuasively. His arguments had great force. He won my clients over.

For me, the test was, how would it work out? Brandeis believed it would work out satisfactorily. I believed it would not. The experiment was tried for five years. The "preferential shop" *did* build up the Union. The power *was* created. There is no doubt about that. If there is a great International Ladies Garment Workers Union today, it is due to Brandeis and to those employers who adopted and actually carried out his plan of the "preferential union shop." It was the one thing that the Union needed upon which to build up its organization and acquire its great power.

V

By the "preferential union shop," Brandeis contributed more to the upbuilding of the International Ladies Garment Workers Union than all the combined efforts of London, Hillquit, Schlesinger and the others. He brought the manufacturers to the union's side as helpers in building up their union. If, however, the Brandeis plan, as we saw it in 1910, turned out to mean a real basis for peace and collaboration on the part of the union with the manufacturers and did result in the maintenance of a "no strike policy," it was worth the price. Upon such a basis, the industry could be built up.

Not very long after the signatures were put to the Protocol,* we ran into the realistic phases of the situation. The disease was the "runaway strike." It came then in the form of the "shop strike." Over and over again the employers called upon the leaders of the International to enforce the "no strike" pledge. The union leaders were unable to perform. It turned out that the International officers were without real power to stop "shop strikes." The leaders down the line were the ones in actual control.

We had precisely the replica of this situation during World War II. The men who control the votes control the destiny of the union. They are the Frank Hagues, the Ed Flynns and the Ed Kellys of the labor unions. This matter of "jobs" gives the clue to an understanding of the problem. One belongs to a political organization to get a job. One belongs to a union to get a job. If one owes his job to the union and the union can hold him in his job, he is no longer dependent on the employer. When that situation develops discipline in the shop tends to break down. When this happened in the cloak and suit industry, it actually resulted in bankruptcy for many of the employers. For five years we tried to build, but our foundations were of shifting sand. Ultimately, the "Big Four," led by Max Meyer, were thrown out of power and a "reactionary group" came in. This group called themselves *realists*. From their point of view the "Big Four" as well as the lawyer hired by the Association, were destroying the industry for the sake of a social experiment! (Neither the "Big Four," nor their lawyer, I am now convinced, adequately appreciated the part gangsterdom was then playing in undermining what we were trying to do. We knew then that Arnold Rothstein was a power. We were aware that the Union had "entertainment committees" and did use strong-armed men. But none of us knew at that time that the eggs of "Murder, Inc." were being hatched right there in that industry. You can understand

* See Chapter 19.

why there were members of the Association who with more realistic knowledge of the underground situation came to the belief that "fire should be fought with fire.")

They became thoroughly dissatisfied with the lawyer, who from their angle, was merely using their industry as a sociological experiment and failed to protect them. They secured control of the Executive Committee and the break came in 1915.

In a few short years, the "fighting fire with fire" policy was tried out. It actually resulted in a judicial condemnation of the employers for contract breaking—in a suit brought by the union.[4] The industry lost completely the public esteem the "Big Four" had built up for it over five years. Some employers learned from this experience. Younger men came to join in wiser leadership. Older men reversed themselves.

VI

During the five year period while the Protocol was in operation, I appeared before the Board of Arbitration on many occasions on behalf of the employers. Brandeis was head of the Board. First, London was my adversary, then Hillquit. (Hillquit was one of the first members of the Board of Arbitration, the nominee of the union.) This Board, it was contemplated, would be a sort of United States Supreme Court for the industry. Like that Court, it was intended to be judicial, deciding *each case on principle*. But here, as I see it, is where we were destined to be disappointed. Obviously, a court that compromises and does not decide, is not a court. There is no assurance to either side that it will get justice. Appeasement is good where the function is *mediation,* but any continuing board of arbitration fails of its purpose if it does not come to real grips with the fundamental principles involved in controversy. Besides, its power is weakened by loss of confidence in it.

As a long-time advocate of arbitration in both the commercial and labor fields, I share the view that conciliation is a highly valuable diplomatic weapon, but if one substitutes for violence and "runaway strikes" a system of *arbitration,* there can be no order in industry unless there are governing principles and *decisions* by a tribunal. Here strengthening of the union will not do the job. *The union as well as the employers must be subject to some control against abuse of power.*[5]

There can be no doubt that Brandeis believed in building a strong union. He was convinced that the employers should carry the onus of lifting up the industry. I am satisfied that at no time did he appreciate adequately what the employers were up against. He did not know then of "Murder, Inc." I must be forgiven if I record my disappointment with the Board of Arbitration. I expected the theory of the United States Supreme Court to be applied in industry. Perhaps in 1910–1915 I expected too much. But I did lead my clients to believe in the expectation.

VII

Brandeis had *convictions*—strong ones. I should like to bring out the difference between him and Dr. Felix Adler on another point. (They married two sisters—the Goldmark girls.)

Louis D. Brandeis was a Zionist. Dr. Felix Adler was not. In the field of Zionism, I prefer the views of Dr. Adler.

I should like here to tell why I do.

Recently, the daughters of Dr. Kaufmann Kohler, Rose and Lillie, presented me with copies of their father's books. I think the views of Dr. Kohler should be revived. I quote from his address on Zionism before the Judeans in 1898:

> "No. We repudiate the idea that Judea is the home of the Jew, which un-homes the Jew all over the wide earth. We shall remain citizens of America, on American soil; of France, on French soil, and of Germany, on German soil, and while fighting for our rights and our liberty, we fight for the cause of the larger justice and larger humanity. This is our duty, and it is anything but brave to shirk it, even if it be at times annoying and difficult." [6]

The son of a rabbi, Dr. Adler, agreed with this great rabbi, Dr. Kohler—one of the greatest leaders the American synagogue has ever seen.

Rabbi Isaac M. Wise, the leader of reformed Judaism in America, rejected Palestine in 1871 as the answer to the persecution of Jews in Central and Eastern Europe and in 1897 he referred to the leaders of Zionism as "the false Messiahs." He was of the opinion that a Jewish state was "foreign to the spirit of the Modern Jew of this land." [7]

I believe those are the views of many Americans of Jewish birth—both inside and outside of the synagogue.

Over forty-seven years ago—to be exact, 1898—Rabbi Kaufmann Kohler analyzed with the clarity of a great seer this whole Zionistic ideology. Here are his words:

> "The fact is that the Jewish spirit never was bound to the soil of Judea. Universality is essential to the making of the Jew. The best parts of the Bible from the Decalogue to the Psalms and the Prophets were written outside of Palestine. The highest philosophy of the Jew points to Greek and Arabian culture. Judaism is cosmopolitan. Under the influence of other civilizations and in contact with other nations, it grew broad and world-embracing; in the narrow confines of Judea it became narrow and exclusive, and so did the Jew." [8]

Had the zealous advocates of Palestine as a national state for the Jews listened to Kaufmann Kohler and Felix Adler, they might have saved the world from some of the tragedies of 1944 in the Orient.

The conflict between the Moslem and the Christian world is probably the most difficult of all the international political problems still to be solved. It calls for the highest kind of statesmanship. If Christian, Arab or Jew be intransigent, the problem will not be solved. Insistence of either upon exclusive rights is perilous. This insistence upon Palestine as a Jewish national state, is, I believe, due to a false Jewish ideology. Dr. Kohler and Dr. Adler had a better point of view.

Another rabbi, formerly of Temple Emanu-El, who has now been in Palestine for twenty-two years, Dr. Judah Leib Magnes [9] said that "it is clear that Palestine will not be constituted as either an Arab state or a Jewish state" and encouragingly believes that in a conciliatory spirit, Arabs, Jews and Christians can be brought together. He quotes an Egyptian Arab for the following:

> "The wheel of history has now come to a full turn, and the new civilization of which mankind is in such desperate need can find its beginnings here again. Two of us together, Arabs and Jews, can do it. We need each other. * * * Together we can develop this important part of the world for the benefit of mankind * * * Have we not leaders of large enough outlook and enough courage to face this task?"

And Magnes adds that "this question is indeed the basic question." But Magnes and some American rabbis do not yet see eye to eye.[10] On February 24, 1945 a letter was written to The New York Times signed by Rabbi Stephen S. Wise, Judith G. Epstein, Rabbi Leon Gellman, David Wertheim and Israel Goldstein. The writers of this letter think that Dr. Magnes' position "is characterized by the mark of appeasement and not by the quality of justice." Their position rests upon the ground that morally the Arabs have nothing to say about the rights of the Jews in Palestine. The contrary view that the Arabs do have something to say with regard to the future of Palestine is not, I think, an attitude of "appeasement." It is an attitude of tolerance for other people's rights. The insistence by the Zionists of exclusive or paramount rights to Palestine comes to clash with the Arabs' claims. Can we expect that the British or the United States will decide against the Arabs and in favor of the Jews? This is the kind of situation which requires recognition of the rights of *two* parties, not one.*

* This chapter was written before the publication of the Anglo-American-Palestine Commission report (May 1, 1946). I found nothing in this report to change the views herein expressed. On the contrary I found much to confirm the danger then clearly visible on the horizon. This report should be carefully read by every interested person, though at this writing, the Zionists and the Arabs are still

Brandeis was the American leader of the Zionist movement. His support is still cited as proof of the soundness of the Jewish Palestine leadership.*

VIII

"The Protocol of Peace, though historically premature, introduced a new and lasting conception of self-government in industry." [11]

Brandeis must be given much of the credit for this result. But would the industry have gone down as it did in 1915–1920 if the Board of Arbitration had followed the principle of deciding cases firmly and clearly? Well, the Council of Conciliation did decide firmly, yet the industry did go down. Was it the *cult of force* that pulled it down? Who is bold enough to say with finality that the constructive labor leadership would have come earlier if the Board of Arbitration under Brandeis had been firmer and more rigorous? For many years we shall be discussing whether Chamberlain's policy in dealing with Germany was good strategy for the British. Was the United States' attitude in dealing with Japan before Pearl Harbor good strategy? In the same fashion there will be many debates and differences of opinion on policy in the garment industry. Was it wise for the Board of Arbitration to placate the union in 1910–1915? I believe it was not. But others will disagree with me, I am sure. And as the lawyer for the employers, I shall of course be subject to the charge of *bias*. But I can give testimony and record the attitude of the employers, not omitting to indicate what were real errors on their part.

* But compare recent "Information Bulletin" of the American Council for Judaism, February, 1946, quoting speeches by Chaim Weizman and others challenging Brandeis' leadership.

CHAPTER EIGHTEEN

Toil away and set the stone
That shall stand when you are gone.
Ask not that another see
The meaning of your masonry.

      * * * *

Grind the gem and dig the well.
For what? For whom? I cannot tell.
The stone may mark a boundary line,
The well may flow, the gem may shine.

But it wage enough for you
To shape them well and set them true.
Of the future who can tell?
Work, my friend, and so farewell.

             JOHN JAY CHAPMAN.

Morris Hillquit

An American statesman in industry—The right to "hire and fire"—The Mayor's Council of Conciliation and its guiding statement of principles.

I

HERE IS LOUIS WALDMAN'S PICTURE of his friend Morris Hillquit:

"Hillquit was in every gesture, in every turn of phrase, a man of wide culture and a scholar. He was a slim, short man with a face of unusual sensitivity and humor. When he talked, he held his hands one above the other and used them as if he were modeling the contours of his ideas." [1]

He suffered from tuberculosis, but would leave his sickbed to fight, then go back to Saranac to recover strength for the next battle.

When I visualize Marshal Stalin, my memory of Hillquit helps me out. He looked something like Stalin—heavy black mustache and black hair—about the size of Stalin, too.

Hillquit ran for Congress—he ran for other offices, too. Of his defeat Hillquit writes:

"On the night of the election the party headquarters and the sidewalks in front of it were thronged with an eager and expectant crowd. As our watchers returned from the polling places reporting the results of the count, which in most instances showed a comfortable lead over my opponents, cheer after cheer went up and joy was unbounded. By midnight we had unofficial returns from all but two election districts. They gave me a plurality of about 500 votes over my nearest opponent, the Republican candidate Isaac Siegel. The two unreported districts were known to be favorable to us, and victory thus seemed assured. But hour after hour passed, and no returns came from the missing election districts. It became obvious that the count was held up for a purpose. While the two tardy election boards were marking time, the local Republican and Democratic bosses were making a deal. We learned of their conference and sensed danger. We stormed the recalcitrant election officials demanding that they proceed with the count and announce the result. Vain effort. They sat there impassively and cynically, chinning, smoking, spitting, doing anything but counting the vote. When we appealed to the police officers stationed in the polling places, they merely shrugged their shoulders. They were powerless to act. Complaints to a city magistrate produced similarly negative results. The petty ward heelers in the 'bi-partisan' election board calmly waited for orders from their respective bosses, and there seemed to be no authority in the city of New York able or willing to interfere with the flagrant and flaunting lawlessness. No crimes are treated in our republic more indulgently, even humorously, than crimes against the elective franchise.

It was late in the afternoon of the next day that the bargain was closed, the returns properly doctored, and the count completed. It gave me 4,192 votes to 4,542 for my Republican opponent and 3,907 for the Democratic candidate. My plurality of about 500 had turned into a shortage of 350 votes." [2]

Hillquit's defense of the Socialist assemblymen, his defense of Johann Most, the anarchist, which he calls his "first cause célèbre" [3] alone entitle him to be rated as first class. A poor boy, he rose from "shirtmaker" to become a courageous, intrepid lawyer.

I first met Morris Hillquit when he was named to the Board of Arbitration by the union under the Protocol of Peace, in the Garment Industry in 1910. Louis Brandeis and Hamilton Holt served as the appointees of both sides. When we came together later as lawyers *vis-à-vis* —into close relationship such as one lawyer has with another where there is continuous representation of interests sometimes conflicting but most often common in aim and purpose—I came to admire him.

In 1914, when Meyer London resigned in disgust over *L'Affaire Hourwich,** Hillquit succeeded him as counsel for the Ladies Garment Workers. But though they both swam in the same sea, Hillquit and London were as different as swordfish is from striped bass.

Hillquit genuinely believed in Socialism. However, in his "Loose Leaves from A Busy Life," Hillquit in recording his "Tilt with Samuel Gompers" sets forth his beliefs:

"The main weakness of American Socialism and American trade-unionism lies in their failure of mutual cooperation. The same condition prevailed in England up to the beginning of the present century with the same result.

I am inclined to believe that recent economic and political development in

* This story is told in Chapter 20.

the United States [he was writing as of 1933–1934] tend to break down the self-imposed barriers between the two movements and that eventually, perhaps shortly, they will reach the same degree of mutual understanding that characterizes the relations of their fellow workers on the other side of the ocean.

When that day comes the Socialist movement of America will attain to the same degree of political strength as the Labor Party in England, and the trade-union movement will infinitely gain in effectiveness." [4]

Dr. Adler came to know Hillquit in the garment situation—saw him in action appearing as the advocate for the union, and met him in close and intimate conference.

Dr. Adler always studied individuals and searched for the unique qualities in every personality. He greatly admired Hillquit, though Adler was one of the foremost critics of Socialism of his day. He believed its *raison d'être,* if it had any, rested in seeking only the material welfare of the individual. Dr. Adler felt, as religious leaders before and since have felt, that "man cannot live by bread alone." To which, of course, the Socialist would reply, "But without bread, he cannot live at all."

Hillquit believed that the welfare of the masses of men was more important than the welfare of the few. He believed that the existing wide gap between the comforts and luxuries of the few and the hardships of the many should not only be bridged, but should be completely eliminated. Dr. Adler agreed that the gap should be bridged, but did not accept the view that all divergencies could or should be eliminated. The theory of equalitarianism was in conflict with his fundamental conviction that the *individual* has a contribution to make all his own. Hence, with all its ugly excrescences—from his point of view—our economic system did provide for initiative and enterprise. That, he believed, was valuable *provided* it were guided always by moral objectives and restraints.

Just because Hillquit was neither fanatical nor bigoted in his Socialism, I think, on balance, he was able to secure more lasting and enduring results for his clients—the labor unions.

He had a realistic sense of what was obtainable.

He wrote in his "Loose Leaves from a Busy Life" concerning the Protocol:

"The most backward and disorganized industry in America adopted a more advanced and enlightened code of labor relations in the form of a collective agreement, styled Perpetual Protocol of Peace.

The Protocol became famous in American labor history * * *

Provisions were made against oppressive treatment of workers and their arbitrary discharge from employment. All grievances and complaints between employers and workers were to be adjusted on their merits by a voluntary industrial court established for that purpose. Strikes and lockouts were outlawed.

The agreement was not limited to a specified time, but was to run perpetually. Any changes or revisions of its terms necessitated by altered conditions were to be made within the framework of the instrument itself." [5]

This is a fine and succinct statement of the purpose of the Protocol. My only qualification to his statement is in the use of the word "perpetual." This word was not used. Since the agreement had no definite term it was a relationship "at will." It could be terminated at will, that is, any time either party should choose to serve notice of termination it was free to do so. But a relationship which provided machinery for revision could, we believe, last for a long time, even though either party could withdraw at any moment. The hope of the framers of the Protocol was that it would last for more than the five years it did last.

And though it died in 1915, it did rise to live again. After it was denounced, the same mutuality of interests which existed in 1915 brought the parties back again to the same kind of collaboration and the same kind of arbitral machinery.

The governing law of industrial relations, Hillquit believed, was not the commercial law he practiced on behalf of his business clients. It was law *still in the making*—new law born out of the industrial needs of the time. *Industrial law*. Hillquit regarded it as a matter of principle that just as capital employed in industry is employed all the year round and payment for the service is a charge upon the industry, so workers who devote their lives to the industry *should be employed all the year round*. Since the garment industry was a seasonal industry, this was not yet a realizable objective. Hence in the intervening period, according to Hillquit, the worker should be protected in his job, and not have to fend for himself for three or four months in the year, idle or looking around for other work.

In 1910–1915, there was in fact little thinking on the part of employer-leaders about unemployment insurance. Few employers thought then of organizing industry on an *all year-round employment basis*.[6] However, Brandeis continually urged us to find work for the non-seasonal periods of the industry. He directed our attention to what his client, the Dennison Company, was doing in Massachusetts. Dennison's "made work" was created to take up the slack period. This was Brandeis' constructive mind working.

Hillquit argued that the worker had a tenure in his job almost if not permanent. The worker had enlisted "for the duration" of the plant. There was no such thing as an unrestricted "right to fire."

From the business point of view the employer required freedom of discipline in the shop. This was the basis of the conflict in the hiring and firing issue. We finally compromised for a time on a "right of reorganization of the shop" at a definite point in each year. At this time, it was recognized by the union that employers should be free to reduce at will and to select their employees as they chose. But the compromise did not work. Instead "shop strikes" became more and more frequent. Long discussions of issues of fact, charges of bad faith and continuous controversy before the Grievance Board followed.

The union was unable to control the "shop strike"—as union leaders even during World War II—in spite of pledges given to the President—were unable to control "runaway strikes." The part of the bargain clear and explicit in the Protocol, the one thing favorable to the employers, was the obligation of the union to prevent all strikes. This commitment was not fulfilled by the union. It seems to be quite clear that in those days the union could not deliver the goods. On the other hand, the result was that the employers cooperated in building a strong union and yet did not secure the very peace essential to the economic progress of the industry. Thus what the employers expected and what led them in 1910 to yield to Brandeis' plea for the "Preferential Union Shop" was not realized. *They did not get what they bargained for.*

II

There was in the Cloak and Suit Manufacturers Association three other leaders besides the "Big Four"—William Fischman, Reuben Sadowsky and Joseph H. Cohen. These leaders were the backbone of "Talmud Torah" on the East Side, the religious schools for Jewish boys and girls; Beth Israel Hospital and similar philanthropies. William Fischman became one of the serious casualties of the industry. He lost his business because he could not run it under the conditions of 1915. These men worked in close cooperation with the "Big Four." In the last analysis, however, their charitable impulses led them to bring pressure to bear almost always for peace. Hence they carried out a policy of appeasement. They, too, believed in carrying umbrellas. They did play a great part in bringing about settlements in the industry.

The issue of the right "to hire and fire" came to a head in 1915, before the Board of Arbitration, then consisting of Louis D. Brandeis, Chairman, Hamilton Holt and William O. Thompson. The Board's decision proved to be highly unsatisfactory to the employers. It brought about a change in administration of the Association. Max Meyer and his colleagues were supplanted by a new "Steering Committee." The "ins" were out and the "outs" were in. The new group had none of the breadth of outlook of their predecessors.

The garment industry in Cleveland, Ohio, was a competitor of New

York. It ran "open shop." E. J. Wile, president of the New York organization, was influenced by the Cleveland group. Those who put Wile in his post as president were convinced that the manufacturers could not live with the union at all under its leadership. They had come to the conviction that conditions were so unbearable that between the devil and the deep blue sea they might as well plunge into the deep blue sea. They decided it was time to tear up the Protocol and fight the union.

This being the mood of the times, they secured majority control of the Executive Board. Following the decision of the Brandeis Board of Arbitration, *the Board officially decided to terminate the Protocol.* The union at once replied by declaring a general strike. The employers locked out all members of the union.

The battle was grave. I have somewhere in the garret, De Cesare's cartoon in the New York Evening "Post" of that day. It is really too grim to hang anywhere. It pictures Death with outstretched arms—one arm over a lowering employer and the other over a starving mother and her babe. Over the employer appears the single word "Bankruptcy" and over the mother and child appears the word "Starvation." Underneath is a broken key, with the word "Protocol." It was a sad but nevertheless true picture of the stark conditions of the industry, after five or six weeks of combined strike and lockout.

Came the time, however, when the employers, under the pressure of the "charity group" thought the war should cease. They were ready now for appeasement. The Board authorized me to see Hillquit. He and I met at the Bar Association at Forty-Fourth Street and devised a plan. Hillquit and I agreed that the union should send a letter to the Association to which the Association would reply favorably, requesting the creation of another tribunal to be appointed by the then Mayor of New York City, John Purroy Mitchel. We agreed upon the text of the letters to be exchanged and the form of the announcement to be made by the Mayor. It was part of our understanding that the appointees by Mayor Mitchel should be *persona grata* to both the union and the manufacturers. We submitted names to each other and the personnel was agreed upon by both Hillquit's clients and mine even before the Mayor issued his call.

On the 28th of June, 1915, the union officially wrote the Association referring to the fact that "the instruments through which our grievances have been settled and our mutual relations have been regulated for the past five years have been destroyed" and now the industry faces "the grave question as to what is to take their place."

"* * * The situation, as we view it, admits of but one answer. Either the employers and workers will get together on a fair and reasonable working agreement for at least the near future, or our industry will find itself involved in an embittered labor struggle, which may spell ruin for many manufacturers, and suffering and privation for tens of thousands of workers and many more thousands of persons, directly or indirectly dependent upon our industry.

The workers fully realize their share of responsibility for such a public calamity, and are ready to make every reasonable effort to avert it. But the responsibility rests upon the manufacturers as fully as upon the workers."

The union then proposed:

"In order to secure a complete and speedy adjustment of all disputes and to avoid any prolonged and fruitless discussions and negotiations * * * our respective contentions be forthwith submitted to a Committee or Board of unbiased persons under the presidency of Mr. Louis D. Brandeis, or Mayor Mitchel, or any other person of recognized standing in the community."

To which the manufacturers replied:

"We are willing to go before a Council of Conciliation, to be made up of disinterested and neutral parties, and to lay our case before them, with the understanding that arbitrable questions may be left to a Board of Arbitration, to be subsequently formed, if necessary."

III

Mayor Mitchel named as members to the Council: the leader of the Society for Ethical Culture, Dr. Felix Adler; a former Judge of the United States Circuit Court of Appeals, Harold G. Noyes; the former Dean of the Columbia Law School, George W. Kirchwey; the City Chamberlain, Henry Bruere; the former head of the Board of Arbitration, Louis D. Brandeis; and the Chairman of the Committee on Arbitration of the Chamber of Commerce of the State of New York, Charles L. Bernheimer. Hillquit and I agreed that Dr. Felix Adler should be chosen as Chairman.

Of course, I could tell my clients everything in executive session and Hillquit could do the same with his clients. But if it had been known to the garment workers generally at that time that Hillquit and I had collaborated so closely, they might have been suspicious even of Hillquit, though he was, indeed, serving them both loyally and efficiently. Some legend had to be invented for home consumption and Benjamin Schlesinger told the story that he personally had persuaded his friend John Purroy Mitchel to make the move. The legend still persists. Now that Hillquit and Schlesinger are both dead, no harm will come if I tell the true story.

The Chairman, Dr. Adler, in opening the public session said:

"We are here on the part of the City representing the community, to tender our friendly offices with a view to industrial peace. And * * * with a view to industrial progress."

After several weeks' hearing and deliberation here is what the council recommended: 7

"* * * the principle of industrial efficiency and that of respect for the essential human rights of the workers should always be applied jointly, priority being assigned to neither. Industrial efficiency may not be sacrificed to the interests of the workers, for how can it be to their interest to destroy the business on which they depend for a living; nor may efficiency be declared paramount to the human rights of the workers, for how in the long run can the industrial efficiency of a country be maintained if the human values of its workers are diminished or destroyed. The delicate adjustment required to reconcile the two principles named must be made. Peace and progress depend upon complete loyalty in the effort to reconcile them."

The Council laid out a definite application of rights and obligations in the relationship between employers and workers. With reference to the freedom of the employers to make selection of workers, to hire and discharge, the Council said:

"1. Under the present competitive system, the principle of industrial efficiency requires that the employer shall be free and unhampered in the performance of the administrative functions which belong to him, and this must be taken to include:
  a) That he is entirely free to select his employees at his discretion.
  b) That he is free to discharge the incompetent, the insubordinate, the inefficient, those unsuited to the shop or those unfaithful to their obligations.
  c) That he is free in good faith to reorganize his shop whenever in his judgment, the conditions of business should make it necessary for him to do so.
  d) That he is free to assign work requiring a superior or special kind of skill to those employees who possess the requisite skill.

With regard to the equal distribution of work and the "right to the job," the Council declared:

  e) That while it is the dictate of common sense, as well as common humanity, in the slack season to distribute work as far as possible equally among wage earners of the same level and character of skill, this practice cannot be held to imply the right to a permanent tenure of employment, either in a given shop or even in the industry as a whole. A clear distinction must be drawn between an ideal aim and a present right."

Thus, Dr. Adler and his colleages worked out an adjustment between ultimate objectives and what was immediately practicable. It was "ladder-like" statesmanship making the ascent, rung by rung. It was the technique of Al Smith in yielding for the time being the "Smith Housing Bank," but continuing to press forward to the ultimate end. Here in these sentences is to be found fruit of the sagacity and idealism for which Dr. Adler was noted. And his colleagues were men who, by reason of their broad experience, could see things in the same light. Since that time, the same principle has been applied by the War Labor Board. In effect, the Council's recommendation reversed the Board of Arbitration—or "modified the decree," as we lawyers say.

The same questions arose during World War II. On May 16, 1944, the War Labor Board decided to punish forty-one former employees employed by the Norge Machine Productions Division of the Borg-Warner Corporation, Muskegon, Michigan. The labor members of the War Labor Board dissenting, the decision came from the public and industrial members. The basis for the decision was precisely the reasoning of the Adler Commission.

Dr. George Taylor,[8] then Chairman of the War Labor Board, condemned the union for its "utter and irresponsible disregard" of its contractual obligations, declared that the decision was a recognition of management's right to discipline employees for cause under the contract *as necessary for the efficient operation of its business."* Dr. Taylor said further that the responsibility for disciplining employees must rest with the management, adding that, "it is the right of the union to see to it that the disciplining of its members is for cause. The union sought to reverse these functions in the present case when it demanded the discharge of an employee fundamentally because of his high rate of production but in successive grievances protesting the employee's rate of production, absenteeism and breaking his machine."

The assumption of such a role by the union, Dr. Taylor said, showed a lack of understanding of the grievance procedure. It was significant, he added, that the forty-one employees themselves "acted to break down the grievance procedure, which could have been invoked in their behalf when they struck in order to prevent the union demand for the discharge of one employee to be handled in an orderly way which would protect his rights."

Finally, in a summary of his conclusions, Dr. Taylor said that:

"* * * management's right to discipline employees for cause is necessary for the efficient operation of its business * * * When the employees in this case struck in violation of the agreement they subjected themselves to discipline by management, * * * to say that management has no right to impose discipline in such a case would impose an insuperable obstacle in the way of management's performance of its essential function."

This is precisely the position which the Adler Council took in principle and precisely the position taken by the employers both before the Council and prior thereto before the Board of Arbitration. Thirty years have not changed the principle nor the essential elements of the problem.

IV

The Adler Council made its recommendations public. The union promptly accepted them. Hillquit saw to that. My job was not so easy. Clearly the employers had won a victory. The reactionary successors of the "Big Four" were not yet in complete control of the Association, but they were well under way toward securing it. Encouraged by the "open shop" manufacturers in other sections of the country, especially their Cleveland competitors, the "New Four" were convinced that they could reject the recommendations of the Adler Council and *break up the Union*. They were willing to risk even public disapproval. They were angered and outraged by the performance of Hourwich and other union leaders, and they felt the public would never understand the situation as they did. While they did not quite take "the public be damned" attitude of some other contemporary business leaders, they did feel that they should fight it out in their own way. Dr. Adler presented the recommendations of the Council to the Executive Committee at a meeting at the Bar Association Building. In the Executive Session which followed, I tried to make it clear that the declaration on the "hiring and firing" issue was a great triumph for the employers. But I am afraid the members were more concerned then with what the union would do with the ruling than with what was said in the recommendations by the Council. There was a prolonged debate and finally the Adler Council won. The recommendations were approved. But there is another story that makes a part of the history of that day. It deals with a "Gentleman's Agreement."

In those hot days of July, in the City Hall before the Adler Council of Conciliation, one of those questions that seemed to be without answer came up. The union had set down as one of its claims, a demand that all piece prices fixed during the truce should be readjusted. The industry was on a "piece price basis." This was a kind of oriental haggling over the price to be paid for each operation on each model. It was one of the great technical difficulties in the industry. The Shop Committee and the employer usually met and when they agreed upon the "piece prices," that became the "labor cost" for the garment for the season.

On such agreements both workers and employers relied. The latter fixed his selling price to his customer on the basis of this cost of labor. The union claimed that in a considerable number of factories, during the period of truce, the "Piece Price Committees" had been put under pressure by the employers and had to submit to their terms. The employers denied that this was the fact. Moreover, they said that once such a reopening of prices was encouraged, it would result in a complete revision throughout the industry and this would ruin the entire season.

This presented a real dilemma. There were hours of discussion before the Adler Council. Finally, Henry Bruere, president of the Bowery Savings Bank, one of the members of the Council, came down from the dais and brought Hillquit and me into a huddle. "You two fellows ought to settle this 'off the record.' Why don't you agree, you, Hillquit, to sift these complaints, pick out only the ones you think have real merit and pass them on to Cohen. And you, Cohen, agree that your clients will take them up and where there has been any 'chiseling,' have them correct it. That's in their own interest, anyway," he said.

This plan Hillquit and I thought had sense to it. Of course, it meant Hillquit had to trust me and my clients. If he withdrew this claim from the Council's consideration, he would be in a position like that of a lawyer who withdraws his rights in an important claim upon the basis of a gentleman's agreement with his adversary that it will be "settled off the record."

We submitted the proposal to the leaders on both sides. It was accepted. Then Hillquit and I drew up a letter which later I was to sign and deliver to him when, as, and if the Council's recommendations were accepted by both sides. This letter was submitted by me to the Committee of the employers. *They approved of it.*

But immediately following the adoption of the resolution of approval of the Adler Council's recommendations, Wile and his associates offered and secured approval of a resolution *forbidding me to give Hillquit the very letter I was under obligation to give him!*

I could not believe these men knew what they were doing. At that moment, technically, they had the power to represent all the members of the Association, but they were not in fact representing them if they did anything like that. I believed an appeal over their heads to the membership at large would have resulted in a reversal of this resolution. At a time when the business end of the industry needed every ounce of public esteem it could muster in its favor in the fight against abuses of union power, to make a record of *business men breaking an agreement*—a "gentleman's agreement," it is true,—but an agreement upon which others had relied and had changed their position, seemed to me to verge on insanity.

At that moment, I was through. My portfolio was gone. I was no longer sure of a "vote of confidence." I could not continue as their lawyer. Wisely or unwisely, I chose to wait awhile, to treat the situation as a mood which could be changed later upon more sober reflection—a temporary obsession not to be cured by immediate head-on collision. I was angry, but I believed the situation called for coolness and patience. It was critical. I am now convinced that the move was part of a deliberate plan to get rid of the lawyer of whom they were very tired. And later they told me that they wanted "a lawyer who would do what we wanted him to do and not one who is always telling us what we should do."

A few days after the public announcement of the employers' acceptance of the Adler Council's recommendations and when the rejoicing of the union and the public had died down, Hillquit called me on the telephone and politely reminded me that I had not sent over the letter. I told him what had happened. (We lawyers keep faith with each other.) He was shocked.

"Morris, if you insist upon the letter, I'll have to resign." "That must not happen," said he. "But I've told my people that the letter was as good as though it were in my pocket." I then said, "The agreement was made. That is the simple fact. The letter is merely *evidence* of the agreement. You have the right to rely upon the *fact* of the agreement." "But I have not even a copy of the draft of the letter." "That can be corrected. You were entitled to it at the time. You shall have it now."

The madness persisted. The Manufacturers Association chose their course. And I chose mine. I got out. They substituted another lawyer. Ultimately, their policy resulted in the first decision ever rendered by a court, denouncing an employers' association for breaking a contract with a union. Under Hillquit's guidance, the union sued the manufacturers and won. The court below was affirmed by the Appellate Division.[9]

V

The hard work done by Dr. Felix Adler and his associates should have produced a constructive result. It did not, at least not for this industry —for a long time to come. On the 26th of April, 1916, Dr. Adler, on behalf of the Council, reported to Mayor Mitchel that "after twenty-three sessions in the hot month of July" and after getting both parties to consent that the agreement arrived at through the recommendations of the Council should last for two years, he (Dr. Adler) "had the mortification of finding that one side refused to abide by the decision"[10] of the Council. This side was the manufacturers!

For a while, as in a recurring quarrel between husband and wife, the Union and the Association did get along—after a fashion. But by January 5th, 1919, bedlam broke loose again. Governor Alfred E. Smith was brought in this time to put out the fire. He appointed another Commission, consisting of representatives of the Union and the Association and representatives of the public. The members were Edward Boyle, Chairman, Charles W. Berry, Adjutant General of the State of New York, Hugh Frayne, General Organizer of the American Federation of Labor, Frances Perkins, later United States Secretary of Labor, Israel Feinberg, Chairman of the Cloakmakers Union, William D. Baldwin, Chairman of the Otis Elevator Company, Saul Singer [11] of the Employers Association and Belle L. Moskowitz.

The Governor's Commission, all concurring, said:

> "A collective bargaining agreement calls for the utmost good faith on both sides to perform, both in letter and spirit, every term and condition thereof, whether it refers to shop strikes on the part of the worker, lockouts on the part of the employers, or the maintenance of its terms as to wages and hours. This board desires to emphasize this point as fundamental in any contractual relationship, and has endeavored to hold the existing contract inviolate in any adjustment it has made of the present difficulty." [12]

Conditions going from bad to worse, in January, 1922, the union brought the suit against the Association to which I have referred. The Special Term Judge, Robert Wagner (later United States Senator from New York) said it was novel "in the respect that for the first time an employees' organization is seeking to restrain their employers' organization from breaking contractual obligation." [13]

The court, after hearing both parties, granted an injunction and required the Association to desist from further violations of its contract with the union. An appeal was taken by the employers to the Appellate Division and that court affirmed the court below saying:

> "Without attempting in good faith to seek a solution of the disputed questions or to remedy the defect, before the time for the commission to report had expired, the Association definitely repudiated the agreement and took effective means to impose its will upon the industry." [14]

The record in the case is replete with evidence of breaches by the union of its contract to preserve peace in the industry. Case after case is cited of failure to respond to the call of the Employers Association to send employees who had gone out on shop strikes back to work. Apparently the court did not find it necessary to deal with this phase of the matter. It put the main blame on the employers.* So did Dr. Adler.

* The lawyers for the union were Morris Hillquit and Samuel Untermyer and for the Association, William Klein, Max D. Steuer and Charles H. Tuttle.

The employers were thus condemned by the public and by the courts *for breaking their agreement!* The "fighting fire with fire" policy turned out to be disastrous. The group who had succeeded the "Big Four" had had their way. Five years of hard work by Max Meyer and his colleagues to build up public good will for the industry had gone up in smoke. The Protocol institutions were dead. Max Meyer and his associates were through.

That is how it seemed then. But "death, where is thy sting?" Out of the grave came victory.

Today, a "Labor Lawyer," Louis Waldman, writes:

"The protocol was, in fact, a remarkable instrument and went beyond the usual economic conditions in most labor agreements. As a means of eradicating the sweatshops a joint board was set up, composed of representatives of employers, workers and the public, with elaborate machinery for periodical inspection of factories and lofts and the abatement of unsanitary conditions. The protocol also made provision against harsh treatment of workers and their summary dismissal from employment." [15]

And in another volume, "Labor in Twentieth Century America," writing of the "Needle Trades," Joel Seidman sums up the experience in this way—a quarter of a century later (1941):

"Though the protocols did not bring permanent peace to the trades that experimented with them, they did lay a solid foundation for unionism and collective bargaining. Under the protocols a substandard, badly sweated industry was raised to fairly decent standards, with the workers rising from serfdom to industrial citizenship. The public was given an insight into the complexities and problems of the industry. Employers and workers alike were left with a clearer realization of their common interests as well as their differences." [16]

VI

Now that we can look with more tolerance upon a Jewish shirtmaker from Riga who rose to leadership at the Bar, we can give him his proper place in the history of his time.

No two lawyers ever differed as much in antecedents, associations or in professional practice as Morris Hillquit and Horace E. Deming. Hillquit was from Riga—Deming was a Yankee from Connecticut. Yet both had the same qualities of soul. They differed in their social and economic outlook and in their backgrounds. Both, however, were *lawyers,* deserving the highest honors of their profession. Neither was ever nominated for nor elected to high office in any Bar Association. No million dollar fees for either—not in any one case nor in many.

CHAPTER NINETEEN

Nulla falsa doctrina est quae non permisceat aliquid veritatis.

There is no false doctrine but mixes up with itself some element of truth.

Meyer London

The epic of a blazing trail-maker—An orator and a poet—The gangster influence in New York—The philosophy of the cult of force.

I

MUSYA PINKENSON was the twelve-year-old son of a noted gynecologist of Kishinev in Russia. A beloved boy who played the violin and thrilled his audience with his rendition of folk tunes. When the Germans seized the family, the father opened his medical kit and took out his needle to jab into his wife and the child so that they might at least pass out of life quietly and painlessly. The mother stopped him and said, "No, darling, you must not do it. Let them do their worst, but you cannot be the murderer of your own family." The doctor put away his needle.

The family did not have to wait long. The Germans came. The father begged them to spare the boy. "My wife and I have already lived our lives—our son is so young and talented."

The Germans were obdurate. Musya turned to the German officer and said, "I have a request to make of you, Mein Herr." "What is it?" "I want to play my violin once more before I die."

The Germans gave a grudging consent. The boy opened his case, took out his violin, tuned it up and placed it under his chin. He lifted the bow and started to play the Russian National Anthem! Enraged, the German officer gave the order "Fire." Musya fell dead on top of his violin.

Maurice Hindus,[1] who reports these events, saw in the City Museum of Krasnodar, capital of the Kuban Cossacks, on the wall dedicated to war heroes, a painting of twelve-year-old Musya Pinkenson playing the violin in the last moments of his life. The boy loved music. He probably knew Strauss' "Till Eulenspiegel," and like Till, he thumbed his nose at his executioner. Grim humor—the humor of a race called "stiff-necked."

Understanding this kind of Russian, I can now understand Meyer London. When I first met him—a small-sized man who wore thick glasses—he had already achieved fame as a great orator. Like Hillquit, he was a lawyer; like Hillquit he was a Socialist. His practice was among the poor. When later he went to Congress, he made a fine record. His oratory had the fire of poetry.

II

Among the immigrants who came over here and found a start in the needle industry were groups who had participated in the Russian revolutionary movement against Czarism. A goodly number were actually members of the Bund—the Jewish group in Russia, allied with the Russian Socialist-Democratic movement. To these men organizations such as the American Federation of Labor or the British labor unions in which collective bargaining was the clearly accepted technique was not satisfactory.

Trade-unionists of the latter type accepted the capitalistic system. Leaders like Gompers frankly dealt with employers on the basis that the employers would continue at the management end. But to the Bundists from Russia, their union, as Seidman puts it, "was a sacred institution." [2]

A call to a union meeting for them took on the same form and was couched in the same language as "the terms of proclamations exhorting the Russian masses to rise against the tyranny of the Czar" [3] and they saw their own pictures as those of "revolutionary heroes who had risked their lives in the struggle against Czardom." [4]

One can appreciate then why typically conservative American trade-unionists could not understand Cahan, the "Forward," or Meyer London. I could not understand them either. And yet London and I could and did find common ground for working together. When, after *L'Affaire Hourwich,** London resigned in disgust as the lawyer for the Union, he was merely playing once more the role of a rebel. This time he revolted, as matter of principle, against those who swung too far to the left. It is easy to see, as I do now, why there were these conflicting forces at work in the Union—one group ready and willing to work even with "a lawyer for capitalists" and another hating the

---

* Hourwich, I believe, left the country and went back to Russia to join the Revolutionary forces.

lawyer and his clients in the bargain. Those who favored collaboration were regarded as traitors to a sacred cause!

III

But something else was going on those days on the East Side of New York. The same East Side that brought out Al Smith and Felix Frankfurter and all the workers in the settlements, developed also a wholly different group. The operations of this group did not fully come to light in 1910–1915.

Eighteen years after these episodes, the full story of what was going on behind the scenes was told. I quote from Seidman:

> "Union leaders and clothing manufacturers went to Mayor James J. Walker and Police Commissioner Edward P. Mulrooney of New York City in the latter part of June, 1931, to ask police protection in their fight against the rackets, which had part of the industry terrorized and intimidated. At these conferences 'The representatives of the union and manufacturers told Mr. Mulrooney of the operations of a gang of racketeers in the clothing industry who have sought to exact tribute both from the union and the employers by injecting themselves into recent disputes in the industry. While demanding money from some individual manufacturers not affiliated with the employers' organizations as protection against the demands of the union for the enforcement of union standards, the gangsters also have sought to extort money from the union as a condition of their non-interference in the disputes and have tried to compel the union to employ them as pickets at non-union shops.' " [5]

It was the manufacturers of men's clothing and the "Amalgamated" —Hillman's union, who joined forces at this time to wipe out this evil. Shortly before, in hearings conducted by Samuel Seabury into the administration of the criminal law under Tammany, it was shown that millinery manufacturers had actually sought and welcomed the aid of underworld characters like Arnold Rothstein, Jacob "Little Augie" Orgen and "Tough Jake" Kurzman. The following excerpt from Judge Seabury's report gives you the picture:

> "In July, 1927, Isidor Fogel, President of the Chelsea Hat Company, was advised that his employes would not be permitted to report for work unless they became unionized. Shortly after receiving this ultimatum, Fogel was visited by one 'Little Augie,' a notorious character in the underworld, who already knew of Fogel's difficulty and suggested that unionization could be avoided on the payment of $2,000 from Fogel to 'Little Augie.' Such payment was agreed upon and made, but before the $2,000 was paid in full 'Little Augie' was shot and killed. In the meantime Fogel was not obliged to unionize his shop. After 'Little Augie' had been killed, Jacob Kurzman, also known as 'Tough Jake,' called on Fogel for the purpose of selling to him the same kind of service that Fogel had received from 'Little Augie.' * * * An arrangement was made whereby 'Tough Jake' was to receive $100 a month, in return for which the Chelsea Hat Company was to continue to be free from interference by the Union. This arrangement was carried out.

In addition to assisting the Chelsea Hat Company, 'Tough Jake' also succeeded 'Little Augie' as protector of the Belleclaire Hat Company and Furst & Maltzman, Inc. He prevented the unionization of the shop of the latter Company by assaulting one Schorr who sought to accomplish this purpose. For the services rendered by 'Tough Jake' in the millinery trade, he received payments aggregating more than $10,000 yearly." [6]

This report showed that the District Attorney had collected similar evidence in twenty-six industries including both men's and women's clothing. The growth of the racketeering movement in these and other industries in New York and the partnership between this movement and the District Attorney's office, to one who had gone through the Devery-Asa Bird Gardiner era in the early nineties, seemed to follow almost the same pattern. And when Thomas E. Dewey became District Attorney of New York and succeeded in securing the conviction of Lepke, at least this writer was reminded of incidents in the careers of Charles S. Whitman and William Travers Jerome.

The gangster, Arnold Rothstein, was the son of a Jewish philanthropist who was associated in charitable work with the three philanthropists in the Cloak Association—William Fischman, Reuben Sadowsky and Joseph H. Cohen. When the industry reached a crisis, in their own way, these philanthropist-manufacturers would go to Arnold Rothstein's father and the old man would intervene.

But in 1910–1915, while one group in the Association was trying to build up, another was tearing down. Gangsters were used by both sides. Business men justified their use. It was really *war*—and war involving actual physical violence—the law of the jungle. It now appears clear that there was no escape until once more a really clean administration of the District Attorney's office could be brought into action.

The Union's wiser leaders awoke finally to the importance of getting from under this destructive yoke. Now if Hillquit or London knew of this evil, they never told me anything about it. And if they knew of it, they must have accepted it as all part of the war. Today, we can understand why in 1915 the "Big Four" were displaced and their policies put in reverse gear by so-called "realists" in the industry. Union leaders must now see it too. During 1910–1915 gangsterism thrived on the leadership of both union leaders and employers and grew more dangerous year by year. Thereafter, both sides succumbed to the influence which undoubtedly ruled the industry.

Roscoe Pound recently analyzed the thinking back of this kind of leadership. He refers to "the confident self-styled advanced thinkers of today" which produced as "the immediate actual result * * * a cult of force."

"A favorite phrase of the realist is 'the brute facts'; a phrase used not in sadness that there should be such facts, but with a certain relish, as if brutality were the test of reality and the discovery of brute facts argued superior intelligence and discernment. In practice this makes force a test in significance. The significant things in the world are force and the satisfaction of material wants."[7]

My experience, not only in this but in other fields, convinces me that Pound is completely right in this diagnosis. It has been the *cult of force* that has dragged us down. In the early days when we were framing the Protocol and trying to make it work, this philosophy of the *cult of force* was shared by many of the leaders on both sides. "You must fight fire with fire." It seemed to come with the very air these men breathed.

IV

It is not difficult now to understand how in the early days of 1900–1920 Russian revolutionists accepted almost as a religion and certainly as a matter of patriotism *the overthrow of government as an objective*. They genuinely believed in continuous class warfare and made their ultimate objective the control of industry *by the working class*. It was difficult for them to stop their program of warfare and substitute in its place a program of peace. Yet they were called upon under the Protocol to operate industrial machinery requiring frank cooperation with employers. All this was in clear conflict with their thinking. It is this machinery that London actually strove to create with us and actually did his best in trying to make workable in 1910–1915. If there could be built up a strong union and a strong employers' group, there was a basis for London's belief and mine that progress could be made. Whatever conflicting interests there were, one thing was clear. Employers and workers had common interests—*the upbuilding of the industry*. It is this finding of the common basis of self-interest that furnished the catalyst for the organization of our own federal union. It took more than one hundred and fifty years and a civil war to teach us that however we may differ—the North from the South—or the West from the East—in "union there is strength." It is not true that self-interest always means conflict. If that were so, there could be no partnerships and no corporations. There could be no United States of America. Intelligent leadership must recognize the area of conflict and search for *common* interests, if there is to be any union. (In later chapters, I shall tell the story of two states, New York and New Jersey, each with conflicting interests, which were brought together in collaboration and have now been operating for nearly a quarter of a century upon the basis of their *common interests*.)

But the technique agreed upon for the settlement of disputes in the garment industry was the technique of *arbitration*. Through arbitration, London and I entertained the hope that there could be built up "case by case" *a common law of industry*. The great Holmes often repeated that "the life of the law has not been logic: it has been experience." [8] And that is true. Experience, constant revision of opinion —is the only sound technique. Felix Adler believed that this was true also in the field of ethics. But the difficulty lay in this human factor —the experience that guides the decisions of courts in large matters of public policy is, too often, the experience of the judge or judges who happen to sit in the case.

In large measure, the opinion of the sitting judge often turns upon his own philosophy of life and it is influenced by his own background. Few judges can take the detached attitude of Judge Charles M. Hough who said to me, after accepting our argument in the Rent Cases, that "Those laws went against my grain, Cohen, but I had to sustain their constitutionality." This detachment from self, this freedom from prejudice, this open-mindedness was the great characteristic of Holmes and Cardozo—both of whom were at once *skeptics* and *believers*.

Few men on the bench and fewer still among arbitrators have the temperament or the training to achieve such an ideal approach. Too many of them were like an English judge I once met—they made up their minds beforehand and never afterwards changed them. [9]

There was involved in this industrial experiment important matters of policy—for one thing, how best to preserve the industry. Hence, there was bound to be plenty of room for differences. There arose, quite naturally, conflicts between those who favored "conciliation" and those who favored "arbitration." I pinned my faith on the ultimate triumph of the arbitral process. If the judicial tribunal would but hew straight to the line and let the chips fall where they might, I felt that we should ultimately triumph.

V

When the "starvation-bankruptcy" crisis was reached in the industry in 1910 and when Richter and I procured the injunction from Judge Goff, the Hebrew Charities of New York and the Jewish philanthropists in the Association took steps to bring about peace. At this time Louis Marshall came onto the scene.

There were clear elements for agreements in the "Preferential Union Shop," the "Joint Board of Sanitary Control" and the proposed Board of Arbitration and the Grievance Committees, *if* the Union were but ready to yield upon these points. I believed they would yield.

In the making of the agreement of 1910, the disciplinary powers of each organization were to be used as a "police force" in the industry. The Manufacturers Association would act upon its own membership by discipline to secure observance of the standards agreed upon and the Union would do the like with its own members. As it turned out later, London's job was much harder than mine.

When London and I met at Louis Marshall's office in August of 1910, both sides had practically agreed upon the terms of the settlement. The Union had capitulated—it had accepted Brandeis' "Preferential Union" shop—it had abandoned the closed shop, at least as a claim, and we two lawyers were ready to take the material before us and whip it into a formal document. Of course, if this had been an ordinary situation, either London or I would have submitted to the other a preliminary draft and then out of amendments suggested by both parties the document would have been worked into final shape. But it was in fact a good thing that Louis Marshall was there. He bridged over what seemed to be a real difficulty. On our side, we were giving up a lot, giving in to what was tantamount to a pledge to build up a strong union. The consideration to us was to be two-fold. *Peace— no strikes* during the existence of the agreement. And second, *enforcement of standards throughout the industry.*

I started to dictate: "This Treaty of Peace . . ." I wanted to stress the idea of peace.

"No, no, no," said London, "that will never do." (He knew his "Bundists.") To go back with a "Treaty of Peace" would mean that he had "sold out to the Bosses."

So he dictated: "This Collective Agreement."

That did not satisfy me. I knew my clients liked "collective agreements" as much as London's clients like "treaties of peace."

It was at this juncture that Louis Marshall showed his shrewdness, the shrewdness of an old rabbi. He said, "Let's call it the *Protocol.* No one will know what that word means except you two lawyers." And so we accepted that solution. The word "Protocol" came to have a broader meaning, but at the start it was just a word of mysterious import.

There has been a lot of loose talk about who was the "Father" of the Protocol. Truth is, that in this instance, as in many others in my experience, there were a good many fathers of the child. But there was but one mother and that mother was *necessity.* To such contributions as were made by Brandeis, Marshall, the employers, the labor leaders and the lawyers for both sides, there must be added the contribution of Judge Goff, because if he had not issued the injunction, the Union would not have yielded and the fight would have gone on.

VI

After the signing of this document, London lent every bit of his energy to making the Protocol a success. Ultimately, like the lawyer for the manufacturers, he went down in defeat. The forces in the union who wanted constant "war" were tearing down while he was building up. Finally, when they gained control, he did what later I did in 1915. London resigned as lawyer for his clients. He lost his portfolio. Once more the poet in him rose above the situation. The dream was over. He would have no more of it. He turned to Socialism and went to Congress.

He was genuine, sincere, selfless. He died poor as a churchmouse. But his funeral cortege resembled in many respects the triumph of a general marching home from victory.[10] He was of the stuff of which martyrs are made.

CHAPTER TWENTY

To walk with erect carriage, a step springy and elastic,
To look with calm gaze or with a flashing eye,
To speak with a full and sonorous voice out of a broad chest,
To confront with your personality all the other personalities of
    the earth.

              A Song of Joys, WALT WHITMAN.

John A. Dyche

*A labor leader trained in English Fabian Socialism
becomes a trade-unionist leader in New York—Resistance to the "all or nothing" rebels—A martyr to principle.*

I

JOHN DYCHE CAME HERE FROM ENGLAND. He worked over there with
the Webbs and leaned towards unionism of the Fabian school. He
was more of a zealot in his trade unionism than in his Socialism. Collective bargaining to him meant frank, open cooperation between
unions and employers. That technique had made great headway in
England and Dyche knew of its success. In this country, under Samuel
Gompers' leadership, it was making progress, too. Gompers believed,
as Dyche did, in *such cooperation between employers and the union.*

William Green, Matthew Woll and other American Federation of
Labor leaders hold this belief today. Such leaders are sometimes
called "conservative." They are against radicals. They prefer to develop the strength of the unions not through governmental tutelage,
but by self-development of the unions and their leaders. The present
day trend toward government power over industrial relations does
not appeal to them. It is contrary to their philosophy.

In 1910, Dyche thought the conservative method could be made to
work in the women's wear industry over here. He was not afraid of
anybody or anything. He could shake his fist in the face of a labor
leader as quickly as he could shake it at an employer. But he could
argue, too. He could write as well as he could speak. He could persuade. He had brains and they functioned.

He became the editor of the "Ladies Garment Worker," the official organ of the International. When the Protocol was signed in 1910, Dyche had his own collective bargaining blueprint to work with. No one knew better than he that what was agreed upon meant performance in good faith by both sides. He knew that bad faith on the part of either would in the end be destructive to both.

Unlike Hillquit, Dyche had great physical strength and endurance. He was nearly six feet tall, had handsome, flashing, keen eyes and attractive black hair. He could hold his own in a physical bout and knew no fear. He would walk right into trouble, as General De Gaulle walked into the Church of Notre Dame in Paris in 1944. Robert Reid, who broadcast the scene for the British Broadcasting Company, was eyewitness and gives this account:

> "He walked straight ahead into what appeared to me to be a hail of fire from somewhere inside the cathedral, somewhere from the galleries up near the vaulted roof. But he went straight ahead without hesitation, his shoulders flung back, and walked right down the central aisle, even while the bullets were pouring around him. It was the most extraordinary example of courage I have ever seen." [1]

This incident will give a picture of John Dyche. He walked right into trouble in the union. De Gaulle is a soldier. But so was John Dyche. De Gaulle was trained to risk his life. John Dyche, too, never thought of personal danger. The world goes forward because of the courage of such men—in civil life as well as on the battlefield.

Dyche had none of Hillquit's caution, none of London's poetry and none of Hillquit's or London's charm. He was a born fighter. He died, as I know, a poor man, trying to make a meager living out of some small business.

II

By 1910, the women's wear industry had grown to a point where it was possible to form a national union. The number of establishments more than doubled in ten years. The capital investment grew from $21,000,000 to $48,000,000. The value of the product grew from $68,000,000 to $160,000,000. The numbers of workers grow from 400,000 to 840,000—I am giving round figures.

In 1911, the workers decided to form an international organization to be made up of workers in Canada as well as in the United States. The union was planned as an *industrial* union to be made up of locals —a union of the crafts. The International procured a charter from the American Federation of Labor. In June of 1900, there were seven local unions forming the basis for the *International*. At that time there was a New York "local," two Philadelphia "locals" and a "local" in

Baltimore. From union sources, I have learned that it started with thirty dollars in its treasury. Neither its president nor its secretary were paid a salary. When the union became more prosperous, the general secretary was voted five dollars per week and later his salary was raised to fifteen.

None of these leaders worked for *pay*. Their ambitions were for large treasuries for the union. The spirit of self-sacrifice and devotion to their work by men such as President Abraham Rosenberg and Secretary Dyche was inspiring. They were pathfinders, these men, they were expendable, and they were blazing in their zeal.

The same kind of inspiration is to be found in the life of Samuel Gompers.[2] If these labor leaders made mistakes, if sometimes they used the wrong methods, it should be remembered that the employers, too, made grievous blunders.

From 1900 to 1910, union activity in the garment industry was primarily revolutionary Russian in its character. On the other side activity on the part of the employers was motivated by each individual building up his own business on the basis of the "brutal facts." One had to sell goods in a keenly competitive market. One had to get his labor as best he could and paid labor as he paid for materials—*on the basis of the market*—as little as necessary. Unorganized labor was at a disadvantage. Trade unionism here came into being because in the bargaining process the individual was distinctly at a disadvantage. Hence *collective bargaining*. That meant trade union bargaining with individual employers. Someone has said that collective bargaining means an agreement where the union expects to get a *bargain!* Until the Protocol came in the needle industries, it was a matter of dealing with the union, on the one side, and an individual employer on the other. *Collective bargaining between a union and an association of employers came in with the Protocol.*

Under Abraham Rosenberg's skillful leadership, supported by Joseph Barondess and Abraham Cahan, the General Strike was declared on July 7, 1910. It immediately gave opportunity for the eloquence of Meyer London—for the statesmanship of Morris Hillquit—and for the masterly leadership of both Rosenberg and Dyche.

III

As already indicated, the pledge of *no strikes* made in 1910 with resort instead to the machinery of arbitration, meant that, just as the "Big Four" in the Association had to deal sharply with recalcitrant employers, so at the union end, too, someone had to do the same with the "runaway shop strike."

John Dyche attacked the local leadership of the union under Abraham Bisno and Dr. Isaac Hourwich because they did not play fair. They encouraged strikes. When the joint board of the Locals charged that union leaders were working in cahoots with the capitalist employers, the "New Post," the organ of the Locals, said that "A union which obtains the support of a manufacturers' association has no moral right to exist." [3] This, of course, was tantamount to advocating the destruction of the Protocol and for no agreements at all with the employers. Dyche retorted by writing in his editorials that this was nothing but "ignorance and dogmatism plus demagogy." [4]

In January, 1913, he wrote in "The Ladies Garment Worker":

"We have had occasion more than once to refer to the discontented and irreconcilable element in our organization. Every organization has this element. By their discontent with prevailing conditions they often do a useful service. * * * But at times this element becomes dangerous, particularly when they fall into the hands of damagogues, who in order to maintain their position in the organization, pander to their prejudices, stir up discontent, and magnify it, and try to force the organization to demand from the employer the impossible * * *"

In the same organ, for November, 1912:

"our people were wise enough to accept what we considered to be a suitable compromise * * * after two years the Organization is much stronger and on a more solid footing than it was two years ago. * * * success in the future will largely depend upon our ability to accept a part of what we demand and keep on clamoring for more. * * * the old story of either 'everything or nothing.' * * * We have been told lately that unless the union will get all that is coming to us * * * the union will remain a 'comedy and a fraud' * * * we have pointed out on several occasions the danger of urging * * * what is physically impossible to get. *It has been our weakness in the past to promise our people more than it was possible to get for them.*"

When in January, 1913, Dyche succeeded in forcing Abraham Bisno out and Dr. Isaac A. Hourwich came in as the representative of the local union, Dyche seemed to have won a victory. It was, however, temporary, for very soon Hourwich developed what Dyche called an insane program for harassing the employers. Hourwich believed in constant litigation. This meant constant friction. He was finally stopped by the decision of the Brandeis Board of Arbitration and Dyche's leadership was sustained.

Now it is not practicable to be a stickler for principle and at the same time keep on good terms with those who are opposed to the principle. One cannot shake one's fist in a colleague's face and say, "You can't do that" and still be popular with him. Outsiders may honor a leader who has the courage of his convictions, but if the fellows who control the votes are told; "I don't give a damn for your support," their hostility is aroused and they just do not get the votes. This is, of course, the story of Wendell L. Willkie in 1944. Independence and courage may result in ultimately affecting a complete change in the program of the party—as it did in Willkie's case —but the leader may go down in great honor and glory and depart! One cannot play the role of critic of his party and at the same time expect to hold party favor. The term "renegade" will be heard behind his back. On the same basis of human action and reaction, Dyche many times heard himself called *"traitor to his union."* But he was not—any more than Willkie was traitor to anybody.

The employers and their lawyer saw Dyche as a brave, outstanding fighter who within his own union stood consistently for principle and in so doing, was helping the union. But that was not the way the union leaders down the line looked at him. John Dyche may be forgotten today, but what he stood for in 1914 is now the accepted policy of the union under the present Dubinsky leadership.

When Meyer London resigned as counsel of the joint board in 1913 and the employers called upon the International to remove Hourwich, they made it clear that they would no longer participate in any proceedings under the Protocol as long as Hourwich continued to represent the union. Dyche then openly declared that the International would not continue as the guarantor of the Protocol if Hourwich remained in power.

Although the joint board was ready to oust Hourwich, they promptly moved for a special convention to impeach both Dyche and Rosenberg on the charge that the International had interfered with the local autonomy of the joint board. Samuel Gompers and John Mitchel were called in to help. Both failed. The employers then threatened a general lockout and the union countered with the threat of a general strike. Dyche was put out of his office in the convention of 1914 and Morris Sigman, former leader of the Industrial Workers of the World, was put in his place. He was forced out of the International and saw his life's work turn to ashes. In such descriptions as the union now permits to be written about Dyche—he is rarely referred to—there are very few expressions of gratitude. In a recent book which undertakes to give the history of the union, all one will find in the index is *"Dyche, John, 7, passim."*

IV

By the fall of 1912, the experiment in Protocol collaboration in the cloak and suit industry was so far accepted by both union and employers that it became the basis for organizing the dress and waist industry—a sister industry to "Cloaks and Suits." There were troubles, but in the language of the workers they would iron themselves out. (They would be "ausgebügled.") Collaboration in the Dress and Waist Industry followed closely the lines of the Protocol in the Cloak and Suit Industry.

At this time, Dyche was at the height of his power. Because the cloak and suit employers believed in Dyche's sincerity, he quickly won his way in the dress and waist industry. There he met a younger group of employers. These men were in close touch with Max Meyer and the other members of the "Big Four," hence they knew how things were progressing in "cloaks."

Among the leaders in the dress and waist industry were Samuel Floersheimer, Jacob J. Goldman, Reuben S. Adler, Henry Wolff and Joseph Dallet. Henry Wolff was a neighbor of mine at White Plains and a fellow member of the Fairview Country Club. On the whole, they were more receptive to new ideas than their seniors in "cloaks." They were, in fact, creating and building a new industry. Goldman was making "Betty Wales" dresses for young women. Henry Wolff specialized in dresses for pregnant women. Floersheimer made fine costumes, appealing to the modish women in the higher income brackets.

Let me pause a moment to survey this branch of the industry. By 1920 the dress industry in volume of output had advanced beyond the older cloak and suit industry. In 1929, the product of the silk dress industry was valued at $900,000,000. In 1934 the silk dress industry in the Metropolitan area employed 87,000 workers in 2,810 shops. In 1940 it declined to 82,000 workers and produced merchandise valued at $350,000,000. At this time the cloak and suit industry employed about 40,000 workers and its annual product was valued at $200,000,000.[5]

I found it relatively easy to work for these men as their lawyer. They were highly sensitive to the influence of public opinion. Their workers were mostly women. Moreover, women interested in women workers generally, began in 1913 to play a vital role in trade-union activity.

Among these women were Jane Addams, Mary Simkhovitch, Lillian D. Wald, Gertrude Barnum, Florence Kelly, Frances Perkins, Mary Elizabeth Dreier and Eleanor Roosevelt. They joined forces with the "shirtwaist" union leaders. It was the beginning of the women's trade-union movement. Their work has never been adequately appreciated by the union. In 1913 the general policy of trade-union activity was to use to the fullest extent the assistance of the outside public, to exploit it thoroughly as a means of keeping the public stirred up and then to exalt the union's own efforts, as though the union alone achieved the results. In private, the union officers looked down upon the outside sympathizers and called them "highbrow butters-in."

In the days of Abraham Rosenberg and John Dyche, the union leaders believed the only way—especially in the case of girls—to hold allegiance to the union was through the *strike*. When I complained once to Rosenberg and Dyche that even after employers had joined the association and were entitled to resumption of peaceful conditions, we found a continuance of shop strikes, Rosenberg replied, "We have to make good union members of the girls, so we must keep them out long enough to realize that it is through the union they are getting the results."

Today, this picture is totally different. With such productions as "Pins and Needles" creating new and interesting opportunities for young men and women—affording them recreational and educational facilities as well as larger opportunities for improving their health— there is a wholly different technique for holding the membership. These modern methods for arousing and keeping the interest of the men and women in this union are highly successful, but the method is wholly different from the ones Rosenberg and Dyche knew in 1910–1912.[6] It is difficult for one not familiar with the conditions of those days to visualize the situation as it then existed. It was the painful lessons learned through trial and error that brought about the change.

The outside women did play a great part. These women—and the writer met them all—were fine, social-minded women. I have always felt that Eleanor Roosevelt's interest in working people began about 1912 in New York City right in the needle industry itself. I have sometimes felt, too, that her husband, though he never participated actively, caught some of this social inspiration from her. It is not im- probable either that the loyalty of President and Mrs. Roosevelt to their friend—the former Secretary of Labor—goes back to comradeship in the shirtwaist industry when Eleanor Roosevelt and Frances Per- kins walked shoulder to shoulder on the picket lines.

Floersheimer, Goldman, Wolff and the other leaders in the dress and waist industry were not unsympathetic to the public phases of their industry. On the contrary, they were quite sensitive to them. Moreover, they knew the value of cultivating public good will. The garments they sold were for women to wear. They did not forget this fact.

Schlesinger's public relation work was by 1913 offset by some work

of similar kind done on the employers' side. In 1913, Floersheimer
and his colleagues were receptive to the building up of Protocol conditions and institutions in their industry that would if possible even
surpass those in the cloak and suit industry.

V

Before calling the general strike in the dress and waist industry in
1913, Rosenberg and Dyche proposed a conference of the leaders of
the manufacturers and the leaders of the union. At this conference,
standards of working conditions to prevail throughout the industry
were to be worked out and the cloak and suit Protocol institutions,
the Board of Arbitration, the Board of Grievances and the Joint Board
of Sanitary Control were to be merged with this younger industry.
Before even the dress and waist manufacturers' association was formed,
the conferences began. There was a table in a room on the top floor
of the Fifth Avenue building around which sat a dozen men—six
representing the union and six the employers.

Hillquit was not there. There were times when because of his ill-
ness he could not attend. London was not there. John Dyche was.
"I am the lawyer for the union here," said he.

Though I was the lawyer for the employers, I was asked to preside.
I have never seen a better tempered conference. There was good fun
—a good deal of chaffing back and forth, but always the serious questions were taken up, one by one, carefully considered and agreed
upon. The test seemed to be for both sides, "Is it fair and will it
work?"

In all these situations, the trick is to find the points of agreement,
the points of possible harmony of interest, despite the points of difference. The story I am about to tell you will give some picture of
Dyche and his ready wit as well as describe the spirit of the conferences. He was really a great joker, but his jokes often had the Lincoln-
like earthiness that characterizes also the humor of Dyche's race.

We were deeply engrossed one evening around that table. The
washroom was more than two hundred feet away. My condition as
chairman was becoming more painful every moment, but I could
not leave the chair. It happened that on that particular evening I was
reminded of the existence of the water retention tank in my system
—several times painfully reminded of it. But if you sit in a conference
of that sort and are presiding, you learn that you cannot leave. You
may fail to "weld" together the pieces if you adjourn.

So I was uncomfortably posted in my chair for over an hour while
both sides battled back and forth on a really difficult point. When it

finally seemed that no solution was in sight, I asked John Dyche to take the chair and I left the room and went down the hall to the washroom. On the way back, I thought over the problem I had left at the conference. Whatever the explanation, I came into the room with what I thought was a good answer. By good fortune, it met the views of all the conferees. Both sides seized upon it and were happy to get it over with. It was written out at once and we all leaned back with satisfaction. We had bridged another difficult crossing. Now we could go on to the next. After the solution was written out, John Dyche turned to me and said, "Mr. Chairman, may I ask where you went when you left the room?" I told him. John burst into laughter and said, "Well, we have had all kinds of solutions in the garment industry, but this is the first washroom solution we have ever had."

When we drew up this Protocol for "Dresses and Waists," agreements were easily arrived at upon the standards which were to govern the institutions under which the parties would jointly operate. Adherence to the Schieffelin-Wald-Moskowitz-Price Board of Sanitary Control was readily agreed upon.

VI

One other important step forward was taken. For several years the National Consumers League had carried out a campaign for their National Consumers Label. The label was in the nature of a certificate assuring the public that in the processing of the article to which it was attached, working and sanitary conditions were found to be satisfactory from the consumers' point of view. Jane Addams and Lillian D. Wald were in the forefront in this label movement.

The Consumers League had been working upon the department stores to get it into operation, but without much success. I had thought about the certificates that were already issued by the Joint Board of Sanitary Control and which were hanging up in the showrooms of the manufacturers. Only the buyers for the department stores saw them.

Having been invited to speak at the National Conference of Charities and Corrections in June of 1912, I presented the new idea along the following lines:

I pointed out that the responsibility for the existence of conditions unsafe for the worker is a responsibility which rests upon the entire community. It should be shifted neither to the shoulders of the employers nor the workers. Moreover, I said that before right standards of living for the community could be made possible, the whole basis of purchase by the consumer would have to be changed. Instead of leaving it a matter of how cheaply the garment could be bought and creating constant demands for bargains, I said we should change the process entirely.

At that time even the most scrupulous buyer of a department store had to shut his eyes to the conditions under which the garment was made. His concern was with the matter of price, style and work. The garment could contain germs of disease. It was none of his business.

The consequences were pressure of two kinds—from the consumer for the lowest prices possible—and from union pressure for higher wages and shorter hours. The manufacturer found himself squeezed between two opposing forces.

I then said:

> "The remedy would seem to be at hand if all the parties would agree to it, that is, the employer, the employee and the public. It is this. Whenever complete and regular inspection of an industry is under way by all three parties, as in the cloak industry, and certificates are issued to shops maintaining adequate standards, the chain of evidence should be carried one link farther—the *garment itself* should be certified by the Board, so that the consumer will know what garment is made under 'Protocol' conditions and what is not. An extensive advertising campaign, conducted by both parties, would inevitably educate the public to a realization of its responsibility for the maintenance of sanitary conditions. The responsibility from consumer to producer would be made direct and real and could not be evaded. A label on each garment would furnish the purchaser with unmistakable evidence of its conformance or non-conformance with the standards of living maintained by the best in the industry." [7]

VII

In 1915, Dyche was put out of the union and I retired as counsel for the employers. I believed then that the White Protocol Label was dead. But note what happened afterwards: Between 1915 and 1935 —an intervening period of twenty years—a miracle occurred. Before the National Industrial Recovery Act was declared unconstitutional by the United States Supreme Court in the so-called "Sick Chicken Case" [8] there was developed, under General Hugh S. Johnson's leadership, an organization of the needle industries which adopted *in toto* all the Protocol principles of joint collaboration between the Union and the employers. This time, however, it was put under the aegis of Uncle Sam—all interests working together. Industrial codes were adopted. *Moreover the label came into play as the most important key piece of the whole machinery for enforcing the industrial codes.* It was called "The Blue Eagle." Under Dr. Price's * administration the "White Protocol Label" had had a brief trial run as the "Prosanis Label." The name changed, but the idea remained the same.

* See Chapter 21.

The unions developed great strength in those days. National Recovery codes were based upon high standards of pay and working conditions. Besides, there was real observance of the codes. NRA labels were issued by various Code Authorities. Indeed, the idea was extended to a far larger field than just the needle industries. Each label carried out the principle of certification. It became proof to the ultimate consumer that the provisions of the code had been observed. When the NRA went down—after the United States Supreme Court decision—there was then founded the "National Coat and Suit Industry Board" and in the millinery industry, the "Millinery Stabilization Commission," of which Max Meyer became the head.

Immediately, these two bodies became representative of the consuming public as well as the employers and workers. They called their label a *Consumers Protection Label*. The public benefited from the higher living standards thus achieved. There was developed a new technique with which to promote industrial peace. There developed a functioning democracy in the place of what had been an autocracy.

VIII

The Protocol created no "anarchical-syndicalist" movement. It was a simple recognition by the three factors—the workers, the employers and the public, that they did have a common interest, and that collaboration could in fact bring about beneficial results for all the parties concerned—precisely the philosophy that Morris Hillquit, Max Meyer, Meyer London, John Dyche, Louis Brandeis and this writer believed in from 1910 to 1915. It all went down to defeat in 1915. The lickings we took then, however, were not to be ultimate defeats of principle. *The ideas were valid.* They have been proving their validity for thirty-five years.

In 1940 the dressmakers' union undertook a promotional campaign in which they expected to raise $1,500,000 to popularize the use of the label. The union itself pledged a contribution of $100,000. The sale of the label was to bring in $1,000,000 annually. In 1940 it was "The New York Creation" label. It was to be sewed on each dress and constitute a certificate that the garment was made under the standards agreed to by the union. Out of this cooperation came the movement to make New York City the world's fashion center.

In the cloak and suit industry under the direction of Samuel Klein, the *label* became the instrument used for promoting not only fine relations between employers and the union, but in addition, better relations between the manufacturers and *retailers*. But in 1910–

1915, the greatest obstacle to the use of the White Protocol Label was the intransigent opposition of the retailers.

The National Cloak and Suit Industry Recovery Board, founded in July, 1935, as a purely voluntary organization was described as "virtually a lineal descendant of the former code authority, operating with much of the same personnel." [9] The Recovery Board extended to all markets and issued its *Consumers Protection Label* in place of the former NRA label. The union has its representatives on the Recovery Board. The agreements made every employer become a member of the Board and use the label and *its workers are instructed not to produce garments without the label.*

To call the Protocol experiment in 1910–1915 "almost a perfect anarcho-syndicalist charter" [10] seems to this writer to display ignorance of the meaning of the words *anarchy* and *syndicalist* (the French movement) as well as the word *charter.* Probably, in the breakup in 1915, no one favored more the open-shop and the anti-Protocol movement than one Cleveland manufacturer. He is now the outstanding leader carrying forward of the use of the Consumer Label!

Alexander Printz, head of the Printz-Biederman Company at Cleveland, on August 24, 1935, issued a public statement outlining the gratifying success of the consumer protection label already achieved. He reported that over a million and a half protection labels had already been sold to the manufacturers and were well received by retailers. He said:

> "I believe this is the first time that labor and employers have united to swing their combined influence to remove the destructive influences from industry.
>
> * * * * * *
>
> The industry, in fact, has capitalized upon a consciousness of the need of cooperative organization * * *" [11]

Printz called this a "unique coalition." By 1935 the work of Max Meyer and the other leaders in 1910–1915 was almost completely forgotten.

In 1944, these same manufacturers tendered Samuel Klein, their representative, a dinner and a gold watch in recognition of his work in bringing these things to pass. Moreover—think of it—an old age pension system *run by the union and the employers has been agreed upon!* * It would seem to be clear that though defeated in 1915, the ideas did re-emerge and triumph thirty years later. John Dyche did not live long enough to see that triumph.

* See the even more advanced work done by the dressmakers under the leadership of Julius Hochman, "A Remarkable Union and Its Leader," Eugene Lyons, in the "New Leader," March 16, 1946. [12]

IX

When in 1913 the representatives of the employers and of the union agreed upon the terms of the Protocol, it was understood that a general strike would be called by the union. The independent employers in the industry were given the choice then of signing separate agreements with the union, or joining with the Floersheimer-Goldman Association. Many of them preferred to join the Association and to participate in its work for the industry, including such fields as the relations of the manufacturers with retailers in the establishment of trade regulations and the like. But when two years later, the reactionaries got control of the Cloak and Suit Association and the "Big Four" were thrown out of power, this "revolt" of the employers spread to the Dress and Waist Association. The fight to break up the union and get away from the "closed shop" was joined in by the Dress and Waist Association.

Obviously, there was no place for a lawyer who disagreed with such a program. Having broken with Wile and his colleagues, the reactionary leaders in "Cloaks and Suits," I broke with the leaders in "Dresses and Waists." Meyer London, you will recall, went through a similar experience with his union clients. You cannot do much as a lawyer, if your clients refuse to follow your advice.

Protocol institutions went down in 1915. In 1935, in different form, through the NRA code relationship, not only the label came into its own, but the whole system of arbitration came back. By 1940 there was created a system of broader collaboration between union leaders and manufacturers.

The experiences between 1915 and 1935 were tragic for the cloak and suit and dress industries. Some of the best firms dropped out. Max Schwarcz' firm dissolved. His partner, Arthur Wolf, went into banking. William Fischman lost everything. The story is but one of many. Max Meyer's firm, Beller & Company, went out of business. Max went into banking. But as I told you earlier, he became the leader in a much larger field.

On the other hand, we can say as Stolberg now says:

"The Protocol generated a new conception of industrial relations. It was hailed as something more than ordinary collective bargaining, indeed as a new era in industrial statesmanship." [13]

It broke down, in Stolberg's opinion,

"for as long as the utopian Protocol of eternal peace remained, as long as the workers could not strike and the bosses could not fire, agreements on the basis of actual power relations were impossible—at least at that stage of economic evolution in the country." [14]

In other words, Max Meyer's work, Morris Hillquit's, Meyer London's, John Dyche's, Louis Brandeis' and the authors were at least by two decades premature! But would the events of the last thirty years have come about save for the efforts of all of us and our faith in an idea?

Mill, in his essay "On Liberty," helps us to understand why *conflict* is essential before a principle finds acceptance.

> "Truth, in the great practical concerns of life, is so much a question of the reconciling and combining of opposites, that very few have minds sufficiently capacious and impartial to make the adjustment with an approach to correctness, and it has to be made by the rough process of a struggle between combatants fighting under hostile banners."

Today the needle trades are in the forefront of the American labor movement. They are idealistic and most generous in their contributions to labor causes. There is now found little talk of class-consciousness, class struggle or cooperative commonwealth. The former class enemies, the employers, are now welcome and proposals to stabilize the union and increase sales and profits as well as wages are carefully considered. The unions have their educational and health programs, have an interest in housing and unemployment benefits and have their own banks and credit unions. [15]

Under the title, "Balance Sheet of Protocolism" Stolberg concedes that "the Protocol of Peace was one of the most important charters in American industrial relations. * * * " He points out as one of the reasons for its failure to function then that "it relied on conciliation instead of arbitration." [16]

The present union leadership, both in men and women's wear—Hillman and Dubinsky—never refer to the *gangster* days and the influence of gangsterism upon the industry. They would like this part of the history to be forgotten. Employers do not refer to those days either. They, too, would like them to be forgotten. Yet, after thirty years' experience and reflection I find one clear explanation for the failures in 1910–1915, more fundamental than anything else. That is the false belief in the *cult of force*. On the other hand, it is but fair to say that the leaders in the industry who succumbed to the blandishments of this philosophy as a short-cut method to reform—on *both* sides—were not alone in this weakness. It was the philosophy of the day. It is the tragic and dramatic revelation of the *effect* of this force philosophy on the battlefield which made us in 1940–1945 appreciate the greater value of the slower processes of *reason*. It would seem that only from the tragedies of defeat do we learn our lessons. Is peace still a utopian dream? If it is for the whole world, it must be for industry, too. But madness cannot continue to rule mankind. Reason must prevail.

Dyche died a brokenhearted and defeated man. He may have been "Utopian," but he had company on both sides. The "Big Four" on the employers' side were "Utopians," too. So was London. So was Hillquit.

So far as Dyche is concerned, it can be truly said that but for his work, the union would not be where it is today. If the union had not had a Dyche, it would not now have a Dubinsky.

CHAPTER TWENTY-ONE

Sic itur ad astra.
Such is the way to the stars; to immortality.

Dr. George M. Price

A doctor devotes his life to the improvement of sanitary conditions in a sweatshop industry—A new labor union tactic is evolved.

I

MY FIRST RECOLLECTION of living quarters in New York City were those at 66 South Fifth Avenue. I must have been six or seven years old then. We walked up three or four flights to our floor—I have forgotten just how many. The trains which we saw from our windows were drawn by steam locomotives. The privy was in the backyard. The washstand was in the hall. When I went to the pantsmaker or the vestmaker or the coatmaker on the East Side to deliver bundles from my father's shop, I found living quarters just like ours.

In those days, tailors sat cross-legged on tables and bent over their sewing, became round shouldered and ofttimes developed tuberculosis —all incidents of their occupation. Very few of these homes ever saw sunlight. Homework in the tenement houses was the rule, not the exception, in the eighties and nineties.

The movement for Tenement House Reform began when Dr. Felix Adler, with the assistance of Dr. E. R. A. Seligman, actually built some modern tenements on Cherry Street. Then came the Neighborhood Guild, under Dr. Stanton Coit; the University Settlement and the Educational Alliance on East Broadway. Things in the way of better living quarters on the East Side began looking up just about the time I was graduated from public school Number Ten on Wooster Street (1885). However, out of these tenements came many of the successful doctors, lawyers, actors, educators and civic leaders of New York. Of course, as we now know, came also the gangsters and the corrupt politicians and the vice carried on with the cooperation of the politicians. The first time our family really had a bathroom was when we moved to 13 St. Marks Place—after I went to work at 55 William Street in 1894 and helped out in the family budget from my fifteen dollars a week.

I draw the picture of these days because it will help the reader to know the opportunities I had for observing at first hand the unwholesome conditions of work and life that prevailed in the tenements of New York City in 1910. Jacob A. Riis described them in his book, "How the Other Half Lives":

> "Take the Second Avenue Elevated Railroad at Chatham Square and ride up half a mile through the sweaters' district. Every open window of the big tenements, that stand like a continuous brick wall on both sides of the way, gives you a glimpse of one of these shops as the train speeds by. Men and women bending over their machines, or ironing clothes at the window, half-naked. * * * The road is like a big gangway through an endless work-room where vast multitudes are forever laboring. Morning, noon, or night, it makes no difference; the scene is always the same." [1]

II

The garment strike of 1910 broke out in July. Among the grievances publicized on behalf of the workers was this very matter of unwholesome working conditions. I needed no proof to convince me of their existence. As most of the employers, too, came from the same kind of living quarters, they needed no proof either. But this material made fine publicity for the Union; Ben Schlesinger took care of all that. It stirred the sympathies of the general public. When, however, we met in the Metropolitan Life Building and took up the agenda of grievances outlined by the Union with Louis Brandeis sitting as Chairman, on our side we waited for some constructive suggestion from the Union. The Union was strong on criticism, but weak on constructive programs. It offered precisely nothing. The responsibility for taking the lead passed to the employers.

With Max Meyer's support, I had won approval for the proposal I presented on the employers' behalf. Simply stated, it was this: The acceptance in principle of *joint responsibility* for the unsanitary and unsafe conditions in the industry, and the development of a method of joint collaboration by the employers and the Union to remove them.

Let there be a Joint Board of Sanitary Control, we proposed, made up of two representatives to be named by the Union, two by the employers and three representing the public, the latter to be chosen by both employers and Union. Let there be a joint survey of the conditions in the Industry, and the creation and establishment of standards —thereafter rigorous enforcement of those standards by *both* parties, to the full extent of their powers—the Union enforcing compliance upon its members, the Association doing the same with its members. All expenses to be paid equally by both sides.

Of course, on our side, we were not unmindful of the importance of doing something constructive in line with the social reform movements in which men like Max Meyer were active in the Ethical Culture movement. Besides, the better concerns in the Industry were already operating their shops in large loft buildings. The "Big Four," for example, knew that most of them could easily comply with the new standards that might be set up. By our plan, the ones lower down in the scale would be obliged to move into better quarters.

The Protocol was definitely not a partnership between capital and labor. It was based in principle upon the simple recognition that both sides had common responsibilities, in their very nature social responsibilities. This was recognized from the very first in the acceptance of the plan for the Joint Board of Sanitary Control. Responsibility *to the public* was one of the fundamental bases for the program. Both sides readily agreed upon the representatives of the public to be named for this Board. William Jay Schieffelin, head of the Citizens Union, Lillian D. Wald of the Nurses' Settlement and Dr. Henry Moskowitz were the appointees.

When it came time to set up the Board, Dr. Schieffelin was made Chairman, and Dr. Moskowitz was made Secretary. Anyone who knew Dr. Schieffelin would know that, like MacGregor, where he sat was always the head of the table. He was the Executive Head of the Citizens Union after R. Fulton Cutting retired. In 1944 he was made Chairman Emeritus of the Citizens Union. We who worked with him know him as a courageous, lovable, public-spirited citizen. Lillian D. Wald's fame in 1910 already had been established by her work on the East Side. Dr. Moskowitz was an assistant leader under Dr. Felix Adler. The employers selected Max Meyer and Ernest J. Wile as their first representatives. The Union selected Dr. George M. Price and Meyer London.

There was no difficulty in getting down to work. From the very start, Dr. Price became the active director. Presently, he resigned as Union representative on the Board and became the Administrative Head of the Institution. A valid idea became a living thing under his capable hands. In those days, we usually organized at a dinner. Dr. Schieffelin knew how to do things of that sort. He lived on 66th Street, off Fifth Avenue. One of those great, handsomely furnished homes of people of real wealth. It made no difference to my friend, Dr. Schieffelin, that he came from a line of aristocrats and that he had married into the

Vanderbilt family. He remained simple. I don't suppose he ever thought of the humor of the situation I am about to describe, but it was quite as good as going to a movie, to have observed us walking up the grand marble staircase to the dining room and seen the butlers in full livery waiting on us at the table. Of course, this was nothing new to Lillian Wald—the intimate friend of the Schiffs and the Warburgs —but there was Henry Moskowitz, an East Side boy, and two or three out and out socialists, representing the Union.

Schieffelin was a good host, still is—full of fun—and he put us all at ease quickly. But looking out of the corner of my eye, I watched the effect on those Socialists. They were good sports, too. One would have supposed they dined formally this way every night in the week. Schieffelin profited much by these contacts with labor union leaders. He came to have great admiration for the work done by organized labor in the garment industries. In the election campaign in 1944 when these labor leaders were attacked, though he was a Republican he announced that he would vote for Franklin D. Roosevelt as a protest against attacks which he regarded as "unsportsmanlike, but also un-American." [2] The Joint Board of Sanitary Control got started at the Schieffelin's gorgeous dinner table.

III

From the very start, the Joint Board was a success. The man who made it a *go* was George M. Price, M.D. He gave up his private practice to devote himself entirely to this job. The point I want to make, is that the Doctor found in this work the supreme satisfaction of his life.

For those who worshipped wealth and power in the gay period from 1910 to 1940, it may be difficult to understand why Dr. Banting spent his life in research and then gave *insulin* to the world with no monetary return to himself, or why Dr. Fleming did the same thing with *penicillin*. But it has been my good fortune to have met many such personalities working unselfishly in public service. Such men and women get their great satisfaction in doing this kind of work. Their joy is greatest when they are able to do it effectively. Most of them could earn much greater financial reward in private service, but they prefer this service for the public. They are in Washington, they are in New York, they are all over in government service. They are in England and they are in Russia. Without such men—competent scientists, engineers—World War II would never have been won by the Allies. Yet, most of them do their work without public recognition. Usually the honors go to the big chiefs who sit in revolving chairs.

In "Life" of October 23, 1944, there is on the cover a bearded bald head, with keen eyes, fine nose. A Soviêt scientist—Alexei Frylov, mechanical engineer. His contributions cover the field of mathematics, naval architecture, in addition to the magnetic and gyro-compass. He had translated Newton's "Principia Mathematica" into Russian. In the same issue can be seen an explorer, several physicists, chemists, geo-chemists, the builder of the first cyclotron to smash the uranium atom, an astronomer, plant biologists, a physiologist, a geologist, a parasitologist, a metallurgist—all faces that make one think of Humboldt, Pasteur and Curie—besides, a few suggestive of great rabbis. Some remind one of Walt Whitman, with his careless, roving beard. These are the men in the service of Russia who developed her great natural resources, gave their best scientific ingenuity to her agricultural problems; made synthetic rubber and found solutions for insect and animal toxins. Most any one of them would be welcomed by the Rockefeller Institute or du Pont or General Motors. They are men of the same type as Dr. George M. Price. His portrait belongs with theirs.

Under Dr. Price's direction, all the cellar shops in the Industry were promptly eliminated. The sanitary conditions of all the others, too, were brought to standards higher even than those required by the city's Health Department. I told in the chapter on John Dyche about the certificates which the Board issued, after inspection of the shops that conformed to the standards of the Joint Board of Sanitary Control.

The Triangle Fire on March 25, 1911, shocked the entire community. It revealed inadequate protection against factory fires. Al Smith then started the Factory Commission and the Factory Laws followed. But even before that tragedy, Dr. Price had made a thorough inspection of the Cloak and Suit Industry, working out adequate regulations to meet all the needs of safety. He was then far in advance of the law on the subject. He helped to shape the new legislation as an adviser to the State Factory Commission.

IV

What kind of man was this Doctor? A Socialist, to be sure, but no *Socialist politician*. He kept away from labor-union politics, internal or external. His thinking apparatus worked at such rapid pace that his speech lagged behind his thoughts. My wife and I and Dr. and Mrs. Price came to be close friends. Later, when the plan for the White-Protocol Label was projected, he got behind it. He believed in it wholeheartedly. He afterwards developed it as the *Prosanis Label*—as a trial flight.

The Doctor died in 1942—much too young. He burned himself up. I saw very little of him after 1917. Like the Red Cross, the Board kept up its work, war or no war. Strikes might come, strikes might go, bitter feelings might develop between the Union and the Association, but the Board of Sanitary Control just kept on going.

Lillian D. Wald, in her "House on Henry Street," said:

> "Since those days [strike of 1910] cloaks are no longer made in New York tenement houses, and the once unhappy, sweated workers, united with other garment-makers, have been lifted into eminence because of the unusual character of their organization."
>
> * * * * * *
>
> "High sanitary standards and a living wage, with reasonable hours of employment, were assured so long as both parties submitted to the terms of the protocol. Whatever changes in the administration of the trade agreement may be made, the protocol has established certain principles invaluable for the present and for future negotiations. The world seemed to have moved since we shuddered over the long hours and the germ-exposed garments in the tenements." [3]

In 1915 Dr. Sigmund S. Goldwater was the Commissioner of Hospitals of New York. In that year, when the Protocol was terminated, he referred to the effectiveness of the work of the Board of Sanitary Control and said:

> "* * * the program of the Joint Board is today the official program of the Department of Health for the sanitary regulation of industry generally. * * * discontinuance of that body is a grave loss to the public health movement." [4]

V

Dr. Price was responsible for the creation of other projects, including the Union Health Center now occupying two floors in a large building in the middle of the garment center. There always is in attendance a visiting nurse service. There is also an organized system of general education in health for the garment workers. For the first time in industry, I believe, there was established a system of medical examination as a prerequisite for membership in a Union. That was Dr. Price's idea. Inevitably it led to reduction in the diseases of the industry—tuberculosis, arthritis, diabetes and nervous ailments. Under his leadership, the Union established a hospital in the country for its members. Its health and vacation program is the result of cooperative agreement between the Dressmakers Union and the four employer associations in the industry applied to 80,000 dressmakers in New York City. Employers contribute 3½% of their payrolls and the annual yield is estimated at $4,000,000. Julius Hochman, general manager of the Dress Joint Board, says:

> "The health fund, as a joint employer-union enterprise, is an integral part of our system of industrial cooperation. It is testimony to our joint concern for the

health and welfare of the workers who are the backbone and foundation of our industry. It is part of our joint program of building our industry, protecting our standards and equipping our market to meet the new developments that will confront us after the war." 5

The widespread effect of Dr. Price's work went beyond the scope of the industry. Undoubtedly, the development of recreational facilities by the Union came in logical sequence from the development of this new kind of Union activity. The vacation spot of the Union workers is a large estate in the Pocono Mountains. The Union leaders boast of it as the largest vacation center in the country—a private lake and every kind of sport, fine musical programs, dramatic and movie entertainment. In short, Dr. Price put Union organization on a higher level of service to its members. To keep up the payment of membership dues, it no longer is necessary to call costly general strikes. Instead, by bringing the members' interest and talents into play, a new Union *esprit de corps* was developed. The member develops a real affection for the organization. Dr. Price aroused this kind of interest. He found his life's work in this new kind of socialized medicine. *He showed the Union the way to be great in this field of service.*

CHAPTER TWENTY-TWO

The reason firm, the temperate will,
Endurance, foresight, strength, and skill.
She Was a Phantom of Delight. WORDSWORTH.

Belle Lindner Moskowitz

A woman blazes trails—Al Smith's close adviser—She meets labor union leaders and hard-boiled employers— The first public relations counsel for the Port of New York Authority.

I

BELLE MOSKOWITZ WAS A BEAUTIFUL WOMAN with great talent. She belonged to the group of women who possessed both brains and charm. Such women have always played great parts in political history. She played several roles in my time.

She married twice. Her first husband was Charles H. Israels. I came to know him in the work of Dr. Peters and the Independent Club of the West Side. He was the nephew of Josef Israels, the great painter. That is how Belle's son comes by the name of Josef Israels II. Charles and Belle had two other children, Carlos—a successful lawyer today, and Miriam, who married an Englishman and now lives abroad. We visited the Israels family first when they lived on the Upper West Side and later when they moved to Park Hill in Yonkers. Conversation always was of high order—a combination always of dreams tempered with reality. After Charles' death, Belle married Dr. Henry Moskowitz, who was one of Dr. Felix Adler's protégés. An East Side boy (I refer to him in the earlier chapters dealing with the Needle Industry), Belle met him when she worked with him at the Educational Alliance on East Broadway. The Alliance brought educational and recreational opportunities to the boys and girls of the East Side.

Belle Moskowitz's activities came to public notice when her name appeared in the newspapers as the leader of the movement to clean up the dance halls of New York City. From then on, she was to be found in the company of Lillian D. Wald, Florence Kelly, Frances Perkins,

Mary Elizabeth Dreier and other leaders of that day. From its very
start she was one of the active personalities in the Women's City Club.
In 1909, she became Chairman of the "Committee on Amusements and
Vacation Resources of Working Groups." The investigation by her
Committee showed that there were more than one hundred dancing
academies in New York City with a usual attendance of 150,000 to
200,000 persons weekly, mostly young men and women. The conditions
of the buildings and rooms in which the academies were conducted
were frequently unsanitary and unsafe and the sale of liquor on the
dancing academy floor became a serious menace, leading to the down-
fall of many otherwise decent girls.

Under Belle Moskowitz's direction, there was presented to the Legislature in 1910, a bill which that year became law. It prohibited the
sale of intoxicants in the hall or in any adjoining room immediately
connected therewith and provided further for the regular inspection
of such places to make sure that they were conducted under whole-
some conditions. The bill went through both Houses, without a roll
call, which meant it was practically unanimous. Its passage was due
entirely to Belle Moskowitz's work.

II

Immediately after the signing of the Protocol in the Dress and Waist
Industry in 1913, it became necessary to organize within the Association a department for the reception and correction of such grievances
as the members of the Union might assert against the employers. Most
of the workers in the industry were girls. Women wore the product of
the industry. It seemed to the younger men in the industry that the
post called for a woman of intelligence and tact, moreover, one who
had the confidence of the public, especially of women.

Mrs. Moskowitz was the best qualified person for the job. The leaders among the employers all thought so. I persuaded her to take the
post. She fully justified all our expectations. She knew just how to
handle the complaints. She understood the Union leaders perfectly.
She understood the employers quite as well. No one could fool her.
Almost always she got the point of the case quickly and if there was a
grievance she promptly adjusted it. Most of the labor leaders sang her
praises loudly, but some of them thought that because she was of the
weaker sex they could wear her down. It must be understood that some
of these labor leaders were just natural born lawyers. They could
argue, argue and argue. They could find points no member of the
Bar would think of. Like some Talmudic debaters, they were pilpulists

—that is, they could find refinements and interpretation and distinctions of argument.

But Solomon Polakoff was Belle Moskowitz's *bête noire*. He tried in every way to wear her down. She never tired. She smiled and smiled and finally would give Polakoff just what he was entitled to and no more. Mrs. Moskowitz went further than the making of day to day adjustments. She studied the Industry as a whole. Her recommendations resulted in a fine piece of research work done by Dr. N. I. Stone. This job was done jointly for both the employers and the Union. The recommendations resulted in improved methods of piece-price-making for the entire Industry.

III

Mrs. Moskowitz advanced from that job to a much bigger one—the close advisor to Al Smith. She interpreted the opinion of women generally to Al and interpreted Al to them. Every executive needs an advisor to sift complex facts for him, someone with whom he can discuss with perfect frankness the many delicate problems which he must decide. Franklin D. Roosevelt, while Governor of New York, had Louis McHenry Howe and Margaret LeHand ("Missie"). All through Governor Smith's four terms as well as during his campaigns Belle Moskowitz was at his side. In its obituary on Governor Smith, the "Herald Tribune" described her position and influence in the following language:

> "And aiding him in every facet of his public life, as general adviser and unofficial Cabinet member, was Mrs. Belle Lindner Moskowitz, a social worker whom he had met in his first campaign for Governor. Mrs. Moskowitz was a chief strategy-maker with Mr. Smith throughout his years in Albany and his Presidential campaign, and after that, until her death in 1933, she remained one of his best friends." [1]

It is not generally known that she urged upon Governor Smith the nomination of Franklin D. Roosevelt for Governor in 1924 to succeed him. In 1919, Governor Smith named a State Reconstruction Commission in which Mrs. Moskowitz and Robert Moses both played leading parts. In 1920, the Commission recommended an entire reorganization of the State government, an executive budget and an increase in the Governor's term of office from two to four years. Their recommendations included streamlining 189 agencies into 20 departments and shortening the statewide ballot. It took Governor Smith from 1922 to 1928 to achieve most of these objectives in the face of a hostile legislature. Finally, by appeal to the people he brought the legislature to submission. In her column "My Day," Eleanor Roosevelt said, under the heading "Al Smith Did Much for State":

> "I have always been grateful to him personally for allowing me the experience of working with Mrs. Belle Moskowitz, who was his close advisor during the years in which he was doing the most constructive work for the people in the State of New York." [2]

Among the members in Governor Smith's unofficial Cabinet there were many disagreements and arguments. Belle's technique was like my mother's in her life with my father. She would let her man rage and storm and after he was all through she would have her quiet say. Al always respected her womanly intuition and foresight.

IV

In 1921, the Port Authority found itself confronted with the need for bringing to the public an adequate knowledge of its work, new as it then was. The public relations counsellor was not then known. But Mrs. Moskowitz took over the job for the Port Authority. She was just as effective in this work as she had been in the Dress and Waist Industry.

Under Chairman Outerbridge's leadership, the Authority created an Educational Council and Mrs. Moskowitz became its Secretary. She brought together about two hundred civic leaders in both States, many of them women. One of the themes was the burden resulting from inefficient transportation methods upon the cost of living. She got up the famous "Mr. Potato" movie. It was widely shown throughout the Port district and was an effective piece of propaganda for Port Authority plans. Mr. Potato was the victim of a "ride" upon which he was taken in a freight car from New Jersey to Brooklyn. He told how slow were his travels and how costly. Belle Moskowitz also inaugurated school essays and school contests on Port Authority subjects. Later, this work was taken over and broadened by Walter Hedden, the Director of the Port Authority's Department of Commerce, assisted by Marion Sanders who did a fine job, too. Philip Hunter and Lorraine Sherwood on WOR later regularly broadcast on Port Authority time. Their talks are always informative and broaden the public knowledge of the institution. Belle Moskowitz, however, was the pathfinder in this field. She prepared simple Question and Answer booklets for general distribution in the schools. If today a new generation knows about the Port Authority it is because of this educational work. Editors had confidence in Mrs. Moskowitz. Hence, she was always successful in securing space for her material. She always knew how to reach the public mind.

When in 1921, the Port Treaty was signed and Congress gave its consent, Belle Moskowitz naturally became liaison officer between Governor Smith and the Port Authority. Hardly a morning passed when she and I did not talk over the phone. She helped the Governor to keep up to the minute on Port Authority activities and she brought us in return the benefit of his judgment.

It was on her initiative that in the pioneer days an invitation to a dinner came from her friend Mrs. Ogden Reid (of the Herald Tribune) to the principal newspaper publishers and editors within the metropolitan district. At this dinner at Mrs. Reid's home, we were able to secure expert advice on how to proceed with all phases of our publicity. Al Smith and Chairman Outerbridge were present. I was there to answer questions. From that day on, we had fine cooperation from the "Times," the "Herald Tribune," the "World," the "Evening Post," the "World-Telegram" and, in New Jersey, the "Newark Evening News." We could always get our side of the story across to the public.

Despite Al Smith's general policy of consulting Belle Moskowitz on all phases of Port Authority activity, both she and I were shocked one day to pick up the morning newspapers and discover that the Governor had named to fill the vacancy caused by Chairman Outerbridge's retirement, a certain Mr. "S". Belle Moskowitz and I both knew this gentleman from our work in the dress and waist industry. He was known throughout the industry for his consistent and steadfast devotion to his own interest. From the publicity that followed, it seemed as though "S" expected to succeed Outerbridge as Chairman of the Authority. The Chairman, however, was named by vote of the whole Board. What did this publicity mean?

I did not speak to the Governor for several weeks after this event. Finally, Belle made it clear to Al what she knew of "S". It was clear that Governor Smith had been "sold a bill of goods." The appointee had been advanced as a great international merchant doing business even with Russia—very much interested in the development of the Port. When the Governor was made thoroughly aware of the danger that might come from the appointment, he told Belle to tell me to watch the gentleman's activities closely, and on the first sign of anything wrong, to let him know and he would find ways of getting rid of him. A vacancy occurred shortly thereafter. Al Smith then did one of his characteristically big things. He sent for another one of his friends and advisers, Raymond V. Ingersoll. He told Raymond that he wanted to put on the Port Board a Brooklyn man, a banker and a man of impeccable honor. In a few days the most surprised man in the whole metropolitan district was Herbert K. Twitchell, the President of The Seamen's Bank for Savings. When the Governor called him and asked him to serve on the Commission as a matter of public interest, he could not understand it. Getting a place of such importance without *political pull!* Was the millenium really in sight? When Commissioner Twitchell came up on the Board, it almost instantly erased the stain of the "S" appointment. But more than that, Twitchell knew the bankers who would bid on our bonds and they knew him. Undoubtedly, the fine price the Authority did get on its first bond issue was influenced by the bankers' confidence in Twitchell as a Commissioner.

Remember Senator Plunkett's theory of "honest graft"? The kind which includes getting inside information on the location of a public improvement and buying land on the basis of the knowledge. Of course, the engineers of the Port Authority kept highly confidential their plans for the approaches to the George Washington Bridge. One day, Commissioner Twitchell came into a meeting very much disturbed and told his colleagues that he had learned from friends in whom he had confidence that the Port Authority "was being sold down the river." A group of speculators were in fact buying real estate in Washington Heights on the basis of "inside information." Of course, Commissioner Twitchell was thoroughly outraged. He never stopped until he finally secured sufficient proof to present to Governor Smith. When Governor Smith got the facts he saw to it that "S" tendered his resignation. As Montague Glass wrote in "Potash and Perlmutter" about one of their salesmen—"He left by mutual consent."

One of the projects included in the plans of the Port Authority was the "Union Inland Terminal," now occupying the whole block from Eighth to Ninth Avenues and from Fifteenth to Sixteenth Streets. The chairman of the committee in charge of planning and building this terminal was "S". It was estimated to cost $16,000,000. The Commissioners were not at all sure then that the railroads wanted the project developed. But during "S's" career, nothing was done effectively to bring the terminal into existence. The project could not be put into effect without a good deal of push behind it. Immediately following the retirement of "S", Belle was this time consulted by Governor Smith in filling the vacancy. She recommended Howard S. Cullman who has been a Commissioner for eighteen years, Vice-Chairman of the Port Authority for eleven years and elected Chairman in February of 1945. Cullman took over the post of Chairman of the Committee on Inland Terminal. He pushed. The project was approved and the building was erected. It can be regarded as a monument to his work as a Commissioner. The engineer who designed the terminal,

John C. Evans, found in him a sympathetic Commissioner with whom to work. There was strong opposition in both New Jersey and New York. Cullman's standing in the community as President of the Beekman Street Hospital, as a member of the firm of Cullman Brothers, tobacco merchants and bankers, brought additional prestige to the Port Authority among business men. Securing this appointment was one of Belle's contributions. In 1945, the Port Authority planned a similar terminal for Newark, New Jersey.

V

The handsome structure that spans the Hudson River, designed by Othmar H. Ammann, the great bridge engineer, could only be located at one particular high point—at the point of the Palisades on the New Jersey side opposite the Washington Heights section of Washington Park. Cass Gilbert was retained as consulting architect. The Gilbert drawings and painting showed the towers of the proposed bridge encased in great masses of concrete in the true classical style, with the bridge fitting into the landscape. But whichever way one turned, one was bound to take up some of the park space on the New York side for the large foundations, and park space is something to be treasured in New York.

There was then functioning the Municipal Art Society; the Society for the Preservation of Historic and Scenic Places, and other organizations interested in preserving and enhancing the beauty of the City's parks. What would these organizations have to say? They might call it a "Park desecration." Our people believed it would really add to the beauty of the City. And it did. But we had to make this clear.

There was created an Advisory Council to the Port Authority which included all the leaders of the various groups. Mrs. Moskowitz arranged for the meetings with them. She saw to it that there was complete disclosure of the bridge plans in advance. The result was that all the organizations endorsed the project. Undoubtedly, Gilbert's fine pictures with the towers covered influenced this. But though the towers were designed in strength adequately to sustain the concrete covering, gradually the engineers got their way. They were quick to admit that Gilbert's design was the more classic, but they insisted throughout that this was a modern bridge and hence should be costumed in modern fashion. And, of course, to be costumed in modern fashion the bridge's supports should be unadorned. We are now in the days when exposure of supports is not regarded as immoral. Accordingly, this natural bridge beauty shows her legs unadorned with concrete or any other kind of stockings. No one today would suggest that it be otherwise.

The engineers have won. The Bridge is a classic "strip tease." Its beauty is enhanced by the extended Riverside Drive and the bridge over Spuyten Duyvil—thanks to Robert Moses and his enterprise. Today, the most beautiful approach to any City in the world is to be found coming down through Yonkers to New York by way of the Saw Mill River Parkway, and Riverside Drive, passing under the George Washington Bridge.

Perhaps the greatest single loss in the whole of Florence is the destruction by the Nazis in 1944 of the Bridge of Santa Trinita, called "the most beautiful bridge in the world." Even before the latter had been destroyed, however, the George Washington Bridge could be called "the most beautiful bridge in the world." Dr. John Lovejoy Elliott said that if the Port Authority had never done anything else but build the George Washington Bridge, it would have justified its entire existence.

Simeon Strunsky reminds us that Wordsworth stood on Waterloo Bridge and said about the Thames view that earth had no fairer sight. But "* * * if there are any fairer approaches or exits of which any world metropolis can boast than this first view of the river looking south from the Henry Hudson Parkway, or looking north from the lower drive to the George Washington Bridge, a person does not remember where." [3] Strunsky advises Wordsworth to come back and stand at the north end of the Henry Hudson Bridge and look south and west. We suggest that while he is about it he go across to Fort Lee to the restaurant over there and get a seat from where he can see the George Washington Bridge itself, or that he ride up and down Riverside Drive at night and see the pearl necklace hung across the Hudson.

The dedication of the bridge was a great event. The President of the United States, the two Governors, four United States Senators, the Mayor of the great City of New York, and a half hundred from all the other cities in the district—all were there. There was a great parade— Army Generals, Navy Admirals, plenty of music, airplanes overhead. My niece from Baltimore had the thrill of her life when our car passed every light, just because we had a police escort and a Rear Admiral under our wing. It was a great show, to be remembered. The man least impressed with the parade was Ammann who designed and constructed the bridge. The real job for him was now over. *Dr.* Ammann if you please—degree duly granted by Columbia for his fine engineering achievement.

My wife and I walked across the bridge, across a narrow plankway before the bridge was completed. The spinning of the cables across the Hudson and the gradual rise of the towers from the New York side was an exciting event in the life of New York.

Now, it happened that a little five-year-old, from her window in a neighboring apartment, watched those cables as they were swung across the river. She was much interested in its bow-like curve. Dad and Mom promised her a ride across the bridge as soon as it was opened. The first day the Bridge was opened to the public—Dad and Mom took little five-year-old for the ride they had promised her. Not a sign of glee, not a childish indication of joy. Only a sad look of disappointment. Mom said, "Don't you like the ride?" The five-year-old replied, "No-o-o." "Why? Are you disappointed?" "Yes—I thought we were going up and down like this [indicating the curve of the cable]."

"Up and down." No, Belle Moskowitz's life was not just one smooth, quiet ride in a cushioned limousine across the George Washington Bridge on a roadway free of all ruts and bumps. She did have a beautiful family life. Her children adored her and she adored them.

In the Garment Industry she took the lickings in stride with the rest of us. In Al Smith's career, she took them with him. I remember the night when the election returns, showing Al's defeat for the Presidency, came in at the Biltmore. She was the last one to concede that he was beaten.

I never saw her angry. Defeat or frustration never soured her. I did envy her almost uncanny instinct for discerning treachery and betrayal before they showed themselves in the open. She could, by smell alone, detect a member of the SODC [4] fraternity even before he showed his face or his hand. If he had a dagger hidden under his coat, by clairvoyance, she saw it. That is a great gift—saves one a lot of shocks if one possesses it.

BOOK VI

NEW TIMES—NEW INSTRUMENTALITIES

CHAPTER TWENTY-THREE

Droit et loyal.

(Just and loyal.) Motto of Dudley, Earl of Leicester

Alexander J. Shamberg

One man's vision and determination starts the building of the first vehicular tunnel—A man of generosity, loyalty and modesty—Shall the states surrender their sovereignty?—The effort to tax state and municipal securities is defeated.

I

HERE WAS A MODEST MAN who liked to do his work always in anonymity. No frills about him. He preferred to let other people get the honors and the glory. Alexander J. Shamberg—to his intimate friends plain *Aleck*.

He is no longer anonymous. His name is attached to a leading case in the field of Income Tax Law, *Commissioner of Internal Revenue* v. *Alexander J. Shamberg*.[1]

Shamberg was a dealer in cattle. His business required him to travel across the Hudson to Jersey City. Here he bought cattle at the stockyards as they came in from the West. Before the "McAdoo Tunnel," Shamberg, like everyone else, crossed the river by ferry.

He was a strong man—the kind one thinks of when visualizing a cattle dealer. But the largest part of him was his heart.

Shamberg was a member of the "Santa Claus Club"—a group of men who obtained from the postmaster each Christmas the names of children who had sent letters to Santa Claus. Shamberg then would personally choose the toys for his group of children, staying at his office until late at night to wrap up the packages. With the assistance of Morris Froelich, Secretary of the Tunnel Commission, he marked each package "From Santa Claus." On Christmas Day they made the rounds. Froelich was given a roll of bills by Shamberg to pay for food or other necessities wherever he found any family in need.

It was Shamberg's habit to carry a lot of money around with him. He never counted bill by bill but merely took the numbers and subtracted the lower from the higher, that is, from XC 567890 to XC 567900 in singles would make exactly ten. Why bother to count bill by bill?

He had earned his money the hard way. He had worked up in the cattle business run by his father and elder brother. On the side, he was a shrewd investor in real estate. During World War I, his services were called upon by the Government as an expert cattle shipper. He supervised the shipping of most of the horses and mules that went to England, France and Belgium. He directed the loading aboard and proper quartering of the animals on the ship.

He loved good food. He knew the restaurants of New York and the headwaiters. Anyone who dined with him was called a sissy if he went light on calories. If he was in the party, he made sure that nobody else would get the check. He bought expensive cigars and distributed them —Coronas—dollar size. It was part of his joy to send fancy cigars around to his friends for birthdays or Christmas. He knew the best vintages of rare wines, and he knew where to get them.

Twice there was a hiatus in the Holland Tunnel Commission's appropriations. Each time he came to the rescue. A month and a half before the opening of the tunnel, when there was no money in the bank to pay the employees, he told Froelich to put a note in the bank for whatever amount was necessary, he would endorse it, but if there was any trouble, he would advance the cash himself! The amount in each instance ran up to four or five thousand dollars. He said, "What's the use of letting the boys suffer?"

He had some bad habits. Like Horace E. Deming, he would come down to the office late in the day and stay until late at night. He would keep Froelich around until after eight o'clock and then they would both go uptown to "Brown's Chop House" or "Jack's" for a bite. Then Shamberg would order a lobster for Froelich to take home to Mrs. Froelich. He would say, "Pass that in the door, and if it stays, you can follow in."

II

I first came to know Shamberg when the Holland Tunnel was *merged* with the Port Authority.

Before then, we had known each other as on the other side of the fence. After the *merger,* when we came together, he as Commissioner of the Port Authority and I as its General Counsel, Shamberg never stopped abusing me, half in earnest, for turning over the Holland

Tunnel to the Port Authority. This was a crime beyond his imagination. Finally, he did admit that the *merger* had been wise. He became a Commissioner of the Port of New York Authority. And that agency acquired more than the Holland Tunnel when it acquired both him and General George R. Dyer, its Chairman.

Alexander J. Shamberg was known for his honesty and frankness. His word could always be relied upon. Besides, his judgment was sound. He had a fine sense of public service. He was influenced, as was Lord Tweedsmuir, by the Walter Bagehot opinion "that the greatest pleasure in life is doing what people say you cannot do, * * *." [2]

The Holland Tunnel is Alexander Shamberg's dream come true. Without his pioneer work, his tact and persistence, we might not be travelling through that tunnel today.

In the hall of the Law Department of the Port Authority is a cartoon by W. A. Rogers which I treasure. It may be a little difficult to visualize the women's fashions of the early twentieth century. Bathing costumes were very different in those days. Slacks and bathing costumes are made up of slightly less than nothing at all now. But thirty-five years ago, some fiend (who should go down in disgrace in history) invented the Hobble-Skirt. The plan of that skirt was to tie the American woman's knees together so closely that in walking she would resemble a Chinese femme.

There came a day when the Hudson River was frozen over for a whole week. No ferry boats could cross the river. There was no coal for New York City. All food supplies were held up. It was then that Rogers drew his cartoon. Father Knickerbocker is laboriously trying to cross on the solid ice. A big sash is tied tight about his knees. He is labeled "Hobbled," with the legend, "Well, I am in the fashion anyway!"

Long before the cartoon appeared, Alexander Shamberg had the *vision* of a way to overcome this handicap—to build a *vehicular* tunnel under the river. The Hudson and Manhattan Railroad (the McAdoo Tunnel) had been driven under the river and the Pennsylvania Railroad was brought through under the river to its great terminal in New York at Thirty-third Street. But how could passengers be taken in automobiles through a tunnel? Wouldn't the gas fumes from the exhausts asphyxiate the passengers? The Public Service Corporation of New Jersey had considered the possibility of a vehicular tunnel as a privately owned and operated venture. Its officers were persuaded it was feasible and profitable. But after all, a tunnel of this kind is a highway and should be publicly owned and operated even if it be built from tolls charged to the users.

Shamberg went to work. Three lawyers were of great help to him. First, his close friend Martin Saxe, member of the New York Senate, who later introduced the necessary legislation. After that, Paul Windels, who afterwards became Counsel for the New York Bridge and Tunnel Commission and on the *"merger"* became Associate Counsel to the Port of New York Authority. And in New Jersey there was James F. Minturn, later Supreme Court Judge, but then a Senator. He handled the legislation in New Jersey for Shamberg.

Of course, there had to be a "study commission"—a Bi-State Commission, created by New York and New Jersey—and there had to be appropriations from each State. At first, the Commission took up the possibilities of building a bridge across the Hudson. By 1913, Shamberg saw that the greater and more immediate need was a downtown connection. But a bridge downtown would be too costly to build. Accordingly, the Commission switched to the tunnel scheme.

It had to be demonstrated that the gas fumes coming from the automobiles passing through the tunnel could be eliminated. Experiments were then made by the Bureau of Mines of the United States Government. A tunnel was built for the test. Driving up the West Side Highway today, one sees near Canal Street two tall brick buildings. These are the New York ventilation towers serving the Holland Tunnel. And going still further uptown, near the entrance to the Lincoln Tunnel, one sees similar towers. An engineer or scientist will want to visit these towers and let one of the operating engineers explain the elaborate system by which the tunnels are ventilated and the precautions taken in case of a break-down.

The tunnel came. It cost $50,000,000. Governor Edge linked up the tunnel with his whole program for highway development in New Jersey, including the building of the bridge at the southern end, connecting Camden, New Jersey, with Philadelphia, Pennsylvania.

In New Jersey, the money, $25,000,000, was raised through a bond issue, behind which, of course, was the State's own credit. In New York, her half was met by annual appropriations over a period of about five years. A total of fifty millions for something highly experimental!

Clifford M. Holland was the engineer in charge of building the tunnel. He died a premature death due to his overwork on the tunnel. The tunnel Commissioners honored him by naming it the "Holland Tunnel." A columnist once said that "you would be fooling yourself if you thought you would get to Holland by going through this tunnel —you wouldn't get any farther than Jersey City."

When the tunnel was opened, it was Aleck Shamberg's great day of triumph. A greater triumph, however, was in store for Shamberg—that was the building of the second tunnel, the *Lincoln Tunnel*. He was not the Chairman of the Commission. He never would take the Chairmanship. His close and intimate friend, General George R. Dyer, was Chairman. He was a military fellow, that General, and cold shivers ran down our spines in the Port Authority when we thought of having someone come in who was reputed to be a military martinet. Later, I came to know the General well and I did not find him a martinet, military or otherwise, I found him a very fair gentleman—a stickler for orderliness and neatness. He once told me that one of his ways of judging the character of an individual, was to look at the condition of his fingernails. From then on, I had my nails manicured regularly.

III

The first tunnel, the Holland Tunnel, was practically authorized at the conference in Al Smith's room in the Executive Mansion the night New York approved of the Eighteenth Amendment. Public opinion in both States was then ready to authorize the building of the first *vehicular tunnel* under the Hudson and to appropriate the necessary funds. Here, too, Al Smith was a tower of strength. There was obstinate and blind opposition from New York City Hall. He beat it down. In 1918, when he was acting-Mayor, he had seen the thousands of tons of coal stored in the break-up-yards in New Jersey, and became impressed with the necessity for some development of the Port that would make such a thing impossible in the future. Accordingly, when he was elected Governor in 1918, he was prepared for the vehicular tunnel project and also for the creation of the Port Authority.

That night at the Executive Mansion at Albany—remember "the wedding ring" story? *—I must confess I was on pins and needles. Almost the whole evening was taken up with the tunnel project. I remember turning to Outerbridge, impatiently, and saying, on the side, "It seems to me they are discussing the matter of one trouser button and buttonhole to save us from disgrace, while we are here to discuss an order for a whole suit of clothes."

But the method to follow was the one I told about in which Al Smith was so effective—rung by rung one builds a ladder and as he builds he goes up the ladder. Changing the figure of speech—foot by foot, we get the first honest-to-goodness vehicular highway connection between New York and New Jersey, and after that is in operation we build another tunnel.

In all his work Shamberg was not only generous, but appreciative

* See Chapter 12.

and loyal. He was aware, as Outerbridge and General Dyer were, that without the help of others, one man can do very little. There are, of course, people in this world who are spoiled by praise, but it pays to take a chance on that. Generosity in the long run does breed generosity. Shamberg was always loyal to *his* boys, so they were loyal to him. If he had any fault, it was in over-loyalty. He was too ready sometimes to forgive serious lapses. Occasionally, when we went uptown after a Port Authority meeting, we talked about things other than tunnels. He loved good music. He loved good books. I have not repeated all the stories of his public contributions—space will not permit that. The truth is simply that he was a noble Roman—a fighter who won real victories. He had many obstacles to overcome. There were efforts of politicians to play the political game. When he came into the Port Authority, his own character became part of the institution and affected it deeply. After he became a Port Authority Commissioner, he saw clearly that the Port Authority's great triumph in its finances would never have been possible save for the rich revenues that came from his tunnel. And he rubbed that in—especially when I was around. But it must be admitted frankly that it is the simple truth. The fine credit of the Port of New York Authority had been established before the "merger" but it was firmly set when the Holland Tunnel revenues came into the general funds.

Shamberg was essentially a realist, but a realist with ideals.

IV

When Kenneth Dayton, my partner at that time, and I, were working on the legislation for the building of the two Staten Island Bridges and the George Washington Bridge by the Port Authority, we struck a snag. That was a limitation on appropriations in the New York State Constitution. No appropriation by any legislature was good for more than two years. We were advised that we had to get a "back-log," that is, advances by the States if we were to finance on tolls and revenues from something not yet in existence. The amount finally agreed upon as such a "back-log" was to be contributed in equal sums by both States—$4,000,000 for the Staten Island Bridges and $10,000,000 for the George Washington Bridge.

The agreement between the two States provided that these sums were to be paid over by the State in five annual installments. The whole cost of the bridges was ultimately to be paid out of their earnings. The bridges were to be, as we called them, *self-liquidating*. But the first lien on revenues was to go to the bondholders who advanced the necessary moneys and the legislation was to provide that the amounts advanced by the States were not to be paid back until the bondholders were fully protected.

Now, how were we going to overcome this difficulty of a five year appropriation with a State Constitution which provided that appropriations were only good for two years?

Kenneth and I finally worked out the plan by which before half of the Holland Tunnel revenues were actually turned in to the Treasury of New York State, the legislature directed the Commissioners to transfer the money to the Port Authority. I suppose a layman reading this will think that it was just a lawyer's way of beating the devil around the stump—but be assured it is perfectly sound in law—and in morals too. We provided for an outright appropriation from the State of New York for a period of two years and for each of the remaining three years a direction from the State to the Tunnel Commissioners to turn over each year the required amount to the Port Authority. When the two States agreed, this all became a binding contract. The provision of the law then could be written into the bonds sold to the public, and the United States Constitution would then protect both the contract between the States and the contract between the States and the bondholders from any impairment of the obligation.[3]

Aleck Shamberg never forgave those devils in the Port Authority for this satanic scheme! For Shamberg knew before anybody else knew it —even those of us who devised the legislative plan—that ultimately it would land the Holland Tunnel in the lap of the Port Authority. He knew the tunnel was going to be a bonanza. But if its revenues were to be gobbled up by the Port Authority, sooner or later that would mean the end of the Holland Tunnel Commission.

V

Now the time came when the Holland Tunnel was overcrowded with traffic. Pressure was then made by business men in midtown New York and from New Jersey to build another tunnel under the Hudson. That is how it came to pass when Morgan F. Larson was Governor of New Jersey and Franklin D. Roosevelt Governor of New York, that both these agencies became competitors—the Port Authority and Shamberg's Tunnel Commission. Two sets of plans were presented to the Executives of the two States, one from the Tunnel group and one from the Port Authority. There were dinners held at the Hotel Roosevelt, presided over by the then Lieutenant-Governor of New York, Herbert H. Lehman, and Governor Morgan F. Larson, of New Jersey.

Finally, Shamberg's fears were realized. The Port Authority had a fine credit. As a public corporation, it could borrow money. It did not have to ask the States for any appropriations or for any State bond issues. On the other hand, the Tunnel Commission had no power to raise money.

So it came to pass that someone behind the scenes suggested to Franklin D. Roosevelt and Herbert H. Lehman that the way to solve the problem was to combine the public bodies into one—increase the number of Port Authority Commissioners from six to twelve—and name some of the Holland Tunnel Commissioners to the Port Authority. Take over the staff and take over the tunnel! The Port Authority engineers had figured it all out. If the States would turn the tunnel over to the Port Authority, that body could raise on its own bond issues fifty million dollars—enough to pay back both States every penny they had put into the tunnel and, on top of that, could raise enough money to build another tunnel. And since logic is logic and business is business, that is just what happened. Each State got back its $25,-000,000. The Port Authority raised the additional money for the Lincoln Tunnel and *presto magico* the public got two tunnels in place of one.

Commissioner Shamberg pretended he was pained. The Port Authority having secured a toe-hold on the revenues of his tunnel, his Commission which really had built the tunnel was now to be washed up and put out of existence! Was there ever any greater offense in all history? I believe that Shamberg said all this with his tongue in his cheek.

Of course, time heals all wounds. Very soon the staff of the Holland Tunnel Commission became a part of the Port Authority. Paul Windels came over as Associate Counsel. Colonel Charles S. Gleim came along with Ole Singstad, its engineer. Morris Froelich became Assistant Secretary of the Port Authority. There came over to the Port Authority staff Dr. Edward Levy, the expert in bends, the disease of the men who work in tunnels. By the way, I owe a personal debt of gratitude to Dr. Levy for taking care of me when I was ill. And the family became a happy one and worked together. Shamberg became the Chairman of the Authority's Construction Committee. When the Port Authority was erected in 1921, Shamberg told Morris Froelich that New York needed such an agency. He said it could do for New York what the Port of London Authority had done for London.

Shamberg became a member of both the Finance Committee and the Personnel Committee of the Authority. He attended every Board and Committee meeting. Presently he found himself exercising a great deal more power and carrying a great deal larger responsibility than he ever had had as a Holland Tunnel Commissioner. Day by day, as he became more active, he saw more dreams come true. Of course, he was right in insisting that there had been no legal merger at all of the two institutions. All that had actually happened was that the Tunnel Commission had been legislated out of office and a new set-up had been made for the Port Authority.

Shamberg enjoyed every minute of his work. Of course he should have been Chairman of the Port Authority and on several occasions would have been elected to that office, if he had not steadfastly refused to take the post. He said simply, "I want to work. I don't want honors." And he would not budge from that position. He was very proud when the Port Authority selected General George R. Dyer as its Chairman. Shamberg was always loyal to his old friend, Frank C. Ferguson, ex-Chairman of the Port Authority whom he had known for years. He was proud of Colonel Gleim, too. After the Colonel finished the Lincoln Tunnel he went into war service. Colonel Gleim played a very considerable part in the building of the Ledo Road in Burma. I venture to believe that the difficulties he had in tunnelling under the Hudson were nothing as compared with his battling of the Japs in the completion of the Ledo Road. The "ground hogs" he found there were of different breed from those he met in the two tunnels.

General Pick, in charge of the engineering work on the Ledo Road, displayed the same kind of persistence in the face of difficulties as was shown by the engineers of the Port Authority. On his first evening in Ledo, General Pick held a staff meeting in the officers' mess hall. This is what he said:

> " 'I've heard the same story all the way from the States,' he said. 'It's always the same; the Ledo road can't be built. Too much mud; too much rain; too much malaria.
> 'From now on we're forgetting this defeatist spirit. The Ledo road is going to be built, mud and rain and malaria be damned!' "[4]

We hope some day Othmar H. Ammann will write the story of the obstacles he met in the building of the George Washington Bridge and John C. Evans will tell the story of the "mud, rain and malaria" he encountered in getting the materials for the first and second tubes of the Lincoln Tunnel. This was a battle with other engineers—army engineers—who were just as determined as he was, until finally they gave in.

But as a matter of historic fact, one found few "defeatists" in the Port Authority staff. There was not a single one in the Law Department—so far as I knew—when I was General Counsel. The "defeatists" were always to be found among those who studied figures and always saw "rocks ahead" and little else. They saw only the "mud, rain and malaria." If they had been dominant, the Port Authority would not be where it had arrived by 1945. It was the "Pick's Pike" faith that brought the Port Authority to its present enviable position.

VI

When the Federal Government decided to test out—as it hoped it could do successfully—and reverse the settled law of the constitutional immunity of State and Municipal bonds from Federal taxation, it picked out a few of the bondholders of the Port Authority as guinea pigs. Among them was Alexander Shamberg.

Of the $500,000,000 of bonds, which had been sold, Shamberg was a considerable buyer in reliance upon the opinion not only of its General Counsel but also of Charles Evans Hughes and of Thomson, Wood & Hoffman, its bond counsel, that they were immune constitutionally and exempt by statute. Shamberg thought the bonds were a good investment. He had the right to believe that they were tax-exempt upon the basis of the decisions of the United States Supreme Court as they then stood, and upon which we lawyers relied in giving our opinions. This move of the Government to reverse the status of the law made Shamberg angry. He was ready to fight. The Government knew the bonds were sold as tax-exempts. Why should they now try to tax them? Out of the seven bondholders chosen by the Government, he was pleased to be selected as the leader and "test pig." He supported the work of the organization of State and Municipal officers who opposed in Congress the efforts of the administration to strike down tax exemption.* He realized that the conflict was in reality between the philosophy of centralization of power as against the principle of local self-government of the states and cities.

But he lived long enough to see the Administration's attempt take a good and decisive beating in Congress. The decision in his favor by the United States Tax Court came before his death, but its affirmance by the United States Circuit Court of Appeals came after his death.

The "test case" began this way:

On March 14, 1941, the Treasury Department announced that it had sent notice of deficiency to seven bondholders of the Port of New York Authority and that this was a "test action" intended ultimately to prove in the courts that the Federal Government has the right under the Constitution to tax the income from State and Municipal securities. It concluded by announcing that if the Supreme Court should uphold its position, the Treasury Department would renew its recom-

* See Chapter 27.

mendation to Congress (1) to abate the payment of back taxes, (2) to exempt outstanding issue from taxation, and (3) to begin the taxation of future issues.

In the brief filed in the United States Supreme Court on behalf of the Shamberg estate signed by George Wharton Pepper, Julius Henry Cohen, John D. M. Hamilton, Leander I. Shelley, Austin J. Tobin and Daniel B. Goldberg, we said:

> "The simple fact is that billions of dollars of bonds have been issued, sold and resold on the basis of the universal understanding that the income from such bonds is by statute exempt from federal taxation. During all the years not a dollar of tax was exacted by an Internal Revenue Collector until, to start a 'test case,' a half dozen bondholders were selected as subjects for experiment. The release cited in the footnote shows that the Treasury hoped to induce this Court to reconsider its previously expressed views and further hoped that, having secured such a reconsideration, the way would be open for an appeal to Congress to repeal the statutory exemption. This is nothing more nor less than an attempt to get this Court to exert a kind of collateral pressure upon Congress after direct pressure during a period of over thirty years had wholly failed. It is significant to note that since 1913 many bills have been introduced into Congress in a vain attempt to repeal the exemption or to launch a constitutional amendment. It is a fair inference from this record that if an act to limit the exemption by excluding 'Authorities' would have had the least chance of success, legislation to effect the limitation would have been proposed long ago. On the contrary, as appears from the treasury release already cited, everybody, including the Commissioner, assumed that the real question intended to be presented in this case is the exemption of the obligations of States and that as long as this is preserved, the exemption of the agent would follow as a matter of course. What was started as a test case has now *degenerated into a mere controversy as to whether the obligations of State Authorities are or are not within the statutory exemption.** This is a mixed question of statutory interpretation and administrative practice which has been dealt with effectively by the Tax Court and by the Circuit Court of Appeals."

On January 2, 1945, the country was handed a New Year's gift in the denial of the Writ of Certiorari. This meant that the United States Supreme Court did not think enough of the arguments of the Government even to hear the case on appeal. That Court made its opinion clear when later it handed down its decision in the so-called Saratoga Springs case—where four opinions were written. It left no doubt as to where the Court stood on the matter of federal taxation of state and municipal bonds.† [5]

Yet for four years we had been hearing that the United States Supreme Court was "packed" against us. That all that was needed was to have the President tell the Court how to decide the case and the Court would so decide. This was not my opinion. I had more respect

* Italics supplied.

† See letter of the author to the New York Times, January 27, 1946, analyzing the opinions of the Justices.

for the Court and I was convinced that the Court was not just "nine fountain pens" for the Chief Executive. [6]

As a matter of fact the judges showed more independence each day and their decisions reflect an honest effort on the part of each member of the Court to find the true and sound basis for decision. They have, however, in many situations now accepted Abbot's principle of "judicially correcting judicial errors." On the other hand, eminent lawyers in 1945 said that no one could prophesy what the Supreme Court would do, since the rule of *stare decisis* has been weakened so materially.[7]

If the United States Supreme Court had followed the dissenting opinion of Judge Jerome Frank in the Circuit Court of Appeals and had held that the Port Authority was not a municipal corporate instrumentality but was a business corporation making "profits," the Authority would then have had to pay income tax on its revenues, the same as any private agency. Throughout the case, it never seemed to me at all probable that after more than twenty years of acceptance of the institution as a public agency and the issuance of half a billion dollars' worth of its bonds sold as "tax free," that the Court would upset all this practice.

Judge Frank's idea that there were "profits" made by the Port Authority was an error. The Port Authority holds all its funds as *trustee* for the two States.

Immediately following the refusal of the United States Supreme Court to reverse the Circuit Court of Appeals, Port Authority bonds went up four points. Within less than a month, they went up ten points, thus clearly indicating the value of the tax exemption feature, a point in controversy between the Government and ourselves in the Shamberg case.

By March 15, 1945, the Port Authority found the market situation so good that it proceeded with refinancing at a lower rate of interest. On March 29, 1945, it sold $12,000,000 of its General and Refunding Bonds, Ninth Series, carrying only a 1½% coupon. The money cost of this issue to the Port Authority was net interest annually 1.534, the lowest rate in its entire history. In addition, the National City Bank and the Chase National Bank took $14,000,000, each bank taking $7,000,000 of General Reserve Notes issued by the Authority at a 1% annual interest rate. This financing enabled the Port Authority to call in $28,422,000 of its 3% bonds otherwise due in 1975. The amount saved was considerable. Of course, interest rates at that time were low and the Authority's credit was superb, but undoubtedly the market reflected the effect of the Government's defeat in the test case.

After the decision in the Saratoga case, on February 19, 1946, an issue of Port Authority bonds were sold at the lowest interest cost ever paid for like securities. On coupon rate of 1¼%, forty-year general and refunding bonds were sold for 97.30 and went to the public at 89¼. Nothing as financially successful as this was ever dreamed of when the Port Authority was first created, or at any time during its first fifteen years of existence.

Yet some lawyers who had confidently predicted defeat for the Authority took the decision in the Shamberg case (1945) with bad grace, saying there still was no telling what Congress might do in the way of repealing the statutory exemption and in that event the Supreme Court would be left free to reverse its previous rulings on the constitutional immunity. Some of these lawyers even went so far as to issue warnings to investors in state and municipal bonds. In the last analysis, investors must rely on the weight they attach to the opinion of law experts based on the law as it stands, while prophecy as to what Congress or the United States Supreme Court may do in the future, will rest upon varying political opinions. In a later chapter * I shall give my reasons for believing that in this important field of public policy, neither the Congress nor the Court will support the centralizing, functional theory of government. On the contrary, the trend now is the other way. It is a sign of the investors' judgment on this point, however, that the bids for the later issues of Port Authority Bonds came from the largest group of distributors of Port Authority Bonds ever brought together. This $12,000,000 bond issue was sold to investors and bought by them as tax exempts. The unqualified official statement in the Authority's public offer contained the following:

"In the opinion of General Counsel and Bond Counsel, the bonds of the Port Authority and the interest thereon are exempt under the Constitution of the United States, as now in force, from any and all taxation (except estate, inheritance and gift taxes) now or hereafter imposed by the United States of America unless the States of New York and New Jersey consent to such taxation; * * * are exempt * * * from any and all real property taxes now or hereafter assessed by either State or by any city, county or political subdivision thereof."

This was consistently my opinion as General Counsel from the time of the very first sale of Port Authority Bonds. My successor, Leander I. Shelley, as Assistant General Counsel, shared these views, and, of course, in the light of the United States Supreme Court action, found no reason for changing his opinion.

* See Chapter 27.

VII

Into the steel that made the towers and cables of the George Washington Bridge have gone many different kinds of iron. Into the towers and cables that sustain the Port Authority have gone many elements of character. Shamberg contributed generosity and loyalty. It was a matter of honor with him that every agreement should be fulfilled—every pledge observed. The other man's case was to be heard, and considered, whether it was a rich contractor claiming "extras" for which, equitably, he was entitled to be paid; or a toll collector or traffic officer under charges by his superior. He believed the standing of the Port Authority would be enhanced by following a policy of breadth. To him any other policy—however much might be gained for the moment—would in the end prove costly.

It so happens that the Port Authority is exempt from suit. That is because it stands as if it were the States themselves. For this reason, it set up a "Court of Claims," that is, a Committee to receive, hear and pass upon claims made by those who asserted any kind of grievance or right against the Authority. *Noblesse oblige.* Precisely because it could not be sued in the courts, it became all the more imperative that it should maintain its reputation for fairness and equity. By reason of his outstanding qualities, it was but natural that Shamberg should be chosen to head the Authority's Committee on Claims.

No matter what other gifts he may possess, the individual falls just short of nobility unless he possesses the two qualities of loyalty and generosity.

CHAPTER TWENTY-FOUR

Avoir du cachet.

To have a distinctive character; to possess qualities that raise one above the common run of men or things.

Eugenius H. Outerbridge

The battle between New York and New Jersey—A business man becomes a great public servant.

I

HOW DOES ONE BECOME A LEADER? Lincoln is reported to have said: "I have not made events; events have made me." My observation is that most of the leaders whose portraits are painted for this gallery made events—events also made them. There is a new science, Sociometry. It has concluded that one must possess at least two things to become a leader—the gift to inspire confidence and the willingness to fight. Outerbridge possessed both of these qualities in generous measure.

Men do not have to possess "glamour" to become leaders. In women we do know that it means charm. Didn't Maggie tell John in Barrie's "What Every Woman Knows"—that if a woman has charm, she has everything? If being liked by other men and having that indefinable gift of making friends is glamour, then Outerbridge had it.

I do not forget that occasion at one of the City Hall Reporters' dinners when Outerbridge was put on the gridiron with a skit "Outerbridge's falling down"—to the tune of "London Bridge Is Falling Down." At the Union Club, in his Church, in the Chamber of Commerce, among bankers, in businessmen's circles generally, he was recognized as a leader of intelligence and character. He was a Director of the Equitable Life Assurance Society, the Delaware and Hudson Railroad Company, the Chase National Bank, and President of the New York Chamber of Commerce.

Outside of Sheffield in England is a place called Oughtibridge and there are traditions to the effect that the family was named after the place—or the place named after the family. Eugenius H. Outerbridge came to New York and founded the well known commission firm of "Harvey & Outerbridge." He also developed "Pantasote," a substitute for leather, with a plant in Passaic, New Jersey. He developed a wallboard product to be used for housing. He called it "Agasote" and operated a plant for making that commodity in Trenton, New Jersey. Thus he was doing business both in New York and in New Jersey.

Next to William Manice, Eugenius H. Outerbridge was the handsomest man I ever knew. He had a florid complexion. He wore English clothes and an English "darby." If one met him on Threadneedle Street in London, one would take him at once for an officer of the Bank of England, or if near Westminster Abbey, for a member of the House of Lords. His mustache was always in curl, a sure sign that the owner is interested in his personal appearance. His barber had a regular customer. A painting of Outerbridge hangs on the walls of the Chamber of Commerce.

Attention to details characterized his work. Some of his friends thought he put in too much time on details. He wrote things out in his own hand. In the files of the Law Department of the Port Authority will be found in his legible hand the original draft of the Principles of the Comprehensive Plan for the Development of the Port, now in the laws of both States.[1]

My memory runs back to the scene in 1921 at 11 Broadway when Outerbridge presided over the conference with the railroad executives. He sat at the head. Close by sat Samuel Rea, President of the Pennsylvania Railroad, a really great railroad leader. Next, Patrick Crowley, President of the New York Central, and then came representatives of the New Haven and other railroads and members of the staff of the Bi-State Commission, Benjamin F. Cresson, Chief Engineer, George W. Goethals, consultant on our staff of engineers. With great tact, on that occasion Outerbridge won concurrence for his principles and discussion was narrowed down to the question of timing—when and how the principles should be made effective. It became clear that they could only become effective as each step became practicable both for the railroads and the Port Authority.

I know of no better description of the basic elements of Outerbridge's nature than those ascribed by Lord Tweedsmuir to his friend Basil Blackwood:

"He was the most cherished and welcome of friends. Whenever he appeared he brought warmth and colour into the air. It is difficult to describe the fascination of his company because it depended on so many subtle things—a peculiar grace and gentleness of manner; a perpetual expectation, as if the world were enormously bigger and more interesting than people thought; * * *"[2]

Outerbridge had realism colored by poetry, a stalwart independence sweetened by courtesy.

On the other hand, Tweedsmuir said of Lord Asquith, " * * * he was immensely intelligent, but he was impercipient. New facts made little impression on his capacious but insensitive mind." [3] Outerbridge was never impercipient. The engineers found it a joy to bring new discoveries to him. The statisticians always found him ready to go deep into their figures. For my own part, the new legal plan I proposed found him cordially percipient and encouraging.

II

My meeting with Outerbridge was what Deming used to call "a lucky happenstance"—lucky for me. Lincoln Steffens has written that the "typical business man is a bad citizen; he is busy." [4] Moreover, his conduct in business is with a people in which political graft was not an unusual practice. Steffens goes on to say:

> "But the bribe we pay to the janitor to prefer our interests to the landlord's, is the little brother of the bribe passed to the alderman to sell a city street, and the father of the airbrake stock assigned to the president of a railroad to have this life-saving invention adopted on his road. And as for graft, railroad passes, saloon and bawdy-house blackmail, all these belong to the same family." [5]

But there were men like Bernheimer, Outerbridge, Cutting and Schieffelin, who did not deserve such castigation. They were genuinely moral and religious men. They conducted their business on a high plane and were good citizens. In the same group were lawyers like Paul Fuller, Charles C. Burlingham, Horace E. Deming and the group of younger lawyers like Abbot, Bard, Tanzer and Dorr. These were the people with whom I lived and worked.

On September 6, 1909, Peary had just sent to the New York Times his preliminary account of his successful discovery of the North Pole. This very day there was organized the "Committee of One Hundred," headed by Eugenius H. Outerbridge. Joseph M. Price, Charles C. Burlingham and William C. Redfield were among the active participants. Their purpose was to secure the election of decent men to govern New York City. The Citizens Union sent three men to that group: William Jay Schieffelin, Francis C. Huntington, and I was the third. As a result of the Committee's work during that summer and fall, the forces for good government won a great triumph and Tammany sustained a crushing defeat.

On Election Day of 1910, there was a clean sweep for Fusion excepting only for the office of Mayor. William J. Gaynor was elected to that office. William A. Prendergast was elected Comptroller, and John Purroy Mitchel was elected President of the Board of Aldermen over John F. Galvin, Chairman of the Port Authority fifteen years later, and Charles S. Whitman was elected District Attorney. Of course, the Citizens Union alone could not have beaten Tammany. The original plans of the Fusion movement contemplated fusion both with the Republicans and with the Hearst forces. But Hearst stood for municipal ownership and operation of subways.

On September 23, 1909, because he could not agree with the Committee's views, Hearst left the conference. The Republicans then nominated for Mayor, Otto T. Bannard, a leading businessman, a man of character but not an advocate of municipal ownership and operation. This result was due entirely to the "tact, wisdom, self-sacrifice and courage displayed by Outerbridge which impressed the Republicans with the necessity of compromise and selecting the very best candidate for the offices in the City." [6] When the City Club on May 19, 1910, presented Outerbridge with a silver centerpiece, those were the exact words used by Isaac N. Seligman. If Hearst had not withdrawn from the Fusion and had supported the ticket, the whole ticket would have been elected. Nevertheless, it was a great triumph.

III

One day in 1917 when the newspapers were reporting important war news, an item appeared of great import to New York businessmen which most of them overlooked. It did not escape Outerbridge. Immediately his imagination made him realize its serious portent. The news item was to the effect that the State of New Jersey had started proceedings before the Interstate Commerce Commission with the objective of imposing a separate "lighterage charge" on freight coming from the West to Manhattan and Brooklyn.

That in itself does not sound so direful, but if one had had Outerbridge's knowledge the suit would really have aroused one to action. A "lighterage charge" would make it more costly to do business on the New York side of the Port than on the New Jersey side. The newspapers later put it editorially—*"splitting the Port."* Anyone who did business in New York would have to pay an additional three cents on every hundred pounds of freight shipped in and out. It would be a handicap, not only with competitors in New Jersey but with others in Philadelphia, Baltimore and even points farther south on the Atlantic coast.

Moreover, its practical consequences might result in an exodus of a very large amount of trade and commerce away from New York to other ports. Railroad rates are still made for long-haul traffic, on the basis of zones, not on cost or distance alone. Within a zone the rate is the same no matter how far out on the periphery one is. Like the five-cent subway fare—one gets the ride for the whole distance from Van Cortlandt Park to Coney Island. Even if one goes only part of the way, the fare is still five cents. New Jersey, under the leadership of a very active citizen, the head of the New Jersey Board of Commerce and Navigation, J. Spencer Smith, was convinced that the existing rate system, as applied to the Port of New York, was all wrong. New Jersey did not get the lighterage, he said, so why should her industries pay the same rate as those who did get it? Of course, there was lighterage along the New Jersey coast too. On the Jersey side some industries, under Spencer's theory, would have had to pay the extra charge. Spencer did not mind that. The thing was complicated further by the fact that there were existing differentials in favor of Baltimore and Philadelphia. Baltimore had a rate of three cents and Philadelphia two cents under New York. Would Baltimore and Philadelphia get a still higher differential?

Let me explain a little more in detail this lighterage business. If one shipped freight from the West on the New York Central it would come all the way on rail, because the New York Central trains ran down the west side of New York on their own tracks. But if one happened to ship by the Pennsylvania or Baltimore & Ohio or Lehigh, whose terminals were on the New Jersey side, there had to be some way of bringing that shipment over to Manhattan. That was by ferry—exactly in the same manner as people who lived in New Jersey travelled to work in New York before the Hudson (McAdoo) tube was built—as some still do. The freight travelled as the suburbanites did, on ferryboats. This process of moving the freight was carried on by taking the freight out of the cars on the New Jersey side, breaking it up, and putting it into barges, and towing the barges across by boat. This was called "lighterage." Or, the whole car could be put right on a flat boat having rails and towed over by the same kind of boat. This was called "car floatage."

The United States Supreme Court had held that carrying the freight over this way, by car float, was in essence just the same as if the carrier had railroad tracks right on the water and rode the cars along on a continuous trip of such imaginary tracks. It said in the *Baltimore & Ohio* case:

"* * * the transportation from Brooklyn to western points is by one continuous transportation by railroad. The mere fact that the physical rails stop at Jersey City does not mean that the railroad transportation there ends. It continues over to Brooklyn by means of car floats, upon which further rails are laid and on which empty and loaded freight cars stand and are transported, so that the rails upon the car floats are brought into contact with the rail ends at Jersey City, and the continuation thereof at Brooklyn, and in this way the transportation by railroad is carried on without interruption from the western points directly to Brooklyn." [7]

From this it can readily be seen that if all the railroads with terminals on the New Jersey side were required to charge an extra three cents per hundred pounds for the ferry ride for freight, the New York Central would get most, if not all, of the rail business. It was the only all rail route to New York.

When in February of 1946 New York was tied up by the tugboat strikes and theaters, clubs, schools and businesses were all closed by emergency orders of the Mayor, this carrying of freight across New York Harbor on barges and lighters brought out dramatically the city's dependence upon "car floatage" and "lighterage."

The editor of "Topics of the Times" [8] took occasion to point out that in 1946 the people had grown away from the picture of New York as "a harbor with tugboats in it." We had indeed become a tunnel-and-tube-and-bridge population. Serious debates "about a thing called the lighterage problem and how the cost of bringing goods over from the Jersey railroad terminals to Manhattan affects the interests of the port of New York"—all such items may have had little interest for the average reader up to that time. But when the tugboat strike brought New York to a standstill—much as a coronary thrombosis can throw even a giant flat on his back, Mr. New Yorker could then understand "why people get excited about lighterage."

IV

However, if in 1917, a New York businessman had a trained and lively imagination like Outerbridge, he would see the peril that lay in this lawsuit by New Jersey against New York over lighterage.

The oldest Chamber of Commerce in the country, tracing its charter way back to King George III, is the Chamber of Commerce of the State of New York. It held and still holds the leadership in all movements for building up and protecting New York's business. It was the pioneer in the movement for building New York's subways.

Outerbridge was then Chairman of the Committee on Harbor and Shipping of the Chamber. Another leader in the Chamber at this time was Irving T. Bush, the creator of the Bush Terminal Company. Quickly Outerbridge and Bush joined forces. They called out all the fire engines.

Bush Terminal had been built and operated on the Brooklyn side of the port, and like all the other Brooklyn terminals was dependent on the continuation of the existing method for fixing freight rates for the Port. This system was called "free lighterage" but "free" was a misleading adjective. The cost was absorbed in the total freight charge. It merely meant there was no extra charge for the lighterage itself. If a department store delivers a package to a customer's door in Westchester he knows this service is not free. The cost is included in the price of the goods.

When Outerbridge and Bush saw the danger of this attempt by New Jersey, they brought the Chamber quickly into action. Of course, they had to have a lawyer. It would be poor grace for me to say now that they should have hired the best Interstate Commerce specialist available. Both thought differently. They were of the opinion that special knowledge of Interstate Commerce law was not needed for the lawyer they should select. They thought a trial lawyer who had some knowledge of the public aspects of the problem should be their selection. (My participation in the "West Side fight" against the New York Central was a matter of public knowledge. I see more clearly now the dangers that can come from inadequate experience. Today I say, "Young men for action—older men for judgment.")

William C. Breed of Breed, Abbott & Morgan, the Bush Company's lawyers, assured Bush that I could be trusted to handle the case. Another friend helped the conspiracy along. He was then the Governor of New York State, Charles S. Whitman, who on Outerbridge's request persuaded the Attorney-General, Egburt Woodbury, to appoint me Special Deputy Attorney-General to represent the State. The Merchants Association had retained as its lawyer Benjamin Lewis Fairchild, who had represented the Association in an earlier case of the same general kind. But he ran for Congress and was elected. The Merchants Association named me to succeed him. I started off then with a whole string of medals, all resulting from getting the first one. With the State, the Chamber of Commerce and the Merchants Association as clients—it was really up to me to make good.

I sent for the petition filed with the Interstate Commerce Commission by our New Jersey friends and began my education. When I dug far enough into the history of the State and its development, including the history of the Erie Canal, one of my colleagues in the case facetiously suggested the story of the farmer in the lunchroom who asked "What soup have you got?" And when the waitress replied, "Oxtail," he remarked, "That's going pretty far back for soup isn't it?" Later my colleague found, as I did, that the complete survey of all the historical factors that had gone into the making and development of the Port made the first postulate for victory in the case, that is, historically, geographically and economically the Port of New York was all of one piece; New York City, Newark, Jersey City, Paterson, Passaic—the entire Metropolitan area. The boundary line drawn by the Hudson which split the territory between two sovereign States had nothing to do with it at all. Ultimately the Interstate Commerce Commission agreed with us.[9] I learned all about DeWitt Clinton's *Big Ditch* and the defeats Clinton took before he got his canal. I learned all about the circumstances that led to Fulton's running the *Claremont* up the Hudson. Also, of the defeat of Livingston's monopoly by the decision of the United States Supreme Court in the great case of *Gibbons* v. *Ogden*.[10] This case, Albert Beveridge said, really made the United States. It was quite clear that these *pathfinders* had made New Jersey as well as New York.

The railroads were represented by able men. The Pennsylvania was represented by George S. Patterson; the New York Central by Clyde Brown; the Lehigh Valley by Richard Warren Barrett; and the Central Railroad of New Jersey by Jackson E. Reynolds. These men were all veterans—experts in the field of Interstate Commerce Law. They must have felt that it was presumptuous for a novice like myself to play so important a role. But it is one of the joys of practicing law with big men that they help the junior along. New Jersey was well represented, too. There was my old friend of law school days, later Dean of the New York University Law School, Frank H. Sommer; George L. Record, the progressive; and former Attorney-General of New Jersey, Robert H. McCarter.

In the courtroom the General loved to dominate. If he could put a young man in his place, that was good sport. In a little while, Bush told Outerbridge that the Chamber ought to charge admission fees for the "show" at the Chamber. Now Outerbridge was a fine gentleman, always courteous as I have said. He was disturbed over this report. The Chamber was host. That was not the way to treat a guest. So he sent me a very nice note. Very tactfully he suggested that perhaps the General's feelings might be hurt by my conduct and he might not think kindly of the Chamber of Commerce. This called for action. I invited both the General and Outerbridge to luncheon at the Bankers Club and after the oysters, I turned Outerbridge's letter over to the General to read. He roared with laughter. Outerbridge then learned that part of the joy of trial work for lawyers is just this kind of "tennis." The General and I became very warm friends. (Later when he was New Jersey counsel for Julius Forstmann and I became Forstmann's counsel in New York, we worked in harness together.)

The Great Hall of the Chamber made an appropriate setting for the hearings. At a small desk under Cadwallader Coldens' portrait sat Wilbur LaRoe, Jr., the Chief Examiner of the Interstate Commerce Commission. Then, in semi-circle arrangement, three large tables—one for the New Jersey lawyers, one for the railroad lawyers, and one for the New York lawyers. Former Attorney-General George Woodward Wickersham retained by the City of New York, and I, sat at a table together. Philadelphia, Baltimore, Norfolk, Boston and other cities had their lawyers at another table. Philadelphia's distinguished lawyer, William A. Glasgow, Jr., came there to protect her interest. The witness sat in a chair to LaRoe's left. We had a good press. Someone brought us a large batch of promotion literature issued in New Jersey in which Newark and other cities urged that because of their proximity to New York, theirs was the one place in which to locate. The story goes that when a resident of Newark went anywhere, he registered as "of New York City."

J. Spencer Smith had to concede on cross-examination the simple truth that New Jersey had actually prospered under the existing system. Spencer made enough admissions that by themselves they were certain to win the case for us. But better still, cross-examination brought J. Spencer Smith over to our side. Shortly after he left the stand, Irving Bush told me he thought we could get a settlement of the case. I advised that we win the case first and then settle.

However, Baltimore was represented by a very fine gentleman of breadth and vision—Herbert Sheridan, Traffic Manager for the Chamber of Commerce of Baltimore. When he was on the witness stand he said this:

> "It may be that had this case been considered in all of the aspects that have been brought to light at this hearing, the complaint would not have been brought as it is presented, but having been presented, I see possibilities for great benefits to follow, in this—if I would not be considered presumptuous in going to this length—a recognition of latent possibilities on the Jersey shore, which are inherent and capable of very great expansion. Recognition on the part of Manhattan of those, together with deserved claim for recognition of what Manhattan has, and so the two, working in harmony, can go on with a plan of expansion and development that would justify the Statue of Liberty at the entrance of the Harbor and win deserved admiration of the entire country." [11]

The simple fact is that there was a great deal of merit in New Jersey's complaint about the costliness of operation of the Port of New York. This very car-floatage and lighterage was a costly operation. It was obvious that it could be cut down, if there were cooperation among the railroads and if there were unification and joint use of terminals, consolidation of shipments, and coordination of the use of carloads—all of this was accepted national policy by the terms of the Transportation Act of 1920.

V

Twenty-five years later the Government brought suit against forty-seven railroad companies charging conspiracy in restraint of trade in violation of the Sherman Anti-Trust Act. In an editorial, the New York "Times" drew attention to the inconsistency between that fight by the Government and the attitude of the Interstate Commerce Commission. It quotes from the Interstate Commerce Commission in the "Fifteen Per Cent Case" decided on October 20, 1931:

> "The records show that in the past decade the railroads have made great strides in improving their service and at the same time operating with greater efficiency and economy. But what they have done * * * has been characterized by continual intensifying of their own competition. At a time when as an industry they have new enemies to face, their warfare with each other has grown more bitter, so that economies in operation have been offset in part by the growth of competitive waste.
>
> All this is contrary to the spirit of the Transportation Act of 1920. Congress then looked beyond the individual railroad to the concept of a national transportation system. It pointed the way, in the consolidation provisions, to the reduction of competitive wastes. It went to the extreme of removing the barriers of restrictive Federal and State anti-trust legislation which might otherwise stand in the way.
>
> Short of consolidations, it opened wide the door to agreements for the pooling of service and of revenue, whenever it could be shown to our satisfaction that such agreements were in the public interest.
>
> Much has been accomplished in the way of unification, but much remains to be done, and the pooling provisions of the law stand almost unused." [12]

Between 1921 and 1931 the same conflicting forces were at work. One, competitive—the other, in the direction of consolidation. The very initiative of the great railroads brought about the creation of such outstanding facilities as New York Central's Forty-second Street Terminal, the Pennsylvania's Terminal at Thirty-third Street, and the great rail tunnel under the Hudson River, and brought into existence also the Hell Gate Bridge one passes under when travelling by boat to Boston. Why should not this Hell Gate Bridge be used by the other railroads? In World War I, the New York Central used this bridge, in spite of the fact that it was built by the Pennsylvania. Frederick Williamson, during World War I, was the representative of the Federal Government in operating all rail facilities in the Port District. Later he became President of the New York Central System. General Williamson told me that this operation during the war was highly successful. In reliance upon this fact, the Port Authority brought proceedings to open up the Hell Gate Bridge to the New York Central Railroad. The Interstate Commerce Commission did not see things our way.

VI

The Great Hall of the Chamber of Commerce of the State of New York in 1917 was the setting for a memorable historic occasion. I suspect that Irving T. Bush and J. Spencer Smith had several lunches before this event came to pass. Governor Edge of New Jersey and Governor Whitman of New York both came to the meeting and made speeches, each pledging his State to a policy of cooperation. Governor Edge in substance repudiated the isolationist policy of his predecessor and said very definitely that he was for cooperation between the two States.

At the luncheon which followed, I was asked to develop a legislative program to facilitate this cooperation. I advised the creation of a "study commission." Later this was worked out in legislation. Three commissioners were to be named from each State, to make a complete survey of all the engineering, commercial and legal phases of the problem. Upon the basis of such study, the Bi-State Commission was required to present to both States a cooperative plan upon which the States could agree—a legal plan as well as an engineering one. On March 2, 1917, Governor Whitman sent to the legislature of New York a message accompanying the bill which Kenneth Dayton and I drew, in which he said:

> "All but two of the trunk lines serving the Port of New York terminate in our neighboring State of New Jersey. This makes it essential that any solution of the Port Problem should include a study of that portion of the Port comprised within the northern part of New Jersey and, while it is beyond question that great benefits will accrue to the State of New York through a comprehensive Port policy, benefits will also accrue to New Jersey."

Benjamin F. Cresson, Chief Engineer for the New Jersey Board of Commerce and Navigation, had been asked on the trial:

> In other words, it is your understanding, as an engineer, that the failure of the West Side to develop is due, in great part, to the lethargy of the people; that physical difficulties are not insuperable, and that if the proper spirit were manifested, the necessary funds provided, and a co-ordination of authority and a central control substituted for the present division a very material advance could be made on the West shore, without a change in the freight rates?"

He replied: "I think that is so." [13]

In my brief filed with the Interstate Commerce Commission as Special Deputy Attorney-General on behalf of the State of New York, as well as for the Chamber of Commerce and the Merchants Association, I wrote:

"Let all hands turn to and co-operate in the solution of this great problem. Its final engineering solution will require the constructive mind of a great engineer (such as that of the man who planned the Panama Canal) and hundreds of millions of dollars (such as was required for the Erie Canal and for the great subway facilities of New York). But if it is to be finally brought about, there must be provided better political organization of the municipalities of New Jersey and legal power on all sides of the harbor to deal collectively with the constructive program that will be evolved. Obviously, this could not have come about before. It required an aroused and awakened New Jersey and New York city whose transit problem had passed the state of initiation and development, and a New York State whose canal problem was well under way of solution. But over and above all other things, it requires a liberal spirit on all *sides* which would break down political barriers, put aside petty rivalries or jealousies, and free itself from the short-sightedness that handicapped DeWitt Clinton in the nineteenth and Irving Bush in the twentieth centuries. * * * The hearings upon this application have already developed healthy elements of co-operation and thus may make of these proceedings a blessing in disguise; but the *grant* of the application—the creation of this 'New Jersey' zone—would destroy the new-born spirit, would paralyze the initiative and palsy the hands of those who would put endeavor into this great work." [14]

VII

It is appropriate that the first bridge which the Port Authority built and which is crossed at the outer periphery of the District, should be called *The Outerbridge Crossing*. It was, indeed, his faith, his vision, his persistence and finally his tactful bringing together of conflicting interests that brought the Port Authority into existence. The bridge is the connecting link between the two States. The name Outerbridge is appropriate for another reason—it is indeed the *Outer Bridge*. But I wonder how many people crossing this bridge from Perth Amboy in New Jersey to Tottenville in Staten Island really know what the name means, really know that it is named after the *pathfinder* who blazed the trail.

The Herald Tribune of November 12, 1932, had this to say:

"He stamped with his organizing ability the character and conduct of that progressive body. His diplomatic skill, his firmness, his judgment, his mastery of intricate problems contributed in large measure to the development of the Port of New York. He received one of the rarest of tributes in the naming of the bridge from Tottenville to Perth Amboy 'The Outerbridge Crossing.' Men are seldom thus honored during life by identification with great public works. In the record of New York Mr. Outerbridge will have an assured rank with her citizens typifying the dignity and prestige of the metropolis."

The legislation creating the "study commission" was passed in New

York and New Jersey in 1917. Governors Whitman and Edge promptly signed the bills.

The legislation created two commissions, one from New Jersey and one from New York. Governor Whitman named William R. Willcox, Eugenius H. Outerbridge and Arthur Curtiss James Commissioners. Governor Edge named J. Spencer Smith, DeWitt Van Buskirk, banker from Bayonne, New Jersey, and Frank R. Ford, senior member of the engineering firm of Ford, Bacon & Davis. The two commissions organized promptly and called themselves the "New York-New Jersey Port and Harbor Development Commission."

Willcox was elected Chairman, J. Spencer Smith was named Vice-Chairman, William Leary, "Old Bill" as we affectionately called him, was made Secretary, Carl A. Ruhlmann was made Assistant-Secretary, Benjamin F. Cresson was made Chief Engineer and General George W. Goethals, of Panama Canal fame, was named Consulting Engineer. I was named Counsel. Edna Goeltz, now Secretary of the Port Authority, came in as Secretary to Chief Engineer Cresson. When I retired in 1942, she and I had a record of the longest period of service to the Port Authority and its predecessor.

In 1917, space was taken at 115 Broadway. The engineers started upon their study. Barely had we organized, when the country was plunged into World War I. There was no such planning in *logistics* as there was in World War II, under the capable direction of General Brehon Somervell. Based very largely upon the lessons learned from the unfortunate experiences in World War I, in 1940 the Army and Navy had a better understanding of what was needed.

In 1917, when we got into World War I, in simple truth, there was chaos in the Port of New York. Shipments came here from all over the country sent by the Navy, by the Army and by the United States Shipping Board. Each department organized and shipped separately. There was no single head. There was no coordination. Everybody shipped. Cars piled up on tracks as far back as Pittsburgh. Great piles of much needed war equipment were dumped along the railroad tracks. Everyone riding in from the West to New York observed it and wondered what would happen. Outerbridge visualized all this and realized what was bound to occur if this "bottle-neck" were continued. Out of his long experience he said one day, "Good God, if this goes on we shall lose the war!" What were we to do? We had great confidence in the President. "Let us go down and see President Wilson and tell him all about it." That is exactly what we did. Willcox, Outerbridge and I went down to the White House. The President was tolerant, quick to take in what we outlined and wholly cooperative. He adopted immediately our recommendation and set in motion the measures we recommended. Our plan was simple: to utilize the staff of engineers of the Bi-State Commission and create a War Board to which would be appointed representatives of each of the Federal departments having anything to do with transportation through the Port of New York.

To achieve this result with the President took only a half-hour. But to the task of working it out, the President assigned the Secretary of War, Newton D. Baker. Now Newton Baker was a lawyer. In World War II as in World War I, the Secretary of War was a lawyer—Henry L. Stimson. In World War II, another lawyer, Robert Patterson, was Under-Secretary. (He was a judge and a good one.) How does it happen that such training equips a man to run a war? But if one knew these three men, Baker, Stimson and Patterson, one would understand that it was their very training in the law that gave them the mental equipment to visualize, to plan and to execute. As Baker and I knew each other from work on committees in the American Bar Association, we had very little difficulty in getting organized.

The first important problem was to secure someone as executive to run the job. For this there was just one person. He was Irving T. Bush, head of the Bush Terminal Company. Outerbridge and I recommended him to Baker. Bush was promptly drafted for the job. Thus was put together "The War Board of the Port of New York." Baker was Chairman. Secretary of the Treasury McAdoo was a member of the Board. Edwin N. Hurley, head of the Shipping Board, was a member, too. As a matter of fact, each Department of the Government having to do with transportation of war supplies was represented.

Our next job was to find offices from which to operate. By that time every inch of space in New York City was taken. There was one building that had been the seat of German plots against the United States. It was the Hamburg-American building at 45 Broadway. It was Outerbridge's idea that it would be poetic justice for the United States Government to take over that building. I was sent to Washington to carry out the war against the Germans and with a little conspiring on the part of Secretary Baker, as well as J. Lionberger Davis, representing the Alien Property Custodian, A. Mitchell Palmer—and some help from the United States Attorney for the Southern District of New York, Francis G. Caffey (later United States District Court Judge), we marched down to 45 Broadway, with forty United States Deputy Marshals and literally threw all the tenants out of the building. (It did not improve my personal relations with the lawyers who had offices in the building at the time. Later on I shall tell how we were punished for our warlike conduct and how we were thrown out ourselves.)

At the time we were planning to go into the building, the United States Shipping Board was actually negotiating with the Hamburg-American Company to rent the first floor of the building. That was droll, wasn't it? I had no difficulty in persuading the representatives of the Shipping Board that there was no sense in paying the Kaiser rent for space we were going to use to beat him. We arranged to give the Shipping Board the first floor and we took the rest of the building. Bush promptly moved into the Chief Executive's office, took down Herr Ballin's picture and put one of Woodrow Wilson in its place. I had a little room next door and was given the title of "Secretary and General Counsel." Then the gold braid began to come in. Each department named someone in uniform to work with us. The best General of the lot was David C. Shanks, head of the Port of Embarkation of New York. But more important than all that, the freight began to move. *The log jam was broken.*

VIII

But here is another incident of World War I. One day, Outerbridge and Bush and I had a long talk at 45 Broadway. Bush and Outerbridge saw clearly that the war was going to be lost for certain if the War Department stuck to its plan for the building of the huge storage and embarkation plant then under way at Newark Bay. This project was estimated to cost about forty million dollars. Bush and Outerbridge knew that Newark Bay was clogged up with ice during the winter and that the land itself was not readily susceptible to the rapid development of a huge plant such as this.

We three went out and inspected the site and were satisfied that the war would be over—and in favor of Germany—before our supplies could be gotten across, at the rate we were going in transshipments abroad. I was sent to inform Secretary Baker about it. He was a little man, smoking a calabash pipe, with his feet stuck up on his desk most of the time and his head hardly visible. To get a full view of his face, I sat at the side of the desk. I told him my story. He looked out of the window and said: "Now what am I to do about this? This whole project has been gone over and over again by the General Staff. These people are supposed to be the experts. Don't I have to rely on my experts?" "Mr. Secretary, would you like to forget for a moment that you are Secretary of War and let us both talk as though we were just lawyers?" "Of course, you know you can always do that with me," he said. Then I said, "What in heck do we care about the experts anyway? When we cross-examine them, don't we have to know more than they do? You come to New York and let your own eyes tell you what you ought to see." He was game. He telephoned the head of the Shipping Board, Edwin Hurley, to get a submarine chaser and in twenty-four hours we met them at New York City and went into Newark Bay. We were there about three hours and we thought we would never get out again. The Bay was clogged with ice. On the return trip, our boat was jammed in the ice. The captain was a clever maneuverer and he did get us out of that ice, or we might have stayed there until the spring thaws came in to release us. But before that, we had taken Baker over the ground. Outerbridge took a three foot piece of pipe that was lying around and stood it on the ground. It disappeared in the soft mud. The visible demonstration was complete. Later, when we got out of that ice jam, we took Baker and Hurley over to South Brooklyn and there they saw a real terminal in operation. It was the Bush Terminal.

That is the story of how, after commandeering Bush, the Government commandeered the Bush Terminal. General Goethals, and Chief Engineer Cresson were immediately put to work, making plans for an additional terminal in South Brooklyn. That was carried through. So was planned and erected Army War Base Number One. Later the Navy built the present huge Naval Base over in South Brooklyn.

When we got that far, there was only one thing lacking—Bush ought to wear a uniform and be given a military title. I think we could have persuaded Secretary Baker to make him a Brigadier General, or as John C. Evans calls such a civilian, a "jigideer brindle." Indeed, I think the then Mrs. Irving T. Bush would have liked both the uniform and the title. I persuaded Bush not to fall for it. I told him if he ever put on a uniform, he would be "in the Army now"—he would always have to take military orders and do what he was told to do.

Then happened one of those things that raises one's blood pressure. Some of the men who did work down in Washington during World War II will sympathize with us. One day Bush received a letter from Secretary Baker. It was polite enough, but it informed Bush that all our functions were to be taken over by a new Board. Philip A. S. Franklin, head of the Cunard Line, was to be the new executive head. And so as punishment for throwing out the tenants of No. 45 Broadway, we were thrown out ourselves. I wrote Secretary Baker a nice letter asking "Why?" No explanation—a military secret. After the war was all over, the truth came to light. Our Ally, the British, had made an arrangement with President Wilson in which in return for Great Britain's assisting with her Navy, she was to have her friends in control of all the shipping from New York. But Outerbridge, Bush and the rest of us were satisfied that but for that trip to Newark Bay with Secretary Baker and the subsequent seizure of the Bush Terminal, the war would have been lost before the United States could be made ready to ship the necessary supplies for our boys abroad. Comparing that experience with what has been done in World War II, it seems nothing short of miraculous. All hail to General Brehon Somervell!

IX

As Chairman of the Port Authority, Outerbridge was called upon to do nearly all the work of the executive. It was like running a bank or a business. The executive had to be on the job all the time. Again it was pioneer work. Though engineers and lawyers were at his call, in the last analysis he was the one person who had to direct the job. It was Outerbridge who had the conferences with the bankers. It was he who conferred with the railway executives. He had to keep six Commissioners in harmony. He was so fair that no decision was ever arrived at until it was unanimous. His task became overwhelming. His own business offices were at 11 Broadway. Recognizing the drain upon his energy, we moved down to the same building.

There came a time when Outerbridge tried to get from under the strain. He was trying to run Harvey and Outerbridge, Pantasote, Agasote, and the Port Authority as well, and do his duty beside on the boards of directors of half a dozen institutions. He decided he had to quit the Port Authority. He sent Governor Smith his resignation. He never received an acknowledgement. When he met the Governor and asked him about the resignation Al looked blankly at him and said, "What resignation?" With his legislative experience, Al had learned what "pigeon-hole" means. He knew the value of Outerbridge to the Commission and felt that he had to keep him at his post. So he stayed until his term expired. No one knew how costly it was until after his death. As the lawyer for his estate, I was the first to discover the truth. He had been very prudent in his younger days and had taken out heavy life insurance for the benefit of his wife and children. On his death, however, we found that he had borrowed up to the hilt on all of his policies. Ethel Boyd Outerbridge, his widow, on my advice, sold their place in Litchfield, Connecticut, and terminated their lease on the Park Avenue apartment. Both loved their homes.

Deming, Ivins, Bernheimer, Outerbridge—all died, leaving small estates. Each declined to give his strength to the job of amassing wealth.

But could it be said they died poor? If the esteem of friends, if the

esteem of the public, if the work they left behind them are weighed
—did they die poor? I challenge any inheritance tax appraiser to put
a value on these imponderables. I assert they all died rich. I assert
they lived richly.

I count myself fortunate that I was privileged to work for and with
each one of them. Certainly their lives offer me no encouragement to
amass a fortune. I put in twenty-five years of service with the Port
Authority and its predecessor and when I retired in 1942 they gave
me a dinner, made some nice speeches, and Chairman Ferguson
handed me a gold pass, entitled "Life Time Pass for Service."

At sixty-nine, I began as a young man, to practice law—a new start.
If ever I had any incentive in the way of making money to do more
than to take care of myself and my wife—we have no children—it is
now completely dissipated. If I can just meet my overhead, pay State
and Federal income taxes, life insurance and possibly begin to pay
off the debts incurred because of the wickedness of the United States
Supreme Court in taxing my Port Authority salary, I shall be content.
I can still follow the example of Deming, Ivins, Bernheimer and
Outerbridge—enjoy good food, good music, good books and good company—and a few, just a few dear, very dear friends. Why should I try
for more?

CHAPTER TWENTY-FIVE

"* * * It's verra good," said the chief engineer, looking along the disheveled dock. "Now, a man judging superfeeically would say we were a wreck, but we know otherwise—by experience."

"Well, I'm glad you've found yourself," said the Steam. "To tell the truth, I was a little tired of talking to all those ribs and stringers. Here's Quarantine. After that we'll go to our wharf and clean up a leetle and—next month we'll do it all over again."

The Ship That Found Herself, RUDYARD KIPLING.

The Port of New York Authority

The daddy of all authorities—How two sovereign states work cooperatively—Frustration and defeat lead to ultimate triumph—Can public ownership and operation be combined with business efficiency?

I

WHY DO PEOPLE MAKE THE MISTAKE of saying the Port *of* Authority? The full name is *The Port of New York Authority*. To shorten it, one could say *The Port Authority*. The name was borrowed from the British. Outerbridge knew about the *Port of London Authority*. So did Shamberg. At the creation of the New York Authority, Shamberg told Morris Froelich that something of the kind was needed for New York.

Outerbridge talked much about the London institution. I learned about it from him. I learned more in London in 1924. I brought pictures back of its handsome building and hung them in the rooms of the Port Authority. Lord Devenport, the Chairman of the Port of London Authority, like Outerbridge, was a businessman. He declined to take the salary equivalent to $30,000 a year attached to his office. The Port Commissioners of London as well as those of Manchester and Liverpool, when I saw them in 1924, advised strongly that we would get better Commissioners if they were not paid. They said that positions without salary would be sought after as posts of honor. On the other hand, if the positions were put on a salary basis, they would most likely become part of the political patronage of the party in power.

I learned also, on my visit, how the title *Authority* came about. This is the story: Lord Devenport and Lloyd George were working on the proposed Act of Parliament, by which they expected to consolidate into one a whole group of London Port bodies. For the name of their baby, "Commission," "Board" and "Agency" were all rejected. These names were all too common. Devenport and George wanted something fresh and new. So Lloyd George said, "Let's wait until we finish the whole bill and then we may get an inspiration." When they had completed the bill they found that nearly every paragraph began with the words "Authority is hereby given." So, Lloyd George said, "Let's call it the Port of London *Authority*." And that is what they did.

It seemed to Outerbridge and me in 1919, that if London could prosper with an *Authority*, New York could do well with one. Besides, the name would have value in selling the bonds which we expected the New York Authority would sometime issue. Port of London Authority Bonds had a market all over the world. The public corporation or public trust was already established in British constructive thinking.

There was a story at the time of the sale of the first issue of Port of New York Authority Bonds that some of them went to the Japanese, who thought that if Port of London Authority Bonds were good, Port of New York Bonds would be just as good. The Port of London Authority had power to collect what in the United States we call "duties," or, as they called them over there, "port dues." Hence, their self-liquidating bonds were well secured by definite revenues. On the other hand, what we were going to do was to "lift ourselves up by our own bootstraps."

II

The recipe for this new creation of ours included some garden varieties of vegetables. There was to be an onion—that is, we were going to be a *public corporation*. Nothing very new about that. In some respects it would be like a city, a town or a village. It would have a separate existence, yet derive its powers from the two States. Then we had to have some potatoes—that is, it was to be a businesslike body, but with none of the usual legal incidents of a business corporation. It was to be responsible only to the two States. *There were to be no stockholders*.

It was clear that New York and New Jersey had to be brought into binding cooperation. Hence there would have to be a compact between the two. This was the *meat and substance* of the concoction we put together. The usual way for two States to work together is to create a commission from each State and both to work in collaboration through such commissions. I consulted my friend, J. DuPratt White in 1919–1920. He was then head of the Palisades Park Commission. That body was then operating as two separate commissions, one from New York and one from New Jersey. I learned from White the inherent weaknesses of an institution so constituted. Real estate as it acquired it, was taken in the name of each separate State. When John D. Rockefeller, Jr., wanted to donate some property to become a permanent part of the great plan for preserving the Palisades, he was confronted with the fact that title to property in New Jersey would go to the State of New Jersey and by the same token property in New York to New York and then be vested in the State. Someday perhaps a legislature might change the policy of the State and dispose of the property in a different direction. That was not so good. Besides, it was a cumbersome process to have two separate commissions meeting as separate bodies, yet at the same time trying to function as one. Ultimately, after the Port Authority had been in existence for some ten or fifteen years, I was asked by the Palisades Park Commission to draw up legislation which would create a *Palisades Park Authority* modeled on the Port Authority. This was done. They profited by our Port Authority experience.

The next question was—how could the two States be bound? That was a real problem. In the Constitution of the United States, there is a provision which, on its face, forbids the making of any treaties between States.[1] However, it had already been held by the United States Supreme Court that two or more states of the Union might cooperate and with the consent of Congress do a great number of things.[2] This compact-method had been used many times before. Indeed, there was in existence a treaty between New York and New Jersey made in 1834 [3] which settled a long standing quarrel between the two States over boundaries and jurisdiction. We decided to take the treaty of 1834 as a basis and erect upon its foundation a supplemental and amendatory agreement.

With an onion and a potato and some meat we made our *stew*. And did it stew! And did we stew! Without a leader like Outerbridge we should have failed utterly.

We started talking about the proposed treaty around 1917. It was not signed until April 20, 1921. Congress gave its consent August 23, 1921. Of course, the name "Authority" was an asset later when we did come to sell our bonds. But it was a severe handicap while we were trying to get the motor started. It sparked, but the engine would not turn over. We got out and pushed. *Authority* must mean something; hence it must mean a *supergovernment!* We became a sort of Halloween spectre to the municipal officials of all the cities within the District. Like the witch in "Hansel and Gretel," we were ready to capture all the little children, push them into our oven and make gingerbread out of them. New York's valuable piers and waterfronts and railroads, even its subways, would surely be gobbled up! When Al Smith, in that memorable legislative hearing in Albany in 1922 in the Assembly Chamber, arose to oppose Mayor Hylan and Comptroller Craig, he opened by saying, "Let's get rid of the fog."

At bottom, the opposition of the Port Authority was based on local and party politics. When we were beaten in New Jersey in 1920, Governor Smith said, "Now let's get this thing approved in the party platforms of both parties in both States. The legislatures will then be bound by these declarations." We went to work on his advice and succeeded. William Leary, our Secretary—an old veteran in Republican politics—helped us with the Republicans in New York. Al Smith did the trick with the Democrats. Other friends helped us in New Jersey. Without political friends in *both* parties in *both* States we should have died before we were born.

However, as fast as we made enemies, we made friends. Make a thing big and broad enough and petty opposition can be beaten down. The appeal to the pride of the States was effective. The opposition of Mayor Hylan and Comptroller Craig naturally led to help from Republicans in both New York and New Jersey. On our side, we had the support of Governor Whitman in New York. In New Jersey we had Governor Edge and Senator Joseph S. Frelinghuysen. When Nathan L. Miller succeeded Al Smith as Governor, he brought his great strength to our side. In the first year of the Miller administration, the legislation was passed in New York. After the Treaty was signed and the Port Authority was created, Nathan L. Miller, Republican, appointed Alfred E. Smith, Democrat, whom he had just defeated for Governor, as one of the first Port Authority Commissioners. Then the motor began to turn and the car began to move forward.

In New Jersey, too, we had good friends. Besides Governor Edge, we had the then Attorney-General, Thomas F. McCran, a first class lawyer. He had run in the Republican primaries for Governor of New Jersey in 1925. Like Al Smith he was defeated, and for the same reason—he was a Catholic. He died shortly afterwards, brokenhearted. But for his untimely death, he would surely have been my associate as New Jersey counsel for the Port Authority. Afterwards, Arthur T. Vanderbilt filled that post and later Russell S. Watson did. Each contributed to the success of the institution. As both were of high standing as lawyers and public leaders, they added to the clearer understanding of the institution in New Jersey—an understanding not always easy to achieve.

At one time I was advised to keep away from Trenton. They did not want any New York lawyer to come down there telling them what *they* should do. In the early days we had the support of Senator Clarence E. Case (later Judge Case), the leader of the New Jersey Senate in 1921. He and Senator Arthur N. Pierson carried the responsibility for passing the initial legislation.

One of our really great aids was John F. Hylan, Mayor of New York City. His persistent and personal attacks upon Outerbridge brought to our side an almost unanimous press—the "Times," "Tribune," "World" and "Telegram"—of course, not the "American." If Hylan was opposed to us, *prima facie,* at least, we were good. We had in New Jersey the support of the powerful "Newark Evening News." It assigned the job of reporting upon our work a very capable newspaper man, John S. Philips, who not only wrote the newspaper reports about us, but its editorials on the subject.

III

In 1921, Edward I. Edwards, then Governor of New Jersey, vetoed the legislation to authorize the signing of the Compact by New Jersey Commissioners. It was passed over his veto. In 1922, after our report came in, he said he had reconsidered his position of the year previously and was now satisfied that the Authority had "dealt justly by the State," (New Jersey) and the plan should be approved. He had already told his friends in New Jersey that he deeply regretted his veto in 1921. It always seemed to me a sign of greatness to admit error, although some even in high places think admission of error is a sign of weakness.

One of the interesting things in the history of the Port Authority is the number of people who came to scoff and remained to pray. Frank C. Ferguson, up to 1945 Chairman of the Port Authority, vigorously opposed its creation in 1921 and appeared with former Attorney-General Robert H. McCarter in opposition before the legislative committee in Trenton. John Milton of New Jersey, later United States Senator, opposed it and afterwards became a Commissioner of the Port Authority—and a good one, too. Mayor Fiorello LaGuardia, while in Congress, denounced the Port Authority and its Counsel. He let loose a whole string of epithets upon our head, all of which can be found duly printed in the Congressional Record of the day. If one read it and believed it, one would get the impression that there was no baser member of the Bar than the lawyer who drew up the treaty. Ogden Mills put a reply to all that in the record. So did Roy Weller. On the twentieth birthday of the Port Authority, Mayor La Guardia praised the Port Authority and even praised its lawyer!

One of our best friends in New Jersey was Senator Joseph S. Frelinghuysen. There came a time when, for sheer lack of votes, we were in for a licking. Senator "Joe" took off his coat and with his secretary Edward S. Bilkey went up and down the State of New Jersey and corralled enough votes in just one week's time to change defeat to victory.

Anyone who read his newspapers in the fall of 1944, would have learned about the huge Union Truck Terminal then in prospect in which the City of New York was working in close cooperation with the Port Authority. Also, of the Produce Market for the West Side, and the crosstown underground tunnel as well. On all of these things the engineers of the Port Authority and of the City worked in close cooperation.

It was Outerbridge's advice always to look ahead for at least fifty years in our planning. Instead of being called a *supergovernment,* by 1940 the Port Authority came to be sought after by municipalities, as in the case of Westchester cities which looked to the Port Authority to save the Boston and Westchester Railroad for them, and by New Jersey municipalities sadly in need of a suburban transit system. Frank Hague, Mayor of Jersey City, became a good friend. He has never tried to influence the Port Authority in the slightest degree in the exercise of its judgment and upon many occasions was helpful.

In spite of the opposition in New Jersey in 1920 and 1921 to the creation of the Port Authority, the Newark Evening News, twenty-five years later (April 22, 1946), editorially favored putting the Port Authority in the airport business through acquisition of the Newark Airport. It reminded its readers that the Interstate Commerce Commission had held in 1917 that, "historically, geographically and commercially, New York and the industrial district in the northern part of New Jersey constitute a single community," hence it argued that this "single community" should now join in the development of the Newark Airport as a community project. It sometimes takes as much as a quarter of a century to establish the soundness of a principle. In that time even the most hostile adversaries may emerge as converts.

IV

One of the most skeptical editorial pages when it dealt with the Port Authority—even long after it was created—was the New York Sun. But I lived to see the "Sun," under the heading "Useful Agency," say that "there is abundant evidence that the Port of New York Authority is usefully serving the metropolitan area."

Those still living who knew the Port Authority twenty-five years ago, must have been as thrilled as I was when reading the New York Times editorial headed "Service to the Port" in its issue of November 18, 1944, or the editorial in the "Sun" of November 20, 1944, "Acknowledging a Debt."

The "Times" noted that his colleagues had a few days before presented Chairman Frank C. Ferguson with a silver medal to commemorate his twenty years of service, the last ten of which were spent as Chairman. The Times compared the ship when Ferguson came aboard with an annual payroll of $200,000 and its annual payroll today of *four and a half millions!* "It is a unique, self-supporting agency" and owes its success largely to "the ability of the distinguished citizens who act as Commissioners and whose only reward is the satisfaction that accrues from the faithful performance" of the "arduous tasks of managing terminal and transportation facilities now valued at $250,-000,000."

Ferguson, in the same editorial, is given "the thanks of the community for having met so efficiently the obligations that accompany leadership in an important public office." If the editors had known as intimately as this writer does, the "headaches" we all had to endure during those twenty years, the tribute would have been even stronger.[4]

But the special value of these editorials is in the clear vindication of the advice received in the twenties from our British friends to make the office of Commissioners of the Port Authority *posts of honor, without salary.* It demonstrates that businessmen here, as in England, can be induced to give of their knowledge, skill and time to such agencies in part-time service. Lord Tweedsmuir in 1939 wrote:

> "But my strongest conviction was that the area of public service should be extended, and that the ordinary citizen should be given the chance of an active share in the work of administration. I believe that the policy represented by organizations like the B.B.C., the Port of London Authority, and the Central Electricity Board was our natural line of development—public utilities privately administered but authorized and ultimately controlled by Government."[5]

The Conservatives in England and the Labor leaders are not so far apart as we think.

Men like Donald Nelson or General William S. Knudsen should find real zest in accepting posts like Authority Commissionerships, giving a part of their time to public service. With a staff of career men giving full time, eagerly pressing forward new projects, the Commissioners can sit at the steering wheel, applying the brakes, or accelerating the speeds—as each situation warrants. The tribute to Ferguson and his colleagues should be an encouragement.

The superiority of the "Authority" method over federal, State and municipal financing lies in an important factor, as that expert in government affairs, Robert Moses, pointed out in December of 1945 when discussing the financing of the Idlewild (New York) Airport and the proposed West Side market:

> "There's a vast difference between computing plans and costs for an ideal airport as a department head, when all your money comes from the city, and, on the other hand, sitting down with cold-blooded underwriters, including fiduciaries who are not taking any risks. * * * If you don't have an authority you don't have to prove anything in particular. Under the present system an official may think he has signed up something good but he won't know if it's a good deal for six, eight or ten years." [6]

Moses could have added that the self-liquidating authority *must keep up its credit*. Hence, it lives in a financial glass bowl. Revenues, costs of operation, and reserves are closely watched by experts for banks, insurance companies and prudent investors and their advisors all over the country. If the authority shows signs of running "into the red," it loses its capacity for borrowing money at low rates of interest. On the other hand, if it is carefully and prudently managed by capable businessmen, it makes its own proud record. The Port of New York Authority has made such an enviable record. It has become a model and example for other similar agencies.

In 1917 to 1921, the principal opposition to the creation of the Port Authority came from the then Mayor of New York City, Hylan, and Charles L. Craig, Comptroller. Craig was always resourceful but in 1920–1921 he made a fine foil for Al Smith's rapier. The briefs that Craig prepared, as well as the answers, are all in that big brown book.[7] But one argument by Al Smith was worth a dozen by Craig any day. What Lord Tweedsmuir has said was applicable to Governor Smith, "I discovered that there was a fine practical wisdom which owed nothing to books and academies." [8]

I shall never forget the Assembly Chamber in 1922. Al was no longer Governor. It was his return visit to Albany. He had come up to put through the legislation approving the so-called "Comprehensive Plan for the Development of the Port of New York." Nearly everybody in Albany turned out to welcome him back to Albany. The Chamber was crowded. We had hung up a map of the Port district in the balcony. For the purpose of showing the costliness of moving freight around the Port, Al traced the weary travels of a lonely cabbage, toiling its way slowly from New Jersey to Brooklyn. When he had worked up the crowded Assembly in the Chamber to a climax of uproarious laughter, he finally said, "When that cabbage gets to Brooklyn *you* can eat it—I won't."

He won the battle for us. The night before he had sat up with Belle Moskowitz and me, getting all the "dope" he needed. He used long backs of envelopes for making notes. You will find a sample of one of them in his book, "Up to Now." He was wholly extemporaneous in his speech, but he had greater gifts of exposition than any layman I have ever met.

Arthur S. Tuttle was then the Chief Engineer for the City. He had drawn up a neat plan for a tunnel to Staten Island which was then offered by the City officials as competitor to the Port Authority plan. Ten years later Arthur Tuttle admitted that it was a mistake and took occasion to praise the Port Authority and its work. Another cartoon I treasure which hangs on the walls of the Law Department of the Port Authority is one showing Mayor Hylan trying to water a garden with a hose all broken and leaking. The garden hose is called "The Staten Island Tube." The legend over it is "All Played Out." When Al Smith finished in Albany with John F. Hylan, and punctured his tires, Hylan was through—so far as we were concerned. Al marched out of the Assembly Chamber as the conquering hero.

V

I must tell how Al Smith became a Port Authority Commissioner. That event should be recorded before time erases memory. The story is simple. When he was Governor, he tried to placate the City Administration by naming its Dock Commissioner, Murray Hulbert, as a Port Authority Commissioner in place of Arthur Curtiss James, an appointee of Governor Whitman. Al told Outerbridge and me that he thought the appointment of Hulbert would help to bring about good will between the Hylan administration and the Port Authority. If Hylan had not been so stupid and Craig so intolerant, Al's move would have been more than a *beau geste*—but it did not work out.

Before we came to the signing of the Port Compact, Hulbert and DeWitt Van Buskirk, Commissioner from New Jersey, came to a deadlock. When it came time for Governor Miller in 1921 to appoint New York Commissioners to the newly created Authority, the Governor discussed the matter with me. He wanted Outerbridge and, of course, wanted him to be the Chairman. He wanted a good man from Brooklyn and he had one in Lewis H. Pounds. But the Governor was puzzled about filling the third place. The only Democrat on the Bi-State Commission was Murray Hulbert. I told Governor Miller that Hulbert had become *persona non grata* to the New Jersey Commissioners. Besides, though he was authorized by the statute to sign the Port treaty on behalf of New York, he never did sign it. "But I cannot avoid naming a Democrat, and Hulbert is the only Democrat on the Commission," said Governor Miller. I said, "Why not appoint a bigger Democrat?" "Who?" I reminded him that at the New York State Bar Association dinner at which he, as Governor-elect, was guest of honor, and his defeated opponent, Al Smith, was also guest, the latter said that being Governor of New York State was a gruelling job. He turned to the Governor-elect and with great sincerity said, "If there is anything I can do to help make your administration a success, Governor, don't hesitate to call on me."

Just a short time before the matter of the appointments to the Port Authority came up, Al had been made president of the United States Trucking Company, with a salary of forty thousand dollars a year. I told Governor Miller that the job of Port Authority Commissioner required knowledge of transportation and Al would probably find the appointment congenial to his new job. In "Up to Now," Governor Smith refers to this incident and says that although he saw a possible conflict between his duty as president of the trucking company and his duty as Port Authority Commissioner, he could not turn Miller down in the light of his prior offer to help him. As the appointment carried no salary, it could not be regarded in any sense as political. Moreover, Governor Miller saw that it would be a fine start for the Port Authority if Commissionerships were dealt with on a broad basis of non-partisanship. As a matter of fact, this precedent was followed later when Governor Herbert H. Lehman, a Democrat, appointed former Governor Charles S. Whitman, a Republican, as a Commissioner.

VI

These two non-political appointments did more than any single thing to give the Port Authority its standing as a non-political body. The appointment by Governor Miller of Al Smith brought to the side of the Port Authority the leader of the Democratic party, respected by everyone, Republicans as well as Democrats, and brought to the institution his rich experience as a legislator and a Governor. J. Spencer Smith was named from New Jersey. In 1921 six Commissioners met at 115 Broadway to organize the Port Authority, while the staff of the Bi-State Commission remained outside.

Some person—who must remain unnamed—sent in two packages neatly done up in white paper and tied with white ribbon, suggestive of pieces of wedding cake—one marked for "Alfred E. Smith" and one for "J. Spencer Smith." Both opened their packages to discover just ordinary boxes of "Smith Brothers' Cough Drops." From then on they laughingly referred to each other as the "Smith Brothers' Cough Drops."

The institution started off with a laugh—the best note in the world for a serious job.

Down at Montauk in the summer of 1944, we went through a hurricane. Perry Duryea's pier was completely destroyed. When I saw Perry the day after, he was smiling. "Are you going to build a new one, Perry?" "Sure," he said. Hurricanes could not stop him or any of the natives at Montauk from carrying on. Hurricanes did not stop the Port Authority either.* Let me tell a bit more about the hurricane down at Montauk in the summer of 1944—the second we went through. My friend, Dr. Otis, has a little cottage down near the Coast Guard station on the ocean. He left our house in the afternoon with word that the coast guards had warned, "She's coming up the coast." That night the hurricane struck Montauk with wild fury. When it cleared next morning, my wife and I drove over to see how the Doctor had come through. (His wife was stuck in New York—no trains.) He had sat up all night. The gale had kept roaring in at a hundred mile an hour clip. Any moment he expected the roof of the house to be blown off and he would have to rush out and bury himself in a foxhole in the lee of the garage. He kept mopping up the floors, as the rain was driven in by the gale—just as we had done over our way at "Red Roof." We found Dr. Otis safe and sound. First thing he did—poet and artist that he is—was to invite us to look at the charging "white horses" of the sea, thirty feet high, as they crashed and thundered up the beach, their foaming crests, in the clear morning sunlight, flashing like millions upon millions of opalescent jewels. It was the Thanksgiving Hymn that follows Storm—in Beethoven's Pastoral Symphony.

Licked? Never. Our answer in the Port Authority was not in language but in spirit the same as General McAuliffe's now famous reply to the Germans' demand for surrender at Bastogne—"Nuts." None of us had studied Karl Von Clausewitz, but we acted on the belief that we could lose a lot of battles and not lose the war. The Von taught the Prussian army that in time of apparent defeat one could call on "fresh

---

* We went through many hurricanes in the Port Authority. The worst one of all was in 1933. Frank C. Ferguson who was then Vice-Chairman, will remember that midnight call on April first. It was no April fool's message—it was real trouble. We had to fasten down the roof and keep washing up the floors as the torrents of water came in through the windows. This storm didn't last for a day—it lasted a long time. But we weathered it!

forces and the natural weakening which every offensive undergoes in the long run may bring about a turn of fortune, or assistance may come from abroad. There is always still time to die." [9] Every good trial lawyer knows that. A witness may go to pieces—something in the way of surprise may be sprung by his adversary. The judge may rule against the trial lawyer and if he is polite but persistent, he may change the judge's mind.

VII

But here I am talking about "Exodus" and we haven't even completed "Genesis!" Wandering around that way, however, is part of the fun I am having in writing this book. History that is just chronology is like the history we were taught in our schooldays—dull. We like much better the "flashback" technique of the movies.

In 1917, the legislatures of the two states had put upon the Bi-State Commission the duty to study the railroad and transportation difficulties of the Port and to work out a physical engineering plan for their solution. In addition, the Commissioners were directed to submit a legal plan.[10]

The problem as it was presented divided itself into two fields for study: methods for cooperation between sovereignties and Interstate and Intrastate Commerce Law.

By December 2, 1918, the results of my study took the form of a report and a proposed draft of a treaty of compact between the two states. I had concluded that the two states could join in an original treaty, or, preferably, one amendatory of and supplementary to the treaty of 1834, and yet could preserve in full the sovereignty of each state. The states could join in a pledge of continuous cooperation in the development of the Port. They could create an agency vested with as little or as great power as the states chose to grant to it. The Authority could be authorized to borrow money upon the credit of the states to the extent that each state was willing to pledge its credit, or the states could authorize the corporate agency to borrow upon its own credit. It was clearly feasible, however, to leave municipal power where it then resided.

My report, a one hundred and forty page volume, covered experiences in international cooperation—the Suez Canal Convention, the Hay-Pauncefote Treaty governing the Panama Canal, the Egyptian Commission on the Public Debt, the Treaty of the Congress of Vienna, the Treaty of London of 1831 among Great Britain, Austria, France, Prussia, Russia and Belgium, dealing with the Scheldt, the International Joint Commission existing between the United States and

Canada, and many other guiding precedents. That exploration trip was an interesting adventure. Figuratively, it took me around the world for about two years.

It is fair to say that though this report received consideration by lawyers in both states, no exception was ever taken to any of its legal premises or conclusions. All the discussion—over four years—centered entirely upon matters of policy, or on matters of detail in the way of protection of each state against the other and protection against abuse of power by the Authority itself.

The heart of the Compact is contained in the simple pledge of co-operation between the two states—"the wedding ring"—and in the creation of the Port Authority as the "municipal corporate instru-mentality" of the two states to effectuate that cooperation. To protect each state against the other, a provision was inserted that two votes from each state was required to make any action valid. Later on, when the Commission was enlarged from six to twelve members, four votes were required from each state. To protect the states from abuse of power by any Commissioner, we put a provision in the Compact, by which each state reserved the right to provide for veto by the Gov-ernor of an action by a Commissioner from his state.

Later, this reserved power was exercised. The legislature of each state passed a bill, requiring the prompt forwarding of the official minutes of the Port Authority to the Governors. If a Governor did not like what the Commissioners were doing, he could say so. Several times in its history, Governors did criticize and when they had a real point, it influenced the Commissioners and sometimes resulted in a reversal on their part.

But my opinions rendered at several critical points in the Author-ity's history were all to the effect that the Governors could not sub-stitute their judgment for the judgment of the Commissioners. They could veto to protect the Compact—not to destroy it. These opinions are now part of the *practical construction* of the legislation, accepted as it has been by one Governor after another—not always cheerfully, I must say. These provisions are, however, a protection to the states against malfeasance or misfeasance on the part of any Commissioner. There is no danger of an abuse of power.

VIII

I must tell of an incident which occurred in 1921, when the legislation for the "Comprehensive Plan" was up for final passage. Without such approval, the work of the Authority would have been halted. This is the legislation which Al Smith supported. We had the votes in both the New York Senate and Assembly.

James J. Walker, later Mayor of New York, was then the minority leader of the Senate. Hylan was still vocal. Since the New York City Senatorial delegation did not want to antagonize Hylan, they decided to support him—even if they were outvoted.

I followed the bill through both Houses and was granted the courtesy of sitting in the Senate Chamber, under the Presiding Officer's desk— where the newspaper men sit. Senator Walker had two moves to make. One was an amendment requiring the approval by the City of New York before any plan could be effectuated, and the other, a bill giving the City of New York power to name two of the three Commissioners. He came over to where I was sitting and told me his problem, and asked for my help. Why not? I told him to offer an amendment to the bill and get the vote on that. Then to move to "discharge the Committee from further consideration" of his own bill—the one Hylan wanted. This would be defeated. He then asked me to draw up the proposed amendment. And I did. When his colleagues asked him who had drawn it and he told them, they were content. Walker made his record and we secured the passage of our bill with Republican votes. Of course, the amendment offered by him was beaten. We both knew it would be. It can be said to his credit that when he became Mayor he worked in hearty cooperation with the Port Authority.

Before this "Comprehensive Plan" was approved by the Commission in 1920, it was submitted to an Advisory Council made up of appointees of Chambers of Commerce and Boards of Trade from both New York and New Jersey. It was at one of the meetings of the Advisory Council that Al Smith (then a Commissioner of the Port Authority) said:

> "We can sit here and talk engineering figures for a year. We can draw plans for five years, but if there isn't a healthy, vigorous determination on the part of localities and organizations, the people generally in the Port district, to make some change in the old-fashioned, worn-out, dilapidated way of doing business in this Port, the figures will amount to nothing. * * * The great problem is to excite enough public opinion behind the plan, or any plan, or the problem itself, so as to make the plan effective when adopted." [11]

To bring about a common understanding in the Port district on both sides of the Hudson, the Commissioners created the Educational Council. This work was taken over by Belle Moskowitz.

Erwin Wilkie Bard said:

> "To pilot these bills unimpaired through the legislatures of two States, and the Congress of the United States was no small feat." [12]

It was not done by any one person, it required support from a host of people. By 1932, however, when the Tunnel Commission was merged with the Port Authority, we might have paraphrased something from Winston Churchill's speech in September, 1944. "What was concealed in 1917 had by 1933 become apparent. What in 1917 was in the egg was now afoot, and what was then a twig was now a great tree."

I must say a little more about the substantial contribution Governor Nathan L. Miller made. It will be recalled that he defeated Al Smith in 1920. In October of that year the New York State Chamber of Commerce had its annual banquet at the Waldorf-Astoria and the Governor-elect was the guest of honor.

Darwin P. Kingsley, then President of the Chamber, was toastmaster. I was its General Counsel. Kingsley had asked me to take half an hour to outline the plan of the Port Compact and the Port Authority. It was the first presentation of the project that Governor Miller had heard. As we were putting on our overcoats in the cloak room after the dinner he said to me, "After the first of the year, I want you to come to Albany and go over this thing with me."

I did go, and in the same room where Al had toasted the passage of the Eighteenth Amendment, Governor Miller—who had been Chief Judge of the Court of Appeals—listened. It took very little argument to persuade him of the soundness of the plan. As a good lawyer he understood thoroughly the principles of law upon which the project was based. In 1920 the Republican leadership in the Senate had not been very strong for the Port Authority plan. But this was changed in 1921. Governor Miller arranged for the conference with the leaders of the Senate and the Assembly. Our bill was passed by both Houses. The Port Compact was signed April 30, 1921.

It seemed appropriate that the ceremonies connected with the signing of this document should take place in the Great Hall of the Chamber of Commerce. That was where the "New York Harbor Case" was tried. That was where Governors Edge and Whitman joined in the pledge of cooperation between the two States. So Charles T. Gwynne, then Executive Secretary of the Chamber, programmed a real party. He thought that the ceremonies should be such as would prove worthy of so important an historic event. Of course, the signing of the treaty in itself was just a formal act. In addition to those authorized to affix their names to it as the official agents of the two States, the scenario pictured by Gwynne called for witnesses, all very prominent.

The official signers were to make speeches, as were each of the attesting witnesses. Naturally, Governor Miller was cast for the star role. He

was to preside. Everything was set up and the press was notified to send
their best reporters. And the day before, Governor Miller telephoned
Secretary Gwynne that he was too busy on gubernatorial matters at
Albany to come down to New York! Did you ever hear of such a thing?
Didn't the man have any romance in his soul? I must say that with all
his ability, Nathan Miller was no showman.

To prevent the affair from becoming a complete fiasco, I got on the
telephone and on bended knees and with tears in my voice, begged the
Governor to come. He came. The treaty was signed. The speeches were
made. I made none. But I got the pen with which the treaty was signed.
The same pen was used in New Jersey when the officers over there
signed the bill authorizing the treaty. Judge Francis Delehanty used
it when he signed the order denying the City an injunction to stop the
execution of the treaty. Oh, I forgot to say, Hylan and his colleagues
at the last moment brought a suit. He took a good drubbing then.

IX

After the decision by the United States Tax Court in our favor in the
Shamberg case, Sanders Shanks, publisher of the "Bond Buyer," referred to me as "The Daddy of the Port Authority." That reminds me
of another story:

When the Army Engineer was conducting a hearing on the then proposed interstate crossing—afterwards named the Goethals Bridge—
Arthur N. Pierson led a supporting delegation. The advocates of the
bridge referred to Arthur fondly as the father of the bridge. Later in
the hearing, a lady who said she was married—but not to Arthur—declared: "If Senator Pierson is the father of this bridge, then I want you
to know I'm its *mother*." She, too, had been a strong advocate of the
project for many years. Each one properly married yet parent of a
child born out of wedlock! What kind of a child was that bridge, anyway? With so many progenitors, there are people who will say what
kind of an institution they think the Port Authority really is. As a
matter of fact, its legitimacy—or the legitimacy of its works—has been
twice the subject of legislative investigation in New Jersey, but, happily, in the end always with creditable outcome to its good name and
repute.

Of course, I would be less than human if I did not like Sanders Shanks'
reference to my responsibility for the paternity of this child. But the
truth is the truth and should be told. You cannot find out by tests of
the father's and the child's blood—as they have a way of doing out on
the Pacific coast—but the record tells the story itself. This child was—
as Chief Justice Van Brunt said in that bastardy case—"the result of

the efforts of no one individual, but rather the efforts of a syndicate."

Here is a list of the leaders who contributed—each of them can rightly be called "Daddy" of the baby. On the New York side, Eugenius H. Outerbridge, Charles S. Whitman, Alfred E. Smith, Nathan L. Miller, Samuel L. Fuller. On the New Jersey side, Walter E. Edge, Joseph S. Frelinghuysen, Clarence E. Case, Arthur N. Pierson, Thomas F. McCran. Let others who will confess to their shame speak up. There were a lot of "daddies" around in 1917–1921. I would not hurt anyone's feelings for the world.

X

Would you like to look at some of my pewter—treasure trove gathered on the way? I am sure I will be forgiven if I quote from Professor Bard's book on "The Port Authority." He worked for several years studying the records before he wrote this book for Columbia University.

> "Finally, a word should be said about the law work of the Port Authority. Julius Henry Cohen has been chief counsel to the Port Authority since its inception. Its legal architecture is largely his work. Under his direction the Port Authority has been signally successful in the courts and its views have generally prevailed with other branches of the government. In a field where direct legal precedents were lacking, the guidance of the Port Authority has required the talents of a flexible and searching legal mind. These are the qualities which he has imparted to his staff. The contribution of the law department has penetrated deeply into all phases of the Port Authority: improvements in the form of construction contracts, the negotiation of multi-risk and use and occupancy insurance policies on the vehicular facilities, the drafting of the basic bond resolution. There has further been a tendency to call upon members of the department for assignments which were not legal at all but of a staff character. Currently the Port Authority's attorneys have been doing most of the work in the campaign of defense for the tax-exempt status of income from bonds such as its own and those of state and local governments." [13]

And in the copy which he gave me he wrote in his own hand:

> "To Julius Henry Cohen, whose brilliant mind conceived the Port of New York Authority and guided its development for better than two decades."

Sidney Lanier once wrote that he was convinced that *"praise* is no ignoble stimulus, and that the artist should not despise it," and "although I am far more independent of praise than formerly, and can do without it perfectly well: yet, when it comes, I keenly enjoy it." [14]

The nice thing about such generous gifts is that the United States Government—and be assured this is the law—cannot collect gift, inheritance or income tax upon them. They just defy the valuation of tax appraisers. And whether they are mere flattery or truth, they are

just as good for one's soul. They are a solace and a comfort to turn to
on a rainy day. And as soldiers and sailors fondle their medals and
ribbons, I fondle mine. For me such gifts are as good a tonic as looking at an LL.D.—which no University ever thought of conferring on
me—or hearing some one call out "Hello, Judge"—a title which nearly
every one seems to confer upon me now, though the nearest I ever got
to judicial office was to sit as a judge with McClelland Barclay and
Clem Keys in a bathing beauty contest at the Surf Club in the summer
of 1942—or as an official Arbitrator on the panel of the motion picture
industry, where the arbitrator is always subject to reversal by some
real-honest-to-goodness ex-judges.

There was a lot of fun in my twenty-five years of service. But there
is a good deal of fun, too, in being released from the restraints that accompany service as a public officer. In such an office, discretion imposes
silence in many matters where there is an urge to speak out.

In 1942 I regained my freedom. Freedom to speak and write as I
pleased. A lawyer in private practice! There is tonic in that surf.

CHAPTER TWENTY-SIX

Imperat aut servit collecta pecunia cuique.
Money is always either our master or our slave.

Samuel L. Fuller

*Wall Street influence—Creative financing—An example
of public spirit combined with expert knowledge of
banking and finance*

I

THERE HANGS ON A WALL in my office a photograph of a check for
$65,122,923.03, dated March 29, 1931, and payable to the Port of New
York Authority. This check represents the proceeds of the $66,000,000
bond issue of the Port of New York Authority for the financing of Inland Terminal Number One and the refinancing of the Holland
Tunnel. The National City Company was the head of the syndicate
which successfully bid for this bond issue.

Under the check is a photograph of a group of eight men, seven
standing behind a desk and one seated. That gray-haired, serious looking fellow, seated, looks like a college professor, but he is not. He is
Charles E. Mitchell, the then Chairman of the National City Company. Behind him, also with serious mien, is Horace C. Sylvester, Jr.,
Vice-Chairman of the same company. On his right, is John F. Galvin,
then the Chairman of the Port of New York Authority. The other
figures in the group are Samuel L. Fuller, William Leary, then Treasurer of the Port Authority, Schuyler N. Rice, Chairman of its Finance
Committee, John Ramsey, then General Manager of the Port Authority. Between Commissioners Rice and Galvin is the General Counsel
of the Port Authority.

The picture of the strong, broad-shouldered, football tackle, with a
chin as pugnacious as "Bill" Leary's mustache, is that of Samuel L.
Fuller. He won his "H" in the battles of his day with the Yale elevens.
Anyone who has known him as I have for more than two decades,
would know that he is one of the gentlest and kindliest of men—

generous to a fault. Because he was one of the pathfinders for the Port Authority—he found the money for us to start with—he deserves a place in this gallery.

Fuller was a successful man, but like most men of the "street," he has taken his lickings. Whenever he was frustrated, he just picked himself up, dusted himself off and went marching again. Fuller, like Horace E. Deming, came of New England stock. Like Deming, too, he was of Andover and Harvard training. His father, Dr. James R. Fuller, a country doctor, practiced in New London, Connecticut, and later in Andover, where the son grew up.

While Sam Fuller did not "take in washing" to work his way through Andover and Harvard, he did support himself and helped his family. He ran the Harvard "Crimson," for one thing. It is good training for a man who expects either to be a lawyer or a banker to go to college, if for nothing else, for the "contacts" he makes. Fuller got both, the training, through working his way, and fine contacts with men of power, wealth and influence. He made friends, because, like Outerbridge, he had personal charm. It is a family secret, which I break, that at one time he had an ambition to become a lawyer, but progress in that field seemed too slow—at least too slow to enable him to marry Constance Greenough, which he wanted very much to do. In his class, Harvard '98, Fuller met William Woodward, later of the Central Hanover Bank, John Prentiss of Hornblower and Weeks and C. Chauncey Stillman. They became valuable friends. In 1917 and 1918 he went through an experience in public service in the United States Shipping Board at Washington and later went across to Italy as a Commissioner of the American Red Cross. He stayed there until World War I was over. King Victor Emmanuel recognized his great contributions to Italy by making him an Honorary Citizen of Rome and conferring upon him the ribbons of the "Order of the Crown of Italy" and the "Order of Maurizio and San Lazario."

When he returned to this country in 1919, he went into business again with his classmate, Herman Kinnicutt, of the firm of Kissel, Kinnicutt & Company, in which he had begun in 1908. He became a Wall Street banker.

I said Fuller was generous. How generous? Ask at Andover who gave it the Memorial Carillon Tower in memory of the Andover boys who lost their lives in World War I. Fuller was a lover of the arts. At his home in Greenwich is a fine collection of paintings and books.

He was a leader in organizing the General Cable Company, the Revere Copper and Brass Company, the Waldorf-Astoria, the General Realty Company, besides doing a considerable bit of government financing for South American Republics like Chile or Colombia. (To have an interesting evening, let Fuller talk about any one of these Latin countries, or of Mexico.) He is still a Wall Street banker, member of the firm of Merrill, Lynch, Pearce, Fenner & Beane, doing a nation-wide business for investors.

Not so long ago, in the early thirties, to say that a man was a "Wall Street banker" was just about enough to push him out of any respectable society. I remember that at the 1932 banquet of the United States Chamber of Commerce in Washington, there was arranged a series of daises—like rungs on a ladder—upon which sat, in tiers, prominent leaders of commerce, industry and banking. As the presiding officer introduced each one by name to take his bow, the president of one of the country's largest banks was called up by name and introduced as "Mr. . . . , Banker." Loud guffaws greeted this announcement.

Of course, there had been abuse of power by some bankers. Anti-*banker* sentiment is no different in essence from anti-*labor*, anti-*Catholic* or anti-*Jewish* bias—people condemn by *generalization*—people judge not on the basis of individual character but by easy generalization. Some bankers did forget, as some labor leaders forget, Lord Acton's maxim—"All power corrupts—and absolute power corrupts absolutely."

Today the pendulum is swinging the other way. Now we generalize about labor leaders. Simeon Strunsky said that "when the Money Power was dethroned after 1930, and the G.H.Q. of financiering moved from Wall Street to Washington, and the New York financial district was as Nineveh and Tyre," [1] it became a day of triumph of the radical CIO Unions. In the chapters on the garment industry we have shown how power in industry can be subject to abuse by labor leaders and employers. Just as clearly subject to abuse is power in the financial world. But as there are labor leaders *and* labor leaders and bosses *and* bosses, there are bankers *and* bankers.

There were in 1932 and there are today men in Wall Street who are not only good bankers but are good citizens as well. I knew such a man intimately in the late nineties, when I was with Horace E. Deming—Cyrus J. Lawrence, one of Deming's clients—respected not only in Wall Street but throughout the country as a banker of integrity.

In 1919 there were men of culture, of vision and of character doing business in Wall Street. Samuel L. Fuller was one of them. I met Fuller through Outerbridge. On the basis of their friendship for each other, Fuller and I became close friends. This friendship has lasted for a quarter of a century.

II

As we had planned, the Port Authority was to be a public enterprise, yet carrying on as a business corporation. To do business it had to have money. What were we to do for money? "Going to lift yourself up by your own bootstraps?"—sneered Craig, Comptroller of New York City.

We needed a strong public opinion too. We needed support from Governors and legislators and we needed fine engineers and fine administrators. But all this would have gotten us nowhere unless we could raise money—real money.

We did get appropriations from the two States of $100,000 a year for the first few years of our existence, but that was just chicken-feed. We needed millions of dollars. *Hundreds of millions.* Through Outerbridge's influence, we made contact with pretty nearly every one of the leaders in the financial world. Samuel L. Fuller took the lead in this work.

It is the simple truth that to be a successful banker one must have imagination and initiative, besides being a fine analyst of facts. One must thoroughly understand human nature and be that rare combination—optimist, realist and skeptic. One must be willing always to back his judgment with money. A legal training will not hurt. There is, for example, Russell Leffingwell, who went from the Cravath law firm to become partner of J. P. Morgan & Company. Dwight Morrow was a lawyer before he became a member of the same firm. Waddill Catchings went from Sullivan & Cromwell, the lawyers, into banking. Their training as lawyers helped each of them become a successful banker. There is one faculty that beyond everything else is indispensable in a "Wall Street man"—he must not be a slave to logic. Lord Tweedsmuir put it this way:

> "The drawback to a completely rational mind is that it is apt to assume that what is flawless in logic is therefore practicable. Milner never made that mistake; he knew too well the stubborn illogiciality of facts. But he seemed to have an instinct for what was possible, an extra sense which must have been due to nature and not to experience * * *" [2]

As the result of my observations, this seems to me the dividing line between the mental processes of the men of enterprise and those who made blueprint programs in Washington during the period from 1933 to about 1944.

III

Fuller in 1920 was like fine whiskey, mellow and aged in the wood. Among other things, he knew how investors reacted to offers of "municipals." He knew all the dealers—Horace Sylvester of the National City Bank, John Linen of the Chase National Bank, and the leading bond men of Lehman Brothers and others. I met most of these men in closer contact when preparing for the trial of the Port Authority case in the United States Tax Court in 1943. I was obliged then to learn more of the intricacies of the marketing of State and Municipal securities and to immerse myself in the thinking "of the Street." I prevailed on one of them, "Chet" Laing of Nuveen & Company, of Chicago, to sit beside me throughout the trial. Fuller and Delmont K. Pfeffer of the National City Bank and Rosewald Armstrong of the Commercial Bank and Trust Company were on my board of tutors in that case. I appreciated then for the first time the amount of knowledge and experience that goes into the handling of a $66,-000,000 bond issue. None of these men is a "blueprint boy." They deal in realities.

The simple truth is that the Port Authority needed Sam Fuller in its pioneer days quite as much as it needed Othmar H. Ammann, the great bridge engineer, or John Evans, its Terminal Engineer, or Walter Hedden, in its Port Planning—or for that matter its lawyers. Ammann, Evans, Hedden, and the whole Law Department of the Port Authority would have achieved precisely nothing if we had not been able to sell Port Authority bonds to the public. Fuller organized the first syndicate to buy our bonds. He sold our bonds to the others in his group before we ever thought of offering them on the market. Later he became the official "Financial Advisor" to the Port Authority and was proud of the title. He gave his advice freely on such matters as the timing of issues, the form of our securities and other intricate phases of financial policy.

At this point I should set down for the record the historical fact that Arthur Anderson and later Dwight Morrow, both of J. P. Morgan & Company, studied our program from the beginning. When it came time for public sale of our first issue of sixteen millions, I was able to bring the Commissioners of the Port Authority the encouraging assurance that if there were no other bidders, the "House of Morgan" would put in a bid for the bonds. The spirit in which this was done was the spirit of *pathfinders*. The members of the firm had confidence in the Port of New York. In addition, they took it as part of their duty to help build up the institution for New York and its business interests.

Sam Fuller and the members of the Morgan firm were close friends and collaborated in the study of the institution and its prospects. *They bet on the Port Authority. And we won!* It turned out that it was not necessary for the Morgan firm to bid. The bidders for our first bonds were: The National City Company, Brown Brothers & Company, Harris, Forbes & Company, Kissel, Kinnicutt & Company (Fuller's firm), and White, Weld & Company. Their bid was 97.25 for bonds bearing a coupon of 4½ per cent, redeemable at 105. This represented an interest cost to the Port Authority of 4.76. The bonds were offered to the public at 100. They were oversubscribed and within twenty-four hours were quoted at 100¼ bid and 101½ asked. That successful bidding was the forerunner of the continuous financial success of the Port Authority.

We went through many crises. General Eisenhower said once that "War is like pushing a heavily loaded wagon up a steep hill in a fog and never knowing when you are going to reach the top. So you have to push like hell all the time." [3] Substitute "Port Authority" for the word "war"—and here in a few words is the entire history of that institution.

IV

There came a time when our piecemeal system of finance nearly strangled us. We had started off with a mere trifle of $16,000,000 with which to build two Staten Island bridges—the Outerbridge Crossing and the Goethals Bridge. These two were financed together. But all subsequent enterprises were treated as separate enterprises, each dependent wholly upon its own revenues to support the bond issues.

Before we even began to issue bonds, Outerbridge created an advisory committee of bankers. Among its members were Albert Strauss of J. & W. Seligman Co., Arthur M. Anderson of J. P. Morgan & Company, James Speyer of Speyer & Company, Jerome J. Hanauer of Kuhn, Loeb & Company, and Samuel L. Fuller. They gave us great help. But most of them were short on experience in legislative matters. Some of them thought it was quite simple to get legislative authority to issue one general bond to cover all the enterprises which we might build— a sort of blanket power of attorney from the two states. Of course, we who had to get the legislation through two states, knew that to get such a grant of power was utterly impossible. We went back to the "rung on rung" ladder method—building up our credit, step by step, as we went along. When Joseph A. McGinnies, Speaker of the Assembly of New York, asked me once why we started with the Staten Island Bridges when the George Washington Bridge was so much more important, I told him frankly that it was because we wanted to begin with something where we were most likely to succeed and the smaller enterprise was the better one for that purpose. If we succeeded, the George Washington Bridge would surely come later. And so it did.

The day we were expecting our first bids, I chanced to meet Jerome J. Hanauer of the Advisory group on Pine Street. He was then bearish on Port Authority bonds. He said we would get no bids and that it was a great mistake to put out an issue secured only by revenues from the bridges. Less than ten years later, Hanauer became a substantial investor in "Ports." Time changes opinions—we found that out.

For the sake of the record, I should tell how we came to the "backlog" method—that is, the advances of money by the two States. It was clear that the States would not be legally bound by the bonds we proposed to issue. But since they were to be issued on behalf of the States, there would be great selling value if the States would indicate in some substantial way their confidence in the enterprise.

After a discouraging conference with the financial advisory committee at the Chamber of Commerce, Outerbridge and I left the meeting with James Speyer. Speyer suggested that we get the States to put in some money, even if it were secondary to the money to be raised on our bonds. When I got to my office, I telephoned immediately to Arthur N. Pierson, then Senator from New Jersey from Union County, the pioneer in New Jersey in this bridge financing legislation. Pierson came right over and we then worked out the schedule of payments to be made by the State as "second monies."

Bard refers to the plan and its efficacy in his book:

> "This plan of mixed financing was original in the United States with the Port of New York Authority. It removed the main stumbling block from the path of autonomously financed public works, the problem of risk capital. Tolls to be levied on the bridges had been estimated to produce sufficient revenue to pay operating costs, interest, and amortization of the entire cost of construction. However, the estimates, from the point of view of the investor, were far from being guarantees. The function of providing the risk capital was performed by the states' contributions. By paying for a part of the construction cost and accepting a junior claim on the revenues, the states permitted the Port Authority to give its bondholders a prior claim on the entire yield of the enterprise. The effect of this on the safety of the private bondholders' investment may be shown by assuming that, in spite of the estimates, the revenue proved insufficient to make the project entirely self-sustaining. By the action of the states, the bondholders would not suffer until there had been a drop of almost twenty-five per cent below the revenue estimates. For this margin of safety they would accept a relatively low coupon rate, since the states would assume the margin share of the risk." [4]

After the Pulaski Skyway was built in New Jersey, however, the revenues of the two Staten Island bridges went down while at the same time those from the Holland Tunnel went up. It was then that it became clear that we should, if it were at all practicable, consolidate the finances of the Port Authority and put all its issues into one single security, supported by all its revenues and surpluses.

To work this out was an exceptionally difficult financial and legal task. The conference with the bankers and their lawyers lasted for almost six months. We finally adopted the "General and Refunding Bond." And in the course of time, these bonds took the place of all the special lien bonds. It is too long a story to be told here, but there were blue days in the Port Authority offices—many of them—before this result was achieved.

Two different approaches developed in our own ranks, one based on fear, the other on faith. Faith was justified, as events subsequently proved. But had we taken the temper of the defeatists, we should have fulfilled their prophecy and gone under. Over the years, the rate of interest the Port Authority has had to pay for its money has steadily gone down. When the merger took place with the Holland Tunnel Commission and the revenues of that facility came over to the Port Authority, it was clear then that revenues and surpluses would be adequate to meet every dollar of the obligations of the Port Authority.

V

In 1942 a new crisis developed. As a result of its war effort the Government cut down the use of gasoline. This naturally reduced the number of vehicles using the facilities of the Port Authority. Some of the conservative members of the staff of the Authority believed then that there would be such a serious decline in its revenues that it would dangerously affect its credit. Once more I did not share their fears. (But my associates did say I was always an incorrigible optimist.) The events of the succeeding years proved that the facilities of the Port Authority were very much needed for trucking war materials under and over the river. *The Port Authority never did go under.*

On September 18, 1944, George Wanders wrote in the financial pages of the Herald Tribune that Port of New York Authority bonds as well as those of the Tri-borough Bridge Authority "are well buttressed and are sure to ride out the dislocations of the war without evil effects. The period of uncertainty which began a year ago, when receipts were alarmingly low and traffic still was on the down-grade, is considered over by financial analysts. Revenues have stabilized at a comfortable level, far above the low figures occasioned by intensive gasoline and tire restriction." Wanders was right in saying, "The demonstrated financial soundness of the state-created agencies under the most adverse condition will lead to a vast expansion of the revenue bond method of financing projects."

The Port Authority has always been blessed with good luck. It has its own special fairy godmother who watches over it. (In a moment of weakness, I expressed it this way: "Handed a lemon, we'll make lemonade out of it.")

When the war came in 1941, Port Authority tunnels and bridges became indispensable thoroughfares for the accommodation of military vehicles and trucks engaged in war work. If the War Production Board had seen the light earlier, it would have permitted the Authority to secure in 1943 the material required for completing the second tube of the Lincoln Tunnel. It was opened February 1, 1945. By November 1st of 1944, 40,000 military vehicles had in one year used the south tube and the Chairman of the Port Authority announced that more than seventy-five per cent of the traffic using this one-half of the projected tunnel as well as the other Port Authority bridges and tunnels was of a nature highly essential to the war effort. In 1943, the south tube was used by 4,500,000 vehicles. The total for 1944 is estimated at 5,500,000.

The New York Times in its financial pages of February 22, 1945, said:

> "The market for the outstanding obligations of the Port of New York Authority and Tri-borough Bridge Authority received its real impetus some weeks ago when the United States Supreme Court ruled that income from those securities was exempt from Federal taxation. The subsequent rise in the market for those issues to new record high levels was generally attributed to that reassurance of tax immunity. However, something basically more substantial even than tax-exemption is the foundation for the current strength in the market for those obligations and that is the obvious margin of safety by which the Port Authority, at least, is covering the interest requirements on its outstanding bonds."

There have been days when some people sold the Port Authority short. Those investors who knew its history profited by picking up some good bargains in "Ports." "Triboro" buyers did even better. In June of 1945 the Port Authority offered to repay the two states the $8,300,000 advanced by them from 1926 to 1928 to aid in the construction of the Outerbridge Crossing and Goethals and Bayonne bridges. The payment would be made in two installments of Port Authority 1½% bonds, due in 1986. Governor Dewey wrote the Port Authority:

> "That you are in a position to go forward with a continuing program of necessary projects of port development and, at the same time, plan to anticipate the repayment of the advances in the amount of $8,300,000 made to you by the two States over the period 1926 to 1928 is a tribute to the prudence and soundness with which you have managed the public affairs entrusted to you."

Governor Edge wrote:

> "The ability of The Port of New York Authority to fund this obligation in this manner, despite the loss of revenues resulting from the wartime curtail-

ment of vehicular traffic, represents a fine attitude of cooperation and responsibility to the two states which created your great organization. On this basis both New Jersey and New York have reason to feel that the trust they have imposed in The Port of New York Authority has been well founded and the resources of the two States have been managed with great care and devotion to the public interests."

VI

When we prepared for the trial of the Shamberg case before the United States Tax Court (Hon. Clarence Opper presiding), we secured some of the best economists on theory in the whole country—led by Dr. Harley L. Lutz of Princeton and many municipal and state officials—all of whom testified to the "differential" in cost to states and cities if "municipals" were made subject to federal taxation. I had, too, the able assistance of Lewis L. Delafield, Jr., no mean expert on "municipals" himself. But I must repeat that the practical men in the field were the best advisers I had. It is the truth that it was they who gave the Port Authority its first nutriment. They brought the baby's milk right to the kitchen door. Without this milk—*no vitamins.*

The Port Authority was not the only baby so fed and nourished by homogenized milk. The financial condition of states and cities was such that the success of the Port Authority method led to creation of Bridge Authorities throughout the country. And this with the help of the Reconstruction Finance Corporation, which encouraged the formation of such instrumentalities—insisting always, as a prerequisite, upon the opinion of Bond Counsel—that such bonds were immune from Federal taxation!

Federal authorities, like the Tennessee Valley Authority, all the Housing Authorities, the St. Lawrence Power Authority, all followed the line of the financial and legislative experience of the pioneer—the Port of New York Authority. It is quite likely that Port Authority technique will be applied in still broader fields to make its employment much more extensive.

Whatever credit is due to others for the creation of the Port Authority, it should never be forgotten that unless it were successfully financed, it would have been a "blueprint" and nothing more. To the "Wall Street bankers," then, go the medal of honor. And to Samuel L. Fuller, "hats off" as the *pathfinder* for them and for us.

CHAPTER TWENTY-SEVEN

TO THE STATES

To the States or any one of them, or any city of the States,
  Resist much, obey little,
Once unquestioning obedience, once fully enslaved,
Once fully enslaved, no nation, State, city of this earth, ever
  afterward resumes her liberty.
                    Leaves of Grass, WALT WHITMAN.

Conference on State Defense

---

*A battle royal between a federal administration and
the states and cities—The states and cities win—So does
the Port Authority.*

I

THE CONFERENCE ON STATE DEFENSE came into being following the
decision of the United States Supreme Court in the *Gerhardt* [1] case.
It is a grouping of Governors, Attorney-Generals, State Treasurers,
Mayors and other officials throughout the country, deeply concerned
over the threat by the United States Government to tax state and
municipal bonds and who organized to fight against it and did so
successfully.

Before the Port of New York Authority sold any of its bonds, I
recommended that it secure the opinion of former Justice Charles
Evans Hughes, who had left the United States Supreme Court to run
for President, and, upon his defeat, returned to the private practice
of law. At once he became the outstanding leader of the American
Bar. We secured it. It may be of interest to know how much of a fee
Judge Hughes received for the opinion holding that our bonds were
immune from federal taxation. It is a matter of record. He charged the
Port Authority $5,000. It might have been four or five times that
amount if the opinion had been rendered to a group of bankers. Judge
Hughes went over all our legislation and agreed that under the law
Port Authority bonds were immune from federal taxation. That was
in 1925. It is not too much to say that not only the $500,000,000 of
bonds which the Port Authority itself has issued, but literally more

than a hundred billion dollars of bonds were sold upon reliance upon the law as it stood when Justice Hughes gave his opinion—and, indeed, as it stands today. The firm of Thomson, Wood & Hoffman (David C. Wood) agreed with us and rendered supporting opinions from time to time on all Port Authority issues. The United States Supreme Court has so decided and it is the law today.

Came a time when the Treasury "boys" persuaded their chief, the Secretary of the Treasury (Henry Morganthau), and he in turn persuaded President Roosevelt, to take the position that the immunity of state and municipal bonds from federal taxation was wrong and should be stopped. This move synchronized with an attack upon the immunity from federal taxation of the salary of public employees.

The Court had held in two cases, the *Rogers*[2] and the *Brush*[3] cases, that employees working for a state or municipal governmental agency were free from federal income taxes on their salaries and by the same reasoning federal employees in similar position were free from state income taxes. We in the Port Authority became convinced from the trend of events that the attack upon the immunity of the salaries would be followed by an attack upon the immunity of the bonds. Furthermore, that it might ultimately involve an attack upon the immunity of state and municipal revenues. Later, in the *O'Keefe*[4] case, the Court decided that the salaries of federal employees were subject to state income taxation. This meant that our adversaries in the Treasury and Justice departments—who were residents of states in which there were income tax laws—had to take the same punishment we did. (I am not at all certain they expected such a boomerang.) It was a defeat not only for Port Authority employees, but for every public employee in the country—school teachers, firemen, policemen, street sweepers. Worse still, it meant that every public employee was liable for back taxes for at least three and perhaps many more years.

Let me explain this. When the Court decides that the law is thus and so, it says that has been the law all along. And when it reverses a prior decision, the prior decision is wiped out completely—erased, expunged, and the taxpayer becomes liable for his acts as though the law now announced were the law when he thought it was otherwise and had acted accordingly. Ordinarily, there are a few exceptions, but a statute does not operate retroactively. There are some cases, where the legislative intent is clear, and no vested or contractual rights being involved, Congress may make a law retroactive. *But with judicial decisions, the situation is different.* The United States Supreme Court is the supreme judicial tribunal of the country, and applying the doctrine of "judicial correction of judicial error" * it may say, as it did in the *Gerhardt* and *O'Keefe* cases, "We were all wrong in our previous decisions. Hence we now reverse ourselves and say that what we said was the law was not the law and never was the law."

In practical effect, it was as if the Court had said to all the public officers and employees, "So sorry if we have caused you any inconvenience by our error. That is too bad, but we have to make decisions even though the heavens fall upon you. You must act like good citizens and take it without flinching."

Now, there is a way out of this dilemma. Judge Cardozo pointed it out clearly in *Great Northern Ry. Co. v. Sunburst Oil & R. Co.,*[5] and we submitted that method to the Court on our motion for reargument.

The papers on the petition for rehearing pointed out that in applying the principle enunciated in *Great Northern Ry. Co. v. Sunburst Oil & R. Co.,* the Court could obviate the harsh consequences that would follow from its decision by the employment of a recognized judicial procedure already approved by the Court.[6] We said:

"A judicial tribunal can restrict the application of its reversal of previous doctrine to such situations as arise after the rendering of the opinion, while applying the reversed doctrine to existing situations which arose in reliance upon existing law."

The opinion in the *Great Northern Ry. Co. v. Sunburst Oil & R. Co.,* by Mr. Justice Cardozo, accented the point that the major obstacle in the way of such an enlightened doctrine was the "ancient dogma that the law declared by its courts had a Platonic or Ideal existence before the act of declaration, in which even the discredited declaration will be viewed as if it had never been, and the reconsidered declaration as law from the beginning."

In his book "The Nature of the Judicial Process," Justice Cardozo said:

"I think it is significant that when the hardship is felt to be too great or to be unnecessary, retrospective operation is withheld. Take the cases where a court of final appeal has declared a statute void, and afterwards, reversing itself, declares the statute valid. Intervening transactions have been governed by the first decision. What shall be said of the validity of such transactions when the decision is overruled? Most courts in a spirit of realism have held that the operation of the statute has been suspended in the interval [citing authorities]. It may be hard to square such a ruling with abstract dogmas and definitions. * * * Where the line of division will some day be located, I will make no attempt to say. I feel assured, however, that its location, wherever it shall be, will be gov-

* See Chapter 1.

erned, not by metaphysical conceptions of the nature of judge-made law, nor by
the fetish of some implacable tenet, such as that of the division of governmental
powers, but by considerations of convenience, of utility, and of the deepest
sentiment of justice." [7]

II

There was another strange thing about the *Gerhardt* decision. The
lawyers who appeared before the Court argued only a simple proposition: "Was the Port Authority engaged in governmental functions
or was it not?" Was it engaged in carrying on "proprietary functions,"
that is, was it engaged in private business?

Golden W. Bell, the Assistant Solicitor-General, who argued for the
Government, answered the Court's question from the bench by saying:
"If the Port Authority is not engaged in proprietary functions, we
concede that Gerhardt's salary is tax-exempt." Nevertheless, the Court
held that though the Port Authority might itself be exempt from taxation, Gerhardt was doing the work of any like employee of a private
business and hence was subject to federal income tax.

Westbrook Pegler was highly elated over this result. It was a day
of triumph for him. He had been denouncing the tax-exemption of
public employees and had labeled them all as "parasitical functionaries." When we had our usual staff garden party up at Fir Cones that
summer, we celebrated our defeat by providing for all the lawyers,
sandwich signs bearing the single legend in large letters: "I am a
Parasitical Functionary." The boys gloried in their shame, while the
girls sang a Gilbert and Sullivan melody as they paraded around. Of
course, there have been parasites in the government service and always
will be. There are also functionaries, that is, men and women who
function in the government service. But without competent and able
men in the public service, the government could not be carried on.
The late Joseph B. Eastman was such an outstanding public servant.
On his death in 1944, Mr. Justice Felix Frankfurter wrote a fine letter
to the New York Times praising him and citing him as an example
of a public official who had done great public service.[8]

The men and women who were "career men and women" and in
office in 1938, planned their lives on the assumption that their salaries
were to be *net*. When taxation went to the limits it did in 1940–1943,
their situation was vitally changed.

If a husband in a state or governmental service told his wife how
much of his salary had to go back to the federal government, of course
she was surprised. He had told her that under the law, his salary was
free from federal tax and when the Court decided the *Brush* and
Rogers cases, he was very confident that that was the law. He could

hardly guess that within two years the United States Supreme Court would somersault the whole thing. His wife might then say: "How could they do a thing like that?" Of course, the publicists of that day would advise him that he was free to leave the public service and go out into private practice again, if he were not satisfied with his *net*. In private life, under similar circumstances, his compensation would be raised—if he were an officer of a corporation—to enable him to meet his increased tax burden. But suppose it were a critical period, and as a public officer he felt a duty to stick to his post, as some men in Washington decided to do. He would determine to break away as soon as he could. Since the decision in the salary cases, the exodus of capable men from public office to private work is already well marked. The movement to encourage men to remain in public service as it was developed in the State Department—a movement in which my friend Frederick M. Davenport [9] did so much good work—received a serious setback when the United States Supreme Court rendered its decisions in the *Gerhardt* and *O'Keefe* cases.

Of course, sooner or later, increases in salaries will have to be made all along the line. It was brought out before his death that President Roosevelt's salary of $75,000 was net—after deduction of taxes—about $27,000, and that the proposed increase of $25,000 would give him only an additional $6,000 a year. By contrast, many a business executive gets a salary of $100,000 and some get as much as $300,000 or $400,000 a year. Others get sizable bonuses, cheerfully paid by the stockholders because they are worth it. Many motion picture stars receive salaries much over $100,000. The same principle applies to United States Supreme Court Justices. Should United States Supreme Court Justices take to writing textbooks on the Constitution in order to add to their income?

Mr. Justice Black said in one of his opinions:

"Public officials in this country * * * are almost universally paid for their services. * * * Without monetary rewards officeholding would necessarily be limited to one class only,—the independently wealthy. Proposals to accomplish such a purpose were deliberately rejected at the very beginning of the Nation's history." [10]

In his "Jefferson Himself," Bernard Mayo reprints an "Analysis of Expenditures from March 4, 1801, to March 4, 1802: * * * Credits, By salary, $25,000, tobacco, $2,974.00, profits of Nailery, supposed about $533.33." [11] There was no deduction from his salary for federal or state income taxation in Jefferson's day.

One conspicuously capable public servant, John Lord O'Brian, found it necessary to resume his private law practice and resign as General Counsel to the War Production Board. Of course, O'Brian earned in private practice from five to ten times what the government paid him. Why should not such a valuable man be kept in public service? [12] Three or four of the most expert men in the Treasury Department went out. Many joined large law firms as "tax experts."

In business, the knowledge of the inner workings of its machinery, of the practices and decisions already made, is all regarded as a capital investment of the employer. Pains are taken to hold on to it. This asset is being lost to the government. Nevertheless salaries will have to be raised. John W. McCormack, majority leader of Congress, made the statement to the House Judiciary Committee that without supplemental fees as a lawyer, he could not remain in Washington and added: "We very much need men of ability, even if they must have more money on which to live—otherwise Congress will become simply a rich man's club." [13]

The "Christian Science Monitor," in an editorial, August 27, 1945, entitled "Top Government Men Paid Too Little," takes the case of Dean Acheson's resignation as an example of the same point and says:

> "It is time, in the eyes of close students of American affairs, that Americans not only approved higher salaries for their representatives and public officials but demanded they get them. Those men can hardly demand it themselves.
>
> * * * * *
>
> Dean Acheson's case is singled out today only because it happens to be the latest and most striking example of America's failure in this matter of Government salaries to grow up to responsibilities."

(Acheson took a 90% cut in his gross income to enter the government service and had to resign or "continue to live in the red.") This is a different editorial point of view than prevailed when the United States Supreme Court decided the *Gerhardt* and *O'Keefe* cases. [14]

This is bound to happen all along the line. The Supreme Court heard no arguments on this point. It reversed its prior decision by taking "judicial notice" of certain factors in public and private employment and ignored a good many others. The worst sufferers are the federal judges, always underpaid. They remain silent simply because they are judges. Yet their nominal salary of $10,000 is worth, after taxes, only $7,650 annually. How can men of such calibre find means to support their families and educate their children on such pay? How can the people secure a capable, high-minded judiciary on such a basis of compensation?

Attorney-General Tom C. Clark testified recently before the Senate

Committee on Civil Service that it is fast becoming very difficult to get outstanding, or even highly qualified lawyers to accept appointments to the federal bench. He said that in the short time he has been in office, five men whom he wanted to recommend have declined to permit him to do so because they could not afford the financial sacrifice inherent in limiting themselves to a salary such as is now paid to judges.[15]

Lawyers understand this situation. A committee of the American Bar Association [16] said:

> "Members of the Federal Judiciary occupy a position which requires the extraordinary legal talent of men of standing and integrity. As one of the three great coordinate departments of the Government, it is their responsibility to interpret and enforce the Constitution and the multitude of Federal laws which affect the welfare of the citizens and the conduct of our Government.
>
> * * * * * *
>
> Federal judges should be chosen from the best members of the profession. Although there is no necessary constant relationship between ability and earnings, it is noteworthy that 10.5 per cent of the lawyers in the country earn more than $9000 per annum. Assuming, as we certainly believe to be the fact, that the Federal Judiciary generally is representative of the very top of the profession, it is clear that these men are being substantially less well compensated than if their abilities had not been devoted to public service. Any continuation of this disparity between compensation and ability must lead inevitably to a situation where judges will be drawn from among those with adequate private incomes or, the really able members of the profession not being able to afford to accept Federal judgeships, relatively incompetent judges will be appointed; either of these events would be extremely unfortunate."

I feel strongly that the Supreme Court decision in the salary cases constituted grave judicial error. The Court has reversed itself many times since 1939. It may do so again.[17] Surely the Court did not foresee the present day consequences of these decisions. Holmes differentiated between a public opinion that was *informed* and one that was not. Certainly a decision that results merely in adding additional revenue, only to pay it out in higher salaries, is not judicial statesmanship. Especially if it results in driving the best men out of public service. Sooner or later its unsoundness will lead to correction by the Court itself if not by congressional and state legislative action. When the wave of centralization dies down, public opinion will swing the other way.

The original basis for the theory of immunity was the principle that the state could only act through *instrumentalities*. And public officers and employees are *instrumentalities*. By reason of such immunity, the state saved millions of dollars by paying capable men *less* than they could earn in private occupations. Today the incentive to such men is to serve *for a while* and then capitalize on the influence and knowledge gained in the public service by responding to the attractiveness of private employment. This is an unhealthy situation for the government. It should retain its competent public servants and get rid of the other ones.

III

The Conference on State Defense succeeded in saving the public employees of the country from the immediate disaster that would have followed from their liability for "back-taxes" by securing appropriate action from Congress. The movement grew to much larger purpose. It became clear to all those who joined in it that the decision would be followed by an administrative program to tax state and municipal bonds.

As I grew up under Deming and Ivins, the move toward the destruction of the states and cities went against my grain. It did not improve my respect for the young geniuses who were throwing away the lessons of the past. This proposed appendectomy, as I saw it, was more likely to kill the patient than cure him. I was convinced that once the country was brought to the realization of what was really involved, a solid public opinion would turn against it. And this is just what happened after 1939. Whether it is called the revival of "states' rights" or not, it is an expression of the deep feeling of the people for local freedom from overlordship.

Over one hundred and fifty years ago, De Tocqueville wrote:

"The American attaches himself to his little community for the same reason that the mountaineer clings to his hills, because the characteristic features of his country are there more distinctly marked; it has a more striking physiognomy." [18]

An utterance from the Pope in his 1944 Christmas message to the world is appropriately described by that gifted writer and seer, Anne O'Hare McCormick, as "one of the historical utterances of the war." [19] To the conviction of the British and American liberals who adhere to the fundamentals of democratic government, the head of the Catholic Church adds his support and bases it, very properly, on the deeper principles of morals and religion involved. It was a comfort to read on Christmas Day in 1944, when the fog was lifting on the Western front, words of deep religious conviction supporting the two wars—the one on the battlefield and the other at home. Said the Pope:

"Moreover—and this is perhaps the most important point—beneath the sinister lightning of the war that encompasses them, in the blazing heat of the furnace that imprisons them, the peoples have, as it were, awakened from a long torpor. They have assumed, in relation to the state and those who govern, a new attitude—one that questions, criticizes, distrusts.

Taught by bitter experience, they are more aggressive in opposing the concentration of dictatorial power that cannot be censured or touched, and call for a system of government more in keeping with the dignity and liberty of the citizens. These multitudes, uneasy, stirred by the war to their innermost depths, are today firmly convinced—at first perhaps in a vague and confused way but already unyielding—that had there been the possibility of censuring and correcting the actions of public authority the world would not have been dragged into the vortex of a disastrous war, and that to avoid for the future the repetition of such a catastrophe we must vest efficient guaranties in the people itself." [20]

IV

The decorations for the triumph of the Conference on State Defense should be awarded to Austin J. Tobin, Secretary of the Conference, then Assistant General Counsel for the Port Authority, and to the members of the staff of the Law Department.[21]

Gradually support came. From Governors, from State Treasurers, from Attorneys-General, from Mayors, from the Leagues of Municipalities, from the American Bar Association, from the American Federation of Labor—until the Treasury "boys" were thoroughly licked in Congress.[22] One of the outstanding contributors was Henry Epstein, Solicitor-General of the State of New York. His address, "The States at the Crossroads," had great influence. The title was obviously appropriate and timely. It was like Paul Revere's call to arms.

Mayor LaGuardia, as head of the organization of municipalities, added his strength. Although financial contributions were received from municipal and public agencies all over the country, the Port of New York Authority and the Tri-borough Bridge Authority were the principal contributors to the expense of this fight. The Attorney-General of New York State, John J. Bennett, and Morris S. Tremaine, its Comptroller, were outstanding supporters. Governor Earl Warren of California, as California's Attorney-General, added his strength, too. Indeed, it is not too much to say that the movement in 1944 of the Governors of the States in the direction of reviving the integrity and sovereignty of the States and their combined resistance to the encroachment of the central government upon the States was, in large measure, due to this stirring up by the Conference on State Defense.

The hearings before the Brown Special Senate Committee and before the Senate Finance Committee and the Ways and Means Committee of the House were managed by members of the Port Authority Law Department. The work constitutes an important part of current American history.

In 1942 I was asked to address the Bar Association of Wilkes-Barre,

Pennsylvania. I took as my subject "Government of the People, By the People and For the People."

> "The time has come no longer to be carried away by discussion of economics. The world has been swept off its feet by the assumption that all our problems are economic. * * * 'God did not unfold the eternal vision to Adam Smith in Manchester nor yet to Karl Marx in the British Museum.' * Government is a matter of dealing with people. It is a matter of sound psychology, and of good morals, rather than a matter of economics. The student of history, the student of the science of government, and the student of psychology and morals, have more to contribute in the solution of these problems than those who have been confined in their thinking within the departmental boundaries of courses in or books on economics.
>
> The world is coming now to the traditional American viewpoint that that government which does not rest upon the consent of the governed is bound to fail; and that even in the case of so-called 'backward peoples' there must be held out to them the promise of self-government at the earliest possible date. At a time when we are seeking to protect ourselves and the other Allied Nations from coercion, we must be sure that there shall not be developed a government of coercion in our own country. Yet, there are people who really believe, and accept as a working philosophy, the new theory that social reforms they wish to see accomplished can and should be accomplished by the practical abolition of the states and the cities, and their subordination—especially in the field of finance and taxation—to the national government."

Some economists are prone to overlook what are essentially *political* and *moral* factors. As early as 1865 John Stuart Mill wrote in his essay "Considerations on Representative Government":

> "It is but a small portion of the public business of a country which can be well done or safely attempted by the central authorities; and even in our own government, the least centralized in Europe, the legislative portion at least of the governing body busies itself far too much with local affairs, employing the supreme power of the state in cutting small knots which there ought to be other and better means of untying. * * *
> It is farther to be remembered that, even supposing the central government to administer through its own officers, its officers do not act at the centre, but in the locality; and however inferior the local public may be to the central, it is the local public alone which has any opportunity of watching them, and it is the local opinion alone which either acts directly upon their own conduct, or calls the attention of the government to the points in which they may require correction." [23]

Thirty years earlier, De Tocqueville said, "A nation may establish a free government, but without municipal institutions it cannot have the spirit of liberty." [24] (I was brought up in this school of thought.)

Both Mill and De Tocqueville recognized clearly that there must be local responsibility, and to meet local responsibility there must be local power. In the nineties, there was no hope of getting good gov-

* Address by Associate Justice Felix Frankfurter at the Inauguration of Dr. Harry N. Wright, Sixth President of the College of the City of New York, September 30, 1942.

ernment in cities until they had secured their home-rule charters and the provisions in state constitutions limiting the interference of the states with their local governments. If one is a *functionalist,* he will concentrate upon devising a national fiscal policy and will come to the conclusion that Professor Edwin R. A. Seligman and his successor, Robert Murray Haig, came to, namely, that there can be no complete control of the financial policy of a country unless the field of income taxation *is wholly national.* I believe that this is fundamentally erroneous thinking.

The late Dr. Gustav Cassel saw this clearly. He wrote:

> "The leadership of the State in economic affairs which advocates of Planned Economy want to establish is, as we have seen, necessarily connected with a bewildering mass of governmental interferences of a steadily cumulative nature. The arbitrariness, the mistakes and the inevitable contradictions of such policy will, as daily experience shows, only strengthen the demand for a more rational coordination of the different measures and, therefore, for unified leadership. For this reason Planned Economy will always tend to develop into Dictatorship.

> * * * * *. *

> Once authoritative control has been established it will not always be possible to limit it to the economic domain. If we allow economic freedom and self-reliance to be destroyed, the powers standing for Liberty will have lost so much in strength that they will not be able to offer any effective resistance against a progressive extension of such destruction to constitutional and public life generally. And if this resistance is gradually given up—perhaps without people ever realizing what is actually going on—such fundamental values as personal liberty, freedom of thought and speech and independence of science are exposed to imminent danger. What stands to be lost is nothing less than the whole of that civilization that we have inherited from generations which once fought hard to lay its foundations and even gave their life for it." [25]

It took the tragic experience of a great war to make realistic the consequences of centralized government and to awaken thinking men everywhere to the danger lurking in the "functional theory of government." The Conference on State Defense was a ringing appeal to the older traditions of democracy. It was an "old man's" view presented to a younger generation and carried on by them with all the élan of youth.

My own feeling is that the dangers that Frederick A. Hayek * fears will be averted in two ways: First, scholars will realize more and more —as Cassel and Hayek do—that the problems of government in democracy are not to be solved by decisions in the field of economics which disregard the governmental phases of the problem. Solutions are to be found only with complete understanding of human nature and of tried methods for securing the widest possible participation of the people in determining governmental policies. Next, there is a renewed

* "The Road to Serfdom."

confidence in the capacity of the people to make sound decisions—the confidence which Jefferson had in a free government of free men. Religious leaders are stressing this point as a point of morals—respect for the inherent quality of man as man.

At a time when problems of sovereignty loom large in international relationship and we are urged to adopt the principle of federalism by granting powers to a supernational government, we must not fail to realize that the preservation of the independence of each sovereignty —except only as it delegates powers—must be tenaciously guarded.

The defeat in the *Gerhardt* and *O'Keefe* cases of the public employees of this country brought them to the side of a great principle. And they won!

CHAPTER TWENTY-EIGHT

The Moving Finger writes; and, having writ,
Moves on; nor all your Piety nor Wit
  Shall lure it back to cancel half a Line,
Nor all your Tears wash out a Word of it.

  Rubaiyat of Omar Khayyam. (FITZGERALD)

St. Lawrence Power Authority

An attempt to bring business and government into cooperation—How water power in the St. Lawrence or in the Tennessee Valley may be developed in the public interest—Failure in New York brings an idea to success in Tennessee—A warning against federalization and domination of the states

I

THE UNITED STATES and Great Britain are both confronted with the problem of dealing with great natural resources—coal and power. In England, as we know, the *public corporation* or *public trust* has long been known and used. In this country the Port Authority is the outstanding example and pioneer. In this country, we fear that extension of the field of public ownership and operation will bring *political* control, with their twins, *patronage* and *graft,* and that this will offset any of the advantages of governmental ownership and operation. Is there a way? We believe there is—an *American* way. The experiences of the St. Lawrence Power Commission from 1930 to 1932 have their scientific value—like a laboratory searching for Radar. It brought lessons worth recording not alone for students of government and economics, but for all who would participate with intelligence in the shaping of governmental policies in this field.

For a century or more, the latent potential energy in the St. Lawrence River has been going to waste. It is still going to waste. For three decades, it has been a football in New York State politics. Between 1900 and 1930 the utility interests and the Republicans in the legislature were in common accord, seeking to secure this power for development by private industry. That is, the existing utility companies. Between the "power interests" and the politicians, the general public was the forgotten man—the man in the middle.

The men who led the corporate interests in New York State were a fine target even in Theodore Roosevelt's days. He went after them with a "big stick!" After Theodore Roosevelt died it became good political strategy in New York for the Republicans to stand by the utility interests. While the conflict between the State and the power companies was running, the hydro-electric power was running, too—to waste.

In 1927 Governor Alfred E. Smith determined that though this was a tough nut to crack, it was clearly his responsibility to do something about it. He did not favor any general program of public ownership and operation of public utilities. He could not reconcile the investment of large sums of the State's money in such enterprises—at least not consistently with his own ideas of State Economy and Budget Reform. On the other hand, he wanted the power developed in the interests of the consuming public.

The St. Lawrence power problem was one of his headaches as Governor. He knew all the political angles of it, from his experience in the Legislature. Al had been a Commissioner of the Port Authority. He had seen its growth and knew about the "Authority Method." Indeed, he had applied it to the "Housing" problem. It was not Al's habit to duck a problem or pass the buck. A problem of that kind was something to be grappled with and mastered.

One day, Belle Moskowitz came down to see me with instructions from the Governor to find out whether or not the *authority method* could be applied in the solution of the St. Lawrence problem. When the Port Authority met its first problems of finance it was obliged to sell its bonds wholly on the basis of *estimates* of the prospective revenues to come from tolls from users. How many vehicles would cross the two Staten Island bridges? What could be charged for tolls? Even at best, no one could be sure of such estimates. Later on, the two Staten Island bridges did go "into the red." By using the Holland Tunnel and the Pulaski Skyway—built later by New Jersey—automobilists could get to the New Jersey coast and points further south more rapidly than over the Staten Island bridges. Because of this situation, unforeseen when the two bridges were planned, traffic from the two bridges was diverted to the Holland Tunnel. The tolls came in to the Port Authority in large volume at the tunnel booths but not at the bridge booths where they fell below expectations.

Of course, applying the authority method to housing, one could be a little more certain how much income would come in. Calculations could be based on actual experience in rental collections. But how about electric power? I advised Governor Smith that the problem might indeed prove to be an easier one to solve—from a practical point of view—than was the case in either the Port Authority bridges or housing. Simply stated, find out first what it will cost to produce the power. Then arrange to market it on the basis of definitive contracts with the public utility companies. On the basis of known revenues which could reasonably be anticipated, a public agency should be able to market *Authority Bonds* at a low rate of interest. This, in a nutshell, was the financial phase of the problem. But the whole problem was not quite as simple as all that—not by any means.

In the first place, the St. Lawrence River runs between the United States and Canada, and Canada has rights in the stream. The State of New York owns part of the stream. Canada, or the Provinces, own the other part—something like the waterway between New York and New Jersey in the Port of New York. There is a treaty between the United States and Canada regulating the flow of water through the St. Lawrence. In consequence, some kind of an understanding must be had with Canada in order to get New York's share of the power.

In the next place, the development of power in the St. Lawrence could be a part of the larger project known as "The St. Lawrence Waterway." The Middle West has always been enthusiastic about the St. Lawrence Waterway. St. Louis Sunday papers print enticing pictures showing great ocean liners stopping at lake ports. On the other hand, if commerce were taken through the proposed St. Lawrence Canal, what would happen to the railroads? What would happen to the commerce of the Port of New York?

But there were still other complications. Who has the right to the power in the St. Lawrence? It is a navigable stream. No dam could be built without the approval of the Federal Government. Under the United States Constitution the Federal Government is given paramount power to regulate interstate commerce and navigation. How then could the State be sure that she would get her share of the revenues from the power when it once was developed? As a matter of fact, the provisions of the "Federal Power Act" make it imperative that a license be procured from the Federal Power Commission before work can begin on a dam in a navigable stream. And the Act is so drawn that once a license is applied for and secured the whole project is subjected to such regulations as the Federal Power Commission would establish. And that result was, of course, the opposite of what New York State desired. Definitely New York did not want Federal control of the power. *It wanted New York State to control it.*

Keep in mind that there were two ways to handle this matter of inter-governmental relationship. Both projects could be tied together —the waterway and the development of hydro-electric power—all in one package, even as a Christmas present, with nice ribbons and seals. If this were done, it would have to have United States Senate approval of a treaty between the United States and Canada and there a two-thirds vote might not be secured. When the package was opened, the Christmas box of candy might all be spoiled. Then again, the project would stand or fall on the merits of the *Waterway Project*—good or bad, as the Senate would see it. New York State might be for the Waterway or it might not. It was clear that up around Watertown, New York, the voters would be *pro,* but down in New York City, they would definitely be *anti.*

On the other hand, if the project were divided into two parts and the State of New York started first with an agreement between itself and Canada (or the Provinces concerned), such an agreement would not require the consent of Congress or the approval of the Senate—as compacts between the States of the Union sometimes do.

Hence, there was presented to Governor Smith this complex phase of national and state policy deeply involved in the problem. A Governor of New York State would naturally prefer to split up the problem and thus make sure of getting the power resources of the State developed at the earliest date by the State itself. If later the same Governor were to become President of the United States—that might be a horse of another color.

In 1929, as a New York State problem, it cried for solution. There was but one way to go about it practically, and that was to follow the experience in dealing with the problems of the Port of New York. First, create a "Study Commission," appoint upon it men who would be expert in the various fields of knowledge involved; organize a staff of competent engineers and marketing experts and select some lawyers to work on the complex legal problems in the situation; study the problem from all points of view and see just how you come out in dollars and cents.

Governor Smith wholeheartedly accepted this recommendation and in the last days of his term tried to put through the necessary legislation. Like the Housing Bank, it was defeated—in Al Smith's term.

II

When Franklin D. Roosevelt succeeded Afred E. Smith as Governor of the State of New York, he found this troublesome problem on his desk. He asked Louis McHenry Howe, his secretary, to study it and make recommendations. The Governor asked me to come to the Executive Chamber in Albany to discuss the Howe plan. Louis Howe was not a lawyer. He did not understand the intricacies of the legal problems involved. I did not like his recommendations and told the Governor so and why. Governor Roosevelt then asked me to submit something in its place, but remarked that he did not want merely to repeat his predecessor's recommendations. I told him that he could go much further and present a more complete plan. In so doing, he would advance to new ground.

I reminded him that hundreds of thousands of dollars were wasted yearly in litigation before the Public Service Commission over power rates in the determination of what constituted reasonable charges to consumers of light and power. *If we could work out a contract with the utilities,* we could save all this litigation. Such a contract could fix a rate of return upon the actual capital invested and above that rate provide for a division between consumers and stockholders, the amount to go to consumers in the form of reduced rates. By this means, preferences in rates could be given to small consumers and farmers and hundreds of thousands of dollars saved in futile rate litigation.

The Governor liked the plan. Later on he became enthusiastic about it—at least I thought he was. My wife remembers, as I do, the day we worked on the scheme in his little office up at Hyde Park. He had invited her to join us and continue her knitting while listening to our conversation. The Governor was then at his best. He was in his most jovial mood—brilliant, scintillating, charming and enthusiastic. Here was a man, paralyzed so he could not walk, taking hold of a man-sized job and understanding all about it. I shall never forget his charm and the way he took hold. We agreed upon the "Study Commission."

III

Chapter 207 of the Laws of New York of 1930 was drawn up by me with the help of Kenneth Dayton, my partner. It provided for the appointment by the Governor of five commissioners to report plans for the development of hydro-electric power in the St. Lawrence River. The first section provided that:

"The natural water power sites in, upon or adjacent to the Saint Lawrence river, owned or controlled by the people of the state or which may hereafter be recovered by them or come within their ownership and control, shall remain inalienable to, and ownership and control shall remain always vested in the people of the state."

Five commissioners were to be appointed by the Governor. They were to report plans not only for the development of the power to be generated at the water power site at the St. Lawrence River, but also a contract for the sale of the power. They were to find their own engineers and legal assistants. They were to consider the reports made by the International Commission of the United States and Canada and the Federal Power Commission and were to recommend a comprehensive plan for the development and operation of the water power resources of the state on the St. Lawrence River by Trustees. All this was to be done under such conditions as to assure fair and impartial treatment of consumers on a basis of charges the lowest compatible with a fair and reasonable return on the cost thereof. If they could not report a plan that would permit the development through a Water Power Authority, they were to submit some other plan.

Two hundred thousand dollars was appropriated. This legislation received a great send-off and was passed with little, if any, opposition in the Legislature.

When it became law, the Governor was called upon to name the commissioners. He asked me to serve as one of them. He consulted me about the other members to be named. I thought he needed a financial man as one commissioner, one who had real familiarity with Authority financing. I suggested Samuel L. Fuller,* who was a close friend of Langdon P. Marvin, former law partner of the Governor. Marvin and Fuller were alumni of Harvard and classmates of the Governor. Governor Roosevelt liked Fuller. To make the commission completely non-partisan, I recommended Frederick M. Davenport, candidate for Governor when Theodore Roosevelt ran as the Progressive candidate for President. Governor Roosevelt knew him well. I had worked with Davenport while he was in Congress on a plan for utilizing the interstate compact method for developing the Colorado River. Davenport and I thought we needed a first-class economist in the New York-St. Lawrence job and suggested Robert Murray Haig, Professor of Economics at Columbia University, whom he knew well. I knew Haig's standing. The Governor knew it, too. So all four were named. The Governor's choice for the fifth member was former Lieutenant-Governor Thomas F. Conway.

We got off to a flying start. We took offices in the Graybar Building. I borrowed a bright office boy from the Port Authority and S. Burton Heath,[1] who had been writing articles on this subject for the New York World-Telegram, became our secretary. Haig became Chairman and I became Vice-Chairman and General Counsel. For our

* See Chapter 26.

legal staff, Kenneth Dayton became Chief of Staff and Charles W. Poletti first assistant. The third member of the law staff was A. Mackay Smith.

As engineer, we secured the services of General Edgar Jadwin, who had made the studies on behalf of the United States Army engineers for the St. Lawrence Waterway. Frederick Stuart Greene, New York's State Engineer, also came in as an adviser. For "The Marketing Board" we secured Colonel John P. Hogan and John Bauer. Each of these two competent men approached the problem from different angles but both finally came out with the same figures and the same recommendations.

On January 15, 1931, the Commissioners made their report to the Governor and the Legislature. Of the two hundred thousand dollar appropriation, they had spent for legal expenses $5,203.24; for engineering, $25,285.36; for economics and marketing, $18,020.86; and for administration, $10,961.20—a total of $59,470.66. They estimated it would cost to print and distribute the report about $80,000. For the first time in history, I believe, a legislative commission returned a substantial part of its appropriation to the State. The report is all nicely bound up in a book bearing the seal of the State of New York, with a lovely olive-brown cover. It covers 206 pages and is full of attractive exhibits. The water power in the St. Lawrence is still undeveloped.

What happened? The majority report was received with public acclaim. The New York Times praised it highly and said:

"In January, 1931, a commission appointed by Governor Roosevelt and headed by Professor Robert Murray Haig of Columbia and Julius Henry Cohen of the Port Authority brought in a report strikingly free from politics, full of common sense, and rooted in sound economics. It proposed to set about the development of the St. Lawrence as a joint enterprise with private and public authorities pooling their resources under effective State direction and control.

Governor Roosevelt was displeased with some of the board's recommendations, particularly its determined opposition to the construction of competing transmission lines, authority for the construction of which he wished to use as a club over the big companies. In the end a compromise bill was adopted, setting up a proposed Power Authority more or less along the lines favored by the commission. When he came to name the trustees of the new Authority the Governor ignored the obvious special qualifications of men like Haig, Cohen and Frederick Davenport and appointed in their place a board headed by Frank P. Walsh, outstanding foe of the utilities. His action was interpreted as significant of his reluctance to make haste to come to terms with the 'Power Trust,' and as presaging the warfare which has since developed on many fronts, but especially in the Tennessee Valley." [2]

The report on the engineering and marketing phases will be found, on examination, to be one of the finest pieces of workmanship ever done professionally on a problem of this kind. The report on the law branch was a good job. (Kenneth Dayton always did a good job.) Charles W. Poletti—afterwards Governor—and Mackay Smith were fine assistants.

The legislation the Commission proposed and that we lawyers drew was enacted by the legislature without the change of a word.[3] The Governor must have been satisfied with the report and the legislation, because he signed the bill. The Republican legislature liked it so well that the Senate amended the bill so as to name all five Commissioners of the post of Commissioners of the Water Power Authority to be created by the Act.

When this amendment was announced in the press, the Governor promptly came out with a statement that he regarded this as an inter-ference with gubernatorial prerogative, and that, if the five men—the very ones he had named to the "Study Commission"—were named in the bill, he would promptly veto it.

We were not responsible for the action of the Senate leaders. We were, of course, flattered by their gesture of confidence in us. There was nothing in the job for us except the opportunity to do a piece of public service. Accordingly, when the Governor made his public state-ment, four of the Commissioners—Haig, Fuller, Davenport and I—im-mediately telegraphed the Senate leaders, asking them to leave our names out of the bill. This the legislature did. The Governor, after the bill was passed, named other men to the Authority.

IV

From the very beginning it was contemplated that the solution of the problem involved frank, open cooperation between the State and pri-vate public-utility interests. That cooperation was actually achieved—or was on its way before we completed our work.

Floyd L. Carlisle, the chairman of the Niagara-Hudson Power Com-pany, came to conferences with us on the basis of "open covenants, openly arrived at." He brought along with him former Judge Joseph M. Proskauer, as his lawyer. Joe and I had been old friends for more than twenty-five years. He had been one of Governor Smith's closest advisors. He could not very well act as counsel to Carlisle and his in-terests and turn his back on the principles for which Al and he had stood. It was a fortunate "happenstance" that the Judge should repre-sent the utilities in dealing with us. It was something of advantage to the State. Before Proskauer accepted the retainer from Carlisle, he told him clearly that he could not accept unless it was understood that he was to follow the line of developing the St. Lawrence in the public interest with reasonable regard for the rights of the company, and to achieve that end, Proskauer advised Carlisle that he undoubtedly would have to agree to state ownership of the dam site. Carlisle retained Proskauer after this *caveat* and cooperated throughout in a most loyal and public-spirited manner.

The policy was so simple and so fair to the State as well as to the public utility interests, that two lawyers could sit down and while protecting their clients' interests, come to a "common denominator." It seemed to me a much less difficult task than I had had in dealing with Morris Hillquit and Meyer London in the Garment Industry. Certainly it was a much easier task than was involved in bringing New York and New Jersey together in the Port compact. Proskauer and I "clicked." So did the four Commissioners and Carlisle. I remember when we were up in Sam Fuller's house in Greenwich, Connecticut—the Commissioners, Joe Proskauer and I—Floyd Carlisle joshed us, saying, "Well, anyway, you fellows are going to make the kind of report the Governor wants." I said, "Mr. Carlisle, you mistake the character of the Commissioners. Not one of them will put his signature to anything he does not believe in. You can count on that."

The majority did keep that in mind throughout all their work. Though the heavens might fall, we would make a report that we could "look squarely in the face" any time, then or later on. Floyd Carlisle, Judge Proskauer, the four Commissioners and the staff were pathfinders of a new trail.

Very early in the conference, we were able to agree that the best way to utilize the St. Lawrence power so as to preserve its direct and indirect economic advantages would be to use a certain portion of it at the site in contiguous industries, and to distribute the balance in the existing market where it could be mingled with power from other sources, such as steam-generated electricity and power from inland streams controlled by storage. In this case, the power from the St. Lawrence could be used on that portion of the load that is continuous, and the fluctuations of daily and seasonal use would be taken by the other more flexible sources.

We also agreed that in addition to direct benefits due to decreased generating costs in the general utility market there would be indirect savings resulting from the fact that where power could be furnished from either water-power of different characteristics, such as the St. Lawrence and regulated interior water-powers, or from steam, the combination of all in the proper proportion would effect substantial savings. These indirect benefits would be shared by the state at large, by industries, by domestic, commercial and rural consumers, as well as by the utilities. The development of industries at the site would bring about increase in population and business and create taxable values. Should distribution be made through existing facilities, the economic benefits would accrue to industries throughout the state. Promotional rate schedules could be established, the average consumption of electricity greatly increased, and the resulting advantages conveyed to the consumers. Railway electrification throughout the state would be stimulated and rural electrification advanced.[4]

V

All these things found their way finally into the report of the majority. The fact that Carlisle and his group were ready to go along, seemed to the four Commissioners to be of great public value. *He and his company had given unmistakable evidence of a new sense of public duty.* So far as we could see, it was time to abandon the use of the "big stick" policy, at least so far as Carlisle's company was concerned. *It was time to cooperate with business—not declare war upon it.*

This conception must be kept in mind in reading the report the Commission made and in any effort to understand the differences in policy that developed later between the Governor and four of his Commissioners.

These differences can be easily summarized. It all fell within a narrow compass. The Governor said he wanted a club—a club which he could wield to force a fair bargain between the utilities and the State. That, of course, meant he favored the policy of cooperation on fair terms. (By signing the bill submitted by the Commissioners, he accepted this policy of collaboration.) The club he would fashion, however, was to vest power in the authority to build, own and operate a complete separate State transmission system with separate distributing stations—all to be operated in competition with the existing privately owned transmission and distributing systems. The Governor said he wanted it to be a club which he could keep in the closet. But obviously if it was to be something to threaten with, it must be something which the "bad boy" would really fear. It must be a real honest-to-goodness first cousin to Theodore Roosevelt's big stick.

The difference between the four Commissioners and the Governor was first, that the majority believed that no club was needed and next, that the club the Governor suggested was in fact no club at all. It resembled more the balloon that clowns use in the circus. The facts developed showed clearly that the only way the enterprise could come out "in the black" was to merge into one operating system the publicly-to-be-owned and the then privately-owned power plants and to use both kinds of facilities at different periods of the year and at different times of the day, as they were needed. An independent state-owned and operated system could only mean *red figures* for the state. The state would have had to put up not less than seventy-five million dollars. Where would this money come from? The people would have to vote upon it and pass either an amendment to the state constitution or approve a separate bond issue. At bottom it is the simple truth that New York State, by and large, is conservative.

In 1931 it was not likely that anyone—even Franklin D. Roosevelt— could persuade a majority of the voters to go all-out for such a major enterprise in Government ownership and operation. Besides, *the plan of cooperating with the utilities offered clear opportunity to get steadily decreasing charges for electric light and power for home owners and farmers.* If the Governor could have been persuaded to follow this line of thought, he could have gone to the people and emphasized the point. He could have readily shown that what he had achieved was in fact a conquest over the utilities—the bad boy had grown good—under his influence.

We remained on good terms with the Governor and along with thousands of others, found occasion later to admire his courage, his insight and his leadership in many fields, especially in the international situation. This matter of water-power in which we disagreed was one in which he consulted other advisors and in the end preferred their advice. As Governor and as President he made his own selection of advisors and changed from time to time. One always takes the risk if chosen to act as an advisor that his client may get someone in his place. "Be a good sport" is one of the rules of the game.

The Majority Report was accepted by the legislature. The bill, precisely as it was prepared, was signed by the Governor and the views expressed in the bill were approved by both the legislature and the Chief Executive. The engineers' studies, the cost studies, the legal plans are all in the report. There they stand!

This writer is of opinion that if David E. Lilienthal had been advisor to the Governor in 1931—and had then the views he now entertains—the course pursued by the Governor would not have been what it was. Perhaps it is not too much to say that in the light of his later experiences, if this matter had been before Franklin D. Roosevelt as Governor of the State of New York in 1944, his judgment would have been different from what it was in 1931. But the seeds were wafted by the breezes to a more favorable Southern soil.

The work of the Tennessee Valley Authority is the best demonstration of the soundness of the policy the four Commissioners recommended and of the practicality of cooperation with the utilities. Under

the skillful leadership of David Lilienthal it is now shown to be entirely possible to achieve several important ends recommended in the
St. Lawrence Commission majority report. *First, a business management of a governmental agency. Next, local management and local interest*—"a new sort of Governmental agency * * * one of which Jefferson as well as Hamilton could consistently approve." [5]

Lilienthal says: "Local delegations don't have to go to Washington
to get an answer where the TVA is involved. The men they want to
see are right in the valley." And the Baltimore "Sun" says editorially,
"Far from withering private enterprise, TVA has afforded the means
for a new variety of new business to spring up in the valley." [6]

The time was ripe in 1921 for the creation of the Port Authority.
Apparently it was not ripe in 1931 for the St. Lawrence Power Author-
ity. But a few years later it was ripe for creation and operation of the
Tennessee Valley Authority.

VI

In 1945 almost everyone agreed that the industrialists of this country
did a fine job in their cooperation with the Government in the war
effort. President Roosevelt in his Chicago address reaffirmed his belief
"in free enterprise and in the profit system." [7] From now on the idea
of cooperation between businessmen, including public utilities, with
Government should find greater support than it received in New York
in 1931. Businessmen cannot be frightened by mere threats and they
are readier now to work in collaboration with Government. Perhaps
1931 was too early to expect such an understanding, but we thought it
was. The time is surely right now for such cooperation. Floyd Carlisle
leaves a fine example behind him.

In "TVA—Democracy on the March," Lilienthal shows how the
principle can be made to work:

> "I find it impossible to comprehend how democracy can be a living reality if
> people are remote from their government and in their daily lives are not made
> a part of it, or if the control and direction of making a living—industry, farm-
> ing, the distribution of goods—is far removed from the stream of life and from
> the local community.
>
> 'Centralization' is no mere technical matter of 'management' of 'bigness versus
> smallness.' We are dealing here with those deep urgencies of the human spirit
> which are embodied in the faith we call 'democracy.' It is precisely here that
> modern life puts America to one of its most severe tests; it is here that the ex-
> perience in this valley laboratory in democratic methods takes on unusual
> meaning.
>   *   *   *   *   *
> For the cumulative effect of overcentralization of administration in a national
> capital is greatly to reduce the effectiveness of government. It is serious enough
> in itself when, because of remoteness and ignorance of local conditions or the

slowness of their operation, laws and programs fail of their purposes. We are threatened, however, with an even more disastrous sequence, the loss of the people's confidence, the very foundation of democratic government. Confidence does not flourish in a 'government continually at a distance and out of sight,' to use the language of Alexander Hamilton, himself a constant advocate of strong central authority.

On the other hand, said Hamilton 'the more the operations of the national authority are intermingled in the ordinary exercise of government, the more the citizens are accustomed to meet with it in the common occurrences of their political life, the more it is familiarized to their sight and to their feelings, the further it enters into those objects which touch the most sensible chords and put into motion the most active springs of the human heart, the greater will be the probability that it will conciliate the respect and attachment of the community.'

When 'the respect and attachment of the community' gives place to uneasiness, fears develop that the granting of further powers may be abused. Ridicule of the capriciousness of some government officials takes the place of pride. Democracy cannot thrive long in an atmosphere of scorn or fear. One of two things ultimately happens: either distrustful citizens, their fears often capitalized upon by selfish men, refuse to yield to the national government the powers which it should have in the common interest; or an arrogant central government imposes its will by force. In either case the substance of democracy has perished." [8]

Here is a warning from a competent source against the dangers of centralization at Washington.

When we were creating the Port of New York Authority, we were urged to make the Federal Government a party by giving the President power to appoint, say, two of the six Commissioners. I was opposed to this viewpoint. I argued that the States must first learn to cooperate with each other before they could cooperate with the Federal Government. If we had given the Federal Government representation in the Port Authority, it would have resulted inevitably in control of the enterprise by the Federal Government. We feared that the consequences that have followed in Canada from centralized control of ports and harbors would take place here in New York. If the development of the Port of New York had been entrusted to a Federal Agency, would we now have all the tunnels and bridges connecting the two states? The record of the enterprise of local Commissioners named to represent the States by the two Governors has proved successful in the case of the Port Authority.

The problem of utilizing hydro-electric power latent in our rivers remains to be solved. *Shall we solve it through centralized authority at Washington or shall we encourage the States to cooperate and furnish the initiative?* [9]

There is now a definite revival of some old-fashioned thinking. How true are De Tocqueville's words today when centralization has made such a dismal and tragic failure in the world.

"Granting, for an instant, that the villages and counties of the United States would be more usefully governed by a central authority which they had never seen than by functionaries taken from among them; admitting, for the sake of argument, that there would be more security in America, and the resources of society would be better employed there, if the whole administration centered in a single arm—still the *political* advantages which the Americans derive from their decentralized system would induce me to prefer it to the contrary plan. It profits me but little, after all, that a vigilant authority always protects the tranquillity of my pleasures and constantly averts all dangers from my path, without my care or concern, if this same authority is the absolute master of my liberty and my life, and if it so monopolizes movement and life that when it languishes everything languishes around it, that when it sleeps everything must sleep, and that when it dies the state itself must perish." [10]

VII

Low-cost housing made very little progress during Governor Smith's term of office, but it made great progress later on. The idea was valid, but *the time* for its effectuation was not yet ripe.

The garment industry tried hard in the Protocol Experiment, fell back, and then went forward again. It took twenty-five years for principles to find fruition. *Time does hold the trump card.*

Remember that the arbitration idea for which Bernheimer fought took three hundred years before it achieved success.

St. Lawrence Power and Tennessee Valley: The method of the *public corporation* combined with business skill and efficiency. *Decentralization*—local initiative avoiding the pitfalls of centralized power. We in America do not need to go to a collectivist state to solve our problems. We can follow an American trail—blazed by Port Authority pioneers. American intelligence combined with American public service will do the trick. America can confound the cynics and the defeatists as she did in World War II. (We can watch out for the tactics of the "double-cross and smear" and overcome them too.) *They* said: "It can't be done." And *we* said—borrowing the slogan from the engineers—*"Here it is!"*

Notes

Chapter 1—Everett v. Abbot

1. "Leadership and the Law School," address by Dean Arthur T. Vanderbilt, January 25, 1944.
2. "Holmes-Pollock Letters," Vol. I, page 16.
3. "Topics of the Times," the New York Times, December 16, 1944.
4. *See:* "The Bar of Other Days," Joseph S. Auerbach.
5. Vol. 26, No. 2, page 104, December, 1916.
6. *United States* v. *Sprague*, 282 U.S. 716, 51 Sup. Ct. 220.

Chapter 3—Res Ipsa Loquitor

1. *Griffen* v. *Manice*, 47 App. Div. 70, reversed 166 N.Y. 188.

Chapter 4—Horace E. Deming

1. "Democracy in America," Alexis DeTocqueville, Vol. I, page 61.
2. *See:* "An American Chronicle," Ray Stannard Baker.
3. William A. Robson in the "Development of Local Government," (page 61) pointed out:

> "the danger which threatens local government most seriously at the present time is the danger of centralization * * *. It is broadly true that national government is already far too congested with matters common to the whole country to be made responsible for the detailed management of even the most vital local affairs."

Dr. Ernest S. Griffith, who taught both at Liverpool University and at Princeton, writes: ("Modern Development of City Government", Vol. 2, pages 554, 555.)

> "In the United Kingdom the two questions—finance and central control—are interlocked through the medium of the grant-in-aid. Broadly speaking, the localities have needed money and have sought it from the central government. The latter have granted the relief in exchange for supervision. The control so secured has been defended, on the one hand, as the corollary of the central financial aid; and on the other hand, as itself desirable. The existence of a possible and apparently sound alternative source of local revenue permits the consideration of central control on its own merits—that is, divorced from its financial aspect."

Comparing the American with the English method, he says: (page 431)

> "Furthermore, the effect of the constitutional supremacy over all legislatures and executives has its roots in the emphasis laid by the Americans upon *popular sovereignty,* and has served to perpetuate this doctrine. To say that the American Government trusts the people is thus historically incorrect; since the doctrine is held that the people *are* the government. Direct government is the last principal manifestation of this, and is the logical outcome of a theory in which the hierarchy of law rests largely in popular hands. The United Kingdom presents a direct contrast. The emphasis has ever been on governing

for the people; and the history has been one of concessions to the people. Thus a distrust of direct methods and a corresponding emphasis on representative government has been kept alive through the supremacy of Parliament. The people of the United States distrust their government and restrict its power: The Government of the United Kingdom has distrusted its people and has been somewhat loath to increase the sphere of popular participation."

4. This fact appears from the Report of the Royal Commission on Income Tax of 1919 submitted to Parliament. An organized body of Treasurers of British Cities complained to this Commission that they were not even accorded the same rights to make deductions which were granted private corporations. Among other things, they were liable for the payment of income tax on the rental value of their public sewers. In response to their plea, the Royal Commission recommended that "sewers and sewer mains should be exempted from liability for income tax assessment," and furthermore recommended allowances of other set-offs "in conformity with the practice obtaining in the case of a private company." In making these recommendations, the Royal Commission pointed out that none of the witnesses raised the fundamental question whether a municipal corporation ought to pay income tax at all, and said that "it might have been in their minds that it would not be expedient to claim exemption from income tax for public bodies which are actually or potentially competitors of private persons or companies carrying on similar trade undertakings." (Minutes of the Royal Commission.)

5. *Matter of Dows*, 167 N.Y. 227; affirmed 60 App. Div. 630; *In re Vanderbilt's Estate*, 50 App. Div. 246, affirmed 163 N.Y. 597; *Alexander E. Orr, et al.* v. *Theodore P. Gilman, etc.*, 183 U.S. 278, 22 Sup. Ct. 213.

6. *See:* New York Times, editorial, August 5, 1945.

7. "The Bar of Other Days," Joseph S. Auerbach, page 302.

8. "Theodore Roosevelt—An Autobiography," pages 311, 312.

9. *Ibid.*, page 312.

10. "Country Lawyer," Bellamy Partridge (Whittlesey House), page 39.

Chapter 5—Dr. Felix Adler

1. The New York Times, July 9, 1944.
A bombshell fell in Rome when it was announced in February, 1945, that the former chief Rabbi of Rome had entered the Catholic Church. To his followers in the synagogue this was nothing short of apostasy. Similarly, in the '70s, Dr. Felix Adler dropped a bombshell when he left the synagogue to become the leader of a new movement. If he had then entered the Catholic Church, he could not have brought upon his head more imprecations than he had to endure. In fairness to Rabbi Zolli, we should listen to what he has to say:

> "Do you think I love the Jews less because I have become a Catholic?
> * * * No, I shall never stop loving the Jews. I did not compare the
> Jewish religion to Catholicism and abandon one for the other."
> ("Time," February 26, 1945).

Zolli's great service to the Jews of Italy, with the aid of the Vatican during World War II should not be forgotten. If he is sincere—and I believe he is—the criticism, if any, must be on the score of his wisdom and judgment. It is announced that he is to write for the Vatican a new book, *Antisemitismo*. Perhaps this great scholar, who had been working inside the Vatican with great benefit to his race is convinced that by "boring from within" he may bring the great power of the Vatican nearer to the goal of tolerance for *all* religions. Judgment, at least, should be suspended until Zolli has really had a chance for his experiment. He may be overconfident in his hope, but who can say today? The event may turn out to mark a turning point in the Catholic Church.

See: New York Times, October 11, 1945. World Jewish Congress makes gift of 20,000,000 lira, the equivalent of $20,000 to the Vatican charities. The gift was urged by the Union of Italian Jewish Communities in recognition of the Holy See's work in rescuing Jews from Fascist and Nazi persecution.

2. "Memoirs of a Superfluous Man," Albert Jay Nock, page 303.

3. *Ibid.*, page 301.

4. "Life and Destiny," Felix Adler, page 13.

5. "Yankee from Olympus," Catherine Drinker Bowen, page xii.

6. *Ibid.*, page xii.

7. *Ibid.*, page xii.

Chapter 6—Dr. John P. Peters

1. "The Ardent Eighties," Gregory Weinstein, pages 124, 125.

2. *See:* "The History of Tammany Hall," Gustavus Myers.

Chapter 7—Dr. Frank Damrosch

1. "The Music Lover's Handbook," Elie Siegmeister, page 17.

2. "Music Comes to America," David Ewen.

3. "Frank Damrosch—Let the People Sing," by Lucy Poate Stebbins and Richard Poate Stebbins, from which I have freely quoted.

Chapter 8—William Travers Jerome

1. "Yankee Lawyer—The Autobiography of Ephraim Tutt," page 111.

2. *Ibid.*, page 110.

3. *Ibid.*, page 110 .

4. "The Evening Post—A Century of Journalism," Allan Nevins, page 546. The author of the quotation, Mrs. Frederick P. Bellamy, wrote under the name of Blanche Wilder, widely known author and poet in those days. She was the sister-in-law of Edward Bellamy, author of "Looking Backwards." At this time, Edwin L. Godkin was editor of the "Post" and Charles A. Dana was editor of the "Sun."

5. "Yankee Lawyer—The Autobiography of Ephraim Tutt," page 71.

6. Association of the Bar of the City of New York Reports, Vol. 55, 1934, page 336.

7. *People* v. *Levin,* 119 App. Div. 233, affirmed 194 N.Y. 554. This conviction was followed by *People* v. *Devine and Ronan; People* v. *Brown and Taub.* These were prosecutions undertaken by me on behalf of organizations of hosiery men, woolens and trimmings men, cotton converters and others.

8. Association of the Bar of the City of New York Reports, Vol. 55, 1934, page 338.

9. *People ex rel. Perkins* v. *Moss,* 187 N.Y. 410, affirming 113 App. Div. 329.

Chapter 9—Theodore Roosevelt

1. *See:* "Fighting Years," Oswald Garrison Villard, page 134.

"The Ghost Talks," Charles Michaelson, pages 88-90, (referring to the methods used by William Randolph Hearst to bring on the Spanish-American War).

Address by Dr. Felix Adler, New York Times, October 24, 1898.

"But now observe the lesson written out in terms of blood, in terms of bereavement and mourning. Shall we then, at last learn the lesson? Shall we remember those brave young men, the hope of whole families, whose lives the country did not require, who were not sacrificed on the altar of patriotism, but on the foul, noisome altar of 'political influence.' And yet I fear, the lesson has not been learned."

Editorial, "A Needless 'War for Humanity'" (referring to address by General Stewart L. Woodward, Minister to Spain), New York Evening Post, October 25, 1898.

2. "Theodore Roosevelt—An Autobiography," page 219.

3. The New York Times, August 15, 1898. On the same day, Reverend Herbert N. Casson, preaching his farewell sermon to the Labor Church at Lynn, Massachusetts said of Theodore Roosevelt that he was "a dangerous man * * *. Because of the war and the thunder this fellow made at El Caney, it is now proposed to make this walking dentist's sign Governor of New York. If this comes true God Help New York. Roosevelt is a bloodless tyrant. He may be called a good man, but he is not what I'd term a Christian."

4. "Theodore Roosevelt—An Autobiography," page 270.

5. *Ibid.*, page 270.

6. In his "Autobiography," the Colonel said that:

"The previous year, the machine or standpat Republicans, who were under the domination of Senator Platt, had come to a complete break with the anti-machine element over the New York mayoralty. This had brought the Republican party to a smash, not only in New York City, but in the State, where the Democratic candidate for Chief Judge of the Court of Appeals, Alton B. Parker, was elected by sixty or eighty thousand majority. * * *

The Republicans realized that the chances were very much against them. Accordingly the leaders were in a chastened mood and ready to nominate any candidate with whom they thought there was a chance of winning." (page 289)

7. *William Barnes* v. *Theodore Roosevelt*, Appellate Division, Fourth Department, Case on Appeal, Vol. 2, pages 648, 649, folios 1944–5.

8. "Theodore Roosevelt—An Autobiography," page 70.

9. *Ibid.*, page 83.

10. *See:* "Roosevelt, the Story of a Friendship," Owen Wister. "The Boys' Life of Theodore Roosevelt," Herman Hagedorn.

11. Paul Fuller was one of the most outstanding representatives of the Independents because to ability he added "stern and unbending devotion to a principle regardless of consequences—or rather, convinced that the consequences of such adherence can be but good, however they may at the moment seem to portend disaster." (New York Evening Post, October 4, 1898.)

12. Paul Fuller, Francis W. Aymar, Theodore Bacon, Clarence A. Barbour, William M. Brundage, John Jay Chapman, A. E. Clark, William Dutcher, Alfred Frank, Charles L. Gardiner, Abner S. Haight, William J. Hillis, Simeon Holroyd, Elias M. Humes, Boudinot Keith, Isaac H. Klein, Robert D. Kohn, John Brooks Leavitt, V. Everett Macy, John G. Milburn, John F. Montignani, Adelbert Moot, Edward D. Page, George S. Perry, Edward R. Rice, Meyer D. Rothschild, William Scott, William Allaire Shortt, Henry Ling Taylor, John De Witt Warner, John W. Weed, Richard W. G. Welling, Ansley Wilcox.

13. New York Herald, September 27, 1898.

14. New York Herald, September 25, 1898.

15. These are all to be found in the New York Public Library, Newspaper Division.

16. *William Barnes* v. *Theodore Roosevelt,* supra, Vol. 4, Exhibit 16 (First), page 2364, folio 7090.

17. *Ibid.,* Vol. 4, page 2356, folio 7068, Exhibit 14.

18. *Ibid.,* Vol. 4, page 2358, folios 7073, 7074, Exhibit 1.

19. *Ibid.,* Vol. 4, page 2358, folio 7074, Exhibit 14.

20. *Ibid.,* Vol. 4, page 2360, folio 7080, Exhibit 14.

21. *Ibid.,* Vol. 1, page 383, folio 1147.

22. *Ibid.*

23. *Ibid.,* Vol. 1, page 378, folios 1133, 1134.

24. *Ibid.,* Vol. 1, page 392, folio 1175.

25. *Ibid.,* Vol. 1, page 392, folio 1176.

26. *Ibid.,* Vol. 1, pages 393, 394, folios 1178, 1180.

27. The New York Times, September 26, 1898.

28. *Barnes* v. *Roosevelt,* supra, Vol. 1, page 4, et seq., folios 12-14.

29. *Ibid.,* Vol. 1, page 5, folio 15.

30. "Essays on Practical Politics," Theodore Roosevelt, pages 59, 60.

31. *Barnes* v. *Roosevelt,* supra, Vol. 1, page 37, folio 110.

32. "Theodore Roosevelt—An Autobiography," page 272.

33. The Independents were not alone in putting trust in the Colonel. The newspapers believed in him until they, too, were disillusioned. This is an interesting phase of the journalistic history of that day. Newspaper men should find it very instructive.

The "Times" said editorially on August 21, 1898 that "No one knows better than the Senator (Platt) that he could do no 'business' with the Colonel." How simple was the editor on that day? But he had a rude awakening a little later, as we shall see. On September 6, he said: "Not that he (Platt) will be able to get from Roosevelt as Governor anything that Roosevelt as Governor ought not to give. That is out of the question."

The "Herald" kept in step with the "Times." On September 24, the "Herald" said editorially, under the title "Embarrassing the Campaign":

> "* * * the Independents should be quiet, not obtrusive. They should silently acquiesce instead of creating embarrassment. It is all well enough to play the role of Jack the Boss Killer when the boss is obstreperous and defiant of public opinion, as bosses are every once in a while, but when 'in the course of human events' the boss does the popular thing, for reasons into which we do not care to pry, then it is bad form to make a fight, because no fight is necessary."

The Boss was virtuous! He had surrendered to the Colonel!

But by October 6, 1898, after the Colonel's speech of acceptance of the Republican nomination, the "Times" was the first to be disillusioned. With pain and chagrin it said:

> "This courageous man, whom the people of this commonwealth have come to respect and admire as a stranger to degrading compromises and as one who would fight to the last ditch for principle, exhibited himself in his reply to the address of notification as a complacent politician willing to assist the rascals of his party in hiding their misdeeds from the sight of the people, stifling his conscience for the sake of harmony, and giving a good character to corrupt men lest he lose votes and endanger his election."

A little later, on October 31, 1898, it said:

> "* * * he has the hardihood to treat the canal frauds as not proved,

* * * and he goes about on terms of campaign intimacy with George Aldridge, the responsible authority of the canal iniquities.

This explodes the Roosevelt myth. The stalwart reformer and fierce foe of public corruption tumbles from his pedestal, and in his place appears the smirking and plausible politician, motley with his many disguises, slippery and evasive, condoning vice, dodging and paltering with a public crime, and consorting familiarly with smirched men."

The newspapers were completely disillusioned by the Colonel's conduct in the campaign. Yet before Roosevelt went all out in support of the machine they were quite as naive as we were in our faith in the Colonel.

34. The New York Times, November 4, 1898.
35. The New York Times, October 26, 1898.
36. The New York Times, September 26, 1898:

"Victor H. Kohn, the business partner of Isaac H. Klein, returned last night from a tour through Rockland, Delaware and Orange Counties, * * *. He said he had no difficulty at all in getting all the signatures he wished. * * * on a single street, and in the small town of Griffin Corners, Delaware County, he said he got the signatures of sixty-nine out of the one hundred voters of the place. He reports a considerable and increasing Independent sentiment, and the only objection he heard urged to Colonel Roosevelt was that it was feared he had sold himself to Platt and would not, therefore, be independent enough."

The reporter had my name wrong. This was my report. These were the counties I covered.

37. "Theodore Roosevelt and His Time," Joseph Bucklin Bishop, Vol. I, page 109.
38. *Ibid.*, page 110.
39. *Ibid.*, page 112.

Chapter 10—William M. Ivins

1. *See:* "The Ghost Talks," Charles Michaelson, "Ideals and Unethical Ethics."
2. The New York Times, July 24, 1915.
3. Ivins was really the father of charter revision for New York City. He followed right along with the work of Deming. In 1907 a commission was appointed by the Legislature of which Ivins was the head. This commission reported January 1, 1908, (National Municipal Review, January, 1912, page 61, et seq.) recommending important changes in the government of the city and advocating the enactment of a home rule charter which should provide simply the outlines of the city government and should also provide for an administrative code containing administrative details and be subject to amendment and amplification by the legislative body of the city. This commission of which he was the head was known as the "Ivins Commission." A special legislative committee known as the "Hammond Committee" reported to the legislature in 1910 and expressed its approval of some of these recommendations, but disagreed with others. Their efforts were consolidated into a bill known as the Hammond Charter. This work was so defective that the legislature declined to pass it.

In November, 1910, a Democratic governor and a Democratic legislature was elected. Mayor Gaynor was the only candidate on the Tammany ticket elected in 1909. With the aim of giving him control of the city government, he developed what was called the Gaynor Charter.

The charter met with serious opposition from all the interests who desired real home rule. Representatives of business and civic organizations fought the bill. These included the City Club, the Allied Real Estate Interests, the Citizens Union, the

Greater New York Taxpayers Conference, the Public Education Association and the Brooklyn League. They charged that the proposed charter violated the principle of home rule by creating mandatory offices. It was full of "jobs" and "jokers" for the benefit of the hungry politicians of Tammany Hall expecting to profit under cover of giving the city a new charter.

The opposition to the bill took the shape of a huge mass meeting in Cooper Union at which Ivins, as chairman of the commission spoke. It was on this occasion that Ivins once more displayed his great power as an orator and his quick wit and acid tongue. As he walked up and down the platform at Cooper Union, he said: "I don't deny that Mayor Gaynor is a capable man. As a matter of fact, he is capable of anything."

4. The New York Times, July 25, 1915.

5. *Ibid.*

6. *Ibid.*

7. *Ibid.*

8. "Theodore Roosevelt and his Time—Shown in His Own Letters," Joseph Bucklin Bishop, Vol. 2, page 366.

9. The New York Times, May 2, 1915.

10. The New York Times, November 1, 1916.

11. *Barnes* v. *Roosevelt,* supra, Vol. 4, page 2361, folio 7081, Exhibit 14.

12. *Ibid.,* pages 2321, et seq., folio 6961, et seq., Exhibit 4.

13. President Roosevelt wrote Herbert Parsons on August 21, 1908, from the White House:

> "I have been carefully going into the Hughes matter since I saw you. I appreciate to the full the force of the arguments urged against his renomination. It is not pleasant for me to support a man who has wantonly behaved badly to the very men who did most in securing his nomination and election. I would not in the least object to his turning them down were that necessary in the public interest, but I do object to its being done wantonly. Moreover I appreciate that he has alienated quite needlessly very many voters, and if we had the right man to put in his place (the right man from the standpoint of getting votes) I should say that it was certainly wise to nominate such a man." *(Barnes* v. *Roosevelt,* supra, Vol. 4, pages 2406, 2407, folios 7218, 7219, Exhibit 45.)

And Parsons wrote the President on August 24, 1908:

> "When Hendricks, Barnes and I saw you the week before, I understood your attitude to be that in view of Hughes' conduct towards them you were unwilling to ask any of your friends to support him.
>
> * * * * * *
>
> It is the man or the party. Many of the people who want Hughes want him because he will destroy the party organization. * * * I believe that an efficient county organization is the one thing necessary to bring better government to New York City. Hughes' course, therefore, I regard as a negation of my efforts of the past three years, and his renomination I shall regard as announcement that such work as I have started in to do is unnecessary." *(Barnes* v. *Roosevelt,* supra, Vol. 4, page 2408, et seq. folios 7222, et seq., Exhibit 46.)

Barnes wrote to Roosevelt July 4, 1910, complaining that Hughes has been endeavoring:

> "to arouse resentment in every locality against the men who have been doing the political work of the Republican party. Some of those men

are the best and most unselfish of men. Some of them are of the meanest and most selfish of men.

It was a gage of battle thrown down which it was my duty to resist, because if I am to remain in the leadership of this county, that leadership must be satisfactory to the Republican people of the county. I cannot be exploited as a machine-made politician or a patronage broker without resisting the charge to the best of my strength." (*Barnes* v. *Roosevelt*, supra, Vol. 1, page 273, folio 817.)

14. "Theodore Roosevelt—An Autobiography," page 275.
15. *Barnes* v. *Roosevelt*, supra, Vol. 1, page 89, folio 266, et seq., Exhibit 2.
16. *Ibid.*, Vol. 1, page 242, folio 726.
17. *Ibid.*, Vol. 1, page 545, folio 1634.
18. *Ibid.*, Vol. 1, page 438, folio 1314.
19. *Ibid.*, Vol. 1, pages 438, et seq., folios 1314, et seq.
20. *Ibid.*, Vol. 4, pages 2533, folios 7597, 7598.
21. *Ibid.*, Vol. 1, pages 604, et seq., folio 1812, et seq.
22. *Ibid.*, Vol. 1, pages 402, 403, folios 1203, 1204, 1205.
23. *Ibid.*, Vol. 2, pages 656, 657, folios 1968, et seq.
24. *Ibid.*, Vol. 4, page 2291, folio 6873.
25. *Ibid.*, Vol. 4, page 2294, folio 6882.
26. *Ibid.*, Vol. 4, page 2297, folio 6889.
27. The New York Times, May 12, 1915.
28. The New York Times, May 8, 1915.
29. The New York Times, May 15, 1915.
30. "Pilgrim's Way, An Essay in Recollection," John Buchan (Lord Tweedsmuir), pages 98, 99.

Chapter 11—Alfred E. Smith

1. "Up to Now," Alfred E. Smith, pages 76, 77.
2. Chapter XI, "The Campaign of 1884."
3. The Citizens Union Legislative Committee was organized in 1904. I was the Chairman from its inception until 1917. In its membership from time to time were: Everett V. Abbot, Albert S. Bard, who succeeded me as Chairman, Hamilton Holt, Goldthwaite H. Dorr, Francis D. Pollak, Laurence A. Tanzer, Robert Louis Hoguet, Henry Winthrop Hardon, Joseph M. Proskauer, Robert Van Iderstine, Walter Lindner, Richard S. Childs, Nicholas Kelley, Clarence M. Lewis, Robert McCurdy Marsh, Emory R. Buckner, Samuel J. Rosensohn, Frank B. Williams.
4. "Up to Now," Alfred E. Smith, page 151.
5. New York Herald Tribune, October 5, 1944.
6. *Ibid.*
7. "Pilgrim's Way, An Essay in Recollection," John Buchan (Lord Tweedsmuir), page 239.
8. *Ibid.*, page 239.
9. "Atlantic Monthly," May, 1927.
10. *See:* "Housing—The Why of Planning," Guy Greer, "Fortune," November, 1944.
11. Legislative Document (1926) "Message from the Governor transmitting Report of the Commission of Housing and Regional Planning for Permanent Housing Relief."
12. Under the Redevelopment Companys Law (Laws of 1942, Chapter 825 as amended by Laws of 1943, Chapter 234.)
13. *Murray* v. *La Guardia*, 291 N.Y. 320, 52 N.E. 2d 884, page 326.
14. *City Housing Authority* v. *Mueller*, 270 N.Y. 333, 339.
15. "Statement on Private Financing of Large-Scale Housing," Frederick H. Ecker, Chairman of the Board, Metropolitan Life Insurance Company, January 18, 1944.

16. *See:* New York Times, July 19, 1945.
17. *See:* New York Times, January 4, 1945.
18. Israel Newman.
19. *See:* New York Times, December 15, 1944, for full declaration.
20. "Up to Now," by Alfred E. Smith.

Chapter 12—Rosalie Loew Whitney

1. New York Times, editorial, November 16, 1944.
2. This movement was the start of the movement for national suffrage. However, on December 9, 1944, Wyoming celebrated the seventy-fifth anniversary of the law granting equal voting rights to women when it was a territory. The pioneer work to achieve this result is credited to Esther Morris, a New York State milliner who went out to a gold mining boomtown in Wyoming. Before the election, on September 2, 1869, she gave a tea party—Wyoming not Boston brand—and publicly pledged the candidates of both parties who were her guests, for the passage of such an act.
3. *See:* New York Times, March 7, 1946.

Chapter 13—I. S. C.

1. *See:* New York Times, December 21, 1945.
2. New York Times, December 25, 1944.
3. *See:* New York Times, September 10, 1944; October 6, 1945.
4. "Keeping Streets Clean," Hon. William H. Edwards, Commissioner of Street Cleaning, City of New York, "Proceedings of the Fourth Annual Conference of Mayors and Other City Officials of the State of New York," page 71.
5. *See:* "Charles B. Stover, His Life and Personality," J. K. Paulding.
6. We mention a few of these pathfinders:
Katherine Day, the predecessor of the Lady, as Chairman of the Committee on Streets of the Women's Municipal League, who joined with her in the original days of street inspection and medal giving.
Marion and Sally Peters, sisters of Dr. John P. Peters, who induced the boys in the clubs attached to Dr. Peters' church to inspect the city's streets and make reports.
Mrs. Charles A. Bryan, who was Chairman of the Committee on Parks of the Riverside Branch of the Women's Municipal League including the work for covering the tracks and adding additional parks and playgrounds to Riverside.
Mrs. Percival Knauth, at whose home the Riverside Branch met.
Frances Peters and the Misses Birdie and Louise Morganstern, who personally inspected the work of parks, streets, transit conditions and comfort stations in subways and elevated railroads.
Mrs. Flora Spiegelberg, not a member of these groups, but who did excellent pioneer work in the same field of refuse collection.
The Parks and Playground Association, Mrs. Arthur Hays Sulzberger, President.
The Outdoor Cleanliness League.

Chapter 14—Charles L. Bernheimer

1. Vice-President, American Arbitration Association.
2. In December, 1942, Mr. Bennett Lord submitted a study of arbitration to the New York Chamber of Commerce, "With Justice for All," in partial fulfillment of the requirements for the degree of Bachelor of Arts to the History Department of Princeton University.
3. New York Times, December 23, 1928.
4. *Park Construction Co.* v. *Independent School District No. 32,* January 17, 1941, 296 N.W. 475 (1941); *Kulukundis Shipping Co., S/A* v. *Amtorg Trading Corporation,* 126 Fed. Reporter (2d) 978.

See: "Arbitration and Public Policy," by this author, "Arbitration Journal," Spring, 1941.

5. *United States Asphalt Refining Co.* v. *Trinidad Lake Petroleum Co.,* 222 Fed. Rep. 1006.

6. Lord Campbell, in *Scott* v. *Avery,* 4 H. L. Cas. 811.

7. *Northampton Gas-Light Co.* v. *Parnell,* 15 C.B. 630, 645, 80 ECL 630, 139 English Reprint 572.

8. Macqueen's Cases on Appeal, pages 3, 4. (Scotch, 1855). Italics supplied.

9. New York Civil Practice Act, Article 84, Sections 1448 to 1469.

10. Revised Statutes of New Jersey (1937) Title 2, Chapter 4, Section 2:40-10 to 2:40-26.

11. United States Statutes at Large, Volume 43, (68th Congress 1923–1925) Chapter 231, Sections 1 to 15 (United States Code Annotated, Title 9).

12. The Court of Appeals of the State of New York, in an opinion rendered January 17, 1946, (In the matter of Feuer Transportation, Inc., Appellant Local Union No. 445 of International Brotherhood of Teamsters, etc. Respondent) written by Associate Judge George C. Medalie, who unfortunately died shortly thereafter, said that the dissatisfaction with the unsatisfactory condition of the law concerning arbitration agreements "was effectively dealt with in 1920 by the enactment of the Arbitration Law after a considerable campaign and with the sponsorship of the Chamber of Commerce of the State of New York, as well as substantial support from the Bar. Under the new statute arbitration became both orderly and enforcible and was made subject in effect to a decree for specific performance. A quarter of a century of its operation has demonstrated its usefulness and general acceptability."

13. "33 Questions," American Arbitration Association.

14. "Contract Settlement Act of 1944," Public Law 395, 78th Congress: Chapter 358-2d Session, S. 1718. The Act contains the following:

> a) Provision for the validation of defective, informal and quasi contracts by contracting agencies; "that the Government agencies shall make a fair settlement of any obligation thereby created or incurred by such agency, whether express or implied, in fact or in law, or in the nature of an implied or quasi contract." (Sec. 17 (b) (3)).
>
> b) Outstanding contracts contained provisions which made the contracting officer of the governmental department the final arbitrator of all disputed questions of fact. This precluded any impartial tribunal to which the controversy should be submitted from completely reviewing the facts and the questions of law in the controversy. This provision in the law was eliminated.
>
> c) Gives the contractor the ultimate right of appeal to "The Appeal Board * * * or to bring suit against the United States * * * in a Court of Claims or in a United States District Court * * *." (Sec. 13(b)(1)(2)).

15. "Yankee from Olympus," Catherine Drinker Bowen, page xii.

16. New York Herald Tribune, December 2, 1944, "Today and Tomorrow," Walter Lippmann.

Chapter 15—Rent Cases

1. *See:* New York Times, August 10, 1945.

2. "Economic History of Ireland in the 18th Century," O'Brien, pages 68, 69. *See:* "Land Tenure in Ireland," Montgomery, pages 90, 91. "Landholding and the Relation of Landlord and Tenant in Various Countries," page 270. "Ireland and England," Turner, page 195. "Agrarian Tenures," Shaw-Lefevre, page 114. *Mitchell* v. *Reed,* 61 N.Y. 124, Dwight Commission adopts the principle of right of renewal as laid down by Sir Francis Hargrave in *Lee* v. *Vernon,* 5 Brown's Parl. Rep. 10 (Irish Reports) March 11, 1776.

3. *See:* "Ozar Haddinim, A Digest of Jewish Law," Eisenstein, pages 129, 130.

"Ozar Yisrael," Vol. IV, page 265. (These volumes are printed in Hebrew and are at the New York Public Library, Department of Semitic Literature.) "Jewish Law in the Modern World," by Nathan Isaacs, formerly Professor of Law and Assistant Dean, University of Cincinnati Law School, 1919-20 Thayer Teaching Fellow at Harvard Law School, in the "Menorah Journal," Vol. VI, No. 5, October, 1920, page 258.

4. Chapters 131-138 of the Laws of 1920 and Chapters 942-952 of the Laws of 1920.

See: Twentieth Century Association, Inc. v. *Waldman,* 294 N.Y. 571, 63 N.E. (2d) 177 (1945). (Emergency Rent Control Laws, Chapter 3 of New York, 1945.)

5. Among other lawyers who participated at that time were David L. Podell, who appeared for the tenants and Lewis M. Isaacs, who was associated with Louis Marshall.

6. "Holmes-Pollock Letters," Vol. 1, page 156.

7. *Block* v. *Hirsh,* 256 U.S. 135 (1921); *Edgar A. Levy Leasing Co. Inc.* v. *Siegel,* 258 U.S. 242 (1922); *Edgar A. Levy Leasing Co. Inc.* v. *Siegel,* 230 N.Y. 634 (1921); affirming 194 App. Div. 482 (1920); *810 West End Avenue* v. *Stern,* 230 N.Y. 652 (1920), reversing 194 App. Div. 482 (1920).

8. We both appeared as Special Deputy Attorneys-General on behalf of the State of New York.

9. *Block* v. *Hirsh,* supra.

10. *Ibid.*

11. 21 Session Cases (4th Series) 21.

See: Discussion in "Commercial Arbitration and the Law" by this author, page 208.

Chapter 16—Max Meyer

1. "The Needle Trades," Joel Seidman, page 97.

2. *A. Beller & Company* v. *Garment Workers' Union, Local No. 61, Industrial Workers of the World, et al.,* New York Law Journal, March 27, 1907.

3. "The Needle Trades," Joel Seidman, page 49.

4. *Ibid.,* page 83.

5. *Ibid.,* pages 246, 247.

6. *See:* First Annual Report, Fashion Institute of Technology, June 7, 1945.

7. "The Needle Trades," Joel Seidman, page 9.

8. "Yankee from Olympus," Catherine Drinker Bowen, page 109.

9. "The Needle Trades," Joel Seidman, page 31.

10. *Ibid.,* page 37.

Chapter 17—Louis D. Brandeis

1. *New State Ice Co.* v. *Liebmann,* 285 U.S. 262, 76 L. Ed. 479.

2. "American Bar Association Journal," February, 1943.

3. "The preferential union shop, which in effect was the closed shop, implied that the worker had the right to his job and that therefore his union had no right to weaken or jeopardize the industry which provided that job." ("Tailor's Progress," Benjamin Stolberg, page 68.)

4. *New State Ice Co.* v. *Liebmann,* supra.

5. *See:* Report of the Committee on Labor Law, (Lawrence Hunt, Chairman) submitted to and approved by the New York State Bar Association at its 68th Annual Meeting, January 20, 1945.

6. "Studies, Addresses and Personal Papers," Dr. Kaufmann Kohler, page 460.

7. *See:* "The Jewish Dilemma," Elmer Berger, pages 238-240.

8. "Studies, Addresses and Personal Papers," Dr. Kaufmann Kohler, pages 458, 459.

9. New York Times, Letters to the Editor, February 17, 1945.

10. *See:* "The Creed of an American Zionist," Rabbi Milton Steinberg, "Atlantic Monthly," February, 1945. Professor William Ernest Hocking's letter to the New

York Times of April 2, 1944 in which he points out the difference between the tentative proposals, "the place of refuge and the National Home" which "are to some extent at odds with each other." He also points out that those who are urging the subordinating of the Arabs' interest—1,000,000 Arabs and 600,000 Jews—"do not explain what they propose to do with the detail that to the Moslems also Jerusalem is a sacred city;" and concludes with the view that "the political Zionists at this moment, as distinct from the cultural Zionists who have built the noble Hebrew university on Mount Scopus and who know what a National Home must be, these political Zionists are the chief enemies of the Jewish interest in the world of to-morrow." Professor Hocking's letter to the New York Herald Tribune, August 26, 1945, "A Jewish National Home." "Abroad," Anne O'Hare McCormick, The New York Times, March 12, 1945.

11. "Tailor's Progress," Benjamin Stolberg, page 202.

Chapter 18—Morris Hillquit

1. "Labor Lawyer," Louis Waldman, pages 99, 100.
2. "Loose Leaves from a Busy Life," Morris Hillquit, pages 117, 118. (Rand School Press.)
3. *Ibid.*, page 120.
4. *Ibid.*, pages 105, 106.
5. *Ibid.*, pages 131, 132.
6. *See:* New York Times, September 21, 1945. "The Parker Manufacturing Company, producers of tool products and wire goods, announced today a wage policy guaranteeing a minimum of 1,800 hours' pay annually to each employe with a record of five years continuous employment."
7. Findings and Recommendations of the Council of Conciliation, handed down July 23, 1915 and accepted by Union and Association August 4, 1915.
8. New York Times, May 5, 1944. (Italics supplied.)
9. *Quinto* v. *Schlesinger,* 201 App. Div. 487.
10. *Ibid.*, folio 186, et seq. of the printed record on appeal.
11. From 1917 to 1919 Saul Singer was Chairman of the Executive Committee of the Cloak, Suit and Skirt Manufacturers Association.
12. *Quinto* v. *Schlesinger,* supra, page 492.
13. *Ibid.*
14. *Ibid.*, page 497.
15. "Labor Lawyer," Louis Waldman, page 30.
16. "The Needle Trades," Joel Seidman, page 113.

Chapter 19—Meyer London

1. New York Herald Tribune, August 29, 1944.
2. "The Needle Trades," Joel Seidman, page 87.
3. *Ibid.*
4. *Ibid.*
5. *Ibid.*, pages 192, 193, (New York Times, June 30, 1931).
6. *Ibid.*, page 195. (The full text of the report is printed in the New York Times, September 1, 1931.)
7. "The Humanities in an Absolutist World," "American Association of University Professors Bulletin," page 205, Summer, 1944, reprinted from the "Classical Journal," October, 1943.
8. "Yankee from Olympus," Catherine Drinker Bowen, page 275.
9. I must tell you a good story. It is the case in which an English judge—Judge Bailache of the English Commercial Court—played the leading role. The case chanced to come up in London in 1924 during the visit of the American and Canadian Bar to London. The simple issue in the case involved the interpretation of the New York State Arbitration Law. Harlan F. Stone, late Chief Justice of the

United States Supreme Court, former Attorney-General George W. Wickersham and Paul D. Cravath, besides several other leaders of the American Bar testified as experts on one side. Together with other lawyers, I appeared on the other side. We had given our testimony on "commission," as we lawyers say. That is, we were examined over in this country and our testimony was to have been read in Court. But the case came up for trial while some of us were in London. As soon as I arrived at the Savoy Hotel, in London, the lawyer for the plaintiff called me and said that Wickersham and Cravath were to appear in person, and he wanted me to appear on the other side. I received a fee for this more than enough to pay the expenses of the entire trip. While we were still there, Judge Bailache decided the case. He decided against us. He and I met at one of the parties at Grey's Inn a day or so afterwards. He told me that he had decided the case. I said, with all the deference I could muster as an American lawyer for an English judge, "Well, then, your Lordship was more persuaded by the reasoning of Messrs. Wickersham and Cravath than by mine." "Not at all, not at all," was the response. "I always make up my mind before I go into Court and once I make up my mind, I never change it."

The argument for establishing courts for the determination of labor disputes as a cure for strikes is made very effectively by Judge John C. Knox of the Federal Court, Southern District of New York. (*See:* New York World-Telegram, October 10, 1945.)

10. *See:* Full account in "An East Side Epic—The Life and Work of Meyer London" by Harry Rogoff, Chapter LIII, "The End of a Noble Life."

Chapter 20—John A. Dyche

1. New York Times, August 26, 1944.
2. "Seventy Years of Life and Labor, An Autobiography," Samuel Gompers.
3. "Tailor's Progress," Benjamin Stolberg, page 81.
4. *Ibid.*, page 81.
5. *See:* "The Needle Trades," Joel Seidman, page 22.
6. *See:* "Workers Education in the United States," Harold V. Faulkner and Mark Starr; "Education Discovers Organized Labor," Mark Starr, pamphlet issued by ILGWU, reprinted from "Current History," October, 1944. "Trade Unions Turn to Art," Mark Starr, "Christian Science Monitor," February 3, 1945.
7. "Control of Sanitary Standards," published by National Conference of Charities and Corrections, 1912.
8. *Schechter Poultry Corp.* v. *U.S.*, 295 U.S. 495, 55 Sup. Ct. 837, 79 L. Ed. 1570.
9. "The Needle Trades," Joel Seidman, page 204.
10. "Tailor's Progress," Benjamin Stolberg, page 68.
11. New York Times, August 25, 1935.
12. *See:* Condensation in the "Reader's Digest," April, 1946.
13. "Tailor's Progress," Benjamin Stolberg, page 68.
14. *Ibid.*, page 89.
15. *See:* "The Needle Trades," Joel Seidman, pages 229, 230.
16. "Tailor's Progress," Benjamin Stolberg, page 91.

Chapter 21—Dr. George M. Price

1. Page 124.
2. Advertisement in the New York Times, November 1, 1944. Dr. Schieffelin was also Adjutant in the Spanish-American War, Colonel of the 15th New York Infantry in 1918, President of the Huguenot Society, President of the National Association of Wholesale Druggists, Trustee of Hampton and Tuskegee Institutes.
3. "The House on Henry Street," Lillian D. Wald, pages 283, 284, 285.
4. Letter to "The New Republic," by S. S. Goldwater, M.D., appearing under heading "Protocol Aided Public Health," July 24, 1915, page 314.
5. New York Times, January 4, 1945.

Chapter 22—Belle L. Moskowitz

1. New York Herald Tribune, October 5, 1944.
2. New York World-Telegram, October 9, 1944.
3. "No Mean City," Simeon Strunsky, page 165.
4. The grand order of *Sons of the Double Cross*. This is a clan to which no one applies for membership. There are no application blanks to be filled in—no references are required. The proposer—there is usually more than one—never vouches for the character of the prospective member. Indeed it is but fair to say that *absence of character* is one of the most certain assurances of getting into the lodge. Officers are chosen on the basis of demonstrated lack of those elementary qualities which men of decency, rich or poor, high or low, well born or otherwise, possess or are supposed to possess. If it can be proved that you are no gentleman, you qualify beyond question.

Chapter 23—Alexander J. Shamberg

1. 3 T. C. 131, affirmed 144 Fed. (2d) 998, certiorari denied, January 2, 1945.
2. "Pilgrim's Way, An Essay in Recollection," John Buchan (Lord Tweedsmuir), page 22.
3. United States Constitution, Article 1, Section 10.
4. Hanson W. Baldwin in the New York Times, February 12, 1945.
5. *State of New York, et al.* v. *United States of America*, 66 Sup. Ct. 310.
6. I delivered an address before the New York State Economic Council on the 9th of February, 1942, "Air Warnings—Domestic." In that address I expressed the view that the Court deserved the confidence and respect of the country and I used this illustration of the nine fountain pens. The Herald Tribune reporter the next day referred to me as having said that I thought the Court was made up of just "nine fountain pens to be wielded by one hand." I had said just the opposite. The Herald Tribune published a correction the next day.
7. *See:* "The Supreme Court:—Principles and Personalities" by Arthur A. Ballantine, "American Bar Association Journal," March, 1945.

Chapter 24—Eugenius H. Outerbridge

1. Chapter 9, Laws of New Jersey, 1922; Chapter 43, Laws of New York, 1922.
2. "Pilgrim's Way, An Essay in Recollection," John Buchan (Lord Tweedsmuir), page 103.
3. *Ibid.*, page 151.
4. "Shame of the Cities," Lincoln Steffens, page 5.
5. *Ibid.*, page 11.
6. New York Times, May 20, 1910.
7. *United States* v. *Baltimore & Ohio Railroad Company*, 231 U.S. 274, 287; 58 L. Ed. 218, 225.
8. New York Times, February 9, 1946.
9. *New York Harbor Case*, No. 8994, 47 I.C.C. 643.
10. 22 U.S. 1, 9 Wheaton 1, 6 L. Ed. 23.
11. *New York Harbor Case*, supra, record, pages 3393, 3394.
12. New York Times, August 30, 1944.
13. *New York Harbor Case*, supra, record, page 503.
14. *Ibid.*, brief on behalf of the State of New York, pages 126, 127.

Chapter 25—The Port of New York Authority

1. United States Constitution, Section 10, Article 1.
2. *See:* "The Compact Clause of the Constitution, A Study in Interstate Adjustments," by Felix Frankfurter and James M. Landis, 34 Yale Law Journal, 685.
3. Treaty of 1834, New York, New Jersey Port and Harbor Development Com-

mission, Joint Report with Comprehensive Plan and Recommendations; 1920, Chapter 8, Laws of New York 1834, Laws of New Jersey, 1833, 34, page 118. Confirmed by the Congress of the United States, June 28, 1834, (U.S. 23, Cong. 1 Sess. Sen. Doc. No. 239).

4. Similar tributes also appear in the Hudson Dispatch, November 21, 1944, the Jersey Journal, November 22, 1944, Newark Evening News, November 18, 1944, Newark Star-Ledger, November 19, 1944 and the New York Sun, November 20, 1944 and the New York Herald Tribune, November 19, 1944.

5. "Pilgrim's Way, An Essay in Recollection," John Buchan (Lord Tweedsmuir), page 231.

6. New York Times, December 21, 1945.

7. Report of the New York and New Jersey Port and Harbor Development Commission.

8. "Pilgrim's Way, An Essay in Recollection," John Buchan (Lord Tweedsmuir), page 119.

9. Quoted by Hanson W. Baldwin, the New York Times, December 27, 1944.

10. *See:* "Administrative Agencies," "What Authority Has an Authority," "Port Accomplishments and Planning of the Port of New York Authority," all by this author. "The Port of New York Authority," by Archibald MacLeish, "Fortune," September, 1933.

11. Port of New York Advisory Council, Stenographic Record of Conference, July 7, 1921, pages 50-52 and Minutes, July 13, 1921, page 3.
See: "The Port of New York Authority," by Erwin Wilkie Bard, page 47, for summary.

12. "The Port of New York Authority," by Erwin Wilkie Bard, page 62.

13. *Ibid.,* pages 304, 305.

14. "Letters of Lanier," by Sidney Lanier, pages 204 and 206.

Chapter 26—Samuel L. Fuller

1. "No Mean City," Simeon Strunsky, page 187.

2. "Pilgrim's Way, An Essay in Recollection," John Buchan (Lord Tweedsmuir), pages 97, 98.

3. New York Herald Tribune, October 27, 1944.

4. "The Port of New York Authority," Erwin Wilkie Bard, pages 231, 232.

Chapter 27—Conference on State Defense

1. *Helvering* v. *Gerhardt,* 304 U.S. 405.

2. *New York ex rel Rogers* v. *Graves,* 299 U.S. 401.

3. *Brush* v. *Commissioner,* 300 U.S. 352.

4. *Graves* v. *New York ex rel O'Keefe,* 306 U.S. 466.

5. *Great Northern Ry. Co.* v. *Sunburst Oil & R. Co.,* 287 U.S. 358.

6. *See:* "The New Guesspotism," by Frank W. Grinnell, "American Bar Association Journal," September, 1944.

7. Page 146, et seq.

8. March 17, 1944.

9. *See:* "Personnel Administration," Vol. 7, January, 1945.

10. *McDonald* v. *Collector of Internal Revenue,* 65 Sup. Ct. 96.

11. "Jefferson Himself, The Personal Narrative of A Many-Sided American," edited by Bernard Mayo, page 236.

12. *See:* "Today in Washington," David Lawrence, New York Sun, December 9, 1944. "In the Nation," Arthur Krock, New York Times, December 8, 1944.

13. New York Times, February 17, 1945.

14. *See:* New York World-Telegram, November 3, 1945 editorial entitled "The Price of Talent."

15. *See:* American Bar Association Journal, December, 1945.

16. Report to the American Bar Association by the Committee on Judicial Salaries on H.R. 2181 introduced by Mr. Hobbs and S. 920 introduced by Senator Wagner, May 8, 1945.

17. *Jones* v. *Opelika*, 316 U.S. 584.

18. "Democracy in America," Alexis DeTocqueville, Vol. 1, page 68.

19. New York Times, December 25, 1944.

20. *Ibid.*

21. These included Mortimer S. Edelstein, Daniel B. Goldberg, Walter P. Caughlan and C. Thomas Schettino, all members of the Law Department of the Port of New York Authority who gave overtime service to the job. It was a night and day and Sunday and holiday job. It was a triumph of *logistics*—the moving of material for a two or three weeks' siege, to Washington and then back again to New York and then back again to Washington—again and again and again. The stenographers of the staff, Rose Lewin, Peggy O'Connell and Anne Zuckerman worked until they were ready to drop in their tracks.

22. The Conference on State Defense was originated by the Attorneys-General of the states on May 31, 1938. The Attorneys-General of the following states were present or represented at the first meeting of the Conference: Connecticut, Delaware, Kansas, Louisiana, Maine, Mississippi, New York, Rhode Island, Washington and West Virginia. The Conference not only included Attorneys-General, but Comptrollers of the states, the United States Conferences of Mayors, the Municipal Finance Officers Association, The National Institute of Municipal Law Officers, the American Municipal Association, the various state Municipal Leagues and the principal associations of state and local employees.

On the hearings before the Special Senate Committee on taxation of Governmental Securities and Salaries, many fiscal officers as well as experts in the municipal bond field testified, pointing out to the committee the dangers inherent in the proposals of the government. Later that year, both houses of Congress rejected the Treasury's attempt to tax state and municipal bonds. The Ways and Means Committee never even reported the proposal to the floor of the House. In 1940 when the matter was actually voted upon in the Senate, the attempt was defeated by vote of 44 to 30—defeated on non-partisan lines. To the brief filed on behalf of the Port of New York Authority, the states and municipalities, the signatures of the Attorneys-General of the following states were attached: Alabama, Arizona, Arkansas, California, Connecticut, Delaware, Florida, Idaho, Illinois, Indiana, Kansas, Kentucky, Louisiana, Maine, Maryland, Massachusetts, Minnesota, Mississippi, Missouri, Montana, Nevada, New Hampshire, New Jersey, New Mexico, New York, North Carolina, North Dakota, Ohio, Oklahoma, Oregon, Pennsylvania, Rhode Island, South Dakota, Tennessee, Utah, Vermont, Virginia, Washington, Wisconsin, Wyoming.

23. "Consideration on Representative Government," John Stuart Mill, page 303.

24. "Democracy in America," Alexis DeTocqueville, page 61.

25. New York Times, January 17, 1945.

Chapter 28—St. Lawrence Power Authority

1. "Yankee Reporter," S. Burton Heath, Chapter 6.

2. New York Times, September 30, 1936.

3. Chapter 772 of the Laws of 1931.

4. Report of the St. Lawrence Power Development Commission, 1931, pages 66, 67, Sections 17, 26.

5. New York Times, January 7, 1945.

6. New York Times, January 7, 1945, "Shall We Have More TVA's?" by David E. Lilienthal.

See: "A Hard Look at TVA," by C. Hartley Grattan, "Harper's," September, 1945. New York Times, October 11, 1945, editorial "Truman at Kentucky Dam." "TVA comes out pretty well after the critics have had their say. The principle that the unified development of a river valley promotes the general welfare has been proven in this instance."

7. New York Times, October 29, 1944.

8. Pages 139, 140, 145.

9. There was hope in 1931 that "bi-State" cooperation could be secured between New York State and the Provinces of Canada. We so reported. (Report of the St. Lawrence Power Development Commission, 1931, pages 36 and 194.) The St. Lawrence Power Authority is not a Federal agency. It is an instrumentality of the State of New York. By the statute incorporating it, it is precluded in applying to any federal agency from waiving any of the State's rights to the Water Power. While the Authority is authorized to "apply to the appropriate agencies and officials of the United States government and/or of the Dominion of Canada or its provinces, including the international joint commissions, for such licenses, permits or approval of its plans or projects as it may deem necessary or advisable," it is provided "that neither the authority nor any trustee, officer or agent thereof shall have the power to waive or surrender for any purpose whatsoever any right of the state of New York, whether sovereign or proprietary in character, in and to the St. Lawrence River, its waters, power, channel, bed or uses, or the right of the state to assert such rights at any future time, and provided further that if for any reason the authority shall fail to secure any such licenses, permit or approval as it may deem necessary or advisable, or shall decide not to make application therefor, it is authorized to institute suit, or to apply to congress for legislation, or take such other action in the premises as it may deem necessary or advisable, in the furtherance of the project and for the protection of its rights and those of the state." (Public Authorities Law of the State of New York, Sec. 1005 (3).)

See: Governor Dewey's message to President Truman demanding guarantee on New York State's rights. Herald Tribune, September 26, 1945. Message from President Truman transmitting the recommendations for approval by the Congress of the agreement of March 19, 1941, between United States and Canada for the development of the Great Lakes-St. Lawrence Basin, October 3, 1945. Proposed agreement recommended by the engineers of the United States for turning over power to the State of New York on the basis of assuming responsibility for the estimated cost of the power development. (Hearings before a Subcommittee of the Committee on Foreign Relations, United States Senate, 72nd Congress, Second Session on S. Res. 278, February 10, 1933, page 1012.) Adverse Report Sen. No. 639, 79th Congress, First Session on Missouri Valley Authority Act, accompanying S. 555, especially pages 12 and 13, dated October 18, 1945. Statement by Major Gen. Francis B. Wilby, retired, chairman of the New York Power Authority for most recent development in this field. (New York Times, March 7, 1946.)

10. "Democracy in America," Alexis DeTocqueville, page 92.

Acknowledgments

Without the help of a number of people, this book would not be in its present form. I make acknowledgment to:

My neighbor at Montauk, Dr. William Bradley Otis, Professor of English and English Literature at the College of the City of New York, author of several excellent works, who lent an encouraging ear to the first readings of the manuscript, scanned the later revisions and made invaluable criticism;

Edward B. Marks, for fifty years publisher of musical hits and to Herbert, his son, an exceptional reviewer of books;

Arthur T. Vanderbilt, Dean of the New York University Law School;

Mortimor S. Gordon, my law associate, for very helpful criticism;

Leo Brady, my associate, for careful reading of the manuscript and saving me from many errors.

John Erskine who read it, made criticism and gave it his blessing.

I owe a large debt to another author—a Doctor of Literature, Will D. Howe, whose recommendations for rearrangement and for cutting made the book a much more readable volume.

To all of these friends, my deep appreciation for their generosity.

Orchids go to Miriam Sloan Mayer, my secretary, for patiently deciphering my handwriting, organizing the material and vigorously criticizing the earlier drafts and to Jean Cobert, her successor, who took hold of the manuscript and cooperated in important details with the publishers.

Appreciation also to Sylvia Friedman who as copyist labored diligently and understandingly.

To Miss Rebecca B. Rankin of the Municipal Reference Library who lent her help on frequent call.

For help in lending me material:

Laurence A. Tanzer
Theodore A. Schorske
Edmund H. Titchenor
Clarence S. Stein
George Gove
Frederick H. Ecker
Morris Froelich
Joseph M. Price
Arthur K. Kuhn
Robert D. Kohn
Eleanor C. Tanzer

We can do scarcely anything at all in this world save through and with the help of others. Recognition of this point, indeed, is one of the objectives of this book. My thanks to all who have helped me in writing it.

Especial acknowledgement to the following publishers for gracious permission to quote from books copyrighted by them:

Columbia University Press. "The Port of New York Authority," by Dr. Erwin Wilkie Bard.

Thomas Y. Crowell Company. "Music Comes to America," by David Ewen.

Doubleday & Company, Inc. "Tailor's Progress," by Benjamin Stolberg.

E. P. Dutton & Co., Inc. "No Mean City," by Simeon Strunsky; "Labor Lawyer," by Louis Waldman.

Harper & Brothers. "Democracy on the March," by David E. Lilienthal; "Considerations on Representative Government," by John Stuart Mill; "Memoirs of a Superfluous Man," by Albert Jay Nock; "The Bar of Other Days," by Joseph S. Auerbach.

Harvard University Press. "Holmes-Pollock Letters."

Henry Holt & Company, Inc. "The House on Henry Street," by Lillian D. Wald.

Houghton Mifflin Company. "Jefferson Himself," by Bernard Mayo.

The International Press. "The Ardent Eighties," by Gregory Weinstein.

Alfred A. Knopf, Inc. "Democracy in America," by Alexis De Tocqueville, Phillips Bradley, editor.

Little, Brown & Company and Atlantic Monthly Press. "Yankee from Olympus," by Catherine Drinker Bowen.

Liveright Publishing Corporation. "The Evening Post—A Century of Journalism," by Allan Nevins.

McIntosh & Otis. "Pilgrim's Way," by John Buchan (Lord Tweedsmuir).

William Morrow & Company, Inc. "Music Lover's Handbook," by Elie Siegmeister.

G. P. Putnam's Sons. "Essays on Practical Politics," by Theodore Roosevelt.

Rand School Press. "Loose Leaves from a Busy Life," by Morris Hillquit.

Rinehart & Company, Inc. "The Needle Trades," by Joel Seidman.

Charles Scribner's Sons. "Yankee Lawyer, The Autobiography of Ephraim Tutt"; "Theodore Roosevelt, An Autobiography"; "Theodore Roosevelt and His Times," by Joseph Bucklin Bishop; "How the Other Half Lives," by Jacob A. Riis; "Letters of Lanier," by Sidney Lanier.

The Viking Press, Inc. "Up to Now," by Alfred E. Smith.

Whittlesey House. "Country Lawyer," by Bellamy Partridge.

And to the following magazine publishers:
    The Atlantic Monthly
    The Classical Journal
    American Association of University Professors Bulletin
    Time, Inc.

And to the following newspapers and press associations:

    New York Herald Tribune
    New York Post
    The Sun
    The New York Times
    New York World-Telegram
    Associated Press
    United Feature Syndicate

Index

Abbot, Nathan, 37, 69
Abbot, Everett V., 3-14, 37, 350
Abbott, Austin, 3
Acheson, Dean, 322
Adams, Franklin P., 123
Adams, Maude, 60
Addams, Jane, 228, 231
Adler, Felix, ix, 12, 32, 40, 53, 59, 66, 75, 77, 87, 119, 152, 168, 169, 183, 185, 188, 198, 199, 203, 207-213, 220, 238, 245, 344, 345
Adler, Helen, 35, 36
Adler, Reuben S., 228
"Agency," 4
Aldridge, George, 348
Alger, Horatio, 108, 109
Alger, Russell Alexander, 75
Allied Real Estate Interests, 348
Amalgamated Clothing Workers, 121
American Arbitration Association, 150, 156, 157, 159, 351, 352
American Association of University Professors Bulletin, 363
American Bar Association, 115, 132, 134, 155, 156, 206, 323, 325, 358
"American Bar Association Journal," 353, 356, 357
American Council for Judaism, 200
American Federation of Labor, 191, 193, 216, 223, 224, 325
American Jewish Committee, 125
American Red Cross, 308
Ammann, Othman H., 123, 251, 252, 265, 311
Amsterdam Avenue "Four Track" Fight, 45
Amtorg Trading Corporation, 351
Anderson, Arthur M., 311, 312
Arbitration, Board of, 205-210, 230
"Arbitration Journal," 352
"Arbitration and Public Policy," 352
"Ardent Eighties, The," 42, 345, 362
Appleton, Charles W., 67
Armstrong, Rosewald, 311
Arndt, Walter, 113
Archbold, John D., 99
Ashley, Clarence D., 3
Associated Press, 363

Association of the Bar of the City of New York, 133, 345
"Atlantic Monthly, The," 116, 363
Auerbach, Joseph S., 343, 344, 362
Austin, Warren R., 159
"Authority," 268, 290, 291
Aymar, Francis W., 346

Babbington-Smith, Constance, 143
Bacon, Selden, 11
Bacon, Theodore, 346
Bagehot, Walter, 259
Bailache, Judge, 354, 355
Baker, Newton D., 284-287
Baker, Ray Stannard, 24, 343
"Balance Sheet of Protocolism," 236
Baldwin, Hanson W., 356, 357
Baldwin, William D., 213
Ballantine, Arthur A., 356
Bannard, Otto T., 274
Barbour, Clarence A., 346
Bard, Albert Sprague, 13, 37, 350
Bard, Erwin Wilkie, 302, 357, 362
Barnes, William, 75, 78, 81, 85-88, 95-97, 99-104, 346, 347
Barnum, Gertrude, 228
Barondess, Joseph, 225
Barrett, Richard Warren, 278
Baruch, Bernard, 158, 159
Bauer, John, 335
Belasco, David, 21
Bell, Golden W., 320
Bellamy, Edward, 345
Bellamy, Mrs. Frederick P., 345
Beller & Company, 180, 181, 235
Bennett, John J., 325
Bennet, William S., 48
Benton, Joel, 43
Berger, Elmer, 353
Bernheimer, Charles L., 138, 149-161, 207, 273, 287, 288, 342
Berry, Charles W., 213
Beveridge, Albert, 278
Bigotry, 127
Bilkey, Edward S., 294
Binkerd, Robert S., 113
Bishop, Joseph Bucklin, 88, 95, 348, 349, 362

Bisno, Abraham, 226
Bi-State Commission, 281, 284, 300
Black, Algernon D., 37
"Black Crook," 109
Black, Frank, 75, 77, 79, 80
Black Horse Cavalry, 45
Black, Hugo, 321
Blackwood, Basil, 272
Blaine, James G., 112
Bliss, Cornelius N., 99
Blume, Paul, 47
"Boodle Alderman," 44
Borden, C. D., 99
Bosler, William D., 67
Boston, Charles A., 37, 38
Bowen, Catherine Drinker, 345, 352-354, 362
Bowers, John M., 96, 103
Boycott, Captain, 163
Boyle, Edward, 213
Braden, J. Noble, 157
Bradley, Phillips, 362
Brady, Leo, 361
Brandeis, Louis D., 182, 183, 185, 190-200, 202, 205, 221, 233, 236, 239
Breed, Abbott & Morgan, 277
Breed, William C., 277
Bridges, Horace, 37
Brooke, Rupert, 116
Brooklyn League, 349
Brown, B. W. B., 93
Brown, Clyde, 278
Bruere, Henry, 207, 211
Brundage, William M., 346
Bryan, Mrs. Charles A., 351
Bryan, William Jennings, 74
Buckner, Emory R., 350
Bull Moose Party, 97
Burlingham, Charles C., 273
"Burn, Burn, Burn, Those Letters," 111
Bush, Irving T., 276, 281, 284-287
Bush Terminal Company, 276, 277, 284
Butler, Benjamin F., 3
Butler, Edmond B., 122
Byrnes, James F., 160

Cade, Jack, 174
Caffey, Francis G., 284
Cahan, Abraham, 187, 191, 216, 225
Cardozo, Benjamin F., 10, 169, 170, 220, 319
Carlisle, Floyd L., 336, 337, 338
Carter, James C., 7
Case, Clarence E., 293
Cassel, Gustav, 327
Casson, Herbert N., 346
Catchings, Waddill, 310

Catholic Church, 344, 345
Caughlin, Walter P., 28, 358
Centralization, 340, 343
Chamber of Commerce, New York State, 141, 149, 153, 156, 157, 159, 162, 174, 271, 276, 278, 281, 302, 351, 352
Chamber of Commerce, United States, 309
Chamberlain, Neville, 200
Chaplin, Stewart, 37
Chapman, John Jay, 30, 76, 77, 80, 82, 87, 90, 346
Childs, Richard S., 350
"Chindits," 151
Choate, Joseph H., 7, 26, 27
Churchill, Winston, 303
CIO, 309
Citizens Union, 12, 65, 76, 84, 86, 87, 92, 112-114, 144, 273, 348, 350
City Club, 29, 42, 84, 112, 113, 274, 348
City Housing Authority, 121, 122, 350
Clark, Alfred Corning, 42
Clark, A. E., 42
Clark, Tom C., 322
Clarke, John Proctor, 69
Classical Journal, The, 363
"Clear it with Sidney," 192
Clearwater, Judge Alfonso T., 4
Cleveland, Grover, 111
Clinton Hall, 3
Cloak and Suit Industry (See Garment Industry), 186, 227, 228, 233, 242
Cloak, Suit and Skirt Manufacturers Association, 181, 184, 193, 205, 212, 221, 354
Cloakmakers Union, 213
Cobert, Jean, 361
Cockran, W. Bourke, 116
Cohalan, Daniel F., 11
Cohen, Ida S., 136-146
Cohen, Joseph H., 182, 205, 218
Cohen, Samuel Conrad, 27
Cohen, William N., 69
Coit, Stanton, 238
College of the City of New York, The, 112, 361
Columbia University, 33, 48, 305
Commercial Arbitration, 149-161
"Commercial Arbitration and the Law," 10, 153, 155, 353
Committee on Labor Law, 353
"Committee of One Hundred," 273
Committee on Parks, 351
Committee on Streets, 351
Consumers Protection Label, 233, 234
"Comprehensive Plan for the Develop-

ment of the Port of New York," 296, 301, 302
Conference on State Defense, 317-328
"Considerations on Representative Government," 326, 362
Cooper Union, 3, 53, 55, 349
Corrigan, Joseph E, 37
Cortelyou, George B., 8, 9
Coudert Brothers, 77
Council of Conciliation, 354
"Country Lawyer," 29, 344, 362
Court of Arbitration, 152, 153
Craig, Charles L., 292, 296, 297, 310
Crain, Thomas C. T., 111
Crane, Frederick E., 93, 170
Contract Settlement Act of 1944, 150, 160, 352
Conway, Thomas F., 334
Cravath, Paul D., 169, 355
Cresson, Benjamin F., 272, 281, 283, 286
Croker, Richard, 86
Cromwell, William Nelson, 29
Crowley, Patrick, 144, 272
Cullman, Howard S., 250, 251
Curie, Madame, 133
Curtis, Sidney, 9
Cutting, Fulton R., 77, 87, 90, 138, 240, 273

Dallet, Joseph, 228
Damrosch, Frank, 50-63, 345
Damrosch, Hetty, 62, 63
Damrosch, Leopold, 51
Damrosch, Walter, 51
Dana, Charles A., 345
Darwin, Charles, 109
Davenport, Frederick M., 90, 321, 334-336
Davies, Stone and Auerbach, 13
Davis, J. Lionberger, 284
Day, Katherine, 351
Dayton, Kenneth, 27, 121, 262, 281, 333, 335, 336
Deane, Joseph G., 21
De Cesare, O. E., 206
De Gaulle, Charles, 161, 224
Delafield, Lewis L., 69, 316
Delehanty, Francis, 304
Delmonico's, 91
Deming, Caroline Sprinstead, 30
Deming, Guy, 22
Deming, Harold, 22
Deming, Horace E., 21-31, 69, 92, 93, 106, 113, 138, 214, 258, 273, 287, 288, 308, 309, 324
Democratic Party, 69, 298
Denison, Lindsay, 66

Dennison Company, The, 204
Depression, The, 145
De Puy, Harriet Adams, 54
Deringer, Anna B., 132
De Tocqueville, Alexis, 23, 324, 326, 341, 343, 359, 362
Davenport, Lord, 289, 290
Dewey, Thomas E., 27, 64, 180, 218, 315, 359
Dewey, Mrs. Thomas E., 143
Dix, John A., 113
Dorr, Goldthwaite H., 12, 350
Doty, Mary S., 54
Dougherty, J. Hampden, 25
Dreier, Mary Elizabeth, 228, 246
Dress, Waist and Millinery Industry (See Garment Industry), 186, 227-231, 246, 248, 249
Drew, John, 60
Dubinsky, David, 187-189, 227, 236, 237
Dudley, John S., 28
Duggan, Stephen P., 179
Dunbar, Paul Lawrence, Housing Project, 121
Dunn, Catherine, 128
Dunning, Sara L., 54
Du Pont, T. Coleman, 99
Duryea, Perry, 299
Dutcher, William, 346
Dyche, John A., 223-237, 242
Dyer, George R., 259, 261, 262, 265

Earle, Mrs. Genevieve, 143
Eastman, Joseph B., 320
Ecker, Frederick H., 122, 123, 350, 361
Economic Club, 133
Edelstein, Mortimer S., 28, 358
Edge, Walter, 117, 118, 260, 281, 283, 292, 303, 305, 315
"Education Discovers Organized Labor," 355
"Education of Henry Adams, The," 119
Educational Alliance, 238, 245
Educational Foundation for the Apparel Industry, 180
Edwards, Edward I., 293
Edwards, William H., 351
Eighteenth Amendment, The, 11, 117, 118, 303
Eisenhower, Dwight D., 312
Eisig, Arthur, 34
Elkus, Abram I., 125
Elliott, John Lovejoy, 34, 37, 119, 252
Ely, Robert Erskine, 133
Embree, William Dean, 67
Emergency Rent Laws, 168, 353
Epstean, Edward, 32

Epstein, Henry, 172, 325
Epstein, Judith G., 199
Equity of Redemption, 164-166, 168
Equity of Renewal, 163, 164, 166, 167
Ethical Culture School, 37, 59
Ethical Culture Society, 33, 34, 36, 37, 53, 61, 63, 77, 168, 207
Evans, John C., 251, 265, 286, 311
Evarts, Choate and Beaman, 13
Evarts, Senator William, 4, 7
Ewen, David, 345, 362

Fairchild, Benjamin Lewis, 277
Fancher, Enoch L., 152, 153
Fashion Institute of Technology, 183, 189
Faulkner, Harold V., 355
Fedden, John, 134
Federal Power Commission, 331, 334
Feinberg, Israel, 213
Ferguson, Frank C., 174, 265, 293, 295, 299
Fiene, Ernest, 183, 184, 185, 187
Fifteenth Ward, 108
55 William Street, 6, 10, 20, 62
"Fighting Years," 49, 345
Filene's, 190
Filene, A. Lincoln, 190
"First Principles," 74
Fischman, William, 182, 205, 218, 235
Fitzmaurice, Robert, 118
Fitzpatrick, Paul, 150, 157, 159, 160
Flammer, J. George, 65
Floersheimer, Samuel, 228, 229, 235
Flynn, Edward, 188, 196
Fogel, Isidor, 217
Foley, James A., 113, 114
Foley, Tom, 110, 111
Folk, James W., 64
Foraker, Burch, 4
Foraker, Frank R., 4
Ford, Bacon & Davis, 283
Ford, Frank R., 283
Forstmann, Julius, 185, 278, 279
Foulke, William Dudley, 25
Frank, Alfred, 346
Frank, Jerome, 172, 268
Frankfurter, Felix, 112, 217, 320, 356
Franklin, Benjamin, 123
Franklin, Philip A. S., 286
Fraser, Robert S., 155
Frayne, Hugh, 213
Free Transfers on Street Railways and Penalties, 46, 47
Frelinghuysen, Joseph S., 292, 294
Friedman, Sylvia, 361
Froelich, Morris, 257, 258, 264, 289, 361

"Fruit and Flower Mission, The," 146
Fuller, James R., 308
Fuller, Paul, 37, 77, 82-84, 87, 90, 273, 346
Fuller, Samuel L., 305, 307-316, 334, 336, 337

Gallup Poll, 170
Galvin, John F., 274, 307
Gans, Howard S., 65
Garbage Disposal in New York City, 137, 138
Gardiner, Asa Bird, 27-30, 218
Gardiner, Charles L., 346
Garment Industry, x, 132, 179-189, 192, 202, 220, 223-237, 239, 253, 337, 342
Garrison, Lloyd McKim, 6, 7, 13
Gary, Postmaster James Albert, 15
"Gay Nineties," The, 47
Gaynor Charter, 348
Gaynor, William J., 144, 273, 348, 349
Gehrung, Fred, 60
Gehrung, George, 51, 60, 61
Gellman, Leon, 199
George, Lloyd, 290
George, Walter F., 159, 160
George Washington Bridge, 124, 250, 253, 262, 265, 270, 312
"Ghost Talks, The," 114, 348
Gifford, Ralph W., 37
Gilbert, Cass, 251
Gilbert, Joseph E., 120
Gilman, Theodore P., 344
Gimbels, 183
Gladstone, Prime Minister, 163
Glasgow, William A., Jr., 279
Glass, Montague, 250
Gleim, Charles S., 264, 265
Godkin, Edwin L., 345
Goeltz, Edna, 133, 283
Goethals, George W., 272, 283, 286
Goff, John W., 110, 131, 194, 220
Goldberg, Caroline, 63
Goldberg, Daniel B., 28, 267, 358
Goldberg, William Victor, 27
Goldman, Jacob J., 228, 229, 235
Goldstein, Israel, 199
Goldstein, Sidney, 28
Goldwater, Dr. Sigmund S., 36, 243, 355
Gompers, Samuel, 187, 191, 216, 223, 225, 227, 355
Good Government Clubs ("Goo Goos"), 12, 73
Goodnow, Frank J., 24
Gordon, Mortimer, 361
Gove, George, 119, 120, 122
"Government of American Cities," 24

"Government of the People, By the People and For the People," 325
Grace, William R., 94
Grand Central Hotel, 111
Grattan, C. Hartley, 358
Great Britain, ix, 24, 286, 329
Greater New York Taxpayers Conference, 349
Green, William, 223
Greer, Guy, 350
Griffith, Ernest S., 343
Grinnell, Frank W., 357
Gross, M. B., 159
Gross, Milt, 123
Grossman, Moses H., 156
Gruber, Abraham, 48, 77, 78, 86, 95
Guthrie, William D., 169-172
Gutman, Abraham L., 34, 37, 168, 169
Gwinn, Ralph W., 27
Gwynne, Charles T., 141, 149, 152, 303, 304

Hagedorn, Herman, 346
Hague, Frank, 188, 196, 294
Haig, Robert Murray, 327, 334, 335
Haight, Abner S., 346
Hall, Marshall, 91
Hallam, Alfred, 54
Halle, Helen, 150
Hamilton, Alexander, 341
Hamilton, John D. M., 267
Hammitt, Joseph, 113
Hammond Charter, 348
Hammond Committee, 348
Hammond, John Henry, 99
Hanauer, Jerome J., 312, 313
Hancock, John, 158-160
Hand, Judge Augustus N., 13
Hand, Learned, 68
Hand, Richard, 68
Harding, Warren G., 31
Hardon, Henry Winthrop, 350
Harren, Marion J., 133
Harrison, Samuel, 61
Hart, Schaffner & Marx, 186, 187
Harvard Law School, 22, 38, 76, 353
Harvard University, 308
Harvey & Outerbridge, 272
Haughwout, J. Ard, 27
Hayek, Frederick A., 327
Hayes, William H., 14
Hayes, John, 13, 14
Hearst, William Randolph, 65, 74, 98, 115, 274, 345
Heath, S. Burton, 334, 358
Hedden, Walter, 248-311
Hellman, Edgar A., 34

Hershkopf, Bernard, 169, 170
Hillis, William J., 346
Hillman, Sidney, 121, 187, 188, 192, 217, 236
Hillquit, Morris, 39, 182, 183, 187, 196, 197, 201-214, 216, 218, 224, 225, 230, 233, 236, 337, 354, 362
Hindus, Maurice, 215
Hinrichs, Frederick W., 85
Historical Memory Versus Logical Memory, 20
Hobble-Skirt, 259
Hochman, Julius, 234, 243
Hocking, William Ernest, 353
Hogan, Frank S., 27
Hogan, John P., 170, 171, 335
Hoguet, Robert Louis, 350
Holland, Clifford M., 260
Holland Tunnel, 117, 258, 260-264, 313, 314, 330
Holmes, Justice Oliver Wendell, 5, 33, 166, 170, 188, 220
Holroyd, Simeon, 346
Holt, Hamilton, 202, 205, 350
Home Rule Amendment, New York, 12
Hornblower, William B., 7
Horowitz, Charles S., 28
Hough, Charles M., 154, 220
Hourwich, Isaac A., 210, 226, 227
Housing, 122, 123, 330, 350
"House on Henry Street," 243, 355, 362
"How the Other Half Lives," 239, 362
Howe, Louis McHenry, 247, 333
Howe, Will D., 361
Hubbard, Elbert, 169
Hudson Guild, The, 146
Hughes, Charles Evans, 5, 47, 68, 97, 113, 155, 266, 317
Hulbert, Murray, 297, 298
Humes, Elias M., 346
Hunt, Lawrence, 353
Hunter, Philip, 143, 248
Huntington, Francis C., 273
Hupper, Roscoe H., 173
Hurley, Edwin N., 284, 286
Hylan, John F., 118, 292, 293, 296, 297, 302, 304

"Ice," 190
Iconophiles, 109
Idlewild Airport, 296
Independent Club of the West Side, The, 43, 245
Industrial Workers of the World (IWW), 180, 227
Ingersoll, Raymond V., 249
Inheritance Tax Law, 25

International Ladies Garment Workers Union, 190, 195, 196, 202, 355
Interstate Commerce Commission, 274, 277, 278, 280, 281, 294
Iroquois Club, 110, 111
Irwin, Wallace, 65
Isaacs, Nathan, 353
Israels, Charles H., 245
Israels, Josef, 245
Israels, Josef II, 245
Iturbi, Jose, 52
Ivins Commission, 348
Ivins, William M., 65, 80, 88, 91-107, 287, 289, 324, 348, 349
Ivins, Wolff & Hoguet, 92

Jacobs, Emma, 146
Jadwin, Edgar, 335
James, Arthur Curtiss, 283, 297
James, Shell and Elkus, 9
"Jefferson Himself," 321, 362
Jefferson, Thomas, 123, 328
Jerome, Lovell, 83
Jerome, William Travers, 16, 64-69, 110, 218
Jessup, Henry W., 37
Johnson, Hiram, 86
Johnson, Hugh S., 232
Joint Board of Sanitary Control, 239, 240, 241, 243
"Judicial Correction of Judicial Error," 11
Juilliard School of Music, The, 51
"Jus Casaca," 167

Keener, William A., 3
Keith, Boudinot, 346
Keller, Frances, 157
Kelley, Nicholas, 350
Kelly, Edward, 188, 196
Kelly, Florence, 228, 245
Kenneson, Ashley, Emley and Rubino, 4
Kieran, John, 133
King, Edward, 53
King, William F., 66
Kingsley, Darwin P., 174, 303
Kinney, Thomas E., 85
Kinnicutt, Herman, 308
Kirchwey, George W., 37, 207
Klein, Isaac H., 77, 346, 348
Klein, Samuel, 183, 184, 187, 189, 233, 234
Klein, William, 213
Knauth, Nachod and Kuhne, 44, 47
Knauth, Mrs. Percival, 351
"Know Your City," 142
Knox, John C., 355

Knudsen, William S., 295
Koenig, Samuel, 4, 73
Kohler, Kaufmann, 198, 199, 353
Kohler, Lillie, 198
Kohler, Rose, 198
Kohn, Robert D., 34, 346, 361
Kohn, Victor H., 348
Kresel, Isidor J., 67
Krock, Arthur, 357
Kuhn, Arthur K., 34, 361
Ku Klux Klan, 127
Kulukundis Shipping Company, 351
Kurzman, "Tough Jake," 217

"Labor Lawyer," 214, 354, 362
Labor Party, 191, 203
L'Affaire Hourwich, 202, 216
"Ladies Garment Worker, The," 224, 226
La Guardia, Fiorello, 24, 125, 140, 179, 293, 294, 325, 350
Laing, Chester ("Chet"), 311
Lamb, Charles, 36
Landis, James M., 356
Lanier, Sidney, 305, 357, 362
Larocque, Joseph, 7
LaRoe, Wilbur, Jr., 279
Larson, Morgan F., 263
"Law and Order in Industry," 185
"Law: Business or Profession? The," 38
Law Reform, 10
Lawrence, Cyrus J., 309
Lawrence, David, 357
Lawyers, 69
League for Political Education, 132
Leary, William, 283, 292, 307
Leavitt, John Brooks, 346
Ledo Road, The, 265
Lee, Abbie S., 54
Lefcourt, A. E., 181
Leffingwell, Russell, 310
Legal Aid Society, The, 134, 135
Legal Ethics Clinic, The, 37
LeHand, Margaret ("Missie"), 247
Lehmaier, James S., 48, 92
Lehman, Herbert H., 127, 132, 179, 263, 264, 298
Lennon, John B., 193
Levy, Edward, 264
Lewin, Rose, 358
Lewis, Clarence M., 350
Lewis, John L., 188
Lexow Committee, 110
"Life of Gladstone, The," 163
"Life of Oliver Cromwell, The," 131
Lighterage Case, 274-280
Lilienthal, David E., 339, 340, 358, 362
"Limited Dividend Corporation," 120

Lincoln Tunnel, 260, 261, 264, 265, 315
Lindabury, John D., 173
Lindner, Walter, 350
Linen, John, 311
Lippmann, Walter, 352
"Little Lost Child," 50
Littleton, Martin W., 63
Lizst, Franz, 51
Local Self-Government, 24
Lockwood, Charles C., 167, 169
Lodge, Henry Cabot, 75, 119
Loeb, William, 104
Loeb, William, Jr., 9
Logistics, 27, 283
London, Meyer, 182, 183, 193, 194, 196, 197, 202, 215-222, 224, 225, 227, 230, 233, 235, 240, 337
"Looking Backwards," 345
"Loose Leaves from A Busy Life," 202, 203, 362
Lord, Bennett, 351
Louisa Alcott Club, The, 146
Low, Seth, 24, 48, 84
Lutz, Harley L., 316
Lyons, Eugene, 234

MacDonald, Ramsay, 116
Mackay, Clarence H., 99
MacKenzie, Emelyn, 133
Macleish, Archibald, 357
MacMahon, Aline, 119
Macy, V. Everett, 346
Magnes, Judah Leib, 199
Manice, Abbot and Perry, 7, 8, 9, 13, 14, 19, 73
Manice, Sarah Remsen, 7
Manice, William, 7, 19, 20
Marks, Edward B., 50, 51, 109, 361
Marks, Herbert, 361
Marquand, Edward G., 54
Marsh, Robert McCurdy, 350
Marshall, Charles C., 116
Marshall, John, 30
Marshall, Louis, 168, 169, 172, 183, 185, 220, 221, 353
Martin, Bernard F., 110
Marvin, Langdon P., 334
"Maw, Maw, Where's My Paw?" 111
Mayer, Miriam Sloan, 361
Mayo, Bernard, 321, 357, 362
McAdoo, William, 65, 275, 284
"McAdoo Tunnel," 257, 259
McCaffery, Sara J. J., 54
McCarter, Robert H., 93, 278, 293
McClellan, George B., 65, 92
McCormack, John W., 322
McCormick, Anne O'Hare, 324, 354

McCran, Thomas F., 292
McGinnies, Joseph A., 312
McGoodale, John, 53
McKane, John Y., 111
McKenna, Joseph, 171, 172
McKinley, William, 8, 74
Medalie, George C., 352
Meitner, Lise, 143
Mellen, Charles S., 99
Merchants Association, The, 277, 282
Merrill, Lynch, Pearce, Fenner & Beane, 309
Metropolis Law School, 3, 5, 73
Metropolitan Life Insurance Company, 121, 122, 350
Metropolitan Opera, 51, 52, 62, 112
Meyer, Max, 179-189, 191, 193, 196, 228, 233-236, 239, 240
Michaelson, Charles, 114, 115, 345, 348
Milburn, John G., 346
Milk Campaign, 115
Mill, John Stuart, 23, 74, 160, 236, 326, 358, 362
Miller, Nathan L., 174, 292, 297, 298, 303-305
Miller, Peckham and Dixon, 7
Millinery Stabilization Commission, 179, 233
Mills, Ogden, 156, 293
Milton, John, 293
Miner, Karl R., 67
Minnevitch, Borrah, 112
Minturn, James F., 260
"Miserables, Les," 109
Missouri Valley Authority Act, 359
Mitchel, John Purroy, 24, 39, 151, 206, 207, 212, 227, 274
Mitchell, Charles E., 307
Montignani, John F., 346
Moot, Adelbert, 346
Morawetz, Victor, 169
Morgan, J. P., & Company, 310-312
Morganstern, Birdie, 146, 351
Morganstern, Louise, 146, 351
Morganthau, Henry, 318
Morris, Esther, 351
Morrow, Dwight, 310, 311
Mosenthal, Theresa, 62
Moses, Robert, 125, 126, 145, 247, 252, 296
Moskowitz, Belle, 132, 167, 213, 231, 245-253, 297, 302, 330
Moskowitz, Henry, 90, 240, 245
Most, Johann, 202
Mulrooney, Edward P., 217
Municipal Art Society, 251
Municipal Reform, 12, 24

"Murder, Inc.," 196, 197
Murphy, Charles F., 75, 85, 86
Murphy, Edward, Jr., 77
Murray, James H., 159, 160
"Music Comes to America," 345, 362
Musical Art Society, 51
Mussolini, 32
Muzzey, David S., 37
"My Day," 248
Myers, Gustavus, 345

Nation, Carrie, 139
National Consumers League, 231
National Industrial Recovery Act, 232-234
National Municipal League, 24, 30
"Nature of the Judicial Process, The," 319
Naumberg, Agnes, 121
"Needle Trades, The," 182, 184, 214, 229, 236, 245, 353-355, 362
Neighborhood Guild, 238
Nelson, Donald, 295
Neumann, Henry, 37
Nevins, Allan, 111, 345, 362
New York Central Railroad Company, 144, 145, 275-277, 280, 281
New York City Housing Authority, 122
New York Civil Practice Act, 352
New York County Lawyers Association, 38
New York Herald-Tribune, 363
New York Life Insurance Company, 68, 174
New York-New Jersey Port and Harbor Development Commission, 117, 283
New York Post, 363
New York State Arbitration Law, 354
New York State Bar Association, 133, 155, 298, 353
New York State Housing Law, 121
New York University, Law School of, 3, 278, 361
New York World-Telegram, 363
Newman, Israel, 350
Niagara-Hudson Power Company, 336
"No Mean City," 139, 356, 357, 362
Nock, Albert Jay, 32, 33, 345, 362
Notman, Winifred, 133
Nott, Charles C., 67
Noyes, Harold G., 207
Nurses' Settlement, 240

O'Brian, John Lord, 321, 322
O'Callaghan, Tom, 134, 135
O'Connell, Peggy, 358
Oddie, Tasker L., 4

Odell, Governor, 77, 78, 79
Ogden, David B., 7
"On Liberty," 236
"On the Witness Stand," 20
O'Neill, Thomas J., 131
Opper, Clarence, 316
Optic, Oliver, 109
Oratorio Society, 51, 61
Orgen, Jacob, "Little Augie," 217
O'Ryan, General John F., 5
Orr, Alexander E., 344
Osborne, Thomas Mott, 77, 85
Otis, William B., 112, 146, 299, 361
Outdoor Cleanliness League, 351
Outerbridge, Ethel Boyd, 287
Outerbridge, Eugenius H., 7, 117, 118, 157, 248, 249, 262, 271-289, 305, 309, 310, 313

Page, Edward D., 346
Palisades Park Authority, 291
Pallme, William, 28
Palmer, A. Mitchell, 284
"Parasitical Functionary," 320
Parker, Alton B., 346
Parkhurst, Charles H., 110
Parks and Playground Association, 351
Parsons, Herbert, 349
Parsons, John E., 7, 19, 26
Parsons, Shepard and Ogden, 7
Partridge, Bellamy, 29, 344, 362
Paskus, Benjamin G., 34
Patterson, George S., 278
Patterson, Robert, 284
Paulding, John K., 53, 351
Pearl Harbor, ix
Pearse, Frederic M. P., 11
Peckham, Wheeler H., 7
Pegler, Westbrook, 320
People's Choral Union, The, 51, 52, 54, 55, 59, 60
People's Singing Classes, The, 51-53, 59, 60
Pepper, George Wharton, 172, 207
Perkins, Charles A., 67
Perkins, Frances, 213, 229, 245
Perkins, George W., 68
Perry, George S., 346
Perry, John Morris, 7, 93
"Peter Cooper Village," 123
Peters, Frances, 48, 351
Peters, John P., 41-49, 144, 245, 351
Peters, Marian, 48, 351
Peters, Sally, 48, 351
Pfeffer, Delmont K., 311
Philbin, Eugene A., 16, 29
Philharmonic Symphony Orchestra, 51

Phillips-Andover, 22
Pierson, Arthur N., 293, 304, 313
Pinkenson, Musya, 215
"Pins and Needles," 184, 229
Place, Ira, 145
Platt, Frank, 94, 96
Platt, Thomas C., 75, 79-81, 86-89, 94, 98-100, 102, 103, 346, 347
Podell, David L., 353
Polakoff, Solomon, 247
Poletti, Charles W., 335, 336
Political Action Committee, 192
"Political Economy," 74
Pollak, Francis D., 350
Pomeroy, John Norton, 3
Pope Pius, 324
"Port Authority, The," 305, 362
Port of London Authority, 290
Port of New York Authority, The, 10, 27, 117, 118, 120, 123, 132, 133, 146, 170, 173, 248, 249, 251, 252, 258-264, 266, 268-270, 279, 281-283, 287-307, 311, 318, 325, 329-331, 335, 341, 357-359
Poses, Lillian L., 133
"Potash and Perlmutter," 250
Potter, Bishop, 42
Pound, Roscoe, 218, 219
Pounds, Lewis H., 297
Pratt, Sereno S., 152
Prendergast, William A., 188, 274
Prentiss, John, 308
Price, George M., 232, 238-244
Price, Joseph M., 34, 273, 361
Prince, David Chandler, 133
Prince, Theodore, 4
"Principia Mathematica," 242
Printz, Alexander, 234
Progressive Party, 89
Proskauer, Joseph M., 12, 121, 125, 172, 336, 337, 350
Protocol Experiment, 342
Public Education Association, 349
Public Service Corporation of New Jersey, 259

Quigg, Lemuel Eli, 75, 77-80, 82, 87-89

Rabinowitz, Aaron, 121
Ramsey, John, 307
Rand, William, 17, 67
Rankin, Rebecca, 361
Ransom, William L., 12
Rea, Samuel, 272
Reconstruction Finance Corporation, 316
Record, George L., 278
Redfield, William C., 273
Reform Club, The, 42

Reid, Mrs. Ogden, 249
Reid, Robert, 224
Reid, Whitelaw, 99
Remsen, Daniel S., 155
Rent Cases, 162-175
Republican Party, 73, 89, 95-97, 99, 349
Res ipsa loquitor, 18, 343
Reynolds, Jackson E., 278
Rice, Edward R., 346
Rice, Schuyler N., 307
Richter, Theodore B., 27, 134, 181, 194, 220
Ricker, Olive, 132
Riegelman, Harold, 120, 121
Riehle, Theodore M., 133
Riis, Jacob A., 239, 362
Ritter, Mortimer C., 183, 184
Robinson, Edward G., 112
Robson, William A., 343
Rockefeller, John D., Jr., 37, 291
Rogers, H. H., 99
Rogers, W. A., 259
Rogers, Will, 22
Rogoff, Harry, 355
Roosevelt, Eleanor, 228, 229, 248
Roosevelt, Franklin D., 104, 125, 127, 151, 192, 229, 241, 247, 263, 264, 318, 324, 332-334, 339
Roosevelt, Theodore, ix, 8, 27-29, 31, 39, 43, 73-90, 96-103, 105, 119, 138, 330, 338, 344, 346-349, 362
Root, Elihu, 3, 7, 95, 114
Rosenberg, Abraham, 182, 225, 227, 229, 230
Rosenberg, James N., 63
Rosenblatt, Isaac, 54
Rosenfeld, Louis, 181, 182, 185
Rosenman, Dorothy, 121
Rosenman, Samuel, 121
Rosensohn, Samuel J., 350
Rothschild, Meyer D., 43, 77, 87, 346
Rothstein, Arnold, 196, 217, 218
Rough Riders, The, 73, 77, 82, 85, 86
Rubin, Mary, 132
Rubino, Henry A., 4, 131
Rudd, Frank, 93
Ruhlmann, Carl A., 283
Russell, John, 44
Russell, Scott, 159

Sadowsky, Reuben, 182, 183, 205, 218
St. James Dramatic Club, 125, 128
St. Lawrence Power Authority, 316, 329-342, 359
St. Lawrence Power Development Commission, 358, 359
St. Lawrence River, 329, 331, 333, 334

St. Michael's Protestant Episcopal Church, 44, 49
St. Patrick's Cathedral, 116, 128
Saks, 183
Sanders, Eleanor Butler, 132
Sanders, Marion, 248
"Santa Claus Club," 257
Sarnoff, David, 162
Saxe, Martin, 260
Schaap, Michael, 4, 90
Schekeler, Charles, 8
Schettino, C. Thomas, 28, 358
Schieffelin, William Jay, 231, 240, 273, 355
Schiff, Jacob H., 84, 241
Schlesinger, Benjamin, 190-192, 196, 207, 229, 239
Schorske, Theodore, 54, 361
Schurz, Carl, 75, 77, 87
Schwarcz, Max, 145, 181, 182, 185, 191, 235
Scott, William, 346
Seabury, Samuel, 217
Seaman, Alfred P. W., 44, 48
Searles, John E., 26
Seidman, Joel, 180, 182-185, 214, 216, 217, 353, 362
Seligman, Edwin R. A., 44, 238, 274, 327
Shamberg, Alexander J., 138, 172, 257-270, 289
"Shame of the Cities," 356
Shanks, David C., 285
Shanks, Sanders, 304
Shelley, Leander I., 27, 267, 269
Shepard, Edward M., 7, 93
Sheridan, Herbert, 279
Sherman Anti-Trust Act, 280
Sherman, John, 74
Sherwood, Lorraine, 248
Shientag, Bernard L., 114
Shortt, William Allaire, 346
"Sick Chicken Case," 232
"Sidewalks of New York, The," 108
Siegmeister, Elie, 50, 345, 362
Sigman, Morris, 227
Silberman, Moses, 181, 185, 191
Silzer, George S., 174
Simkhovitch, Mary, 228
Simonson, Gustave, 60, 74
Singer, Saul, 213, 354
Singstad, Ole, 264
Skehan, Rosaleen, 133
Smith, Alfred E., 108-128, 149, 152, 167, 185, 208, 213, 217, 242, 247, 249, 250, 252, 261, 287, 292, 296-298, 303, 305, 330-332, 336, 342, 350, 351, 362
Smith, A. Mackay, 335

Smith, Catherine Dunn, 128
"Smith Housing Bank," 120, 132, 205, 332
Smith, J. Spencer, 173, 275, 279, 281, 283, 298
Smith, Tom, 116
Socialism, 202, 203, 222, 223
Society for the Preservation of Historic and Scenic Places, 251
Sokolsky, George, 126
Somervell, General Brehon, 27, 283, 287
Sommer, Frank H., 4, 278
Sons of the Double Cross, 356
Spanish-American War, ix, 74, 115, 345, 355
Spellman, Cardinal Francis, 128
Spencer, Herbert, 74, 109
Speyer, James, 312, 313
Spiegelberg, Flora, 351
Sprague case, 11
Stalin, Marshal, 201
Stanchfield, John B., 136
Stapler, Henry B. B., 46-47
Stapleton, Luke, 170
Stare Decisis, 10
Starr, Mark, 355
Staten Island Bridges, 262, 312, 313, 330
Stebbins, Lucy Poate, 58, 345
Stebbins, Richard Poate, 58, 345
Steffens, Lincoln, 24, 139, 273, 356
Stein, Clarence S., 119-122, 361
Stein, Fred M., 66
Steinberg, Milton, 353
Steinbrink, Meier, 93
Stenography, 8
Steuer, Max D., 136, 213
Stillman, C. Chauncey, 308
Stimson, Henry L., 284
Stokes, Thomas L., 127
Stokowsky, Olga Samaroff, 52
Stolberg, Benjamin, 235, 236, 353-355, 362
Stone, Harlan F., 354
Stone, N. I., 247
Stotesbury, E. T., 99
Stover, Charles B., 53, 144, 145, 151, 351
Strauss, Albert, 312
Strauss, Isidore, 183
Strauss, Nathan, 183
Straus, Oscar S., 47, 113
Street Cleaning Department (Department of Sanitation), 138, 139
Strong, William L., 24, 138
Strunsky, Simeon, 139, 252, 309, 356, 362
Stryker, Lloyd Paul, 67
"Stuyvesant Town," 121
Sullivan & Cromwell, 310

Sulzberger, Arthur Hays, 44
Sulzberger, Mrs. Arthur Hays, 351
Sulzberger, Cyrus L., 44
Sun, The, 363
Sylvester, Horace C., Jr., 307, 311
Symphonic Orchestras, 51

Taft, William Howard, 171, 172, 173, 175
Tammany Hall, 27, 65, 76, 110, 116, 349
Tanzer, Eleanor C., 361
Tanzer, Laurence A., 12, 350, 361
Tariffs and Subsidies, 43
Taylor, Deems, 51
Taylor, George, 209
Taylor, Henry Ling, 346
Taylor, Robert C., 15-17, 60, 67, 69
Temple Emanu-El, 199
Tenement House Reform, 238
Tennessee Valley Authority, 316, 339, 340
Terry, Katherine, 133
Thayer, Ezra R., 38
"They All Had Glamour," 50
"They All Sang," 50
Thomas, Abner C., 5, 6
Thompson, William O., 205
Thomson, Wood & Hoffman, 266, 318
Tilden, Samuel J., 3
"Tilt with Samuel Gompers," 202
Time, Inc., 363
Titchenor, Edmund H., 84, 85, 361
Tobin, Austin J., 28, 267, 325
Tod, J. Kennedy, 84
"Topics of the Times," 276
Torts, 4
Totalitarianism, 124
Tracy, Benjamin F., 93, 96
Trade and Commerce Bar Association, 133
"Trade Unions Turn to Art," 355
Train, Arthur, 17, 31, 64, 67
"Transit Reform Committee of 100," 45
Transportation Act of 1920, 280
Tremaine, Morris S., 325
Triangle Fire, 113, 242
Tri-Borough Bridge Authority, 314, 325
Trowbridge, Isabelle, 133
Trowbridge, Lawrence W., 113
Truman, Harry S., 359
Tucker, Preble, 83
Tuttle, Arthur S., 297
Tuttle, Charles H., 213
"TVA—Democracy on the March," 340, 362
Tweed, Harrison, 133, 134
Tweedsmuir, Lord (John Buchan), 107, 116, 259, 272, 273, 294, 296, 310, 350, 356, 357, 362

Twilight Club, The, 43
Twitchell, Herbert K., 250

Ulmann, Albert, 108, 140
"Union Inland Terminal," 250
United Feature Syndicate, 363
United States Arbitration Act, 155, 156
United States Supreme Court, 11, 12, 25, 26, 30, 124
University of Cincinnati Law School, 353
University Settlement, The, 53, 238
UNNRA, 132
Untermyer, Samuel, 28, 69, 172, 213
"Up to Now," 297, 298, 362

Van Brunt, Judge Arthur H., 14, 304
Van Buskirk, DeWitt, 283, 297
Vanderbilt, Arthur T., 292, 343, 361
Van Iderstine, Robert, 350
Van Wyck, Robert A., 65, 87
Vatican, 344
Verne, Jules, 109
Villard, Oswald Garrison, 49, 345
Von Briesen, Arthur, 134
Von Clausewitz, Karl, 299

Wagner Act, 194
Wagner, Robert, 113, 114, 213, 358
Wainright, J. Mayhew, 104, 173
Wold, Lillian D., 228, 231, 240, 243, 245, 355, 362
Waldman, Louis, 201, 214, 354, 362
Walker, James J., 217, 302
Walsh, Frank P., 335
Wanders, George, 314
War Contract Termination Act, 158
War Labor Board, 209
War Production Board, 315, 322
Warburg, Felix, 241
Waring, George E., Jr., 85, 138, 140, 144
Warner, John DeWitt, 43, 47, 346
Warren, Earl, 325
Watson, Russell S., 292
Webster, Daniel, 30
Weed, John W., 346
Weinstein, Gregory, 43, 345, 362
Weizman, Chaim, 200
Welfare Island, 146
Weller, Roy, 293
Welling, Richard W. G., 346
Wertheim, David, 199
"What Every Woman Knows," 271
White, J. DuPratt, 291
White House, The, 31, 99, 101, 128, 283
Whiteside, George W., 67
Whitman, Alfred A., 44, 64

Whitman, Charles S., 100, 218, 274, 277, 281, 283, 292, 298, 303, 305
Whitney, Edward B., 43, 46, 47
Whitney, Rosalie Loew, 131-136
Whitney, Travis, 47, 112, 134
Wickersham, George W., 173, 279, 355
Wilby, Francis B., 359
Wilcox, Ansley, 28, 346
Wile, E. J., 206, 240
Willcox, William R., 117, 283
Williams, Frank B., 350
Williamson, Frederick, 145, 280
Willkie, Wendell L., 159, 227
Wilson, Oren E., 85
Wilson, Woodrow, 283-286
Windels, Paul, 264
Wingate's Raiders, 151
Wise, Edmond E., 37
Wise, Isaac M., 198
Wise, Stephen S., 199
Wister, Owen, 346
WNYC, 142
Wolf, Arthur, 235
Wolff, Harry, 96
Wolff, Henry, 228, 229
Woll, Matthew, 223
Women's City Club, 246
Women's Municipal League, 62, 140, 142, 143, 351
Women, Prejudice against, 133

Woman's Suffrage, 131, 133
Wood, David C., 318
Wood, Leonard, 75
Woodbury, Egburt, 277
Woodruff, Clinton Rogers, 24
Woodruff, Timothy, 75
Woodward, Stewart L., 74, 346
Woodward, William, 308
Worcester, Francis J., 47
"Workers Education in the United States," 355
Worksman, William, 28
World Jewish Congress, 345
World War I, ix, 32, 89, 145, 157, 158, 162, 167, 258, 280, 283-285
World War II, ix, 27, 133, 143, 157, 162, 196, 205, 209, 241, 283, 284, 286, 287, 342
Wright, Harry N., 326

Yale Law Journal, 11
"Yankee from Olympus," 345, 352-354, 362
Yerkes, C. T., 75

Zaretsky, 187-189
Zionism, 198, 199, 200
Zolli, Anton, 344
Zorn, Burton, 11, 27
Zuckerman, Anne, 358